Operating Systems

ROHIT KHURANA
Founder & CEO
ITLESL, New Delhi

VIKAS® PUBLISHING HOUSE PVT LTD

Vikas® Publishing House Pvt Ltd
E-28, Sector-8, **Noida**-201301 (UP)
Phone: 0120-4078900 • Fax: 4078999
Regd. Office: 576, Masjid Road, Jangpura, **New Delhi**-110 014

E-mail: *helpline@vikaspublishing.com* • *Website: www.vikaspublishing.com*

- **Bengaluru** : First Floor, N.S. Bhawan, 4th Cross, 4th Main, Gandhi Nagar, Bengaluru-560 009
  • Ph. 080-2220 4639, 2228 1254
- **Chennai** : Damodhar Centre, New No. 62, Old No. 59, Nelson Manickam Road, Aminjikarai,
  Chennai-600 029 • Ph. 044-2374 4547, 2374 6090
- **Kolkata** : P-51/1, CIT Road, Scheme-52, Kolkata-700 014 • Ph. 033-2286 6995, 2286 6996
- **Mumbai** : 67/68, 3rd Floor, Aditya Industrial Estate, Chincholi Bunder, Malad (West),
  Mumbai-400 064 • Ph. 022-2877 2545, 2876 8301

Distributors:

UBS PUBLISHERS' DISTRIBUTORS PVT LTD
5, Ansari Road, **New Delhi**-110 002
• Ph. 011-2327 3601, 2326 6646 • Fax: 2327 6593, 2327 4261
E-mail: ubspd@ubspd.com   Website: www.gobookshopping.com

- **Ahmedabad** : 1st Floor, Shop No. 133-134, Aust Laxmi, Apparel Park, Outside Dariyapur Gate,
  Ahmedabad-380 016 • Ph. 079-29092241, 29092248, 29092258
- **Bengaluru** : Crescent No. 148, 1st Floor, Mysore Road, Bengaluru-560 026 • Ph. 080-26756377, 26756362
  • Fax: 080-26756462
- **Bhopal** : Z-18, M P Nagar, Zone-1, Bhopal-462 011 • Ph. 0755-4203 183, 4203 193
- **Bhubaneshwar** : Ist Floor 145, Cuttack Road, Bhubaneshwar-751 006 • Ph. 0674-2314 446
- **Chennai** : 60, Nelson Manickam Road, Aminjikarai, Chennai-600 029 • Ph. 044-2374 6222
- **Coimbatore** : 2nd & 3rd Floor, Sri Guru Towers, No. 1-7, Sathy Road, Cross III, Gandhipuram,
  Coimbatore-641 012
- **Ernakulam** : No. 40/8199A, 1st Floor, Public Library Building, Convent Road, Ernakulam-682 035
  • Ph. 0484-2353901, 2373901, 2363905, 4064706 • Fax: 0484-236551
- **Guwahati** : 1st Floor, House No.4, Kanaklata Path, Lachit Nagar, Bharalupar, Guwahati-781 007
- **Hyderabad** : 3rd Floor, Alekhya Jagadish Chambers, H. No. 4-1-1058, Boggulkunta, Tilak Road,
  Hyderabad-500 001 • Ph. 040-2475 4472 / 73 / 74
- **Kolkata** : 8/1-B, Chowringhee Lane, Kolkata-700 016 • Ph. 033-2252 1821, 2252 2910
- **Lucknow** : 9 Ashok Nagar, Near Pratibha Press, Gautam Buddha Marg, Latush Road, Lucknow-226 001
  • Ph. 0522-2294 134, 3014 010
- **Mumbai** : 2nd Floor, Apeejay Chambers, 5 Wallace Street, Fort, Mumbai-400 001
  • Ph. 022-6637 6922-3, 6610 2069 • Fax: 6637 6921
- **Patna** : GF, Western Side, Annapoorna Complex, Naya Tola, Patna-800 004
  • Ph. 0612-2672 856, 2673 973
- **Pune** : 680 Budhwar Peth, 2nd Floor, Appa Balwant Chowk, Pune-411 002 • Ph. 020-2446 1653,
  2443 3976

First Edition 2011

Vikas® is the registered trademark of Vikas Publishing House Pvt Ltd
Copyright © ITL Education Solution Ltd

Printed at Print Links, Delhi-110095

*I would like to dedicate this book to my uncle, Shri G K Jaju,
for his understanding, constant support and trust in me.
He has always inspired me to aim higher and achieve bigger.
He has been a great friend, philosopher and guide.*

Preface

The era of computer revolution began almost 50 years ago and since then, the developments in the field have been very rapid. Every sphere of human activity has been affected by developments. An essential part of every computer is the operating system, which provides a platform for the proper usage of computer resources during the operation of a computer. Therefore, we believe that operating systems must be understood by everyone who uses a computer.

Operating Systems is an insightful work elaborating on the fundamentals as well as advanced topics in the discipline. Keeping the needs of the students in mind, this work offers an in-depth coverage of concepts, design and functions of an operating system irrespective of the hardware that will house it. With neat illustrations, examples and presentation of difficult concepts in the simplest form, the USP of this book lies in it being extremely student-friendly.

Based upon the updated university curriculum, this book caters to BTech Computer Science and Engineering (IV semester) students, who would find the introductory and advanced discussions highly informative and enriching. *Operating Systems* is a great guide for self-paced learning and will go a long way in equipping budding system programmers with the right knowledge and expertise.

Text Layout

The text is organised into 12 chapters.

- *Chapter 1* introduces operating system, its services and structure. Also, it provides an insight into the organization of computer system.
- *Chapter 2* deals essentially with the basic concepts of processes such as process scheduling, operations on processes and communication between processes.
- *Chapter 3* helps to understand the need and advantages of threads, various multithreading models as well as threading issues.
- *Chapter 4* spells out the scheduling criteria and different types of scheduling algorithms. It also discusses several issues regarding scheduling in multiprocessor and real-time systems.
- *Chapter 5* throws light on several methods used for achieving synchronization among cooperating processes.
- *Chapter 6* describes the deadlock situation and the conditions that lead to it. It also provides methods for handling deadlocks.

- *Chapter 7* familiarizes the reader with the different memory management strategies used for contiguous and non-contiguous memory allocation.
- *Chapter 8* introduces the concept of virtual memory. It also discusses how virtual memory is implemented using demand paging.
- *Chapter 9* acquaints the readers with the basic concepts of files, including file types, attributes and access methods. It also describes the concept of file-system mounting.
- *Chapter 10* explores how the files and directories are implemented. The management of free space on the disk is explained as well.
- *Chapter 11* discusses system I/O in detail, including the I/O system design, interfaces, and functions.
- *Chapter 12* explains disk scheduling algorithms, disk management, swap-space management and RAID. It also introduces the concept of stable and tertiary storage.

Happy reading!

Rohit Khurana
Founder & CEO
ITLESL, New Delhi
itlesl@rediffmail.com

Acknowledgement

In all my efforts towards making this book a reality, my special thanks goes to my technical and editorial team, without whom this work would not have achieved its desired level of excellence. I sincerely extend my thanks to my research and development team for devoting their time and relentless effort in bringing out this high quality book. I convey my gratitude to my publisher Vikas Publishing House Pvt Ltd for sharing this dream and giving all the support in realizing it.

In our attempt towards further improvement, I welcome you all to send your feedback to *itlesl@rediffmail.com*. I will highly appreciate all your constructive comments.

I hope you will enjoy reading the book and hope it proves to be a good resource for all.

Author

Contents

Syllabi – Book Mapping

Anna University

(Chennai/Coimbatore/Tirunelveli/Tiruchirappalli)

(SEM IV, Common to CSE & IT)

Syllabus	Mapping in the book: Unit/Chapter
UNIT I PROCESSES AND THREADS Introduction to operating systems – review of computer organization – operating system structures – system calls – system programs – system structure – virtual machines. Processes: Process concept – process scheduling – operations on processes –cooperating processes – interprocess communication – communication in client-server systems. Case study: IPC in Linux. Threads: Multi-threading models – threading issues. Case Study: Pthreads library	1, 2, 3
UNIT II PROCESS SCHEDULING AND SYNCHRONIZATION CPU Scheduling: Scheduling criteria – scheduling algorithms – multiple-processor scheduling – real time scheduling – algorithm evaluation. Case study: Process scheduling in Linux. Process Synchronization: The critical-section problem – synchronization hardware – semaphores – classic problems of synchronization – critical regions – monitors. Deadlock: System model – deadlock characterization – Methods for handling deadlocks – deadlock prevention – deadlock avoidance – deadlock detection – recovery from deadlock.	4, 5, 6
UNIT III STORAGE MANAGEMENT Memory Management: Background – swapping – contiguous memory allocation – paging – segmentation – segmentation with paging. Virtual Memory: Background – demand paging – process creation – page replacement – allocation of frames – thrashing. Case Study: Memory management in Linux	7, 8
UNIT IV FILE SYSTEMS File-System Interface: File concept – access methods – directory structure – file system mounting – protection. File-System Implementation: Directory implementation – allocation methods – free-space management – efficiency and performance – recovery – log-structured file systems. Case studies: File system in Linux – file system in Windows XP	9, 10
UNIT V I/O SYSTEMS I/O Systems – I/O Hardware – application I/O interface – kernel I/O subsystem –streams – performance. Mass-Storage Structure: Disk scheduling – disk management – swap-space management – RAID – disk attachment – stable storage – tertiary storage. Case study: I/O in Linux	11, 12

Chapter

01

Introduction to Operating Systems

Learning Objectives

After reading this chapter, you will be able to:

- ☐ Understand the term operating system
- ☐ Describe the basic computer organization
- ☐ Explain architecture of computer system
- ☐ Describe operations of operating system
- ☐ List the services provided by the operating system
- ☐ Explain different types of system calls
- ☐ List different categories of system programs
- ☐ Discuss various ways of structuring an operating system
- ☐ Understand the concept of virtual machines

1.1 INTRODUCTION

A computer system consists of two main components: hardware and software. The hardware components include Central Processing Unit (CPU), memory and input/output (I/O) devices. The software part comprises system and application programs, such as compilers, text editors, word processors, spreadsheets, database systems, etc. An application program is developed by an application programmer in some programming language.

The application programmers and the end users (users who interact with the application programs to solve their problems) are generally not concerned with the details of the computer hardware and hence do not directly interact with it. Thus, to use the various hardware components, the application programs and the users need an intermediate layer that provides a convenient interface to use the system. This layer is referred to as an operating system.

1.2 OPERATING SYSTEM

In simple terms, the operating system is defined as a program that is running at all times on the computer (usually called the **kernel**). It is a program that acts as an interface between the computer users and the computer hardware (see Figure 1.1). It manages the computer hardware and controls and coordinates the use of hardware among various application programs. The operating system also provides a way in which the various computer resources, such as hardware, software and the data can be used in a proper and efficient manner.

An operating system has two main objectives: convenience and efficiency. An operating system is designed in such a way that it makes the computer system more convenient to use and allows the system resources to be used in an efficient manner. Some operating systems are designed for convenience (for example, PC operating systems), some for efficiency (for example, mainframe operating systems) and some for the combination of both.

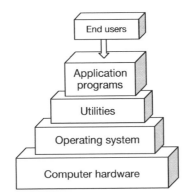

Figure 1.1: Components of a Computer System

An operating system can be compared to a government. Though like a government, it does not perform any useful function by itself, but it provides an environment for the other programs so that they can do useful work. There are two viewpoints from which we can understand the role of an operating system: the user point of view and the system point of view.

User View

In case of a stand-alone environment, where a single user sits in front of a personal computer, the operating system is designed basically for the ease of use and some attention is paid to system performance. However, since these systems are designed for a single user to monopolize the resources, there is no sharing of hardware and software among multiple users. Therefore, no attention is paid to resource utilization.

In case of a networked environment, where multiple users share resources and may exchange information, the operating system is designed for resource utilization. In this case, the operating system ensures that the available processor time, memory and I/O devices are used efficiently, and no individual user tries to monopolize the system resources. In case, the various users are connected to a mainframe or a minicomputer via their terminals, no attention is paid to usability of individual systems. However, in case the users are connected to the servers via their workstations, a compromise between individual usability and resource utilization is made while designing the operating system.

In case of hand-held systems, the operating system is basically designed for individual usability as these systems are mostly stand-alone units for individual users. Finally, the computers which have little or no user view, such as embedded systems, the operating system for such systems is basically designed to ensure that these system will run without user intervention.

System View

As discussed earlier, the computer system consists of many resources, such as CPU time, memory and I/O devices, which are required to solve a computing problem. It is the responsibility of the operating system to manage these resources, and allocate them to various programs and users in a way such that the computer system can be operated in an efficient and fair manner. Thus, from the system's point of view, the operating system primarily acts as a **resource allocator**.

The operating system also acts as a control program that manages the execution of user programs to avoid errors and improper use of computer system. It also controls the I/O devices and their operations.

CHECK YOUR PROGRESS

1. What are the two viewpoints from which we can understand the role of an operating system?
2. The operating system acts as a:
   (a) Resource allocator   (b) Control program
   (c) Interface   (d) All of these
3. The two main objectives of an operating system are _____ and _____.
4. Operating system does not make the computer system more convenient to use. (True or False)

1.3 REVIEW OF COMPUTER ORGANIZATION

These days a computer system basically consists of one or more processors (CPUs), several device controllers and the memory. All these components are connected through a common bus that provides access to shared memory. Each device controller acts as an interface between a particular I/O device and the operating system. Thus, a device controller plays an important role in operating that particular device. For example, the disk controller helps in operating disks, USB controller in operating mouse, keyboard and printer, graphics adapter in operating monitor, sound card in operating audio devices, and so on. In order to access the shared memory, the memory controller is also provided that synchronizes the access to the memory. The interconnection of various components via a common bus is shown in Figure 1.2.

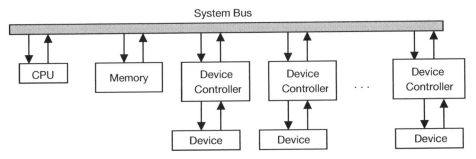

Figure 1.2: Bus Interconnection

1.3.1 Computer System Operation

When the system boots up, the initial program that runs on the system is known as **bootstrap program**. The bootstrap program is typically stored in Read-Only Memory (ROM) or Electrically Erasable Programmable ROM (EEPROM). During the booting process, all the aspects of the system, such as CPU registers, device controllers and memory contents are initialized and then the operating system is loaded into the memory. Once the operating system is loaded, the first process, such as 'init' is executed and operating system then waits for some event to occur.

The event notification is done with the help of an **interrupt** that is fired either by the hardware or the software. When the hardware needs to trigger an interrupt, it can do so by sending a signal to the CPU via the system bus. When the software needs to trigger an interrupt, it can do so with the help of **system call** (or **monitor call**).

Whenever an interrupt is fired, the CPU stops executing the current task and jumps to a predefined location in the kernel's address space, which contains the starting address of the service routine for the interrupt (known as **interrupt handler**). It then executes the interrupt handler and once the execution is completed, the CPU resumes the task that it was previously doing.

To quickly handle the interrupts, a table of pointers to interrupt routines is used. The table contains the addresses of the interrupt handlers for the various devices and is generally stored in the low memory (say first 100 locations or so). The interrupt routine can be called indirectly with the help of this table. This array of addresses is known as **interrupt vector**. The interrupt vector is further indexed by a unique device number, given with the interrupt request, to provide the address of the interrupt handler for the interrupting device.

1.3.2 Storage Structure

Whenever a program needs to be executed, it must be first loaded into the main memory (called **Random Access Memory** or **RAM**). RAM is the only storage area that can be directly accessed by the CPU. RAM consists of an array of memory words, where each word has its unique address. The two instructions, namely, `load` and `store` are used to interact with the memory.

- The load instruction is used to move a word from main memory to a CPU register.
- The store instruction is used to move the content of the CPU register to the main memory.

We know that a program is basically a set of instructions that are executed to complete a given task. The execution of the program instructions takes place in the CPU registers, which are used as temporary storage areas and have limited storage space. Usually, an instruction execution cycle consists of the following steps.

1. Whenever the CPU needs to execute an instruction, it first fetches it from the main memory and stores it in Instruction Register (IR).
2. Once the instruction has been loaded into the IR, the control unit examines and decodes the fetched instruction.
3. After decoding the instruction, the operands (if required) are fetched from the main memory and stored in one of the internal registers.
4. The instruction is executed on the operands and the result is stored back to the main memory.

Since RAM is the only storage area that can be directly accessed by the CPU, ideally all the programs and data should be stored in the main memory permanently for fast execution and better system performance. But, practically it is not possible because RAM is expensive and offers limited storage capacity. Secondly, it is volatile in nature, that is, it loses its contents when power supply is switched off.

Therefore, we need some storage area that can hold large amount of data permanently. Such type of storage is called **secondary storage**. Secondary storage is non-volatile in nature, that is, the data is permanently stored, and survives power failure and system crashes. However, data on the secondary storage are not directly accessed by the CPU. Therefore, it needs to be transferred to the main memory so that the CPU can access it. **Magnetic disk** (generally called disk) is the primary form of secondary storage that enables storage of enormous amount of data. It is used to hold on-line data for long term.

In addition to RAM and magnetic disk, some other form of storage devices also exist, which include cache memory, flash memory, optical discs and magnetic tapes. The basic function of all the storage devices is to store the data. However, they differ in terms of their speed, cost, storage capacity and volatility. On the basis of their characteristics, such as cost per unit of data and speed with which data can be accessed, they can be arranged in a hierarchical manner as shown in Figure 1.3.

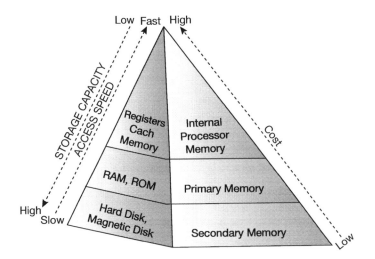

Figure 1.3: Memory Hierarchy

1.3.3 I/O Structure

Handling I/O devices is one of the main functions of an operating system. A significant portion of code of operating system is dedicated to manage I/O. One reason for this is the varying nature of I/O devices. The operating system must issue commands to the devices, catch interrupts, handle errors, and provide an interface between the devices and the rest of the system.

As already mentioned, a computer system consists of one or more processors and multiple device controllers that are connected through a common bus. Each device controller controls a specific type of device and depending on the device controller one or more devices may be attached to it. For example, a Small Computer System Interface (SCSI) controller may have seven or more devices attached to it. To perform its job, device controller maintains some local buffer storage and a set of special-purpose registers. The operating systems usually have a **device driver** for each device controller. The role of device driver is to present an interface between the device and the rest of the system. This interface should be uniform, that is, it should be same for all the devices to the possible extent.

To start an I/O operation, the device driver loads the appropriate registers within the device controller, which in turn examines the contents of registers to determine the action to be taken. Suppose, the action is to read the data from the keyboard, the controller starts transferring data from the device to its local buffer. Upon completion of data transfer, the controller informs the device driver (by generating an interrupt) that the transfer has been completed. The device driver then returns the control along with the data or pointer to the data to the operating system. This form of I/O is interrupt-driven I/O and this scheme wastes CPU's time because CPU requests data from the device controller one byte at a time. Thus, it is not feasible to transfer a large amount of data with this scheme.

To solve this problem, another scheme, that is, **Direct Memory Access (DMA)** is commonly used. In this scheme, after setting up the registers to inform the controller to know what to transfer and where, the CPU is free to perform other tasks. The device controller can now complete its job, that is, transfer a complete block of data between its local buffer and memory without CPU intervention. Once the block of data has transferred, an interrupt is generated to inform the device driver that the operation has completed.

1.4 COMPUTER SYSTEM ARCHITECTURE

Depending on the number of processors used in the system, a computer system can be categorized mainly into one of the two types: single processor system or multiprocessor system.

1.4.1 Single Processor Systems

Single processor systems consist of one main CPU that can execute a general-purpose instruction set, which includes instructions from user processes. Other than the one main CPU, most systems also have some special-purpose processors. These special-purpose processors may be in the form of device-specific processors, such as disk, keyboard, etc., or in mainframes, they may be I/O processors that move data among the system components. Note that the special-purpose processors execute a limited instruction set and do not execute instructions from the user processes. Further, the use of special-purpose processors does not turn a single-processor system into a multiprocessor system.

In some systems, the special-purpose processors are managed by the operating systems, and in others, they are low-level components built into the hardware. In the former case, the operating system monitors their status and sends them information for their next task. For example, the main CPU sends requests to access the disk to a disk controller microprocessor, which implements its own disk queue and disk scheduling algorithm. Doing this, the main CPU is relieved from the disk scheduling overhead. In the latter case, these special-purpose processors do their tasks autonomously and the operating system cannot communicate with them.

1.4.2 Multiprocessor Systems

As the name suggests, the multiprocessor systems (also known as **parallel systems** or **tightly coupled systems**) consist of multiple processors in close communication in a sense that they share the computer bus and even the system clock, memory, and peripheral devices. The main advantage of multiprocessor systems is that they increase the system throughput by getting more work done in less time. Another benefit is that it is more economic to have a single multiprocessor system than to have multiple single-processor systems. In addition, the multiprocessor systems are more reliable. If one out of N processors fails, then the remaining N-1 processors share the work of the failed processor amongst them and thereby preventing the failure of the entire system.

Multiprocessor systems are of two types, namely, symmetric and asymmetric. In **symmetric multiprocessing systems**, all the processors are identical and perform identical functions. Each processor runs an identical copy of the operating system and these copies interact with each other as and when required. All processors in symmetric multiprocessor system are peers—no master-slave relationship exists between them. On the other hand, in **asymmetric multiprocessing systems**, processors are different and each of them performs a specific task. One processor controls the entire system and hence, it is known as **master processor**. Other processors, known as **slave processors**, either wait for the master's instructions to perform any task or have predefined tasks. This scheme defines a master-slave relationship. The main disadvantage of asymmetric multiprocessing systems is that the failure of the master processor brings the entire system to a halt. Figure 1.4 shows symmetric and asymmetric multiprocessor system.

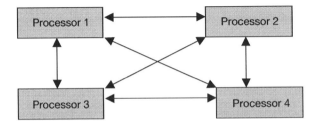

(a) Symmetric Multiprocessing System

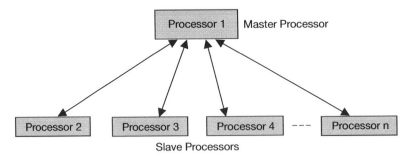

(b) Asymmetric Multiprocessing System

Figure 1.4: Symmetric and Asymmetric Multiprocessing Systems

CHECK YOUR PROGRESS

12. What are the two types of multiprocessor systems? Define any one of them.
13. In which forms, the special-purpose processors may be in the single processor system.
14. The main advantage of multiprocessor systems is that they increase the _____ .
15. The use of special-purpose processors turns a single processor system into a multiprocessor system. (True or False)

1.5 OPERATING SYSTEM STRUCTURE

Though, internally the operating systems vary greatly in their framework as they are organized along many different lines, but still there are some features that are common in them. This section discusses some of these commonalities. One of the most common features of operating systems is that they support multiprogramming. The execution of multiple jobs in an interleaved manner is known as **multiprogramming**.

Execution of a single job cannot keep the CPU and the I/O devices busy at all times because during its execution it sometimes requires CPU and sometimes requires I/O devices but not both at the same time. Hence, when the program is busy with CPU, the I/O devices have to wait and when the program is busy with I/O devices, the CPU remains idle.

For example, consider two jobs P_1 and P_2 such that both of them require CPU time and I/O time alternatively. The serial execution of P_1 and P_2 is shown in Figure 1.6(a). The shaded boxes show the CPU activity of the jobs and white boxes show their I/O activity. It is clear from the figure that when P_1 is busy in its I/O activity, the CPU is idle even if P_2 is ready for execution.

In case of multiprogramming systems, the jobs are organized in such a way that the CPU always has one to execute. This increases the CPU utilization by minimizing the CPU idle time. The basic idea behind multiprogramming is that the operating system loads multiple jobs into the memory from the job pool on the disk. The operating systems then pick up one job amongst them and start executing it. When job needs to perform some other activity, such as an I/O activity, the operating system simply picks up another job and starts executing it. When this job needs to perform some other activity, the operating system switches to the third job and so on. When the I/O activity of the job is finished, it gets the CPU back. Therefore, as long as there is at least one job to execute, the CPU will never remain idle. The memory layout for a multiprogrammed system is shown in Figure 1.5.

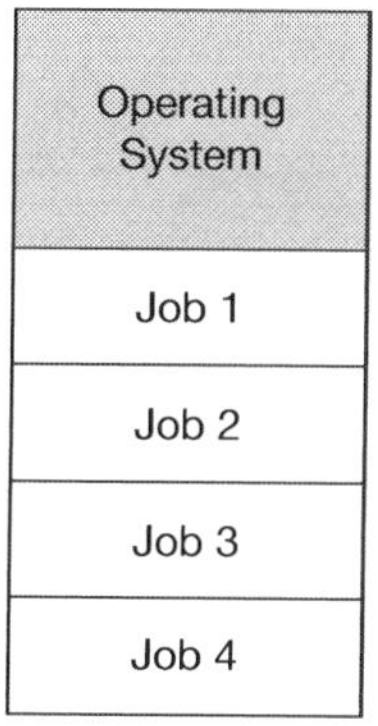

Figure 1.5: Memory Layout for a Multiprogrammed System

Figure 1.6(b) shows the multiprogrammed execution of jobs P_1 and P_2, both are assumed to be in memory and waiting to get CPU time. Further assume that job P_1 gets the CPU time first. When P_1 needs to perform its I/O activity, the CPU starts executing P_2. When P_2 needs to perform I/O activity, the CPU again switches to P_1 and so on. This type of execution of multiple processes is known as **concurrent execution**.

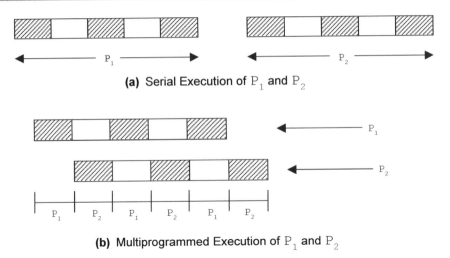

(a) Serial Execution of P_1 and P_2

(b) Multiprogrammed Execution of P_1 and P_2

Figure 1.6: Serial and Multiprogrammed Execution

Note that for simplicity we have considered the multiprogrammed execution of only two processes P_1 and P_2, but in general there are more than two processes that compete for system resources at any point of time. The number of processes competing to get the system resources in multiprogramming environment is known as **degree of multiprogramming**. In general, higher is the degree of multiprogramming, more will be the resource utilization.

In multiprogrammed systems, the operating system is responsible to make decisions for the users. When a job enters into the system, it is kept in the job pool on the disk which contains all those jobs that are waiting for the allocation of main memory. If there is not enough memory to accommodate all these jobs, then the operating system must select among them to be loaded into the main memory. Making this decision is known as **job scheduling**, which is discussed in *Chapter 04*. To keep multiple jobs in the main memory at the same time, some kind of memory management is required, which is discussed in detail in *Chapter 07*. Moreover, if multiple jobs in the main memory are ready for execution at the same time, the operating system must choose one of them. Making this decision is known as **CPU scheduling**, which is discussed in *Chapter 04*.

Multiprogrammed systems allow the operating system to handle multiple jobs at a time, but they do not allow users to interact with the computer system. An extension of multiprogrammed systems is **time-sharing systems** (or **multitasking**) in which multiple users are allowed to interact with the system through their terminals. Each user is assigned a fixed time-slot in which he or she can interact with the system. The user interacts with the system by giving instructions to the operating system or to a program using an input device, such as keyboard or a mouse and then waits for the immediate response. The **response time** should be short—typically less than one second. The CPU in time-sharing systems switches so rapidly from one user to another that each user gets the impression that only he or she is working on the system, even though the system is being shared among multiple users. A typical time-sharing system is shown in Figure 1.7.

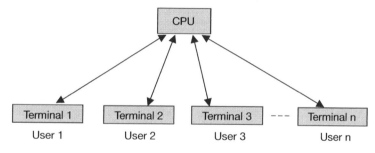

Figure 1.7: Time-sharing System

The main advantage of time-sharing systems is that they provide a convenient environment in which the users can develop and execute their programs. They provide quicker response time, and allow users to debug their program interactively under the control of a debugging program. Moreover, the users are allowed to share the system resources in such a way that each user gets an impression that he or she has all the resources to himself or herself.

The time-sharing systems are even more complex than multiprogrammed systems. Time-sharing provides a mechanism for concurrent execution, which requires CPU scheduling to be more sophisticated. Most time-sharing systems make use of round robin scheduling algorithm in which each program is given a system-defined time slice for its execution. When this time slice gets over and the program still requires CPU for its execution, it is interrupted by the operating system and is placed at the end of the queue of waiting programs. Memory management in time-sharing systems must provide isolation and protection of multiple programs residing simultaneously in the main memory. I/O management in time-sharing system must be sophisticated enough to cope with multiple users and devices.

Though the concept of time-sharing was demonstrated in early 1960s, but since it was expensive and difficult to implement at that time, they were not in use until the early 1970s. However, these days, most of the systems are time sharing.

CHECK YOUR PROGRESS

16. Why execution of a single program cannot keep the CPU and I/O busy at all times?
17. What is the basic idea behind multiprogramming?
18. The job pool on the disk contains all those jobs that are _____.
19. Which of the following is false?
    (a) Time-sharing system provides quicker response time than multiprogramming system.
    (b) Multiprogrammed systems are more complex than time-sharing systems.
    (c) Time-sharing system is an extension of multiprogrammed system.
    (d) In time-sharing system, each user is assigned a fixed time slot.

1.6 OPERATING SYSTEM OPERATIONS

As discussed earlier, modern operating systems are interrupt driven. When there is no work to do, that is, no processes for execution, no I/O activities and no user to whom to respond, the operating system will sit idle. Whenever an event occurs, it is signalled by triggering an interrupt or a trap. For each type of interrupt, there exists a code segment in the operating system that specifies the actions to be taken. The part of the operating system called **Interrupt Service Routine (ISR)** executes the appropriate code segment to deal with the interrupt.

In case of multiprogrammed environment, the computer resources are shared among several programs simultaneously. Though the sharing of resources improves the resource utilization, it also increases the problems. An error in one user program can adversely affect the execution of other programs. It may also happen that the erroneous program modifies another program, or data of another program or the operating system itself. Without the protection against such type of errors, only one process must be allowed to execute at a time.

However, to improve the resource utilization, it is necessary to allow resource sharing among several programs simultaneously. Therefore, to handle such environment, the operating system must be designed in such a way that it should ensure that an incorrect program does not affect the execution of other programs or the operating system itself.

1.6.1 Dual-mode Operation

In order to ensure the proper functioning of the computer system, the operating system, and all other programs and their data must be protected against the incorrect programs. To achieve this protection, two modes of operations, namely, **user mode** and **monitor mode** (also known as **supervisor mode**, **system mode**, **kernel mode** or **privileged mode**) are specified. A mode bit is associated with the computer hardware to indicate the current mode of operation. The value '1' indicates the user mode and '0' indicates the monitor mode. When the mode bit is 1, it implies that the execution is being done on behalf of the user and when it is 0, it implies that the execution is being done on behalf of the operating system.

When the system gets started (or booted), it is in monitor mode. Then the operating system is loaded and the user processes are started in the user mode. When a trap or an interrupt occurs, the hardware switches from user mode to the monitor mode by changing the mode bit value to 0. Therefore, whenever the operating system has the control on the computer, it is in the monitor mode. Whenever the control needs to be passed to the user program, the hardware must change the mode to the user mode before passing the control to the user program.

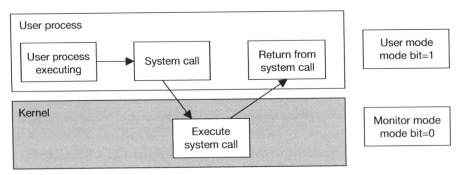

Figure 1.8: Dual-Mode Operation

This dual mode of operation helps in protecting the operating system and the other programs, from malicious programs. To achieve this protection, some of the machine instructions that may cause harm are designated as **privileged instructions**. These privileged instructions are allowed to be executed only in the monitor mode. If an attempt is made to execute a privileged instruction in user mode, the hardware treats it as an illegal instruction and traps it to the operating system without executing it. The instruction used to switch from kernel mode to user mode is an example of a privileged instruction.

> **Note:**   Recent operating systems, such as Windows 2000 and IBM OS/2 provide greater protection for the operating system by supporting privileged instructions.

1.6.2 Timer

When a process starts executing, then it is quite possible that it gets stuck in an infinite loop and never returns the control to the operating system. Therefore, it is necessary to prevent a user program from gaining the control of the system for an infinite time. For this, a **timer** is maintained, which interrupts the system after a specified period. This period can be fixed or variable. A **variable timer** is usually implemented by a fixed-rate clock and a counter.

It is the responsibility of the operating system to set the counter which is decremented with every clock tick. Whenever the value of counter reaches 0, an interrupt occurs. In this way the timer prevents a user program from running too long. Initially, when a program starts, a counter is initialized with the amount of time that a program is allowed to run. The value of counter is decremented by 1 with each clock tick and once it becomes negative, the operating system terminates the program for exceeding the assigned time limit. Note that the instructions that modify the operations of the timer are also designated as privileged instructions.

CHECK YOUR PROGRESS

20. What problems may arise when resources are shared among several programs?
21. To achieve protection, some of the machine instructions that may harm are designated as _____.
22. When system gets started, it is in _____ mode.
23. A variable timer is usually implemented by a fixed-rate clock and a counter. (True or False)

1.7 OPERATING SYSTEM SERVICES

Almost all the user programs need an environment in which they can be executed. In addition, they need a set of services using which the burden of programming reduces and it becomes easier. For instance, programmer should not be bothered about how memory is allocated to their programs, where their programs are loaded in memory during execution, how multiple programs are managed and executed, how their programs are organized in files to reside on disk, etc. Providing this environment in which programs can be executed and the set of services to user programs are the operating system's responsibilities. One set of operating-system services provides functions to help the user. These services include the following.

- **User interface:** Providing a User Interface (UI) to interact with users is essential for an operating system. This interface can be in one of the several forms. One is **command line interface**, in which users interact with the operating system by typing commands. Another is **batch interface**, in which several commands and directives to control those commands are collected into files which are then executed. Another is **Graphical User Interface (GUI)**, in which users interact with the system with a pointing device, such as a mouse.
- **Program execution:** The system must allocate memory to the user programs and then load these programs into memory so that they can be executed. The programs must be able to terminate either normally or abnormally.
- **I/O operations:** Almost all the programs require I/O involving a file or an I/O device. For efficiency and protection, the operating system must provide a means to perform I/O instead of leaving it for users to handle I/O devices directly.
- **File-system manipulation:** Often, programs need to manipulate files and directories, such as creating a new file, writing contents to a file, deleting or searching a file by providing its name, etc. Some programs may also need to manage permissions for files or directories to allow or deny other programs requests to access these files or directories.
- **Communication:** A process executing in one computer may need to exchange information with the processes executing on the same computer or on a different computer connected via a computer network. The information is moved between processes by the operating system.
- **Error detection:** There is always a possibility of occurrence of error in the computer system. Error may occur in the CPU, memory, I/O devices or in user program. Examples of errors include an attempt to access an illegal memory location, power failure, link failure on a network, too long use of CPU by a user program, etc. The operating system must be constantly aware of possible errors and should take appropriate action in the event of occurrence of error to ensure correct and consistent computing.

As we know, multiple programs may be executed concurrently each of which may require multiple resources during their execution. Therefore, providing another set of services that helps allocating resources to programs in some order is necessary for an operating system. These services exist not for helping user instead to ensure the efficient and secure execution of programs.

- **Resource allocation:** In case of multiprogramming, many programs execute concurrently, each of which require many different types of resources, such as CPU cycles, memory, I/O devices, etc. Therefore, in such an environment, operating system must allocate resources to programs in a manner such that resources are utilized efficiently and no program should wait forever for other programs to complete their execution.
- **Protection and security:** Protection involves ensuring controlled access to the system resources. In a multiuser or a networked computer system, the owner of information may

want to protect information. When several processes execute concurrently, a process should not be allowed to interfere with other processes or with the operating system itself. Security involves protecting the system from unauthorized users. To provide security, each user should authenticate himself or herself to the system before accessing system resources. A common means of authenticating users is username/password mechanism.

- **Accounting:** We may want to keep track of usage of system resources by each individual user. This information may be used for accounting so that users can be billed or for accumulating usage statistics, which is valuable for researchers.

CHECK YOUR PROGRESS

24. List some services the operating system should provide to help the users.
25. Why error detection is important?
26. We may want to keep track of usage system resources. (True or False)
27. Operating system must allocate resources to the programs in a manner such that resources are utilized _____.

1.8 USER OPERATING SYSTEM INTERFACE

Providing an interface to interact with the users is essential for an operating system. Earlier operating systems provide users with the command line interface or character based interface. This interface enables users to interact with operating system by entering commands to which it responds. On the other hand, most operating systems nowadays provide GUI in addition to character-based interface. GUI enables users to interact with the operating system by clicking mouse buttons.

1.8.1 Command Line Interface

As mentioned, this interface enables users to interact with the operating system by typing commands. These commands are then interpreted and executed in order to provide response to the user. The MS-DOS is the most commonly used operating system that provides command line interface. Figure 1.9 shows MS-DOS command line interface. Some operating systems provide more than one command line interface, therefore, on such systems, command line interfaces are called **shells**. For example, UNIX provides C shell, Bourne shell, Korn shell, etc.

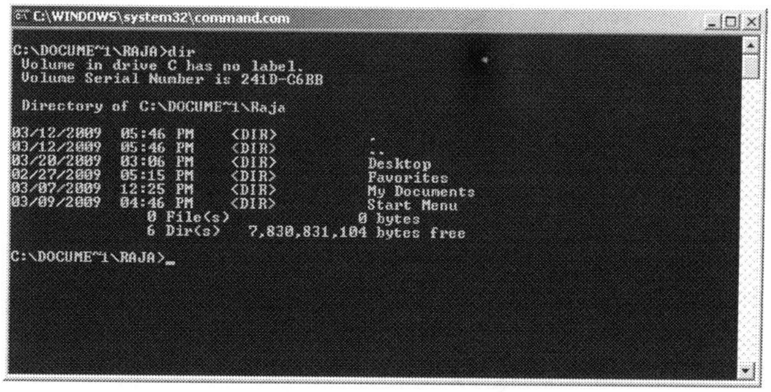

Figure 1.9: MS-DOS Command Line Interface

Generally, the commands that can be given perform some operations on a file, such as creation, deletion, printing, executing and so on. These commands can be implemented in two ways. In the first method, the code to execute the commands could be included in the interface itself. Now, whenever a command is issued by the user, the interface jumps to a section of its code and makes the appropriate system call. Since the code for the commands is included in the interface itself, adding new commands require changing the interface. In addition, the size of interface increases with each new command.

Alternatively, system programs can be developed that include the code for most commands. In this case, the interface has no idea about the command implementation; instead it just uses the command to locate the file and then load and executes it. The UNIX operating system follows this approach, therefore, a command in UNIX would search a file with that name, load it in memory and then executes it. For example, the command

```
cp file1.txt file2.txt
```

interprets cp as the file name, searches it and load it in the memory for execution. The command cp creates a copy of a given file. In the above command, file1.txt and file2.txt are the name of the source and the destination files and they are treated as parameters during execution of the command cp. It means a copy of file1.txt is created and named as file2.txt.

With this approach, the new commands can be added to the system easily by creating new system files. The names of the files will then serve the command name. Since adding new files do not require changing the interface, the size of the interface remains unchanged and small.

1.8.2 Graphical User Interfaces

Since in command line interface users interact by issuing certain commands, there is always a chance of committing a mistake. For example, opening a file might require the user to enter the path where the file actually resides. Any mistake in entering the path will prevent the user to open the file.

An alternative and more user friendly method to interface with the operating system is graphical user interface. GUI provides a rectangular area of screen called **Window** in which files, programs, directories and system functions are represented as small images or symbols called **icons**. In addition, various **menus** are provided which list actions or commands to be performed by the user. Such interface enables users to interact with operating system by moving mouse to position the mouse cursor and clicking on some icon or menu option. Depending upon the position of mouse cursor and the button (left or right) clicked on the mouse, some action is performed, such as opening of a file, execution of a program, appearing of a menu, etc.

UNIX, Apple Macintosh (Mac OS) and various versions of Microsoft Windows, including version 1.0, are some examples of operating systems that provide GUI. Many operating systems provide users with both command line interface and GUI, and it depends on person's personal choice to choose from and work with. Many UNIX programmers prefer to use command line interface because it is faster to work with and provides powerful capabilities, whereas, almost all Window users use GUI. GUI of Microsoft Windows XP is shown in Figure 1.10.

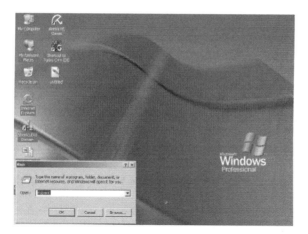

Figure 1.10: GUI of Microsoft Windows XP

1.9 SYSTEM CALLS

As mentioned, providing services to the user programs come under the operating system's responsibilities. User programs interface to these services through system calls. In other words, user programs take these services from operating system by making system calls. These calls are similar to a procedure call except that it switches the mode of execution from user mode to kernel mode and invokes the operating system. The operating system then determines what the user program actually asks or wants, performs the system call and returns the control back to the instruction following the system call. The user program now again proceeds in the user mode.

To understand how system calls are used in command line interface, let's take an example of a program that opens a file and writes some data in it. Suppose the file name and the data to be written on it is provided by the user during the execution of the program. This program performs a sequence of system call during its execution. First, it makes a system call to prompt a message on screen to ask the user to provide the file name and the data to be written on the file. Then, the user provides the file name and the data by typing it through keyboard and reading this from keyboard again needs a system call. With having the file name, the program attempts to open the required file, for which another system call needs to be made. Once the file is opened, the data is written to the file (requires a system call) and then the file is closed (another system call). Finally, a system call is performed to prompt the user with a message to inform that task is completed successfully.

The above discussion explains the use of system calls during normal operation, however, error could occur during any operation. For instance, when the program attempts to open the file, an error, such as file not found, hardware failure, file protection violation, etc., could occur. In this situation, the program cannot proceed with its normal behaviour, instead, it should prompt an appropriate message on the screen (a system call needed) and then terminate abnormally (another system call).

As now, it is clear that even the simple programs make heavy use of operating system services through system calls. In general, the services offered by these calls include creation and termination (or deletion) of processes, creation, deletion, reading, writing, opening and closing files, management of directories, and carrying out input and output. In fact, the set of services that are offered through system calls determines a significant part of the operating system's responsibilities. Here note that each system call may have same or different name in different operating systems.

1.9.1 Types of System Calls

All the system calls provided by an operating system can be roughly grouped into following five major categories.

- **Process management:** The system calls under this category include the calls to create a new process, terminate a process, setting and retrieving process attributes (such as process priority, its maximum allowable execution time, etc), forcing a process to wait for some time or some event to occur, etc.
- **File management:** The system calls under this category include the calls to create, delete, open, close, read and write a file.
- **Device management:** The system calls under this category include the calls to request for device, releasing it and performing some operations (such as read or write) with the device.
- **Information maintenance:** The system calls under this category include the calls to return information about the system, such as system's current data and time, number of current users, version of operating system, amount of free memory, etc.
- **Communications:** The system calls under this category include the calls to open and close communication connection, reading and writing messages, etc.

CHECK YOUR PROGRESS

28. How users interact with operating system using command line interface?
29. What are shells?
30. A user-friendly method to interface with the operating system is _____.
31. Many UNIX programmers prefer to use GUI. (True or False)
32. Which of the following does not provide GUI?
    (a) MS-DOS   (b) UNIX
    (c) Apple Macintosh   (d) None of these
33. For what purpose, system calls are used?
34. The set of services offered through system calls determines a significant part of the operating system's responsibilities. (True or False)

1.10 SYSTEM PROGRAMS

In addition to system calls, modern systems also provide a variety of system programs. These programs act as an interface between the operating system and the application programs. They provide an environment in which application programs can be developed and executed in a convenient manner. They can be classified into the following categories.

- **File management:** The system programs under this category provide commands, such as cut/copy, dump, list, print, etc., to perform various operations on files and directories.
- **File modification:** The system programs under this category allow creating or modifying the contents of a file stored on disk or some other storage device. Text editor is a system program that belongs to this category.

- **Communications:** The system programs under this category enable communication among different users, processes or systems by establishing virtual connections between them. With the help of these programs, a user can send messages to other users, log on some remote systems or transfer data from other system to its own system.
- **Status information:** The system programs under this category are used to present the status of the computer system, such as system date and time, number of users connected, CPU utilization, disk and memory usage, configuration information, etc.
- **Programming language support:** Nowadays, several programming languages support different system programs, such as compilers, assemblers and interpreters. These system programs are generally provided to the users along with the operating system.
- **Program loading and execution:** After a user program has been complied, it needs to be loaded in main memory for execution. The task of loading a program into the memory is performed by the loader, a system program. A system may provide different loaders, including absolute loaders, relocatable loaders, overlay loaders, etc. In addition, the successful execution of the program also requires debugging, which is performed by **debugger**—another system program under this category.

1.11 SYSTEM STRUCTURE

Every operating system has its own internal structure in terms of file arrangement, memory management, storage management, etc., and the entire performance of the system depends on its structure. The internal structure of operating system provides an idea of how the components of operating system are interconnected and blended into kernel. This section discusses various system structures that have evolved with time.

1.11.1 Simple Structure

The elementary approach to structure an operating system is simple structure. In this approach, the structure of the operating system was not well defined. MS-DOS is an operating system designed with this approach. Initially, it was designed as a small-size, simple and with limited scope but grew beyond its scope with time. It was designed with the idea of providing more functionality within less space, therefore, it was not carefully divided into modules. Figure 1.11 shows the structure of MS-DOS system.

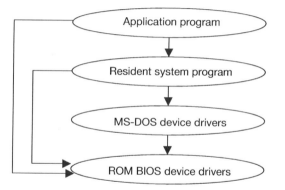

Figure 1.11: Structure of MS-DOS System

Though MS-DOS has a limited structuring, there is no clear separation between the different interfaces and level of functionality. For example, application programs can directly call the basic I/O routines to read/write data on disk instead of going through a series of interfaces. This exemption makes the MS-DOS system susceptible to malicious programs which may lead to system crash. Moreover, due to lack of hardware protection and dual-mode operation in Intel 8088 system (for which MS-DOS system was developed), the base hardware was directly accessible to the application programs.

1.11.2 Layered Approach

In layered approach, the operating system is organized as a hierarchy of layers with each layer built on the top of the layer below it. The topmost layer is the user interface while the bottommost layer is the hardware. Each layer has a well-defined function and comprises data structures and a set of routines. The layers are constructed in such a manner that a typical layer (say, layer n) is able to invoke operations on its lower layers and the operations of layer n can be invoked by its higher layers.

'THE system' was the first layer-based operating system developed in 1968 by E W Dijkstra and his students. This operating system consisted of six layers (0–5) and each layer had a predefined function as shown in Figure 1.12.

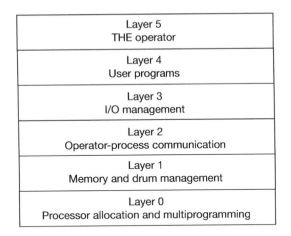

Figure 1.12: Layers in THE System

The layered design of operating system provides some benefits, which are as follows:

- It simplifies the debugging and verification of the system. As the lowest layer uses merely the base hardware, it can be debugged without pertaining to the rest of the system. Once it has been verified, its correct functioning can be assumed while the second layer is being verified. Similarly, each higher level layer can be debugged independent of the lower layer. If during verification, any bug is found, it will be on the layer being debugged as lower layers have already been verified.
- It supports information hiding. Each higher level layer is required to know only what operations the lower layers provide and not how they are being implemented.

The layered approach has some limitations too, which are as follows:

- As each higher level layer is allowed to use only its lower level layers, the layers must be defined carefully. For example, the device driver of physical disk must be defined at a layer below the one containing memory management routines. This is because memory management needs to use the physical disk.
- The time taken in executing a system call is much longer as compared to that of non-layered systems. This is because any request by the user has to pass through a number of layers before the action could be taken. As a result, system overhead increases and efficiency deceases.

1.11.3 Microkernels

Initially, the size of kernel was small; with Berkley UNIX (BSD), began the era of large kernels. Large kernel implies support for large number of system calls some of which are used very rarely. Moreover, large kernels are more error-prone and difficult to maintain. To overcome these problems, an approach called **microkernel** was developed that emphasized on modularizing the kernel. The idea is to remove the less essential components from the kernel and keeping only a subset of mechanisms typically included in a kernel thereby, reducing its size as well as number of system calls. The components moved outside the kernel are implemented either as system or user level programs. Mach system and OS X are the examples of operating systems designed with microkernel approach.

The main advantage of microkernel approach is that the operating system can be extended easily; the addition of new services in the user space does not cause any changes at the kernel level. In addition, microkernel offers high security and reliability as most services are running as user processes rather than kernel processes. Thus, if any of the running services fail, the rest of the system remains unaffected.

> **Note:** Though in microkernel approach the size of the kernel was reduced, still there is an issue regarding which services to be included in the kernel and which services to be implemented at the user level.

1.11.4 Modules

The module approach employs object-oriented programming techniques to design a modular kernel. In this approach, the operating system is organized around a core kernel and other loadable modules that can be linked dynamically with the kernel either at boot time or at run time. The idea is to make the kernel providing only core services while certain services can be added dynamically. An example of module-based operating system is Solaris, which consists of core kernel and seven loadable kernel modules: scheduling classes, file systems, loadable system calls, executable formats, streams modules, miscellaneous, and device and bus drivers.

The modular approach is similar to layered approach in the sense that each kernel module has well-defined interfaces. However, it is more flexible than layered approach as each module is free to call any other module.

1.12 VIRTUAL MACHINES

Virtual machine is nothing but the identical copy of the bare hardware, including CPU, disks, I/O devices, interrupts, etc. It allows each user to run operating system or software packages of his own choice on a single machine, thereby, creating an illusion that each user has its own machine.

The Virtual Machine Operating System (VMOS) creates several virtual machines by partitioning the resources of the real machine. The operating system uses the CPU scheduling and virtual memory concept to create an appearance that each running process has its own processor as well own virtual memory (see Figure 1.13). The spooling and file system are used to create illusion of each user having own card reader and line printer.

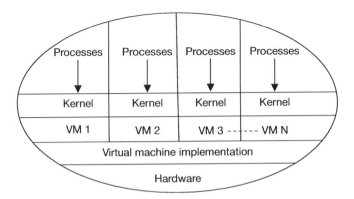

Figure 1.13: Virtual Machine Structure

The virtual memory approach provides the following benefits.

- Using virtual machines does not result in any extra overhead and performance degradation as each virtual machine has same architecture as that of real machine.
- Generally, while developing the operating system, the normal functioning of the current system is to be halted. However, by using virtual machine system, each system programmer can be provided with his own virtual machine for system development. Thus, there is no need to interrupt the normal system operation.
- The VMOS keeps the virtual machines isolated from one another. This results in protection of system resources.

CHECK YOUR PROGRESS

35. Mention different categories of system programs.
36. What is the main idea behind the microkernel approach?
37. THE operating system comprises five layers. (True or False)
38. The _____ creates several virtual machines by partitioning the resources of the real machine.

Let Us Summarize

1. The operating system is defined as a program that is running at all times on the computer (usually called the kernel). It is a program that acts as an interface between the computer users and the computer hardware.

2. An operating system is designed in such a way that it makes the computer system more convenient to use and allows the system to use its resources in an efficient manner.

3. There are two viewpoints from which we can understand the role of an operating system: the user point of view and the system point of view.

4. In case of a stand-alone environment, where a single user sits in front of a personal computer, the operating system is designed basically for the ease of use and some attention is also paid to system performance.

5. In case of a networked environment, where multiple users share resources and may exchange information, the operating system is designed for resource utilization.

6. In case of hand held systems, the operating system is basically designed for individual usability as these systems are mostly stand-alone units for individual users.

7. From the system's point of view, the operating system primarily acts as a resource allocator.

8. The operating system also acts as a control program that manages the execution of user programs to avoid errors and improper use of computer system.

9. These days a computer system basically consists of one or more processors (CPUs), several device controllers and the memory. All these components are connected through a common bus that provides access to shared memory

10. When the system boots up, the initial program that runs on the system is known as bootstrap program.

11. The event notification is done with the help of an interrupt which is fired either by the hardware or the software.

12. Whenever a program needs to be executed, it must be first loaded into the main memory (called random access memory or RAM).

13. The two instructions, namely, load and store are used to interact with the memory.

14. The execution of the program instructions takes place in the CPU registers, which are used as temporary storage areas and have limited storage space.

15. RAM is expensive, offers limited storage capacity and is volatile in nature, that is, it loses its contents when power supply is switched off.

16. Secondary storage is non-volatile in nature, that is, the data is permanently stored, and survives power failure and system crashes.

17. Magnetic disk (generally called disk) is the primary form of secondary storage that enables storage of enormous amount of data.

18. A significant portion of code of operating system is dedicated to manage I/O. One reason for this is the varying nature of I/O devices.

19. Each device controller controls a specific type of device and depending on the type of device controller one or more devices may be attached to it.

20. Interrupt-driven I/O wastes CPU's time because CPU requests data from the device controller one byte at a time. To solve this problem, another scheme, that is, Direct Memory Access (DMA) is commonly used.

21. Depending on the number of processors used in the system, a computer system can be categorized mainly into one of the two types: single processor system or multiprocessor system.

22. Single processor systems consist of one main CPU that can execute a general-purpose instruction set, which includes instructions from user processes. Other than the one main CPU, most systems also have some special-purpose processors.

23. The multiprocessor systems (also known as parallel systems or tightly coupled systems) consist of multiple processors in close communication in a sense that they share the computer bus and even the system clock, memory, and peripheral devices.

24. Multiprocessor systems are of two types, namely, symmetric and asymmetric.

25. One of the most common features of operating systems is that they support multiprogramming. The execution of multiple jobs in an interleaved manner is known as multiprogramming.

26. In case of multiprogrammed systems, the jobs are organized in such a way that the CPU always has one to execute. This increases the CPU utilization by minimizing the CPU idle time.

27. The number of processes competing to get the system resources in multiprogramming environment is known as degree of multiprogramming.

28. When a job enters into the system, it is kept in the job pool on the disk which contains all those jobs that are waiting for the allocation of main memory.

29. An extension of multiprogrammed systems is time-sharing systems (or multitasking) in which multiple users are allowed to interact with the system through their terminals.

30. The CPU in time-sharing systems switches so rapidly from one user to another that each user gets the impression that only he or she is working on the system, even though the system is being shared among multiple users.

31. Time-sharing provides a mechanism for concurrent execution, which requires CPU scheduling to be more sophisticated.

32. In order to ensure the proper functioning of the computer system, the operating system, and all other programs and their data must be protected against the incorrect programs. To achieve this protection, two modes of operations, namely, user mode and monitor mode (also known as supervisor mode, system mode, kernel mode or privileged mode) are specified.

33. Some of the machine instructions that may cause harm are designated as privileged instructions. These privileged instructions are allowed to be executed only in the monitor mode.

34. It is necessary to prevent a user program from gaining the control of the system for an infinite time. For this, a timer is maintained, which interrupts the system after a specified period.

35. Providing the environment in which programs can be executed and the set of services to user programs are the operating system's responsibilities. One set of operating-system services provides functions to help the user.

36. Another set of services that helps allocating resources to programs in some order is necessary for an operating system. These services exist not for helping user, instead to ensure the efficient and secure execution of programs.

37. The command line interface enables users to interact with operating system by entering commands to which it responds.

38. GUI enables users to interact with the operating system by clicking mouse buttons.

39. User programs interface to the services provided by the operating system through system calls. In other words, user programs take these services from operating system by making system calls. These calls are similar to a procedure call except that it switches the mode of execution from user mode to kernel mode and invokes the operating system.

40. All the system calls provided by an operating system can be roughly grouped into following five major categories, namely, process management, file management, device management, information maintenance and communication.

41. The system programs act as an interface between the operating system and the application programs. They provide an environment in which application programs can be developed and executed in a convenient manner.

42. Every operating system has its own internal structure in terms of file arrangement, memory management, storage management, etc., and the entire performance of the system depends on its structure. Various system structures have evolved with time, including simple structure, layered structure, microkernel and modules.

43. Virtual machine is nothing but the identical copy of the bare hardware, including CPU, disks, I/O devices, interrupts, etc. It allows each user to run operating system or software packages of his own choice on a single machine, thereby, creating an illusion that each user has its own machine.

 ## ANSWERS TO 'CHECK YOUR PROGRESS'

1. The two viewpoints from which we can understand the role of an operating system are user point of view and the system point of view.
2. (d)
3. Convenience, efficiency
4. False
5. Device controller acts as an interface between a particular I/O device and the operating system. In other words, a device controller plays an important role in operating that particular device.
6. Whenever an interrupt is fired, the CPU stops executing the current task and jumps to a predefined location in the kernel's address space, which contains the starting address of the service routine for the interrupt (known as interrupt handler). It then executes the interrupt handler and once the execution is completed, the CPU resumes the task that it was previously doing.
7. An instruction execution cycle consists of the following steps.
   (i)   Whenever the CPU needs to execute an instruction, it first fetches it from the main memory and stores it in Instruction Register (IR).
   (ii) Once the instruction has been loaded into the IR, the control unit examines and decodes the fetched instruction.
   (iii) After decoding the instruction, the operands (if required) are fetched from the main memory and stored in one of the internal registers.
   (iv) The instruction is executed on the operands and the result is stored back to the main memory.
8. (c)
9. Bootstrap program
10. Storage devices
11. True
12. Multiprocessor systems are of two types, namely, symmetric and asymmetric. In symmetric multiprocessing systems, all the processors are identical and perform identical functions. Each processor runs an identical copy of the operating system and these copies interact with each other as and when required. All processors in symmetric multiprocessor system are peers—no master-slave relationship exists between them.
13. The special-purpose processors may be in the form of device-specific processors, such as disk, keyboard, etc., or in mainframes, they may be I/O processors that move data among system components. Note that the special-purpose processors execute a limited instruction set and do not execute instructions from the user processes.
14. System throughput
15. False

16. Execution of a single program cannot keep the CPU and the I/O devices busy at all times because during its execution it sometimes requires CPU and sometimes requires I/O devices but not both at the same time. Hence, when the program is busy with CPU, the I/O devices have to wait and when the program is busy with I/O devices, the CPU remains idle.

17. The basic idea behind multiprogramming is that the operating system loads multiple jobs into the memory from the job pool (the jobs kept on the disk). The jobs are organized in such a way that the CPU always has one job to execute. This increases the CPU utilization by minimizing the CPU idle time.

18. Waiting for the allocation of main memory

19. (b)

20. Though the sharing of resources has improved the resource utilization, it has also increased the problems. In single-user system, an error in a currently running program can cause problems for that program only as it is the only active program at that point of time. However, when the resources are shared among several programs, then an error in one program can adversely affect the execution of other programs. It may also happen that an erroneous program modifies another program, or data of another program or the operating system itself.

21. Privileged instructions

22. Monitor

23. True

24. One set of operating system services provides function to help the user. These services, include user interface, program execution, I/O operations, file system manipulation, communication and error detection.

25. There is always a possibility of occurrence of error in the computer system. Error may occur in the CPU, memory, I/O devices or in user program. Examples of errors include an attempt to access an illegal memory location, power failure, link failure on a network, too long use of CPU by a user program, etc. The operating system must be constantly aware of possible errors, and should take appropriate action in the event of occurrence of error to ensure correct and consistent computing.

26. True

27. Efficiently

28. The command line interface enables users to interact with the operating system by typing commands. These commands are then interpreted and executed in order to provide response to the users.

29. Some operating systems provide more than one command line interface, therefore, on such systems, command line interfaces are called shells.

30. Graphical user interface

31. False

32. (a)

33. User programs interface to the services provided by the operating system through system calls. In other words, user programs take these services from operating system by making system calls. These calls are similar to a procedure call except that it switches the mode of execution from user mode to kernel mode and invokes the operating system.

34. True

35. Different categories of system programs include file management, file modification, communications, status information, programming language support, and program loading and execution.

36. The idea behind microkernel approach is to remove the less essential components from the kernel and keeping only a subset of mechanisms typically included in a kernel, thereby, reducing its size as well as number of system calls.
37. False
38 Virtual machine operating system

TEST YOURSELF

1. Describe the two viewpoints from which we can understand the role of an operating system.
2. How computer system handles interrupts? Also discuss how interrupts can be handled quickly?
3. Discuss the storage structure of computer system.
4. How an I/O operation is handled by the system?
5. Describe single processor and multiprocessor systems.
6. Write short note on the following:
    (a) Direct memory access
    (b) Multiprogramming
    (c) Time-sharing systems
    (d) Dual-mode operation
    (e) Command line interface
    (f) Virtual machines
7. Why maintaining a timer is important?
8. Discuss the set of services the operating system should provide.
9. How GUI is better than command line interface?
10. What are system calls? Describe the use of system calls with the help of an example.
11. Explain various categories of system programs.
12. Discuss various system structures that have evolved with time.

Chapter 02

Processes

Learning Objectives

After reading this chapter, you will be able to:

- ☐ Understand the basic concepts of processes
- ☐ Discuss about various states of a process and the transition between these states
- ☐ Define the term process scheduling
- ☐ Explain various operations that can be performed on processes
- ☐ Understand the concept of cooperating process
- ☐ Provide an overview of interprocess communication
- ☐ Explain different mechanisms used for communication in client-server environment
- ☐ Explore some of the interprocess facilities provided by Linux

2.1 INTRODUCTION

In yesteryears, there was a boundation of loading only one program at a time into the main memory for execution. This program was very multifaceted and resourceful as it had access to all the computer resources, such as memory, CPU time, I/O devices and so on. As the time went by, improvements were accepted as new systems incorporate a variety of new and powerful features that dramatically improved the efficiency and functionality of the overall system. Modern computer systems corroborate multiprogramming, which allows a number of programs to reside in the main memory at the same time. These programs can be executed concurrently, thereby, requiring the system resources to be shared among them. Multiprogrammed systems need to distinguish among the multiple executing programs, which is accomplished with the concept of a process (also called **task** on some systems). A **process** is a program under execution or we can say an executing set of machine instructions. A process can be either a **system process** executing the system's code or a **user process** executing the user's code.

When multiple processes run on a system concurrently and more than one process requires CPU at the same time, then it becomes essential to select any one process to which the CPU can be allocated. To serve this purpose, scheduling is required. Moreover, the multiple processes running on a system also need to intercommunicate in order to reciprocate some data or information. This kind of intercommunication between several processes is referred to as **InterProcess Communication (IPC)**.

2.2 PROCESS CONCEPTS

In this section, we will discuss some basic concepts of processes.

2.2.1 The Process

As stated earlier, a program undergoing execution is termed as a process. There is a hairline difference between the program and process in the sense that a program is a passive entity that does not initiate anything by itself, whereas, a process is an active entity that performs all the actions specified in a particular program. A process comprises not only the program code (known as **text section**) but also a set of global variables (known as **data section**) and the Process Control Block (PCB). The process control block (discussed in detail further in this section) of a process contains some additional information about the process, like a program counter, to specify the current activity in progress, the contents of CPU's registers, a process stack to store temporary data, like function parameters, local variables used in a function, return addresses, etc.

> **Note:** The set of instructions, data and stack together form the address space of a process.

There can be either one-to-one or one-to-many relationship between programs and processes. A one-to-one relationship exists in case only a single instance of a program is running on the system. On the other hand, if the multiple instances of a single program are running simultaneously or when a concurrent program (a program that requires some of its parts to be executed concurrently) is being run, there exists one-to-many relationship between programs and processes. In this case, the text section of the multiple instances will be same but the data section will be different.

One important thing to notice about the processes is that some processes involve higher computation than I/O operations, thereby, demanding more use of CPU than I/O devices during their lifetime. Such processes where the speed of execution is governed by CPU are called **CPU bound** or **compute bound**. Contrastive to this, are some processes that involve a lot of I/O operations as compared to computation during their lifetime. Such processes where the speed of execution is governed by the I/O device not by the CPU are called **I/O bound**.

2.2.2 Process States

Each process in the operating system is tagged with a 'state' variable—an integer value that helps the operating system to decide what to do with the process. It also indicates the nature of the current activity in a process. A process may be in one of the following states depending on the current activity of the process.

- **New:** A process is said to be in 'new' state if it is being created.
- **Ready:** A process is said to be in 'ready' state if it is ready for the execution and waiting for the CPU to be allocated to it.
- **Running:** A process is said to be in 'running' state if CPU has been allocated to it and it is being executed.
- **Waiting:** A process is said to be in 'waiting' state (also called 'blocked' state) if it has been blocked by some event. Unless that event occurs, the process cannot continue its execution. Examples of such blocking events are completion of some I/O operation, reception of a signal, etc. Note that a process in waiting state is unable to run even if the CPU is available.
- **Terminated:** A process is said to be in 'terminated' state if it has completed its execution normally or it has been terminated abnormally by the operating system because of some error or killed by some other process.

> **Note:** On a single processor system, only one process may be in running state at one time, however, in a multiprocessor system with m CPUs, at most m processes may be in running state at one time.

Each process undergoes changes in states during its lifetime. The change in state of a process is known as **state transition** of a process. Generally, it is caused by the occurrence of some event in the system. There are many possible state transitions (see Figure 2.1) that may crop up along with their possible causes are as follows:

- **New → Ready:** This transition takes place if a new process has been loaded into the main memory and it is waiting for the CPU to be allocated to it.
- **Ready → Running:** This transition takes place if the CPU has been allocated to a ready process and it has started its execution.
- **Running → Ready:** This transition may occur if
  - the time-slice of the currently running process has expired
  - some higher priority process gets ready for execution, etc.

In this case, the CPU is preempted from the currently executing process and allocated to some another ready process.

- **Running → Waiting:** This transition may take place if the currently running process
  - needs to perform some I/O operation
  - has to wait for a message or some action from another process
  - requests for some other resource

In this case, the CPU gets freed by the process and can be allocated to some another ready process.

- **Running → Terminated:** This transition takes place if the currently running process
  - has completed its task and requests to the operating system for its termination
  - is terminated by its parent in case the function performed by it is no longer required
  - is terminated by the kernel because it has exceeded its resource usage limit or involved in a deadlock

In this case, the CPU is preempted from the currently running process and allocated to some another ready process.

- **Waiting → Ready:** This transition takes place if an event (for example, I/O completion, signal reception, synchronization operation, etc.) for which the process was waiting, has occurred.

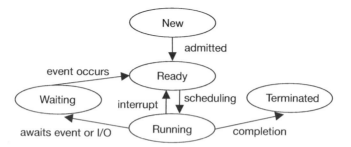

Figure 2.1: Process State Transition Diagram

2.2.3 Process Control Block (PCB)

To keep track of all the processes in the system, the operating system maintains a structurally organized table called **process table** that includes an entry for each process. This entry is called **Process Control Block** (PCB)—a data structure created by the operating system for representing a process. A process control block stores descriptive information pertaining to a process, such as its state, program counter, memory management information, information about its scheduling, allocated resources, accounting information, etc., that is required to control and manage a particular process. The basic purpose of PCB is to indicate the so far progress of a process. Some of the important fields stored in a PCB are as follows:

- **Process ID:** Each process is assigned a unique identification number called **process identifier** (PID) by the operating system at the time of its creation. PID is used to refer the process in the operating system.
- **Process state:** It stores the current state of a process that can be new, ready, running, waiting or terminated.
- **Parent process ID:** It stores the PID of the parent, if the process has been created by some other process.
- **Child process IDs:** It stores the PIDs of all the child processes of a parent process.
- **Program counter:** It contains the address of the instruction that is to be executed next in the process. Whenever CPU switches from one process to another, the program counter

of the old process is saved so that the operating system could resume with the same instruction whenever the old process is restarted.

- **Event information:** If the process is in waiting state then this field contains the information about the event for which the process is waiting to happen. For example, if the process is waiting for an I/O device, then this field stores the ID of that device.
- **Memory management information:** It includes information related to the memory configuration for a process, such as the value of base and limit registers, the page tables (if paging memory management technique has been used) or the segment tables (if segmentation memory management technique has been used). The memory management techniques are discussed in detail in *Chapter 07*.
- **CPU registers:** It stores the contents of index registers, general purpose registers, condition code information, etc., at the time when the CPU was last freed by the process or preempted from the process.
- **CPU scheduling information:** It includes information used by the scheduling algorithms, such as the process priority number (in case the priority scheduling is to be used for the process), the pointers to appropriate scheduling queues depending upon the current state of the process, the time when CPU was last allocated to the process, etc. CPU scheduling is discussed in detail in *Chapter 04*.
- **I/O status:** It includes information, such as I/O devices allocated to a process, pointers to the files opened by the process for I/O, the current position in the files, etc.

CHECK YOUR PROGRESS
1. A process comprises _____ , _____ and _____ .
2. Which of the following state transition is not possible?
   (a) Ready → Running   (b) Running → Waiting
   (c) Ready → Waiting   (d) Waiting → Ready
3. What does a process control block contain?
4. The set of instructions, data and stack together form the address space of a process. (True or False)

2.3 PROCESS SCHEDULING

The main objective of multiprogramming is to keep the jobs organized in such a manner that CPU has always one to execute. This confirms that CPU is utilized to the maximum level by reducing its idle time. This purpose can be jolly well achieved by keeping the CPU busy at all the times. This implies that some process must always be running on the CPU. However, when two or more processes compete for the CPU at the same time then choice has to be made which process to allocate the CPU next. This procedure of determining the next process to be executed on the CPU is called **process scheduling** and the module of operating system that makes this decision is called the **scheduler**.

2.3.1 Scheduling Queues

For scheduling purposes, there exist different queues in the system that are as follows:

- **Job queue:** As the processes enter the system for execution, they are massed into a queue called job queue (or **input queue**) on a mass storage device, such as hard disk.
- **Ready queue:** From the job queue, the processes which are ready for the execution are shifted into the main memory. In the main memory, these processes are kept into a queue called ready queue. In other words, the ready queue contains all those processes that are waiting for the CPU.
- **Device queue:** For each I/O device in the system, a separate queue called device queue is maintained. The process that needs to perform I/O during its execution is kept into the queue of that specific I/O device and waits there until it is served by the device.

Generally, both the ready queue and device queue are maintained as linked lists that contain PCBs of the processes in the queue as their nodes. Each PCB includes a pointer to the PCB of the next process in the queue (see Figure 2.2). In addition, the header node of the queue contains pointers to the PCBs of the first and last process in the queue.

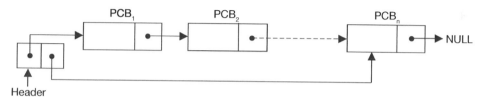

Figure 2.2: Ready Queue and Device Queue Maintained as Linked List

Whenever a process in the job queue becomes ready to execute, it is brought into the ready queue where it waits for the CPU allocation. Once CPU is allocated to it (that is, the process switches to the running state), the following transitions may occur.

- If the process needs to perform some I/O operation during its execution, it is removed from the ready queue and put into the appropriate device queue. After the process completes its I/O operation and is ready for the execution, it is switched from the device queue to ready queue.
- If an interrupt occurs, the CPU can be forcibly taken away from the currently executing process and the process has to wait until the interrupt is handled. After that the process is put back into the ready queue.
- If the time-slice (in case of time-sharing systems) of the process has expired, the process is put back into the ready queue.
- If the process creates a new process and has to wait until the child process terminates, the parent process is suspended. After the execution of child process, it is again put back into the ready queue.
- If the process has successfully completed its task, it is terminated. The PCB and all the resources allocated to the process are deallocated.

All these transitions can be represented with the help of a queuing diagram as shown in Figure 2.3.

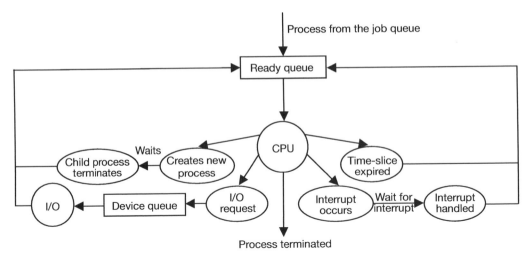

Figure 2.3: Queueing Diagram

> **Note:** In a single processor system, since there can be only one running process at a time, there is no need to maintain a queue for the running processes.

2.3.2 Types of Schedulers

The following types of schedulers (see Figure 2.4) may coexist in a complex operating system.

- **Long-term scheduler:** also known as **job scheduler** or **admission scheduler** works with the job queue. It selects the next process to be executed from the job queue and loads it into the main memory for execution. The long-term scheduler must select the processes in such a way that some of the processes are CPU bound while others are I/O bound. This is because if all the processes are CPU bound, then the devices will remain unused most of the time. On the other hand, if all the processes are I/O bound then CPU will remain idle most of the time. Thus, to achieve the best performance, a balanced mix of CPU bound and I/O bound processes must be selected. The main objective of this scheduler is to control the degree of multiprogramming (that is, the number of processes in the ready queue) in order to keep the processor utilization at the desired level. For this, the long-term scheduler may admit new processes in the ready queue in case of poor processor utilization or may reduce the rate of admission of processes in the ready queue in case the processor utilization is high. In addition, the long-term scheduler is generally invoked only when a process exits from the system. Thus, the frequency of invocation of long-term scheduler depends on the system and workload, and is much lower than other two types of schedulers.
- **Short-term scheduler:** also known as **CPU scheduler** or **process scheduler** selects a process from the ready queue and allocates CPU to it. This scheduler is required to be invoked frequently as compared to long-term scheduler. This is because generally a process executes for a short period and then it may have to wait either for I/O or

some other reason. At that time, CPU scheduler must select some other process and allocate CPU to it. Thus, the CPU scheduler must be fast in order to provide the least time gap between executions.

- **Medium-term scheduler:** also known as **swapper** comes into play whenever a process is to be removed from the ready queue (or from the CPU in case it is being executed) thereby reducing the degree of multiprogramming. This process is stored at some space on the hard disk and later brought into the memory to restart execution from the point where it left off. This task of temporarily switching a process in and out of main memory is known as **swapping** (discussed in detail in *Chapter 07*). The medium-term scheduler selects a process among the partially executed or unexecuted swapped-out processes and swaps it in the main memory. The medium-term scheduler is usually invoked when there is some unoccupied space in the memory made by the termination of a process or if the supply of ready processes reduces below a specified limit.

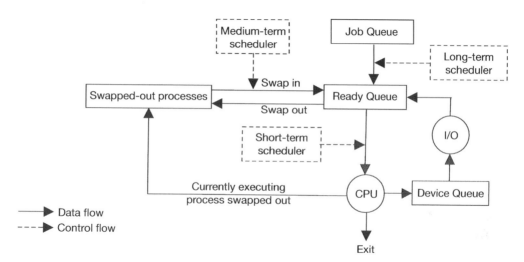

Figure 2.4: Types of Schedulers

2.3.3 Context Switch

Transferring the control of CPU from one process to another demands for saving the context of the currently running process and loading the context of another ready process. This mechanism of saving and restoring the context is known as **context switch**. The portion of the process control block, including the process state, memory management information and CPU scheduling information together constitute the **context** (also called **state information**) of a process. Context switch may occur due to a number of reasons some of which are as follows:

- The current process terminates and exits from the system.
- The time-slice of the current process expires.
- The process has to wait for I/O or some other resource.

- Some higher priority process enters the system.
- The process relinquishes the CPU by invoking some system call.

Context switching is performed in two steps, which are as follows:

1. **Save context:** In this step, the kernel saves the context of the currently executing process in its PCB of the process so that it may restore this context later when its processing is done and the execution of the suspended process can be resumed.
2. **Restore context:** In this step, the kernel loads the saved context of a different process that is to be executed next. Note that if the process to be executed is newly created and CPU has not yet been allocated to it, there will be no saved context. In this case, the kernel loads the context of the new process. However, if the process to be executed was in waiting state due to I/O or some other reason, there will be saved context that can be restored.

One of the major detriments of using context switching is that it incurs a huge cost to the system in terms of real time and CPU cycles because the system does not perform any productive work during switching. Therefore, context switching should be generally refrained from as far as possible; otherwise, it would amount to reckless use of time. Figure 2.5 shows context switching between two processes P_1 and P_2.

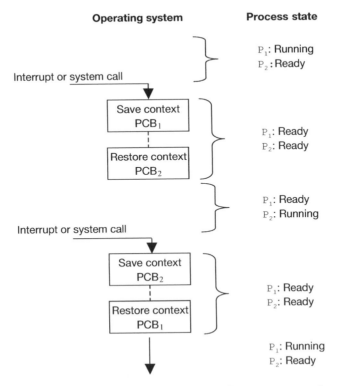

Figure 2.5: Context Switching between Processes P_1 and P_2

2.4 OPERATIONS ON PROCESSES

There are innumerable operations that can be performed on processes, such as creating, terminating, suspending or resuming a process, etc. To successfully execute these operations, the operating system provides run-time services (or system calls) for the process management. The user may invoke these system calls either directly by embedding the process supervisory calls in the user's program or indirectly by typing commands on the terminal which are translated by the system into system calls. In this section, we will discuss only process creation and termination operations.

2.4.1 Process Creation

Whenever an operating system is booted, a number of processes (system processes) are created automatically. Out of these, some involve user interaction (called **foreground processes**) while others are not related with any user but still perform some specific function (called **background processes**). In addition to system processes, new processes can be created afterward as well. Sometimes, a user process may need to create one or more processes during its execution. It can do the same by invoking the process creation system call (for example, `CreateProcess()` in Windows and `fork()` in UNIX which tells the operating system to create a new process. This task of creating a new process on the request of some another process is called **process spawning**. The process that spawns a new process is called **parent process**, whereas, the spawned process is called the **child process** (or **sub process**). The newly created process can further create new processes, thereby, generating hierarchy of processes.

Whenever a process creates a child process, there are chances of innumerable likelihoods that may arise depending on the operating system installed. Some of these likelihoods are as follows:

- Either the parent and child process may run concurrently (**asynchronous process creation**) or the parent process may wait until the child process completes its task and terminates (**synchronous process creation**).
- The newly created process may be the duplicate of the parent process in that case it contains a copy of the address space of its parent. On the other hand, the child process may have a new program loaded into its address space.

- The child process may be restricted to a subset of resources available to the parent process or the child process may obtain its resources directly from the operating system. In the former case, the resources being used by the parent process need to be divided or shared among its various child processes.

> **Note:** Every time a process creates a new process, the `PID` of the child process is passed to the parent process.

2.4.2 Process Termination

Depending upon the condition, a process may be terminated either normally or forcibly by some another process. Normal termination occurs when the process completes its task and invokes an appropriate system call (for example, `ExitProcess()` in Windows and `exit()` in UNIX) to tell the operating system that it is finished. As a result, all the resources held by the process are deallocated, the process returns output data (if any) to its parent and finally, the process is removed from the memory by deleting its PCB from the process table.

> **Note:** A process that no longer exists but still its PCB has not been removed from the process table is known as a zombie process.

Contrary to this, a process may cause abnormal termination of some another process. For this, the process invokes an appropriate system call (for example, `TerminateProcess()` in Windows and `kill()` in UNIX) that tells the operating system to kill some other process. Generally, the parent process can invoke such a system call to terminate its child process. This usually happens because of the following reasons.

- Cascading termination in which the termination (whether normal or forced) of a process causes the termination of all its children. On some operating systems, a child process is not allowed to execute when its parent is being terminated. In such cases, the operating system initiates cascading termination.
- The task that was being performed by the child process is not required.
- The child process has used up the resources allocated to it more than that it was permitted.

2.5 COOPERATING PROCESSES

The processes that coexist in the memory at some time are called **concurrent processes**. The concurrent processes may either be independent or cooperating. The **independent** (also called **competitors**) processes, as the name implies, do not share any kind of information or data with each other. They just compete with each other for the resources, like CPU, I/O devices, etc., that are required to accomplish their operations. The **cooperating** (also called **interacting**) processes, on the other hand, need to exchange data or information with each other. In other words, we can say a cooperating process is the one that can affect or be affected by the actions of other concurrent processes. The need of cooperation among processes arises because of the following reasons.

- Several processes may need access to the same information. This requires the operating system to provide a means for concurrent access to the desired information.

- If a computer system has multiple processing elements (for example, multiple CPUs or multiple I/O channels), we can make a task to execute faster by breaking it into various subtasks and running each of them in parallel.
- The environment supporting cooperating processes will help a single user to carry out multiple tasks at the same time. For example, a single user may be opening, printing and compiling at the same time.
- The system's functions can be divided into different processes and threads in order to construct the system in a modular fashion.

2.6 INTERPROCESS COMMUNICATION

The cooperating processes require some mechanism to exchange data or pass information to each other. One such mechanism is InterProcess Communication (IPC)—a very useful facility provided by the operating system—that allows the processes running on a single system to communicate with each other. Two basic communication models for providing IPC are **shared memory systems** and **message passing systems**. In the former model, a part of memory is shared among the cooperating processes. The processes that need to exchange data or information can do so by writing to and reading from this shared memory. However, in the latter model, the cooperating processes communicate by sending and receiving messages from each other. The communication using message passing is very time consuming as compared to shared memory. This is because the message passing system is implemented with the help of operating system calls and thus, it requires a major involvement of kernel. On the other hand, in shared memory systems, system calls are used only to set up the shared memory area. Once the shared area is set up, no further kernel intervention is required.

2.6.1 Shared Memory Systems

In shared memory systems, the process that needs to communicate with other processes creates a shared memory segment in its own address space. Other processes can communicate with this process by attaching its shared memory segment along with their address space. All the communicating processes can read or write data through this shared area. Note that these processes must be synchronized so that no two processes should be able to access the shared area simultaneously. Figure 2.6 shows a shared memory communication model.

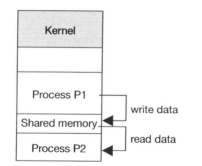

Figure 2.6: Shared Memory Communication Model

To understand the concept of shared memory systems, consider a common example of cooperating processes known as **producer consumer** problem. In this problem, there are two processes, one is `producer` that produces the items and other is `consumer` that consumes the items produced by the `producer`. These two processes need to run concurrently thereby requiring communication with each other. One possible solution to this problem can be provided through shared memory. Both the `producer` and `consumer` processes are made to share a common **buffer** between them. The `producer` fills the buffer by placing the produced items in it and the `consumer` vacates the buffer by consuming these items.

The buffer shared between `producer` and `consumer` may be bounded or unbounded. In bounded buffer, the size of buffer is fixed therefore `producer` has to wait in case the buffer is full and `consumer` has to wait in case the buffer is empty. On the other hand, in unbounded buffer, there is no limit on the buffer size. Thus, only `consumer` has to wait in case there is no item to be consumed. However, `producer` need not wait and it may continuously produce items.

Note: In case of bounded buffer, the producer consumer problem is also known as bounded buffer problem.

To implement the bounded buffer problem using shared memory, consider the shared buffer consists of N slots with each capable of storing an item. Further assume that the buffer is implemented as a circular array having two pointers `in` and `out`. The pointer `in` points to the next free slot in the buffer and the pointer `out` points to the slot containing the next item to be consumed. Initially, both `in` and `out` are set to zero. The following code written in C language illustrates the implementation of shared area.

```
#define size 100;      /* N=100 */
int buffer[size];
int in=0;
int out=0;
```

To implement the producer process, a local variable `item_produced` is used that stores the newly produced item. The `producer` produces an item, places it in the buffer at the position denoted by `in` and updates the value of `in`. It continues to do so as long as buffer is not full. Once the buffer gets full, that is, when `(in + 1) % size == out`, it goes to the waiting state and remains in that state until some slot becomes free in the buffer (that is, until `consumer` removes some item from the buffer). The following code illustrates the implementation of the producer process.

```
int item_produced;
while(1)
{
        item_produced = produce_item();
                /* calling procedure to produce an item */
        while(((in + 1) % size) != out)
        {               /* check if buffer is not full */
            buffer[in] = item_produced;
```

```
                     /* put item into the buffer */
          in = (in + 1) % size;
                     /* update in to point to next free slot */
     }
}
```

Likewise, to put into the effect the consumer process, a local variable item_consumed is used that stores the item to be consumed. The consumer removes an item from the position denoted by out in the buffer, updates the value of out and consumes that item. It continues to do so as long as the buffer is not empty. Once the buffer gets empty, that is, when in == out, it goes to the waiting state and remains in that state until producer places some item in the buffer. The following code illustrates the implementation of the consumer process.

```
int item_consumed;
while(1)
{
     while(in != out)    /* check if buffer is not empty */
     {
          item_consumed = buffer[out];
                     /* remove item from the buffer */
          out = (out + 1) % size; /* update out to point */
                     /* to the next item to be consumed */
     }
     consume_item(item_consumed);
                /* calling procedure to consume an item */
}
```

> **Note:** For the sake of simplicity, we have assumed that the item in the buffer is of type integer and the implementation of procedures for producing or consuming items is not shown here.

This solution to bounded buffer problem permits to have at most size-1 items in the buffer at the same time. In order to have size items in the buffer at the same time, we will need to develop a different solution. In addition, this solution does not address to how to implement the synchronization between producer and consumer. Both the solution and the synchronization are discussed in *Chapter 05*.

2.6.2 Message Passing Systems

In message passing systems, two system calls, send() and receive() are used. The sender process (say, P_1) sends the message to the operating system by invoking the send() system call. The operating system stores this message in the buffer area until the receive() system call is invoked by the receiver process (say, P_2). After that the operating system delivers this message to P_2. In case there is no message available for P_2 when it invokes the receive() system call, the operating system blocks it until some message arrives for it. On the other hand, if a number of messages arrive for P_2, the operating system puts them in a queue and delivers them in FIFO order upon the invocation of `receive()` call (one for each process) by P_2. Figure 2.7 shows the message passing communication model.

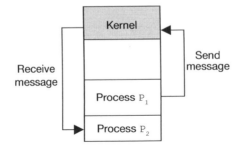

Figure 2.7: Message Passing Communication Model

In message passing, it is not necessary for the communicating processes to reside on the same computer rather they may reside on different computers connected via network (a distributed environment). Therefore, whenever two processes want to communicate, a communication link must be established between them. At the physical level, the communication link may be implemented via shared variables or bus or the network, etc. However, at the logical level, some features related with the implementation of communication link arise, which are discussed here.

Type of Communication

Processes may communicate with each other directly or indirectly.

In the **direct communication**, processes address each other by their `PID` assigned to them by the operating system. For example, if a process P_1 wants to send a message to process P_2, then the system calls `send()` and `receive()` will be defined as follows:

- `send(PID₂, message)`
- `receive(PID₁, message)`

Since, both sender and receiver process need to know each other's `PID`, this type of communication is known as symmetric direct communication. However, asymmetry in addressing can be represented by making only the sender process to address the receiver process by its `PID` but the receiver process need not know the `PID` of the sender process. In case of asymmetric direct communication, the calls `send()` and `receive()` will be defined as follows:

- `send(PID₂, message)`
- `receive(id, message)`

Now, when operating system delivers a message to process P_2 upon the invocation of a `receive()` call by it, the parameter `id` is replaced with the `PID` of the sender process.

In **indirect communication**, messages are sent and received via **mailbox** (also known as **port**)—a repository of interprocess messages. A mailbox, as the name implies, is just like a post box into which messages sent by the processes can be stored and removed by other processes. The different characteristics of a mailbox are as follows:

- Each mailbox has a unique ID and the processes communicate with each other through a number of mailboxes.
- The process that creates the mailbox is the owner of mailbox and only this process can receive messages from it. Other processes can only send messages to it. In other words, there can be multiple senders but a single recipient for a mailbox.
- The process that knows the ID of a mailbox can send messages to it.
- Besides a user process, the operating system may also own a mailbox. In this case, the operating system may allow the processes to create or delete a mailbox, send and receive messages via mailbox. The process that creates the mailbox becomes the owner of that mailbox and may receive messages through this mailbox. However, with time, other processes can also be made to receive messages through this mailbox by passing ownership to them.

The system calls to send a message to a mailbox (say, X) and receive a message from a mailbox will be defined as follows:

- `send(X, message)`
- `receive(X, message)`

As stated earlier, a communication link must exist between processes before starting the communication. The communication link exhibits different properties in direct and indirect communication, which are discussed in Table 2.1.

Table 2.1: Comparison of Direct and Indirect Communication

Direct Communication	*Indirect Communication*
• There exists only one link between each pair of communicating processes.	• There may be multiple links between each pair of communicating processes, where each link corresponds to exactly one mailbox.
• A link is associated with just two processes.	• A link may be associated with more than two processes.
• The link is established automatically between the communicating processes, provided the sender process knows the `PID` of the receiver process.	• The communication link can be established between two processes only if both the communicating processes share a mailbox with each other.

Synchronization

Messages can be sent or received either **synchronously** or **asynchronously**, also called **blocking** or **non-blocking**, respectively. Various design options for implementing `send()` and `receive()` calls are as follows:

- **Blocking send:** If a process (say, P_1) invokes `send()` call to send a message to another process (say, P_2) or to a mailbox, the operating system blocks P_1 until the message is received by P_2 or by the mailbox.

- **Blocking receive:** If there is no message available for P_2 when it invokes the `receive()` system call, the operating system blocks it until some message arrives for it.
- **Non-blocking send:** P_1 sends the message and continues to perform its operation without waiting for the message delivery by P_2 or by mailbox.
- **Non-blocking receive:** When P_2 invokes a `receive()` call, it either gets a valid message if some message is available for it or `NULL` if there is no message available for it.

Buffering

As discussed earlier, the messages sent by a process are temporarily stored in a temporary queue (also called **buffer**) by the operating system before delivering them to the recipient. This buffer can be implemented in a variety of ways, which are as follows:

- **No buffering:** The capacity of buffer is zero, that is, no messages may wait in the queue. This implies the sender process has to wait until the message is received by the receiver process.
- **Bounded buffer:** The capacity of the buffer is fixed, say m, that is, at most m processes may wait in the queue at a time. When there are less than m messages waiting in the queue and a new message arrives, it is added in the queue. The sender process need not wait and it can resume its operation. However, if the queue is full, the sender process is blocked until some space becomes available in the queue.
- **Unbounded buffer:** The buffer has an unlimited capacity, that is, an infinite number of messages can be stored in the queue. In this case, the sender process gets never blocked.

2.7 COMMUNICATION IN CLIENT-SERVER SYSTEMS

So far we have discussed about the communication mechanism for the processes running on a single system. However, in an environment (for example, client-server architecture) where processes are running on separate systems connected via network, a different mechanism is required to enable the communication. In this section, we will discuss some mechanisms that facilitate remote communications.

2.7.1 Sockets

Socket is defined as an end point of the communication path between two processes. Each of the communicating processes creates a socket and these sockets are to be connected to enable the communication. Socket is identified by a combination of IP address and the port number. The IP address is used to identify the machine on the network and the port number is used to identify the desired service on that machine.

Usually, a machine provides a variety of services, such as electronic mail, Telnet, FTP, etc. To differentiate among these services, each service is assigned with a unique port number. To avail some specific service on a machine, first it is required to connect to machine and then connect to the port assigned for that service. Note that the port numbers less than 1024 are considered well known and are reserved for standard services. For example, the port number used for Telnet is 23.

Sockets employ client-server architecture. The server listens to a socket bound to a specific port for a client to make connection request. Whenever a client process requests for a connection, it is assigned a port number (greater than 1024) by the host computer (say M). Using this port number and the IP address of host M, the client socket is created. For example, if the client on host M having IP address (125.61.15.7) wants to connect to Telnet server (listening to port number 23) having IP address (112.56.71.8), it may be assigned a port number 1345. Thus, the client socket and server socket used for the communication will be (125.61.15.7:1345) and (112.56.71.8:23), respectively, as shown in the Figure 2.8.

Figure 2.8: Communication between Sockets

Note that each connection between client and server employs a unique pair of sockets. That is, if another client on host M wants to connect to Telnet server, it must be assigned a port number different from 1345 (but greater than 1024).

2.7.2 Remote Procedure Calls (RPC)

RPC, as the name implies, is a communication mechanism that allows a process to call a procedure on a remote system connected via network. The calling process (client) can call the procedure on the remote host (server) in the same way as it would call the local procedure. The syntax of RPC call is very similar to conventional procedure call as given below:

```
Call <Procedure_id> (<List of parameters>);
```

The RPC system facilitates the communication between client and server by providing a stub on both client and server. For each remote procedure, the RPC system provides a separate stub on the client side. When the client process wants to invoke a remote procedure, the RPC call is implemented in the following steps.

1. The RPC system invokes the stub for the remote procedure on the client, passing to it the parameters that are to be passed further to the remote procedure. The client process is suspended from execution until completion of the call.
2. The client stub performs parameter marshalling, which involves packaging the parameters into a machine-independent form so that they can be transmitted over the network. It now prepares a message containing the identifier of the procedure to be executed and the marshalled parameters.
3. The client stub sends the message to the server. After the message has been sent, the client stub blocks until it gets reply to its message.
4. The corresponding stub on the server side receives the message and converts the parameters into a machine-specific form suitable for the server.
5. The server stub invokes the desired procedure, passing parameters to it. The server stub is suspended from execution until completion of the call.
6. The procedure executes and the results are returned to the server stub.
7. The server stub converts the results into a machine-independent form and prepares a message.
8. The server stub sends the message containing the results to the client stub.
9. The client stub converts the results into machine-specific form suitable for client.
10. The client stub forwards the results to the client process. With this, the execution of RPC is completed and now, the client process can continue its execution.

Figure 2.9 depicts all the steps involved in execution of RPC.

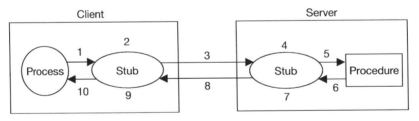

Figure 2.9: Implementation of RPC

2.7.3 Remote Method Invocation (RMI)

RMI is a Java-based approach that facilitates remote communication between programs written in the Java programming language. It allows an object executing in one Java Virtual Machine (JVM) to invoke methods on an object executing in another Java virtual machine either on the same computer or on some remote host connected via network.

To enable the communication between client and server using RMI, the remote methods must be transparent both to the client and the server. For this, RMI implements the remote objects using stubs and skeletons. A **stub** is a client-side proxy for a remote object while a **skeleton** is the server-side proxy for the remote object. On the client side, the stub acts on behalf of the actual remote object. Whenever a client process wishes to invoke a remote method, the stub for the remote object is called. This stub prepares a parcel that contains the name of the method to be invoked on the server along with the marshalled parameters and sends it to the server. At the server, the skeleton for the remote object receives the parcel, unmarshalls the parameters and invokes the desired method. After the execution of the method on the server, the skeleton prepares a parcel containing the marshalled return value (or exception, if any) and sends it to the client. The client stub then unmarshalls the return value and forwards it to the client. Figure 2.10 shows the RMI communication.

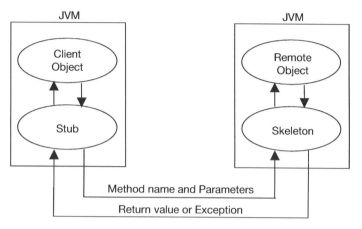

Figure 2.10: RMI Communication

2.8 CASE STUDY: IPC IN LINUX

Generally, a process needs to communicate with another process either to inform it about occurrence of some event or to exchange some data or information. The Linux operating system is empowered with various InterProcess Communication (IPC) facilities, some of which are discussed in this section.

Signals

A signal is the most basic communication mechanism that is used to alert a process to the occurrence of some event, such as abnormal termination or floating point exception. It does not carry any information rather it simply indicates that an event has occurred. When a process sends a signal to another process, the execution of the receiving process is suspended to handle the signal as in case of interrupt.

Linux offers a wide range of signals to indicate different events. A majority of signals are sent from the kernel to user processes while some can be used by the user processes to communicate with each other. However, the kernel does not use signals to communicate with a process running in kernel mode; instead a wait-queue mechanism is used to enable kernel-mode processes to convey each other about incoming asynchronous events. This mechanism allows several processes to wait for a single event by maintaining a queue for each event. Whenever a process needs to wait for the completion of a particular event, it sleeps in the wait queue associated with that event. After the event has happened, all the processes in the wait queue are awakened.

Pipes

Pipe is the standard communication mechanism that enables the transfer of data between processes. It provides a means of one-way communication between related processes. Each pipe has a read end and a write end. The data written at the write end of the pipe can be seen (read) through the read end. When the writer process writes to the pipe, stream of bytes are copied to the shared buffer, whereas at the time of reading, bytes are copied from the shared buffer. Though both the reader and writer processes may run concurrently, the access to pipe must be synchronized. Linux must ensure that only one process (either writer or reader) is accessing the pipe at a time. To synchronize the processes, Linux uses locks and wait queues; each end of pipe is associated with a wait queue.

Whenever the writer process requests for writing to pipe, Linux locks the pipe for it if and only if there is enough space as well as the pipe is not locked for the reader process. Once the writer process gains access to pipe, bytes are copied into it. However, if the pipe is full or locked for the reader process, the writer process sleeps in the wait queue at write end and remains there unless it is not awakened by the reader. After the data has been written to the pipe, the pipe is unlocked and any sleeping readers in the wait queue at read end are awakened. A similar process follows at the time of reading from the pipe.

A variation of pipe that Linux supports is **named pipe**, also called **FIFO**. As the name implies, in FIFOs, data written first to the pipe is read first. They employ same data structures as used in pipes as well as are handled in the same way. However unlike pipes, they are persistent and exist in the file system. Any process can use them provided it has appropriate access rights. Before starting to use a FIFO, it needs to be opened and similarly, after use it needs to be closed. However, Linux must ensure that a writer process opens the FIFO before the reader process and a reader process does not attempt to read from before the writer process has written to.

Shared Memory

Shared memory is another means of communication that allows cooperating process to pass data to each other. This mechanism enables a memory segment to be shared between two or more processes. As discussed in *Section 2.6.1*, one process creates the shared memory segment while others can read/write through it by attaching the shared memory segment along with their address space. Like other mechanisms, Linux must ensure the synchronization among communicating processes so that no two processes access the shared area simultaneously.

Shared memory is a faster means of communication as compared to other methods; however, it does not provide synchronization among different processes by its own. For this, it is to be used with some other IPC mechanism that offers synchronization.

Let Us Summarize

1. A process is a program under execution or we can say an executing set of machine instructions. It can be either a system process executing the system's code or a user process executing the user's code.

2. A process comprises not only the program code (known as text section) but also a set of global variables (known as data section) and the Process Control Block (PCB).

3. The set of instructions, data and stack together form the address space of a process.

4. The processes that involve more computation than I/O operations, thereby, demanding more use of CPU than I/O devices during their lifetime are called CPU bound or compute bound processes.

5. The processes that involve a lot of I/O operations as compared to computation during their lifetime are called I/O bound processes.

6. Each process is labelled with a 'state' variable—an integer value that helps the operating system to decide what to do with the process. It indicates the nature of the current activity in a process.

7. The various possible states for a process are new, ready, running, waiting and terminated.

8. The change in state of a process is known as state transition of a process and is caused by the occurrence of some event in the system.

9. To keep track of all the processes in the system, the operating system maintains a table called process table that includes an entry for each process. This entry is called Process Control Block (PCB).

10. A process control block stores descriptive information pertaining to a process, such as its state, program counter, memory management information, information about its scheduling, allocated resources, accounting information, etc., that is required to control the process.

11. The procedure of determining the next process to be executed on the CPU is called process scheduling and the module of operating system that makes this decision is called the scheduler.

12. As the processes enter the system for execution, they are kept into a queue called job queue (or input queue).

13. From the job queue, the processes which are ready for the execution are brought into the main memory. In the main memory, these processes are kept into a queue called ready queue.

14. For each I/O device in the system, a separate queue called device queue is maintained. The process that needs to perform I/O during its execution is kept into the queue of that specific I/O device and waits there until it is served by the device.

15. The long-term scheduler also known as job scheduler or admission scheduler selects the next process to be executed from the job queue and loads it into the main memory for execution.

16. The short-term scheduler also known as CPU scheduler or process scheduler selects a process from the ready queue and allocates CPU to it.

17. The medium-term scheduler also known as swapper selects a process among the partially executed or unexecuted swapped-out processes and swaps it in the main memory.

18. Transferring the control of CPU from one process to another demands for saving the context of the currently running process and loading the context of another ready process. This task of saving and restoring the context is known as context switch.

19. The portion of the process control block, including the process state, memory management information and CPU scheduling information together constitute the context (also called state information) of a process.

20. A user process may create one or more processes during its execution by invoking the process creation system call.

21. The task of creating a new process on the request of some another process is called process spawning. The process that spawns a new process is called parent process, whereas, the spawned process is called the child process.

22. When a process is terminated, all the resources held by the process are deallocated, the process returns output data (if any) to its parent and finally, the process is removed from the memory by deleting its PCB from the process table.

23. A process that no longer exists but still its PCB is not removed from the process table is known as a zombie process.

24. The processes that coexist in the memory at some time are called concurrent processes. The concurrent processes may either be independent or cooperating.

25. The independent (also called competitors) processes, as the name implies, do not share any kind of information or data with each other.

26. The cooperating (also called interacting) processes, on the other hand, need to exchange data or information with each other.

27. The cooperating processes require some mechanism to communicate with each other. One such mechanism is InterProcess Communication (IPC)—a facility provided by the operating system.

28. Two basic communication models for providing IPC are shared memory systems and message passing systems.

29. In shared memory systems, a part of memory is shared among the cooperating processes. The processes that need to exchange data or information can do so by writing to and reading from this shared memory.

30. In message passing systems, cooperating processes communicate by sending and receiving messages from each other. The system calls, `send()` and `receive()` are used to send and receive messages, respectively.

31. A process running on a system can communicate with another process running on remote system connected via network with the help of communication mechanisms, including sockets, Remote Procedure Call (RPC) and Remote Method Invocation (RMI).

32. Socket is defined as an endpoint of the communication path between two processes. Each of the communicating processes creates a socket and these sockets are to be connected to enable the communication.

33. RPC, as the name implies, is a communication mechanism that allows a process to call a procedure on a remote system connected via network. The calling process (client) can call the procedure on the remote host (server) in the same way as it would call the local procedure.

34. RMI is a Java-based approach that facilitates remote communication between programs written in the Java programming language. It allows an object executing in one Java Virtual Machine (JVM) to invoke methods on an object executing in another Java virtual machine either on the same computer or on some remote host connected via network.

35. The Linux operating system is empowered with various interprocess facilities, some of which are signals, pipes and shared memory.

36. A signal is the most basic communication mechanism that is used to alert a process to the occurrence of some event, such as abnormal termination or floating point exception. It does not carry any information rather it simply indicates that an event has occurred.

37. Pipe is the standard communication mechanism that enables the transfer of data between processes. It provides a means of one-way communication between related processes. Each pipe has a read end and a write end. The data written at the write end of the pipe can be seen (read) through the read end.

38. Shared memory is another means of communication that allows cooperating process to pass data to each other. This mechanism enables a memory segment to be shared between two or more processes.

 ## ANSWERS TO 'CHECK YOUR PROGRESS'

1. Text section, data section, process control block
2. (c)
3. A process control block contains descriptive information pertaining to a process, such as its state, program counter, memory management information, information about its scheduling, allocated resources, accounting information, etc., that is required to control the process.
4. True
5. The procedure of determining the next process to be executed on the CPU is called process scheduling.
6. If the process needs to perform some I/O operation during its execution, it is removed from the ready queue and put into the appropriate device queue. After the process completes its I/O operation and is ready for the execution, it is switched from the device queue to ready queue.
7. Save context, restore context
8. (b)
9. False
10. The task of creating a new process on the request of some another process is called process spawning.
11. Zombie process
12. In symmetric direct communication, both sender and receiver process need to know each other's PID. On the other hand, in asymmetric direct communication, only the sender process needs to know PID of the receiver process but the receiver process need not know the PID of the sender process.
13. (d)
14. IP address, port number
15. False
16. (a)

TEST YOURSELF

1. Distinguish between CPU bound and I/O bound process.
2. Discuss the various states of a process.
3. Describe the events under which state transitions between ready, running and waiting take place.
4. List three important fields stored in a process control block.
5. Distinguish among long-term scheduler, short-term scheduler and medium-term scheduler.
6. What is context switching? How it is performed and what is its disadvantage?
7. Describe the different models used for interprocess communication. Which one is better?
8. In message passing systems, the processes can communicate directly or indirectly. Compare both the ways.
9. Write a short note on the following:
   (a) Remote method invocation
   (b) Signals in Linux
   (c) Difference between pipes and named pipes
10. Consider the indirect communication method where mailboxes are used.
    (a) Suppose a process P wants to wait for two messages, one from mailbox M and other from mailbox N.
    (b) Suppose P wants to wait for one message from mailbox M or from mailbox N (or from both).
    What will be the sequence of execution of `send()` and `receive()` calls in both cases?

Chapter

03

Threads

3.1 INTRODUCTION

In conventional operating systems, each process has a single thread of control, that is, the process is able to perform only one task at a time. To implement multiprogramming, multiple processes with each having a separate address space may be created and CPU may be switched back and forth among them to create the illusion that the processes are running in parallel. But as discussed in previous chapter, process creation and switching is very time consuming and resource intensive and thus, incurs an overhead to the system. Therefore, many modern operating systems employ **multithreading** that allows a process to have multiple threads of control within the same address space. These threads may run in parallel, thereby, enabling the process to perform multiple tasks at a time.

3.2 BASIC CONCEPTS

A **thread** is defined as the fundamental unit of CPU utilization. Multiple threads of the same process share with each other the code section, data section and other resources, including list of open files, child processes, signals, etc., of the process. In addition, each thread has its own ID, stack, set of registers and program counter.

Though a thread, like a process, is also a unit of program execution, there are certain differences between the two:

- A thread is a subset of a process, that is, a thread is dependent on the process, whereas, the processes may be independent.
- Each child process has a separate address space from that of its parent while the threads belonging to the same process share the address space of the process.
- Switching among threads is considerably faster than the process switching and incurs less overhead. This is because the resource state is to be switched only when switching to a thread belonging to a different process.

> **Note:**   The traditional processes are termed heavy weight while a thread is referred to as Light Weight Process (LWP).

3.2.1 Advantages of Threads

The major advantage that threads provide over processes is the low overhead during switching (as discussed in the previous section). In addition, threads offer some other advantages, which are as follows:

- **Computational speedup:** On a uniprocessor system, a process can be executed speedily by creating multiple threads in the process and executing them in a quasi-parallel manner (that is, by rapidly switching the CPU among multiple threads).
- **Economy:** Thread creation is more economical than the process creation. Every time a process is created, some memory and resources are required to be allocated to it. On the other hand, threads share the resources of the process to which they belong, so there is no need to allocate memory and resource at the time of thread creation.
- **Efficient communication:** As different threads of a process share the same address space, communication among them can be made via the shared memory. There is no need to execute system calls, which cause extra overhead.
- **Proper utilization of multiprocessor architecture:** In multiprocessor systems, threads prove more useful than processes. Multiple threads of a single process can be made to run on different CPUs at the same time, thereby, achieving real parallelism. In contrast, a single process can run only on one CPU regardless of the number of available CPUs.
- **Responsiveness:** In case of interactive processes, the major performance criteria is the response time. If such a process is multithreaded, a part of the process (thread) is able to run even if some other part of the process is blocked. As a result, responsiveness of the process to the user is increased.

3.2.2 Implementation of Threads

Threads can be implemented in different ways depending on the extent to which the process and the operating system knows about them. Here, we will discuss two methods for implementing threads, namely, kernel-level and user-level threads.

Kernel-level Threads

The kernel-level threads are implemented by the kernel. The kernel is responsible for creating, scheduling and managing threads in the kernel space. It maintains a **thread table** in addition to the process table within the kernel space that holds the program counter, stack pointer, registers, state, etc., of each thread in the system. Whenever a process wishes to create or terminate a new thread, it initiates a system call to the kernel. In response, the kernel creates or terminates the thread by modifying the thread table. Many modern operating systems, including Solaris 2, Windows 2000 and Windows NT provide support for kernel-level threads.

Advantages

- In a multiprocessor environment, multiple kernel-level threads belonging to a process can be scheduled to run simultaneously on different CPUs, thereby, resulting in computation speedup.
- As the threads are managed directly by the kernel, if one thread issues a system call that blocks it, the kernel can choose another thread to run either from the same process (to which the blocked thread belongs) or from some different process.

Disadvantages

- The cost of creating and destroying threads in the kernel is relatively greater than that of user-level threads.
- The kernel performs switching between the threads, which incurs overhead to the system.

User-level Threads

The user-level threads are implemented by a thread library associated with the code of a process. The thread library provides support for creating, scheduling and managing threads in the user space without any involvement from the kernel. Thus, the kernel is unaware of the existence of threads in a process; it is concerned only with managing single-threaded process. Whenever a process wishes to create or terminate a thread, it can do so by calling an appropriate function from the thread library without the need of kernel intervention. Moreover, each process maintains its own thread table that keeps track of the threads belonging to that process and the kernel maintains only the process table. POSIX threads or Pthreads, Solaris 2 UI-threads and Mach C-threads are some of the user thread libraries.

Advantages

- The user-level threads can be created and managed at a faster speed as compared to kernel-level threads.
- The thread switching overhead is smaller as it is performed by the thread library and there is no need to issue the system call.

- The thread library can schedule threads within a process using a scheduling policy that best suits to the process's nature. For example, for a real-time process, a priority-based scheduling policy can be used. On the other hand, for a multithreaded Web server, round-robin scheduling can be used.

Disadvantages

- At most one user-level thread can be in operation at one time, which limits the degree of parallelism.
- If one user-level thread issues a blocking system call, the kernel blocks the whole process to which the thread belongs even there is some other thread that is ready to run. This is because the kernel does not know the difference between a thread and a process; it simply treats a thread like a process.

CHECK YOUR PROGRESS

1. _____ allows a process to have multiple threads of control within the same address space.
2. Why does the switching among threads incur less overhead as compared to process switching?
3. Name some operating systems that provide support for kernel-level threads.
4. In case of user-level threads, the kernel maintains a thread table to keep track of user-level threads. (True or False)

3.3 MULTITHREADING MODELS

Many systems support a hybrid thread model that contains both user-level and kernel-level threads along with a relationship between these threads. There may exist different types of relationship between user-level and kernel-level threads, each resulting in a specific multithreading model. In this section, we will discuss three common multithreading models.

3.3.1 Many-to-One (M:1) Model

In this model, the kernel creates only one kernel-level thread in each process and the multiple user-level threads (created by thread library) of the process are associated with this kernel-level thread (see Figure 3.1). As the threads are managed in the user space, this model produces a similar effect as that of user-level threads. An example of a thread library that employs this model is Green threads available for Solaris 2.

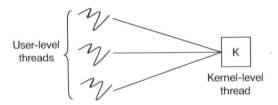

Figure 3.1: Many-to-One (M:1) Model

Advantages

● It incurs a low switching overhead as kernel is not involved while switching between threads.

Disadvantages

● If one user-level thread issues a blocking system call, the kernel blocks the whole parent process.
● As the kernel-level thread can be accessed by only one user-level thread at a time, multiple user-level threads cannot run in parallel on multiple CPUs, thereby, resulting in low concurrency.

3.3.2 One-to-One (1:1) Model

In this model, each user-level thread is associated with a kernel-level thread (see Figure 3.2). The threads are managed by the kernel; therefore, this model provides an effect similar to kernel-level threads. Many modern operating systems, such as Windows 2000 and Windows NT employ this model.

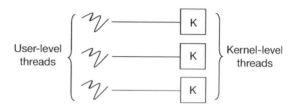

Figure 3.2: One-to-One (1:1) Model

Advantages

● Multiple threads can run in parallel on multiple CPUs in a multiprocessor environment and thus, greater concurrency is achieved.
● As each user-level thread is mapped into a different kernel-level thread, blocking of one user-level thread does not cause other user-level threads to block.

Disadvantages

● It results in high switching overhead due to involvement of kernel in switching.
● Most implementations of this model restrict on the number of threads that can be created in a process. This is because whenever a user-level thread is created in a process, a corresponding kernel-level thread is also required to be created. The creation of many kernel-level threads incurs an overhead to the system, thereby, degrading the performance.

3.3.3 Many-to-Many (M:M) Model

In this model, many user-level threads are associated with many kernel-level threads with the number of kernel-level threads being equal to or less than that of user-level threads (see Figure 3.3). This implies that more than one user-level threads may be associated with same kernel-level thread. This model overcomes the limitations of both many-to-one and one-to-one models. The operating systems, including Solaris 2 and Tru64 UNIX, employ this model.

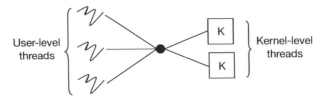

Figure 3.3: Many-to-Many (M:M) Model

Advantages

- Many user-level threads can be made to run in parallel on different CPUs by mapping each user-level thread to a different kernel-level thread.
- Blocking of one user-level thread does not result in the blockage of other user-level threads that are mapped into different kernel-level threads.
- Switching between user-level threads associated with same kernel-level thread does not incur much overhead.
- There is no restriction on the number of user-level threads that can be created in a process; as many user-level threads as required can be created.

Disadvantages

- The implementation of this model is very complex.

3.4 THREADING ISSUES

While multithreaded programs are executed, a number of issues arise. In this section, we will discuss some of these issues.

3.4.1 `fork()` and `exec()` System Calls

Recall from the previous chapter the usage of `fork()` and `exec()` system calls. Whenever a process invokes the `fork()` system call, a new (child) process is created that is the exact duplicate of its parent process. The child process executes the same code as that of its parent. However, if it requires to load some another program in its address space, it can do so by invoking the `exec()` system call, passing the name of desired program as a parameter to it.

In case of multithreaded programs, the semantics of `fork()` and `exec()` system calls are somewhat different. Here, the question arises whether the newly created thread (upon invocation of `fork()` by one thread) should contain all the threads of the process to which the invoking thread belongs or only the invoking thread. In response to this, many UNIX system offer two versions of `fork()` system call: one to duplicate all the threads and another to duplicate only the invoking thread.

The selection of a particular version of `fork()` system call to be invoked depends on the application. If the newly created process is to invoke `exec()` system call immediately after the `fork()` system call, it is unnecessary to duplicate all the threads. Thus, the latter version of `fork()` should be used. On the other hand, if the newly created process does not require to invoke `exec()` after `fork()`, all threads should be duplicated. Therefore, the former version of `fork()` should be used.

3.4.2 Thread Cancellation

The procedure of terminating a thread before it completes its execution is known as **thread cancellation** and the thread that is to be cancelled is known as **target thread**. Thread cancellation may be performed in any of the following ways:

- **Asynchronous cancellation:** In this type of cancellation, the target thread is terminated immediately after any thread indicates its cancellation. The operating system may acquire the resources allocated to the cancelled thread but not necessarily all the resources. Thus, asynchronous thread cancellation may not release a system-wide resource, thereby, leaving the system in an inconsistent state. Many operating systems support asynchronous thread cancellation.
- **Deferred Cancellation:** In this type of cancellation, the target thread is not terminated immediately rather it checks at regular intervals whether it should be terminated. Thus, the target thread gets the opportunity to terminate itself in an orderly manner. Deferred cancellation ensures system consistency by defining points in the code of a thread where it can safely be cancelled. Whenever the target thread determines that it should be terminated, it first checks whether it can safely be terminated. If so, the target thread terminates; otherwise, its cancellation may be deferred until it executes up to safe point.

3.4.3 Thread-specific Data

As we know that the threads of a process share the process's data with each other. But sometimes a thread may require having its own copy of certain data, termed as **thread-specific data**. For example, consider an airline reservation application in which a separate thread is created to handle each client's request for flight reservation. Each request may be assigned a unique ID in order to distinguish among multiple clients. Now, to relate each thread with the ID of request it is handling, we would need thread-specific data.

3.5 CASE STUDY: PTHREADS LIBRARY

Pthreads refer to thread extensions of POSIX standard (IEEE 1003.1c) that provide the programmers an API for thread creation and management. The Pthreads library can be implemented either in the kernel space or in the user space as per the operating system's designer choice. It comprises different functions that are used for managing Pthreads. In this section, we will discuss some of these functions.

3.5.1 Creating a Pthread

A process can create a Pthread by calling the `pthread_create()` function. The syntax of this function is as follows:

```
pthread_create (ptr_id, attr, start_routine, arg);
```

Where
ptr_id is a pointer to the memory location where the id of Pthread will be stored.
attr specifies an attributes object that defines the attributes to be used in Pthread creation.
start_routine is the routine to be executed by the newly created Pthread.
arg is the single argument that is passed to the pthread during its creation.

Once a Pthread has been created, it starts executing the start_routine function within the environment of the process which has created it.

3.5.2 Terminating a Pthread

A Pthread can terminate under any of the following circumstances.

- When it calls the pthread_exit (status_code) function.
- After it returns from its start_routine, because then pthread_exit() function is called implicitly.
- When some other Pthread cancels it by calling the pthread_cancel() function.
- When the process that has created it terminates.

3.5.3 Detaching a Pthread

A Pthread can be detached from other Pthreads by calling the pthread_detach() function. The syntax of this function is as follows:

        pthread_detach(<pthread_id>);

Where
pthread_id is the id of the Pthread which is to be detached (target thread).

Note that no other Pthreads can synchronize their activities with the detached Pthread. However, the detached Pthread continues to run until it gets terminated.

3.5.4 Waiting for Termination of a Pthread

A Pthread can wait for another Pthread to complete before its termination by calling the pthread_join() function. The syntax of this function is as follows:

        pthread_join(<pthread_id>, adr(x));

Where
<pthread_id> is the id of the Pthread whose termination is awaited.
adr(x) is the address of the variable x in which the status of the target Pthread is to be stored.

Following points should be kept in mind while using the pthread_join() function.

- The Pthread that has invoked the pthread_join() function remains suspended until the targeted Pthread terminates.
- The pthread_join() function cannot be used for a detached Pthread.
- No two Pthreads can invoke the pthread_join() function for each other as it will result in a deadlock.

Note: Generally, the implementation of Pthread library is limited only to UNIX-based systems, for example, Solaris 2 and not supported on Windows.

CHECK YOUR PROGRESS

5. List some advantages of one-to-one multithreading model.
6. _____ and _____ operating systems employ many-to-may multithreading model.
7. The procedure of terminating a thread while it is in midst of its execution is known as _____.
8. A thread may require having its own copy of certain data, termed as thread-specific data. (True or False)
9. What are Pthreads?
10. The Pthreads library can be implemented either in the kernel space or in the user space. (True or False)

Let Us Summarize

1. Many modern operating systems employ multithreading that allows a process to have multiple threads of control within the same address space. These threads may run in parallel, thereby, enabling the process to perform multiple tasks at a time.
2. A thread is defined as the fundamental unit of CPU utilization. Multiple threads of the same process share with each other the code section, data section and other resources, including list of open files, child processes, signals, etc., of the process. In addition, each thread has its own ID, stack, set of registers and program counter.
3. The major advantage that threads provide over processes is the low overhead during switching. In addition, threads offer some other advantages which include computational speedup, economy, efficient communication, proper utilization of multiprocessor architecture and responsiveness.
4. Threads can be implemented in different ways depending on the extent to which the process and the operating system knows about them. Two common methods for implementing threads include kernel-level and user-level threads.
5. The kernel-level threads are implemented by the kernel. The kernel is responsible for creating, scheduling and managing threads in the kernel space.
6. The user-level threads are implemented by a thread library associated with the code of a process. The thread library provides support for creating, scheduling and managing threads in the user space without any involvement from the kernel.
7. Many systems support a hybrid thread model that contains both user-level and kernel-level threads along with a relationship between these threads. There may exist different types of relationship between user-level and kernel-level threads, each resulting in a specific multithreading model. Three common multithreading models are many-to-one, one-to-one and many-to-many model.
8. In many-to-one multithreading model, the kernel creates only one kernel-level thread in each process and the multiple user-level threads (created by thread library) of the process are associated with this kernel-level thread.
9. In one-to-one multithreading model, each user-level thread is associated with a kernel-level thread.

10. In many-to-many multithreading model, many user-level threads are associated with many kernel-level threads with the number of kernel-level threads being equal to or less than that of user-level threads.
11. The procedure of terminating a thread while it is in midst of its execution is known as thread cancellation and the thread that is to be cancelled is known as target thread. Thread cancellation may be performed in two ways: asynchronous cancellation and deferred cancellation.
12. Pthreads refer to thread extensions of POSIX standard (IEEE 1003.1c) that provide the programmers an API for thread creation and management.

ANSWERS TO 'CHECK YOUR PROGRESS'

1. Multithreading
2. Switching among threads incurs less overhead because the resource state is to be switched only when switching to a thread belonging to a different process.
3. The operating systems, including Solaris 2, Windows 2000 and Windows NT, provide support for kernel-level threads.
4. False
5. The advantages of one-to-one multithreading model are as follows:
   ● Multiple threads can run in parallel on multiple CPUs in a multiprocessor environment and thus, greater concurrency is achieved.
   ● As each user-level thread is mapped into a different kernel-level thread, blocking of one user-level thread does not cause other user-level threads to block.
6. Solaris 2, Tru64 UNIX
7. Thread cancellation
8. True
9. Pthreads refer to thread extensions of POSIX standard (IEEE 1003.1c) that provide the programmers an API for thread creation and management.
10. True

TEST YOURSELF

1. Define thread. How it is different from a process?
2. List some advantages of threads over the traditional processes.
3. Differentiate between kernel-level and user-level threads. Which one is preferred over another and under what circumstances?
4. Describe some issues related with multithreaded programs.
5. How does the many-to-many multithreading model overcome the limitations of many-to-one and one-to-one models?
6. Explain some functions provided by Pthreads library.

Chapter 04

CPU Scheduling

Learning Objectives

After reading this chapter, you will be able to:

☐ Understand the basic concepts of scheduling

☐ Discuss the criteria for scheduling

☐ Explain various scheduling algorithms

☐ Discuss scheduling for multiprocessor systems

☐ Explain real-time scheduling

☐ Evaluate various scheduling algorithms

☐ Explore how scheduling is performed in Linux

4.1 INTRODUCTION

As discussed in *Chapter 02*, CPU scheduling is the procedure employed for deciding as to which of the ready processes, the CPU should be allocated. CPU scheduling plays a pivotal role in the basic framework of the operating system owing to the fact that the CPU is one of the primary resources of the computer system. The algorithm used by the scheduler to carry out the selection of a process for execution is known as **scheduling algorithm**. A number of scheduling algorithms are available for CPU scheduling. Each scheduling algorithm influences the resource utilization, overall system performance and quality of service provided to the user. Therefore, one has to reason out a number of criteria to be considered while selecting an algorithm on a particular system.

4.2 SCHEDULING CONCEPTS

Before we start discussing about the scheduling criteria and scheduling algorithms comprehensively, we will first take into account some relatively important concepts of scheduling which are mentioned underneath.

4.2.1 Process Behaviour

CPU scheduling is greatly affected by how a process behaves during its execution. Almost all the processes continue to switch between CPU (for processing) and I/O devices (for performing I/O) during their execution. The time period elapsed in processing before performing the next I/O operation is known as **CPU burst** and the time period elapsed in performing I/O before the next CPU burst is known as **I/O burst**. Generally, the process execution starts with a CPU burst, followed by an I/O burst, then again by a CPU burst and so on until the termination of the process. Thus, we can say the process execution comprises alternate cycles of CPU and I/O burst. Figure 4.1 shows the sequence of CPU and I/O bursts upon the execution of the following code segment written in C language.

```
i=1;                    /* CPU burst */
sum=0;
scanf("%d", &num);      /* I/O burst */
while (i <= 10 )         /*CPU burst */
{
    sum += num * i;
    i = i + 1;
}
printf("%d", sum);      /* I/O burst */
```

Figure 4.1: Alternate Cycles of CPU and I/O Bursts

The length of CPU and I/O burst varies from process to process depending on whether the process is CPU bound or I/O bound. If the process is CPU bound, it will have longer CPU bursts as compared to I/O bursts and vice versa in case the process is I/O bound. From the scheduling perspective, only the length of CPU burst is taken into consideration and not the length of I/O burst.

4.2.2 When to Schedule

An important facet of scheduling is to determine when the scheduler should make scheduling decisions. The following circumstances may require the scheduler to make scheduling decisions.

- When a process switches from running to waiting state. This situation may occur in case the process has to wait for I/O or the termination of its child process or some another reason. In such situations, the scheduler has to select some ready process for execution.

- When a process switches from running to ready state due to occurrence of an interrupt. In such situations, the scheduler may decide to run a process from the ready queue. If the interrupt was caused by some I/O device that has now completed its task, the scheduler may choose the process that was blocked waiting for the I/O.
- When a process switches from waiting state to ready state, for example, in case the process has completed its I/O operation. In such situations, the scheduler may select either the process that has now come to the ready state or the current process may be continued.
- When a process terminates and exits the system. In this case, the scheduler has to select a process for execution from the set of ready processes.

4.2.3 Dispatcher

The CPU scheduler only selects a process to be executed next on the CPU but it cannot assign CPU to the selected process. The function of setting up the execution of the selected process on the CPU is performed by another module of the operating system, known as **dispatcher**. The dispatcher involves the following three steps to perform this function.

1. Context switching is performed. The kernel saves the context of currently running process and restores the saved state of the process selected by the CPU scheduler. In case the process selected by the short-term scheduler is new, the kernel loads its context.
2. The system switches from the kernel mode to user mode as a user process is to be executed.
3. The execution of the user process selected by the CPU scheduler is started by transferring the control either to the instruction that was supposed to be executed at the time the process was interrupted or to the first instruction if the process is going to be executed for the first time after its creation.

> **Note:** The amount of time required by the dispatcher to suspend execution of one process and resume execution of another process is known as dispatch latency. Low dispatch latency implies faster start of process execution.

4.3 SCHEDULING CRITERIA

The scheduler must consider the following performance measures and optimization criteria in order to maximize the performance of the system.

- **Fairness:** It is defined as the degree to which each process is getting an equal chance to execute. The scheduler must ensure that each process should get a fair share of CPU time. However, it may treat different categories of processes (batch, real-time or interactive) in a different manner.
- **CPU utilization:** It is defined as the percentage of time the CPU is busy in executing processes. For higher utilization, CPU must be kept as busy as possible, that is, there must be some process running at all times.

- **Balanced utilization:** It is defined as the percentage of time when all the system resources are busy. It considers not only the CPU utilization but also the utilization of I/O devices, memory and other resources. To get more work done by the system, the CPU and I/O devices must be kept running simultaneously. For this, it is desirable to load a mixture of CPU bound and I/O bound processes in the memory.
- **Throughput:** It is defined as the total number of processes that a system can execute per unit of time. By and large, it depends on the average length of the processes to be executed. For the systems running long processes, throughput will be less as compared to the systems running short processes.
- **Turnaround time:** It is defined as the amount of time that has rolled by from the time of creation to the termination of a process. To put it differently, it is the difference between the time a process enters the system and the time it exits from the system. It includes all the time the process has spent waiting to enter into ready queue, within ready queue to get CPU, running on CPU and in I/O queues. It is inversely proportional to throughput, that is, more the turnaround time, less will be the throughput.
- **Waiting time:** It is defined as the time used up by a process while waiting in the ready queue. However, it does not take into account the execution time or time consumed for I/O. In practice, waiting time is more accurate measure as compared to turnaround time.
- **Response time:** It is defined as the time elapsed between the user initiates a request and the system starts responding to this request. For interactive systems, it is one of the best metric employed to gauge the performance. This is because in such systems, only the speed with which the system responds to user's request matters and not the time it takes to output the response.

The basic purpose of a CPU scheduling algorithm is that it should tend to maximize fairness, CPU utilization, balanced utilization and throughput, and minimize turnaround, waiting and response time. Practically speaking, no scheduling algorithm optimizes all the scheduling criteria. Thus, in general, the performance of an algorithm is evaluated on the basis of average measures. For example, an algorithm that minimizes the average waiting time is considered as a good algorithm because this improves the overall efficiency of the system. However, in case of response time, minimizing the average is not a good criterion rather the variance in the response time of the processes should be minimized. This is because it is not desirable to have a process with long response time as compared to other processes.

CHECK YOUR PROGRESS

1. The process execution comprises an alternate cycles of _____ and _____.
2. What is the function of dispatcher?
3. Balanced utilization is defined as the percentage of time the CPU is busy in executing processes. (True or False)
4. _____ is defined as time elapsed between the user submits a request and the system starts responding to this request.
   (a) Response time   (b) Waiting time
   (c) Turnaround time   (d) None of these

4.4 SCHEDULING ALGORITHMS

A wide variety of algorithms are used for the CPU scheduling. These scheduling algorithms fall into two categories, namely, non-preemptive and preemptive.

- **Non-preemptive scheduling algorithms:** Once the CPU is allocated to a process, it cannot be taken back until the process voluntarily releases it (in case the process has to wait for I/O or some other event) or the process terminates. In other words, we can say the decision to schedule a process is made only when the currently running process either switches to the waiting state or terminates. In both cases, the CPU executes some other process from the set of ready processes.
- **Preemptive scheduling algorithms:** The CPU can be forcibly taken back from the currently running process before its completion and allocated to some other process. The preempted process is put back in the ready queue and resumes its execution when it is scheduled again. Thus, a process may be scheduled many times before its completion. In preemptive scheduling, the decision to schedule another process is made whenever an interrupt occurs causing the currently running process to switch to ready state or a process having higher priority than the currently running process which is ready to execute.

> **Note:** A non-preemptive scheduling algorithm is also known as a cooperative or voluntary scheduling algorithm.

4.4.1 First-Come First-Served (FCFS) Scheduling

FCFS is one of the simplest scheduling algorithms. As the name implies, the processes are executed in the order of their arrival in the ready queue, which means the process that enters the ready queue first gets the CPU first. FCFS is a non-preemptive scheduling algorithm. Therefore, once a process gets the CPU, it retains the control of CPU until it gets blocked or terminates.

To implement FCFS scheduling, the implementation of ready queue is managed as a FIFO (First-in First-out) queue. When the first process enters the ready queue, it immediately gets the CPU and starts executing. Meanwhile, other processes enter the system and are added to the end of queue by inserting their PCBs in the queue. When the currently running process completes or gets blocked, the CPU is allocated to the process at the front of the queue and its PCB is removed from the queue. In case a currently running process was blocked and later it comes to the ready state, its PCB is linked to the end of queue.

Example 4.1:

Consider four processes P_1, P_2, P_3 and P_4 with their arrival times and required CPU burst (in milliseconds) as shown in the following table.

Process	P_1	P_2	P_3	P_4
Arrival time	0	2	3	5
CPU burst (ms)	15	6	7	5

How will these processes be scheduled according to FCFS scheduling algorithm? Compute the average waiting time and average turnaround time.

Solution:

The processes will be scheduled as depicted in the following Gantt chart.

P_1	P_2	P_3	P_4
0　　　　15	21	28	33

Initially, P_1 enters the ready queue at $t = 0$ and CPU is allocated to it. While P_1 is executing, P_2, P_3 and P_4 enter the ready queue at $t = 2$, $t = 3$, and $t = 5$, respectively. When P_1 completes CPU is allocated to P_2 as it has entered before P_3 and P_4. When P_2 completes, P_3 gets the CPU after which P_4 gets the CPU.

Waiting time for $P_1 = 0$ ms as P_1 starts immediately

Waiting time for $P_2 = (15 - 2) = 13$ ms as P_2 enters at $t = 2$ and starts at $t = 15$

Waiting time for $P_3 = (21 - 3) = 18$ ms as P_3 enters at $t = 3$ and starts at $t = 21$

Waiting time for $P_4 = (28 - 5) = 23$ ms as P_4 enters at $t = 5$ and starts at $t = 28$

Average waiting time $= (0 + 13 + 18 + 23)/4 = 13.5$ ms

Turnaround time for $P_1 = (15 - 0) = 15$ ms as P_1 enters at $t = 0$ and exits at $t = 15$

Turnaround time for $P_2 = (21 - 2) = 19$ ms as P_2 enters at $t = 2$ and exits at $t = 21$

Turnaround time for $P_3 = (28 - 3) = 25$ ms as P_3 enters at $t = 3$ and exits at $t = 28$

Turnaround time for $P_4 = (33 - 5) = 28$ ms as P_4 enters at $t = 5$ and exits at $t = 33$

Average turnaround time $= (15 + 19 + 25 + 28)/4 = 21.75$ ms

The performance of FCFS scheduling algorithm largely depends on the order of arrival of processes in the ready queue. That is, whether the processes having long CPU burst enter before those having short CPU burst or vice versa. To illustrate this, assume that the processes (shown in Example 4.1) enter the ready queue in the order P_4, P_2, P_3 and P_1. Now, the processes will be scheduled as shown in the following Gantt chart.

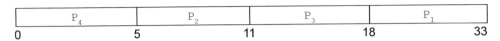

P_4	P_2	P_3	P_1
0　　　　5	11	18	33

Average waiting time $= (0 + (5 - 2) + (11 - 3) + (18 - 5))/4 = 6$ ms

Average turnaround time $= ((5 - 0) + (11 - 2) + (18 - 3) + (33 - 5))/4 = 14.25$ ms

It is clear that if the processes having shorter CPU burst execute before those having longer CPU burst, the average waiting and turnaround time may reduce significantly.

Advantages

● It is easier to understand and implement as processes are simply to be added at the end and removed from the front of queue. No process from in between the queue is required to be accessed.

- It is well suited for batch systems where the longer time periods for each process are often acceptable.

Disadvantages

- The average waiting time is not minimal. Therefore, this scheduling algorithm is never recommended where performance is a major issue.
- It reduces the CPU and I/O devices utilization under some circumstances. For example, assume that there is one long CPU bound process and many short I/O bound processes in the ready queue. Now, it may happen that while the CPU bound process is executing, the I/O bound processes complete their I/O and come to the ready queue for execution. There they have to wait for the CPU bound process to release the CPU and the I/O devices also remain idle during this time. When the CPU bound process needs to perform I/O, it comes to the device queue and the CPU is allocated to I/O bound processes. As the I/O bound processes require a little CPU burst, they execute quickly and come back to the device queue, thereby, leaving the CPU idle. Then the CPU bound process enters the ready queue and is allocated the CPU which again makes the I/O processes waiting in ready queue at some point of time. This happens again and again until the CPU bound process is done which results in low CPU and I/O devices utilization.
- It is not suitable for time sharing systems where each process should get the same amount of CPU time.

4.4.2 Shortest Job First (SJF) Scheduling

The shortest job first also known as **Shortest Process Next (SPN)** or **Shortest Request Next (SRN)** is a non-preemptive scheduling algorithm that schedules the processes according to the length of CPU burst they require. At any point of time, among all the ready processes, the one having the shortest CPU burst is scheduled first. Thus, a process has to wait until all the processes shorter than it have been executed. In case two processes have the same CPU burst, they are scheduled in the FCFS order.

Example 4.2:

Consider four processes P_1, P_2, P_3 and P_4 with their arrival times and required CPU burst (in milliseconds) as shown in the following table.

Process	P_1	P_2	P_3	P_4
Arrival time	0	1	3	4
CPU burst (ms)	7	5	2	3

How will these processes be scheduled according to SJF scheduling algorithm? Compute the average waiting time and average turnaround time.

Solution:

The processes will be scheduled as depicted in the following Gantt chart.

P_1	P_3	P_4	P_2
0 7	9	12	17

Initially, P_1 enters the ready queue at $t = 0$ and gets the CPU as there are no other processes in the queue. While it is executing, P_2, P_3 and P_4 enter the queue at $t = 1$,

$t = 3$ and $t = 4$, respectively. When CPU becomes free, that is, at $t = 7$, it is allocated to P_3 because it is having the shortest CPU burst among the three processes. When P_3 gets completed, CPU is allocated first to P_4 and then to P_2.

Waiting time for $P_1 = 0$ ms as P_1 starts immediately

Waiting time for $P_2 = (12 - 1) = 11$ ms as P_2 enters at $t = 1$ and starts at $t = 12$

Waiting time for $P_3 = (7 - 3) = 4$ ms as P_3 enters at $t = 3$ and starts at $t = 7$

Waiting time for $P_4 = (9 - 4) = 5$ ms as P_4 enters at $t = 4$ and starts at $t = 9$

Average waiting time $= (0 + 11 + 4 + 5)/4 = 5$ ms

Turnaround time for $P_1 = (7 - 0) = 7$ ms as P_1 enters at $t = 0$ and exits at $t = 7$

Turnaround time for $P_2 = (17 - 1) = 16$ ms as P_2 enters at $t = 1$ and exits at $t = 17$

Turnaround time for $P_3 = (9 - 3) = 6$ ms as P_3 enters at $t = 3$ and exits at $t = 9$

Turnaround time for $P_4 = (12 - 4) = 8$ ms as P_4 enters at $t = 4$ and exits at $t = 12$

Average turnaround time $= (7 + 16 + 6 + 8)/4 = 9.25$ ms

Advantages

- It eliminates the variance in waiting and turnaround times. In fact, it is optimal with respect to average waiting time if all processes are available at the same time. This is due to the fact that short processes are made to run before the long ones which decreases the waiting time for short processes and increases the waiting time for long processes. However, the reduction in waiting time is more than the increment and thus, the average waiting time decreases.

Disadvantages

- It is difficult to implement as it needs to know the length of CPU burst of processes in advance. In practice, having the prior knowledge of required processing time of processes is difficult. Many systems expect users to provide estimates of CPU burst of processes which may not always be correct.
- It does not favor the processes having longer CPU burst. This is because as long as the short processes continue to enter the ready queue, the long processes will not be allowed to get the CPU. This results in starvation of long processes.

4.4.3 Shortest Remaining Time Next (SRTN) Scheduling

The shortest remaining time next also known as **Shortest Time to Go (STG)** is a preemptive version of the SJF scheduling algorithm. It takes into account the length of remaining CPU burst of the processes rather than the whole length in order to schedule them. The scheduler always chooses the process for execution that has the shortest remaining processing time. While a process is being executed, the CPU can be taken back from it and assigned to some newly arrived process if the CPU burst of the new process is shorter than its remaining CPU burst. Notice that if at any point of time, the remaining CPU burst of two processes becomes equal; they are scheduled in the FCFS order.

Example 4.3:

Consider the same set of processes, their arrival times and CPU burst as shown in Example 4.2. How will these processes be scheduled according to SRTN scheduling algorithm? Compute the average waiting time and average turnaround time.

Solution:

The processes will be scheduled as depicted in the following Gantt chart.

P_1	P_2	P_3	P_2	P_4	P_1

0   1   3   5   8   11   17

Initially, P_1 enters the ready queue at $t = 0$ and gets the CPU as there are no other processes in the queue. While it is executing, at time $t = 1$, P_2 with CPU burst of 5 ms enters the queue. At that time the remaining CPU burst of P_1 is 6 ms which is greater than that of P_2. Therefore, the CPU is taken back from P_1 and allocated to P_2. During execution of P_2, P_3 enters at $t = 3$ with a CPU burst of 2 ms. Again CPU is switched from P_2 to P_3 as the remaining CPU burst of P_2 at $t = 3$ is 3 ms which is greater than that of P_3. However, when at time $t = 4$, P_4 with CPU burst of 3 ms enters the queue, the CPU is not assigned to it because at that time the remaining CPU burst of currently running process (that is, P_3) is 1 ms which is shorter than that of P_4. When P_3 completes, there are three processes P_1 (6 ms), P_2 (3 ms) and P_4 (3 ms) in the queue. To break the tie between P_2 and P_4, the scheduler takes into consideration their arrival order and the CPU is allocated first to P_2, then to P_4 and finally, to P_1.

Waiting time for $P_1 = (11 - 1) = 10$ ms as P_1 enters at $t = 0$, executes for 1 ms, preempts at $t = 1$ and then resumes at $t = 11$

Waiting time for $P_2 = (5 - 2 - 1) = 2$ ms as P_2 enters at $t = 1$, executes for 2 ms, preempts at $t = 3$ and then resumes at $t = 5$

Waiting time for $P_3 = 0$ ms as P_3 enters at $t = 3$, starts immediately and executes completely

Waiting time for $P_4 = (8 - 4) = 4$ ms as P_4 enters at $t = 4$, starts at $t = 8$ and executes completely

Average waiting time $= (10 + 2 + 0 + 4)/4 = 4$ ms

Turnaround time for $P_1 = (17 - 0) = 17$ ms as P_1 enters at $t = 0$ and exits at $t = 17$
Turnaround time for $P_2 = (8 - 1) = 7$ ms as P_2 enters at $t = 1$ and exits at $t = 8$
Turnaround time for $P_3 = (5 - 3) = 2$ ms as P_3 enters at $t = 3$ and exits at $t = 5$
Turnaround time for $P_4 = (11 - 4) = 7$ ms as P_4 enters at $t = 4$ and exits at $t = 11$

Average turnaround time $= (17 + 7 + 2 + 7)/4 = 8.25$ ms

Advantages

- A long process that is near to its completion may be favoured over the short processes entering the system. This results in an improvement in the turnaround time of the long process.

Disadvantages

- Like SJF, it also requires an estimate of the next CPU burst of a process in advance.
- Favouring a long process nearing its completion over the several short processes entering the system may affect the turnaround times of short processes.
- It favours only those long processes that are just about to complete and not those who have just started their operation. Thus, starvation of long processes still may occur.

4.4.4 Priority Based Scheduling

In priority based scheduling algorithm, each process is assigned a priority and the higher priority processes are scheduled before the lower priority processes. At any point of time, the process having the highest priority among all the ready processes is scheduled first. In case two processes are having the same priority, they are executed in the FCFS order.

The priority scheduling may be either preemptive or non-preemptive. The choice is made whenever a new process enters the ready queue while some process is executing. If the newly arrived process has the higher priority than the currently running process, the preemptive priority scheduling algorithm preempts the currently running process and allocates CPU to the new process. On the other hand, the non-preemptive scheduling algorithm allows the currently running process to complete its execution and the new process has to wait for the CPU.

> **Note:** Both SJF and SRTN are special cases of priority based scheduling where priority of a process is equal to inverse of the next CPU burst. Lower is the CPU burst, higher will be the priority.

A major design issue related with priority scheduling is how to compute priorities of the processes. The priority can be assigned to a process either internally defined by the system depending on the process's characteristics, such as memory usage, I/O frequency, usage cost, etc., or externally defined by the user executing that process.

Example 4.4:

Consider four processes P_1, P_2, P_3 and P_4 with their arrival times, required CPU burst (in milliseconds) and priorities as shown in the following table.

Process	P_1	P_2	P_3	P_4
Arrival time	0	1	3	4
CPU burst (ms)	7	4	3	2
Priority	4	3	1	2

Assuming that the lower priority number means the higher priority, how will these processes be scheduled according to non-preemptive as well as preemptive priority scheduling algorithm? Compute the average waiting time and average turnaround time in both cases.

Solution:

Non-preemptive priority scheduling algorithm

The processes will be scheduled as depicted in the following Gantt chart.

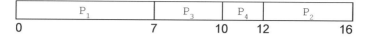

Initially, P_1 enters the ready queue at $t = 0$ and gets the CPU as there are no other processes in the queue. While it is executing, P_2, P_3 and P_4 enter the queue at $t = 1$, $t = 3$ and $t = 4$, respectively. When CPU becomes free, that is, at $t = 7$, it is allocated to P_3 because it is having the highest priority (that is, 1) among the three processes. When P_3 completes, CPU is allocated to the next lower priority process, that is, P_4 and finally, the lowest priority process P_2 is executed.

Waiting time for $P_1 = 0$ ms as P_1 starts immediately

Waiting time for $P_2 = (12 - 1) = 11$ ms as P_2 enters at $t = 1$ and starts at $t = 12$

Waiting time for $P_3 = (7 - 3) = 4$ ms as P_3 enters at $t = 3$ and starts at $t = 7$

Waiting time for $P_4 = (10 - 4) = 6$ ms as P_4 enters at $t = 4$ and starts at $t = 10$

Average waiting time $= (0 + 11 + 4 + 6)/4 = 5.25$ ms

Turnaround time for $P_1 = (7 - 0) = 7$ ms as P_1 enters at $t = 0$ and exits at $t = 7$

Turnaround time for $P_2 = (16 - 1) = 15$ ms as P_2 enters at $t = 1$ and exits at $t = 16$

Turnaround time for $P_3 = (10 - 3) = 7$ ms as P_3 enters at $t = 3$ and exits at $t = 10$

Turnaround time for $P_4 = (12 - 4) = 8$ ms as P_4 enters at $t = 4$ and exits at $t = 12$

Average turnaround time $= (7 + 15 + 7 + 8)/4 = 9.25$ ms

Preemptive priority scheduling algorithm

The processes will be scheduled as depicted in the following Gantt chart.

P_1	P_3	P_4	P_3	P_3	P_2
0 1	3	6	8	10	16

Initially, P_1 of priority 4 enters the ready queue at $t = 0$ and gets the CPU as there are no other processes in the queue. While it is executing, at time $t = 1$, P_2 of priority 3 greater than that of currently running process P_1, enters the queue. Therefore, P_1 is preempted (with remaining CPU burst of 6 ms) and the CPU is allocated to P_2. During execution of P_2, P_3 of priority 1 enters at $t = 3$. Again CPU is switched from P_2 (with remaining CPU burst of 2 ms) to P_3 as the priority of P_3 is greater than that of P_2. However, when at time $t = 4$, P_4 of priority 2 enters the queue, the CPU is not assigned to it because it has lower priority than currently running process P_3. When P_3 completes, there are three processes P_1, P_2 and P_4 in the ready queue having priorities 4, 3 and 2, respectively. The CPU is allocated first to P_4, then to P_2 and finally to P_1.

Waiting time for $P_1 = (10 - 1) = 9$ ms as P_1 enters at $t = 0$, executes for 1 ms, preempts at $t = 1$ and then resumes at $t = 11$

Waiting time for $P_2 = (8 - 2 - 1) = 5$ ms as P_2 enters at $t = 1$, executes for 2 ms, preempts at $t = 3$ and then resumes at $t = 8$

Waiting time for P_3 = 0 ms as P_3 enters at t = 3, starts immediately and executes completely

Waiting time for P_4 = (6 − 4) = 2 ms as P_4 enters at t = 4, starts at t = 6 and executes completely

Average waiting time = (9 + 5 + 0 + 2)/4 = 4 ms

Turnaround time for P_1 = (16 − 0) = 16 ms as P_1 enters at t = 0 and exits at t = 16

Turnaround time for P_2 = (10 − 1) = 9 ms as P_2 enters at t = 1 and exits at t = 10

Turnaround time for P_3 = (6 − 3) = 3 ms as P_3 enters at t = 3 and exits at t = 6

Turnaround time for P_4 = (8 − 4) = 4 ms as P_4 enters at t = 4 and exits at t = 8

Average turnaround time = (16 + 9 + 3 + 4)/4 = 8 ms

Advantages

- Important processes are never made to wait because of the execution of less important processes.

Disadvantages

- It suffers from the problem of starvation of lower priority processes, since the continuous arrival of higher priority processes will prevent lower priority processes indefinitely from acquiring the CPU. One possible solution to this problem is **aging** which is a process of gradually increasing the priority of a low priority process with increase in its waiting time. If the priority of a low priority process is increased after each fixed time of interval, it is ensured that at some time it will become a highest priority process and get executed.

CHECK YOUR PROGRESS

5. What is the difference between non-preemptive and preemptive scheduling algorithm?
6. FCFS is well suited for batch systems but not suitable for time sharing systems. (True or False)
7. Consider four processes P_1, P_2, P_3 and P_4 with CPU burst of 7 ms, 10 ms, 4 ms and 2 ms, respectively. Which of the following processes will be executed first according to SJF scheduling algorithm?
    (a) P_1 (b) P_2
    (c) P_3 (d) P_4
8. How are priorities assigned to processes in a priority scheduling algorithm?

4.4.5 Highest Response Ratio Next (HRN) Scheduling

The highest response ratio next scheduling is a non-preemptive scheduling algorithm that schedules the processes according to their response ratio. Whenever CPU becomes available, the process having the highest value of response ratio among all the ready processes is scheduled next. The response ratio of a process in the queue is computed by using the following equation.

$$\text{Response ratio} = \frac{(\text{Time since arrival} + \text{CPU burst})}{\text{CPU burst}}$$

Initially, when a process enters, its response ratio is 1. It goes on increasing at the rate of (1/CPU burst) as the process's waiting time increases.

Example 4.5:

Consider four processes P_1, P_2, P_3 and P_4 with their arrival times and required CPU burst (in milliseconds) as shown in the following table.

Process	P_1	P_2	P_3	P_4
Arrival time	0	2	3	4
CPU burst (ms)	3	4	5	2

How will these processes be scheduled according to HRN scheduling algorithm? Compute the average waiting time and average turnaround time.

Solution:

The processes will be scheduled as depicted in the following Gantt chart.

P_1	P_2	P_4	P_3

0   3   7   9   14

Initially, P_1 enters the ready queue at $t = 0$ and CPU is allocated to it. By the time P_1 completes, P_2 and P_3 have arrived at $t = 2$ and $t = 3$, respectively. At $t = 3$, the response ratio of P_2 is $((3-2)+4)/4 = 1.25$ and of P_3 is 1 as it has just arrived. Therefore P_2 is scheduled next. During execution of P_2, P_4 enters the queue at $t = 4$. When P_2 completes at $t = 7$, the response ratio of P_3 is $((7-3)+5)/5 = 1.8$ and of P_4 is $((7-4)+2)/2 = 2.5$. As P_4 has higher response ratio, the CPU is allocated to it and after its completion, P_3 is executed.

Waiting time for $P_1 = 0$ ms as P_1 starts immediately
Waiting time for $P_2 = (3 - 2) = 1$ ms as P_2 enters at $t = 2$ and starts at $t = 3$
Waiting time for $P_3 = (9 - 3) = 6$ ms as P_2 enters at $t = 3$ and starts at $t = 9$
Waiting time for $P_4 = (7 - 4) = 3$ ms as P_4 enters at $t = 4$ and starts at $t = 7$

Average waiting time $= (0 + 1 + 6 + 3)/4 = 2.5$ ms

Turnaround time for $P_1 = (3 - 0) = 3$ ms as P_1 enters at $t = 0$ and exits at $t = 3$
Turnaround time for $P_2 = (7 - 2) = 5$ ms as P_2 enters at $t = 2$ and exits at $t = 7$
Turnaround time for $P_3 = (14 - 3) = 11$ ms as P_3 enters at $t = 3$ and exits at $t = 14$
Turnaround time for $P_4 = (9 - 4) = 5$ ms as P_4 enters at $t = 4$ and exits at $t = 9$

Average turnaround time $= (3 + 5 + 11 + 5)/4 = 6$ ms

Advantages

- It favours short processes. This is because with increase in waiting time, the response ratio of short processes increases speedily as compared to long processes. Thus, they are scheduled earlier than long processes.
- Unlike SJF, starvation does not occur since with increase in waiting time, the response ratio of long processes also increases and eventually they are scheduled.

Disadvantages

- Like SJF and SRTN, it also requires an estimate of the expected service time (CPU burst) of a process.

4.4.6 Round Robin (RR) Scheduling

The round robin scheduling is one of the most widely used preemptive scheduling algorithms which considers all the processes as equally important and treats them in a favourable manner. Each process in the ready queue gets a fixed amount of CPU time (generally from 10 to 100 milliseconds) known as **time slice** or **time quantum** for its execution. If the process does not execute completely till the end of time slice, it is preempted and the CPU is allocated to the next process in the ready queue. However, if the process blocks or terminates before the time slice expires, the CPU is switched to the next process in the ready queue at that moment only.

To implement the round robin scheduling algorithm, the ready queue is treated as a circular queue. All the processes arriving in the ready queue are put at the end of queue. The CPU is allocated to the first process in the queue and the process executes until its time slice expires. If the CPU burst of the process being executed is less than one time quantum, the process itself releases the CPU and is deleted from the queue. The CPU is then allocated to the next process in the queue. However, if the process does not execute completely within the time slice, an interrupt occurs when the time slice expires. The currently running process is preempted, put back at the end of the queue and the CPU is allocated to the next process in the queue. The preempted process again gets the CPU after all the processes before it in the queue have been allocated their CPU time slice. The whole process continues until all the processes in queue have been executed.

Example 4.6:

Consider four processes P_1, P_2, P_3 and P_4 with their arrival times and required CPU burst (in milliseconds) as shown in the following table.

Process	P_1	P_2	P_3	P_4
Arrival time	0	1	3	4
CPU burst (ms)	10	5	2	3

Assuming that the time slice is 3 ms, how will these processes be scheduled according to round robin scheduling algorithm? Compute the average waiting time and average turnaround time.

Solution:

The processes will be scheduled as depicted in the following Gantt chart.

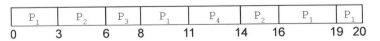

Initially, P_1 enters the ready queue at $t=0$ and gets the CPU for 3 ms. While it executes, P_2 and P_3 enter the queue at $t=1$ and $t=3$, respectively. Since, P_1 does not execute within 3 ms, an interrupt occurs when the time slice gets over. P_1 is preempted (with remaining

CPU burst of 7 ms), put back in the queue after P_3 because P_4 has not entered yet and the CPU is allocated to P_2. During execution of P_2, P_4 enters in the queue at $t = 4$ and put at the end of queue after P_1. When P_2 times out, it is preempted (with remaining CPU burst of 2 ms) and put back at the end of queue after P_4. The CPU is allocated to the next process in the queue, that is, to P_3 and it executes completely before the time slice expires. Thus, the CPU is allocated to the next process in the queue which is P_1. P_1 again executes for 3 ms, then preempted (with remaining CPU burst of 4 ms) and put back at the end of the queue after P_2 and the CPU is allocated to P_4. P_4 executes completely within the time slice and the CPU is allocated to next process in the queue, that is, P_2. As P_2 completes before the time out occurs, the CPU is switched to P_1 at $t = 16$ for another 3 ms. When the time slice expires, CPU is again allocated to P_1 as it is the only process in the queue.

Waiting time for $P_1 = (5+5) = 10$ ms as P_1 enters at $t = 0$, starts immediately, waits for $t = 3$ to $t = 8$ and then again waits for $t = 11$ to $t = 16$

Waiting time for $P_2 = (3 - 1 + 8) = 10$ ms as P_2 enters at $t = 1$, starts at $t = 3$, waits for $t = 6$ to $t = 14$ and then resumes at $t = 14$

Waiting time for $P_3 = (6 - 3) = 3$ ms as P_3 enters at $t = 3$, starts at $t = 6$ and executes completely

Waiting time for $P_4 = (11 - 4) = 7$ ms as P_4 enters at $t = 4$, starts at $t = 11$ and executes completely

Average waiting time $= (10 + 10 + 3 + 7)/4 = 7.5$ ms

Turnaround time for $P_1 = (20 - 0) = 20$ ms as P_1 enters at $t = 0$ and exits at $t = 20$

Turnaround time for $P_2 = (16 - 1) = 15$ ms as P_2 enters at $t = 1$ and exits at $t = 16$

Turnaround time for $P_3 = (8 - 3) = 5$ ms as P_3 enters at $t = 3$ and exits at $t = 8$

Turnaround time for $P_4 = (14 - 4) = 10$ ms as P_4 enters at $t = 4$ and exits at $t = 14$

Average turnaround time $= (20 + 15 + 5 + 10)/4 = 12.5$ ms

The performance of round robin scheduling is greatly affected by the size of the time quantum. If the time quantum is too small, a number of context switches occur which in turn increase the system overhead. The more time will be spent in performing context switching rather than executing the processes. On the other hand, if the time quantum is too large, the performance of round robin simply degrades to FCFS.

Note: If the time quantum is too small, say 1 μs, the round robin scheduling is called processor sharing.

Advantages

- It is efficient for time sharing systems where the CPU time is divided among the competing processes.
- It increases the fairness among the processes.

Disadvantages

- The processes (even the short processes) may take long time to execute. This decreases the system throughput.

- It requires some extra hardware support, such as a timer, to cause interrupt after each time out.

> **Note:** Ideally, the size of time quantum should be such that 80% of the processes could complete their execution within one time quantum.

4.4.7 Multilevel Queue Scheduling

The multilevel queue scheduling is designed for the environments where the processes can be categorized into different groups on the basis of their different response time requirements or different scheduling needs. One possible categorization may be based on whether the process is a system process, batch process or an interactive process (see Figure 4.2). Each group of processes is associated with a specific priority. For example, the system processes may have the highest priority, whereas, the batch processes may have the least priority.

To implement multilevel scheduling algorithm, the ready queue is partitioned into as many separate queues as there are groups. Whenever a new process enters, it is assigned permanently to one of the ready queues depending on its properties, such as memory requirements, type and priority. Each ready queue has its own scheduling algorithm. For example, for batch processes, FCFS scheduling algorithm may be used and for interactive processes, one may use the round robin scheduling algorithm. In addition, the processes in higher priority queues are executed before those in lower priority queues. This implies no batch process can run unless all the system processes and interactive processes have been executed completely. Moreover, if a process enters into a higher priority queue while a process in lower priority queue is executing, then the lower priority process would be preempted in order to allocate the CPU to the higher priority process.

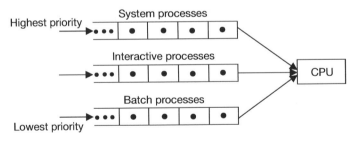

Figure 4.2: Multilevel Queue Scheduling

Advantages

- Processes are permanently assigned to their respective queues and do not move between queues. This results in low scheduling overhead.

Disadvantages

- The processes in lower priority queues may have to starve for CPU in case processes are continuously arriving in higher priority queues. One possible way to prevent starvation is to time slice among the queues. Each queue gets a certain share of CPU time which it schedules among the processes in it. Note that the time slice of different priority queues may differ.

4.4.8 Multilevel Feedback Queue Scheduling

The multilevel feedback queue scheduling also known as **multilevel adaptive scheduling** is an improved version of multilevel queue scheduling algorithm. In this scheduling algorithm, processes are not permanently assigned to queues; instead they are allowed to move between the queues. The decision to move a process between queues is based on the time taken by it in execution so far and its waiting time. If a process uses too much CPU time, it is moved to a lower priority queue. Similarly, a process that has been waiting for too long in a lower priority queue is moved to a higher priority queue in order to avoid starvation.

To understand this algorithm, consider a multilevel feedback queue scheduler (see Figure 4.3) with three queues, namely, Q_1, Q_2 and Q_3. Further, assume that the queues Q_1 and Q_2 employ round robin scheduling algorithm with time quantum of 5 ms and 10 ms, respectively while in queue Q_3, the processes are scheduled in FCFS order. The scheduler first executes all processes in Q_1. When Q_1 is empty, the scheduler executes the processes in Q_2. Finally, when both Q_1 and Q_2 are empty, the processes in Q_3 are executed. While executing processes in Q_2, if a new process arrives in Q_1, the currently executing process is preempted and the new process starts executing. Similarly, a process arriving in Q_2 preempts a process executing in Q_3. Initially, when a process enters into ready queue; it is placed in Q_1 where it is allocated the CPU for 5 ms. If the process finishes its execution within 5 ms, it exits from the queue. Otherwise, it is preempted and placed at the end of Q_2. Here, it is allocated the CPU for 10 ms (if Q_1 is empty) and still if it does not finish, it is preempted and placed at the end of Q_3.

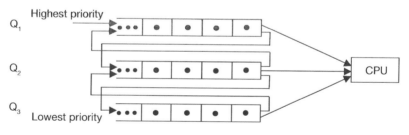

Figure 4.3: Multilevel Feedback Queue Scheduling

Example 4.7:

Consider four processes P_1, P_2, P_3 and P_4 with their arrival times and required CPU burst (in milliseconds) as shown in the following table.

Process	P_1	P_2	P_3	P_4
Arrival time	0	12	25	32
CPU burst (ms)	25	18	4	10

Assume that there are three ready queues Q_1, Q_2 and Q_3. The CPU time slice for Q_1 and Q_2 is 5 ms and 10 ms, respectively and in Q_3, processes are scheduled on FCFS basis. How will these processes be scheduled according to multilevel feedback queue scheduling algorithm? Compute the average waiting time and average turnaround time.

Solution:

The processes will be scheduled as depicted in the following Gantt chart.

P_1 Q_1	P_1 Q_2	P_2 Q_1	P_1 Q_2	P_3 Q_1	P_2 Q_2	P_4 Q_1	P_1 Q_2	P_2 Q_2	P_4 Q_2

```
0    5        12      17        25   29  32      37     42             52    57
```

Initially, P_1 enters the system at $t = 0$, placed in Q_1 and allocated the CPU for 5 ms. Since, it does not execute completely, it is moved to Q_2 at $t = 5$. Now Q_1 is empty so the scheduler picks up the process from the head of Q_2. Since, P_1 is the only process in Q_2, it is again allocated the CPU for 10 ms. But during its execution, P_2 enters Q_1 at $t = 12$, therefore P_1 is preempted and P_2 starts executing. At $t = 17$, P_2 is moved to Q_2 and placed after P_1. The CPU is allocated to the first process in Q_2, that is, P_1. While P_1 is executing, P_3 enters Q_1 at $t = 25$ so P_1 is preempted, placed after P_2 in Q_2 and P_3 starts executing. As P_3 executes completely within time slice, the scheduler picks up the first process in Q_2 which is P_2 at $t = 29$. While P_2 is executing, P_4 enters Q_1 at $t = 32$ because of which P_2 is preempted and placed after P_1 in Q_2. The CPU is assigned to P_4 for 5 ms and at $t = 37$, P_4 is moved to Q_2 and placed after P_2. At the same time, the CPU is allocated to P_1 (first process in Q_2). When it completes at $t = 42$, the next process in Q_2 which is P_2, starts executing. When it completes, the last process in Q_2, that is, P_4 is executed.

Waiting time for P_1 = (5+12) = 17 ms as P_1 first waits for $t = 12$ to $t = 17$ and then again waits for $t = 25$ to $t = 37$

Waiting time for P_2 = (12+10) = 22 ms as P_2 first waits for $t = 17$ to $t = 29$ and then again waits for $t = 32$ to $t = 42$

Waiting time for P_3 = 0 ms as P_3 enters at $t = 25$, starts immediately and executes completely

Waiting time for P_4 = (52 − 37) = 15 ms as P_4 waits for $t = 37$ to $t = 52$

Average waiting time = (17 + 22 + 0 + 15)/4 = 13.5 ms

Turnaround time for P_1 = (42 − 0) = 42 ms as P_1 enters at $t = 0$ and exits at $t = 42$

Turnaround time for P_2 = (52 − 12) = 40 ms as P_2 enters at $t = 12$ and exits at $t = 52$

Turnaround time for P_3 = (29 − 25) = 4 ms as P_3 enters at $t = 25$ and exits at $t = 29$

Turnaround time for P_4 = (57 − 32) = 25 ms as P_4 enters at $t = 32$ and exits at $t = 57$

Average turnaround time = (42 + 40 + 4 + 25)/4 = 27.75 ms

Advantages

- It is fair to I/O bound (short) processes as these processes need not wait too long and are executed quickly.
- It prevents starvation by moving a lower priority process to a higher priority queue if it has been waiting for too long.

Disadvantages

- It is the most complex scheduling algorithm.

- Moving the processes between queues causes a number of context switches which results in an increased overhead.
- The turnaround time for long processes may increase significantly.

4.5 MULTIPLE PROCESSOR SCHEDULING

So far we have discussed the scheduling of a single processor among a number of processes in the queue. In case of having more than one processor, different scheduling mechanisms need to be incorporated. In this section, we will concentrate on homogeneous multiprocessor systems which mean the systems in which all processors are identical in terms of their functionality and any process in the queue can be assigned to any available processor.

The scheduling criteria for multiprocessor scheduling are same as that for single processor scheduling. But there are also some new considerations which are discussed here.

4.5.1 Implementation of Ready Queue

In multiprocessor systems, the ready queue can be implemented in two ways. Either there may be a separate ready queue for each processor (see Figure 4.4(a)) or there may be a single shared ready queue for all the processors (see Figure 4.4(b)). In the former case, it may happen that at any moment the ready queue of one processor is empty while the other processor is very busy in executing processes. To prevent this situation, the latter approach is preferred in which all the processes enter into one queue and scheduled on any available processor.

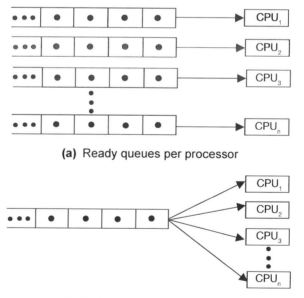

(a) Ready queues per processor

(b) A single shared ready queue

Figure 4.4: Implementation of Ready Queue in Multiprocessor Systems

4.5.2 Scheduling Approaches

The next issue is how to schedule the processes from the ready queue to multiple processors. For this, one of following scheduling approaches may be used.

- **Symmetric Multi Processing (SMP):** In this approach, each processor is self-scheduling. For each processor, the scheduler selects a process for execution from the ready queue. Since, multiple processors need to access common data structure, this approach necessitates synchronization among multiple processors. This is required so that no two processors could select the same process and no process is lost from the ready queue.
- **Asymmetric multiprocessing:** This approach is based on the master-slave structure among the processors. The responsibility of making scheduling decisions, I/O processing and other system activities is up to only one processor (called master), and other processors (called slaves) simply execute the user's code. Whenever some processor becomes available, the master processor examines the ready queue and selects a process for it. This approach is easier to implement than symmetric multiprocessing as only one processor has access to the system data structures. But at the same time, this approach is inefficient because a number of processes may block the master processor.

4.5.3 Load Balancing

On SMP systems having a private ready queue for each processor, it might happen at a certain moment of time that one or more processors are sitting idle while others are overloaded with a number of processes waiting for them. Thus, in order to achieve the better utilization of multiple processors, load balancing is required which means to keep the workload evenly distributed among multiple processors. There are two techniques to perform load balancing, namely, push migration and pull migration.

In **push migration** technique, the load is balanced by periodically checking the load of each processor and shifting the processes from the ready queues of overloaded processors to that of less overloaded or idle processors. On the other hand, in **pull migration** technique, the idle processor itself pulls a waiting process from a busy processor.

> **Note:** Load balancing is often unnecessary on SMP systems with a single shared ready queue.

4.5.4 Processor Affinity

Processor affinity means an effort to make a process to run on the same processor it was executed last time. Whenever a process executes on a processor, the data most recently accessed by it is kept in the cache memory of that processor. Next time if the process is run on the same processor, then most if its memory accesses are satisfied in the cache memory only and as a result the process execution speeds up. However, if the process is run on some different processor next time, the cache of the older processor becomes invalid and the cache of the new processor is to be repopulated. As a result, the process execution is delayed. Thus, an attempt should be made by the operating system to run a process on the same processor each time instead of migrating it to some another processor.

When an operating system tries to make a process to run on the same processor but does not guarantee to always do so, it is referred to as **soft affinity**. On the other hand, when an operating system provides system calls that force a process to run on the same processor, it is referred to as **hard affinity**. In soft affinity, there is a possibility of process migration from one processor to another, whereas in hard affinity, the process is never migrated to some another processor.

CHECK YOUR PROGRESS

9. How is the response ratio of a process computed?
10. The round robin scheduling is efficient for _____ .
    (a) Batch systems   (b) Time sharing systems
    (c) Real-time systems   (d) None of these
11. What should be the ideal size of time quantum?
12. How does multilevel scheduling result in low scheduling overhead?
13. How does the multilevel feedback queue scheduling provide an improvement over multilevel queue scheduling?
14. Two techniques used to perform load balancing in multiprocessor systems are _____ and _____ .
15. In symmetric multiprocessing scheduling approach, the responsibility of making scheduling decisions is up to only one processor. (True or False)
16. What is the main difference between soft affinity and hard affinity?

4.6 REAL-TIME SCHEDULING

In real-time systems, the correctness of the computations not only depends on the output of the computation but also on the time at which the output is generated. A real-time system has well-defined and fixed time constraints. If these time constraints are not met, the system is said to be failed in spite of producing the correct output. Thus, the main aim of real-time systems is to generate the correct result within its certain time constraints. The real-time systems are of two types: hard real-time systems and soft real-time systems.

4.6.1 Hard Real-time Systems

In hard real-time systems, a process must be accomplished within the specified deadlines; otherwise, undesirable results may be produced. A process serviced after its deadline has crossed does not make any sense. Industrial control and robotics are the examples of hard real-time systems.

In hard-real time systems, the scheduler requires a process to declare its deadline requirements before entering into the system. Then it employs a technique known as **admission control** algorithm to decide whether the process should be admitted. The process is admitted if the scheduler can ensure that it will be accomplished by its deadline; otherwise it is rejected. The scheduler can give assurance of process completion on time only if knows the exact time taken by each function of operating system to perform and each function is guaranteed to be performed within that amount of time. But practically, it is not possible to provide such assurance in case of systems with secondary storage and virtual memory. This is because in such systems the amount of time to execute a process may vary. Thus, hard real-time systems are composed of special purpose software running on hardware committed to their vital processes.

4.6.2 Soft Real-time Systems

In soft real-time systems, the requirements are less strict; it is not mandatory to meet the deadline. A real-time process always gets the priority over other tasks and retains the priority until its completion. If the deadline could not be met due to any reason, then it is possible to reschedule the task and complete it. Multimedia, virtual reality and advanced scientific applications, such as undersea exploration come under the category of soft real-time systems.

The implementation of scheduling in soft real-time systems requires the following properties to be considered:

- The system must employ preemptive priority based scheduling and real-time processes must be assigned higher priority than non real-time processes. Also, the priority of the real-time processes must not change during their lifetime.
- The dispatch latency must be low so that a runable real-time process could start as early as possible.

The system can guarantee the first property by prohibiting aging (discussed in *Section* 4.4.4) on real-time processes thereby, preserving their priority. However, guaranteeing the second property is somewhat difficult. This is because most operating system are constrained to wait for the completion of some system call or I/O operation before context switching a process thereby, resulting in high dispatch latency.

One way to keep dispatch latency low is to provide **preemptive kernels**, which allows the preemption of a process running in kernel mode. A number of approaches can be used to make the kernel preemptive; two of them are as follows:

- The first approach is to place preemption points at the safe locations (where the kernel data is not being modified) in the kernel. A preemption point determines whether there is a high-priority process ready for execution. If so, the kernel process is preempted, context switching is performed and the high-priority process is made to run. After the high-priority process has been executed, the preempted process is rescheduled.
- Since the first approach allows a kernel process to be preempted only at preemption points, a high-priority process may have to wait while the process is executing in unsafe locations. As a result, dispatch latency would be large. Thus, an alternative approach is to make the kernel process preemptible at all times. However to facilitate this, this approach needs to employ some synchronization mechanisms. These mechanisms ensure the protection of kernel data from modification by the high-priority process if it comes when the process to be preempted is updating the kernel data. This approach is efficient and used widely.

The aforementioned approaches suffer from **priority inversion** problem. This problem occurs when the high-priority process requires accessing (read/write) the kernel data currently being accessed by some low-priority process or a chain of low-priority processes. In such a case, the high-priority process is forced to wait for the low-priority process or processes to complete their execution thereby, resulting in large dispatch latency.

The priority inversion problem can be overcome using the **priority inheritance protocol**. This protocol allows the low-priority processes that are currently accessing the resources required by the high-priority process to inherit higher priority until they finish their work with the required resource. Once they have finished with the resource, their priorities revert to the original ones.

4.7 ALGORITHM EVALUATION

In *Section 4.4*, we have studied various scheduling algorithms. But, now the issue arises on the selection of a scheduling algorithm for a particular system. For this, we need to evaluate the performance of different scheduling algorithms under given system workload and find out the most suitable one for the system. This section discusses some commonly used methods to evaluate scheduling algorithms.

4.7.1 Deterministic Modelling

Deterministic modelling is the simplest and direct method used to compare the performance of different scheduling algorithms on the basis of some specific criteria. It takes into account the prespecified system workload and measures the performance of each scheduling algorithm for that workload.

For example, consider a system with workload as shown below. We have to select an algorithm out of FCFS, SJF and RR (with time slice 8 ms), which results in minimum average waiting time.

Process	P_1	P_2	P_3	P_4
Arrival time	0	1	3	4
CPU burst (ms)	7	15	2	5

According to FCFS, SJF and RR scheduling algorithms, the processes will be scheduled as depicted in the following Gantt charts.

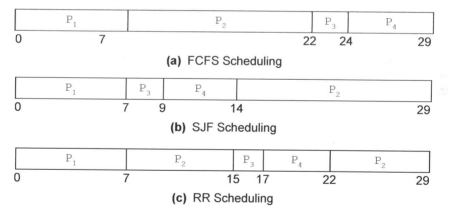

(a) FCFS Scheduling

(b) SJF Scheduling

(c) RR Scheduling

According to FCFS, the average waiting time = (0 + 6 + 19 + 20)/4 = 11.25 ms
According to SJF, the average waiting time = (0 + 13 + 4 + 5)/4 = 5.5 ms
According to RR, the average waiting time = (0 + 13 + 12 + 13)/4 = 9.5 ms

From the above calculation, we can study the comparative performance of scheduling algorithms. SJF scheduling algorithm results in average waiting time less than half of that in FCFS while the RR scheduling results in an intermediate value. Thus, for the given system workload, SJF scheduling will work best.

Though the deterministic modelling returns exact measures to compare the performance of scheduling algorithms, it requires the exact processing requirements of processes to be provided as input. Thus, deterministic modelling is suitable for systems in which same programs may run again and again thereby, providing exact measures of CPU bursts and I/O bursts of processes.

4.7.2 Queuing Models

Generally, there is no fixed set of processes that run on systems; thus, it is not possible to measure the exact processing requirements of processes. However, we can measure the distributions of CPU bursts and I/O bursts during the lifetime of processes and derive a mathematical formula that identifies the probability of a specific CPU burst. Similarly, the arrival rate of processes in the system can also be approximated.

The use of mathematical models for evaluating performance of various systems led to the development of **queuing theory**, a branch of mathematics. The fundamental model of queuing theory is identical to the computer system model. Each computer system is represented as a set of servers (such as CPU, I/O devices, etc.) with each server having its own queue. For example, CPU has a ready queue and an I/O device has a device queue associated with itself. By having knowledge of arrival rates of processes in each queue and service rates of processes, we can find out the average length of queue, average waiting time of processes in the queue, etc.

For example, consider L denotes the average queue length, W denotes the average waiting time of a process in the queue and α denotes the average arrival rate of processes in the queue. The relationship between L, W and α can be expressed by the Little's formula, as given below:

$$L = \alpha \times w$$

This formula is based on the following facts:

- During the time a process waits in the queue (W), ($\alpha \times w$) new processes enter into the queue.
- The system is in steady state, that is, the number of processes exiting from the queue is equal to the number of processes entering into the queue.

> **Note:**   The performance evaluation using the queuing theory is known as queuing analysis.

In spite of the fact that queuing analysis provides a mathematical formula to evaluate the performance of scheduling algorithms, it suffers from few limitations. We can use queuing analysis for only limited classes of scheduling algorithms, not for all. Moreover, it is based on approximations; therefore, the accuracy of calculated results depends on how closely the approximations match with the real system.

4.7.3 Simulations

Simulations are the more accurate method of evaluating algorithms that mimic the dynamic behaviour of a real computer system over time. The computer system model is programmed and all the major components of system are represented by the data structures. The simulator employs a variable representing a clock. As the clock is incremented, the current system state is changed to reflect the changed actions of processes, scheduler,

I/O devices, etc. While the simulation executes, the system parameters that affect the performance of scheduling algorithms, such as CPU burst I/O burst and so on, are gathered and recorded.

The data to drive the simulation can be generated using the **trace tapes**, which are created by monitoring the system under study and recording the events taking place. The sequence of recorded events is then used to drive the simulation. Although trace tapes is the easier method to compare the performance of two different scheduling algorithms for the same set of real inputs, they need a vast amount of storage space. Moreover, simulation requires a lot of computer time; this makes it an expensive method.

4.8 CASE STUDY: PROCESS SCHEDULING IN LINUX

Linux has two separate classes of processes: real-time and non–real-time and the real-time processes are given priority over non-real-time processes. The real-time processes are assigned priorities ranging from 0 to 99 (that is, 100) where 0 denotes the highest priority. On the other hand, the priorities assigned to non-real-time processes range from 100 to 139 (that is, 40) where 100 denotes the highest priority. Thus, Linux supports total 140 priority levels.

In Linux, the real–time processes can be scheduled in two ways: First-Come First-Served (FCFS) and Round Robin (RR) within each priority level (0-99). Accordingly, it provides two real-time scheduling classes, one for real-time FCFS processes and another for real-time RR processes. Within each scheduling class, each process has a priority assigned to it and the CPU is always allocated to the process having the highest priority. Note that a real-time FCFS process has higher priority than a real-time RR process and it cannot be preempted until it terminates, or blocks, or voluntarily exits. On the other hand, a real-time RR process is associated with a time slice and thus, is preemptable by the clock.

Though Linux scheduler ensures to serve a real-time process before non-real-time processes, the kernel cannot guarantee how rapidly the process will be scheduled once it becomes ready for execution. This is because the Linux kernel is non-preemptive; a process running in kernel mode cannot be preempted, even if a real-time process with a higher priority is ready to run. Thus, Linux offers soft real-time scheduling rather than hard.

The non–real-time processes in Linux are scheduled in a time sharing manner. But the notion of time slice differs from that of conventional time sharing algorithm. In Linux, the time slice of a process varies according to its priority; higher priority implies larger time slice. For instance, the processes with priority 100 may get a time slice of 800 ms while the processes with priority 139 may get 5 ms. Moreover, a process can use its time slice over a period of time in accordance with its priority.

The Linux scheduler uses a runqueue data structure that contains the runnable processes. As Linux supports SMP, each processor has its own runqueue data structure. Further, each runqueue maintains two arrays: active and expired, which are indexed from 0 to 139 corresponding to 140 priority levels (see Figure 4.5). The active array contains the processes that have their time slices remaining and the expired array contains the processes that have exhausted their time slices. In each of these arrays, the ith position points to the list of processes with priority i.

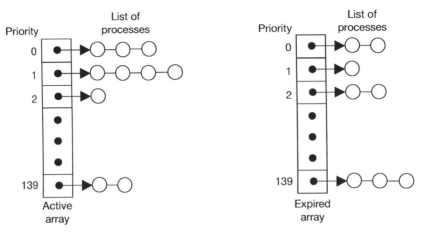

Figure 4.5: Active and Expired Arrays

At any instant, the scheduler selects a process with the highest priority (say, P) from the active array for execution. After the process P has executed for its time slice but still not finished, it is moved to the expired array. However, if the process gets blocked (due to wait for some event) before its time slice expires, it is put back in the active array with its time slice decremented by the amount of CPU time it has already taken. Once the awaited event has occurred, the blocked process can be resumed. After all the processes in the active array have exhausted their time slices (that is, active array is empty), the active and expired arrays are exchanged; active array now becomes the expired array and vice versa. This way the processes are scheduled in Linux.

CHECK YOUR PROGRESS

17. The real-time systems are of two types, namely, _____ and _____.
18. A preemptive kernel helps to keep the dispatch latency low. (True or False)
19. Describe the Little's formula.
20. What do the active array and expired array in Linux contain?

Let Us Summarize

1. The algorithm used by the scheduler to carry out the selection of a process for execution is known as scheduling algorithm.
2. The time period elapsed in processing before performing the next I/O operation is known as CPU burst.
3. The time period elapsed in performing I/O before the next CPU burst is known as I/O burst.
4. The module of the operating system that performs the function of setting up the execution of the selected process on the CPU is known as dispatcher.
5. For scheduling purposes, the scheduler may consider some performance measures and optimization criteria which include fairness, CPU utilization, balanced utilization, throughput, waiting time, turnaround time and response time.

6. A wide variety of algorithms are used for the CPU scheduling. These scheduling algorithms fall into two categories, namely, non-preemptive and preemptive.

7. In non-preemptive scheduling algorithms, once the CPU is allocated to a process, it cannot be taken back until the process voluntarily releases it or the process terminates.

8. In preemptive scheduling algorithms, the CPU can be forcibly taken back from the currently running process before its completion and allocated to some other process.

9. FCFS is one of the simplest non-preemptive scheduling algorithms in which the processes are executed in the order of their arrival in the ready queue.

10. The shortest job first also known as shortest process next or shortest request next is a non-preemptive scheduling algorithm that schedules the processes according to the length of CPU burst they require.

11. The shortest remaining time next also known as shortest time to go is a preemptive version of the SJF scheduling algorithm. It takes into account the length of remaining CPU burst of the processes rather than the whole length in order to schedule them.

12. In priority based scheduling algorithm, each process is assigned a priority and the higher priority processes are scheduled before the lower priority processes.

13. The highest response ratio next scheduling is a non-preemptive scheduling algorithm that schedules the processes according to their response ratio. Whenever CPU becomes available, the process having the highest value of response ratio among all the ready processes is scheduled next.

14. The round robin scheduling is one of the most widely used preemptive scheduling algorithms in which each process in the ready queue gets a fixed amount of CPU time (generally from 10 to 100 milliseconds) known as time slice or time quantum for its execution.

15. The multilevel queue scheduling is designed for the environments where the processes can be categorized into different groups on the basis of their different response time requirements or different scheduling needs.

16. The multilevel feedback queue scheduling also known as multilevel adaptive scheduling is an improved version of multilevel queue scheduling algorithm. In this scheduling algorithm, processes are not permanently assigned to queues; instead they are allowed to move between the queues.

17. In multiprocessor systems, the ready queue can be implemented in two ways. Either there may be a separate ready queue for each processor or there may be a single shared ready queue for all the processors.

18. In symmetric multiprocessing scheduling approach, each processor is self-scheduling. For each processor, the scheduler selects a process for execution from the ready queue.

19. In asymmetric multiprocessing scheduling approach, the responsibility of making scheduling decisions, I/O processing and other system activities is up to only one processor (called master), and other processors (called slaves) simply execute the user's code.

20. A real-time system has well-defined and fixed time constraints. If these time constraints are not met, the system is said to be failed in spite of producing the correct output. It is of two types: hard real-time system and soft real-time system.

21. In hard real-time systems, the scheduler requires a process to declare its deadline requirements before entering into the system. Then it employs a technique known as admission control algorithm to decide whether the process should be admitted.

22. In soft real-time systems, the requirements are less strict; it is not mandatory to meet the deadlines. A real-time process always gets the priority over other tasks and retains the priority until its completion. If the deadline could not be met due to any reason, then it is possible to reschedule the task and complete it.

23. To select a scheduling algorithm for a particular system, we need to evaluate the performance of different scheduling algorithms under given system workload and find out the most suitable one for the system. Some of the commonly used evaluation methods are deterministic modelling, queuing models and simulations.

ANSWERS TO 'CHECK YOUR PROGRESS'

1. CPU burst, I/O burst
2. The dispatcher is a module of the operating system whose function is to set up the execution of the process selected by the short-term scheduler on the CPU.
3. False
4. (a)
5. In non-preemptive scheduling algorithms, once the CPU is allocated to a process, it cannot be taken back until the process voluntarily releases it or the process terminates. On the other hand, in preemptive scheduling algorithms, the CPU can be forcibly taken back from the currently running process before its completion and allocated to some other process.
6. True
7. (d)
8. The priority can be assigned to a process either internally defined by the system depending on the process's characteristics, such as memory usage, I/O frequency, usage cost, etc., or externally defined by the user executing that process.
9. The Response Ratio (RR) of a process in the queue is computed by using the following equation.

$$\text{Response ratio (RR)} = \frac{(\text{Time since arrival} + \text{CPU burst})}{\text{CPU burst}}$$

10. (b)
11. Ideally, the size of time quantum should be such that 80% of the processes could complete their execution within one time quantum.
12. The multilevel scheduling results in low scheduling overhead as the processes are permanently assigned to their respective queues and do not move between queues.
13. In multilevel feedback scheduling algorithm, processes are not permanently assigned to queues; instead they are allowed to move between the queues.
14. push migration, pull migration
15. False
16. In soft affinity, there is a possibility of process migration from one processor to another, whereas, in hard affinity, the process is never migrated to some another processor.
17. Hard real-time systems , soft real-time systems
18. True
19. The Little's formula identifies the relationship between the average queue length (L), average waiting time of a process in the queue (W) and the average arrival rate of the processes in the queue (α). This formula is expressed as:

$$L = \alpha \times W$$

20. The active array contains the processes that have their time slices remaining and the expired array contains the processes that have exhausted their time slices.

 ## TEST YOURSELF

1. Distinguish between non-preemptive and preemptive scheduling algorithms.
2. Define throughput, turnaround time, waiting time and response time.
3. List the situations that may require the scheduler to make scheduling decisions.
4. Explain the relation (if any) between the following pairs of scheduling algorithms.
   (a) Round robin and FCFS
   (b) Multilevel feedback queue and FCFS
   (c) SJF and SRTN
   (d) SRTN and priority based
5. Which non-preemptive scheduling algorithms suffer from starvation and under what conditions?
6. Consider five processes P_1, P_2, P_3, P_4 and P_5 with their arrival times, required CPU burst (in milliseconds), and priorities as shown in the following table.

Process	P_1	P_2	P_3	P_4	P_5
Arrival time	0	1	4	4	5
CPU burst (ms)	10	6	4	2	5
Priority	4	4	1	2	4

Assume that the lower priority number means the higher priority. Compute the average waiting time and average turnaround time of processes for each of the following scheduling algorithms. Also determine which of the following scheduling algorithms result in minimum waiting time.
   (a) FCFS
   (b) SJF
   (c) HRN
   (d) Non-preemptive priority based
7. Consider the same set of processes as shown in **Question 6**. Compute the average waiting time and average turnaround time of processes for each of the following scheduling algorithms.
   (a) SRTN
   (b) Preemptive priority based
   (c) Round robin (if CPU time slice is 2 ms)
   Compare the performance of these scheduling algorithms with each other.
8. Which of the following scheduling algorithms favor the I/O bound processes and how?
   (a) Multilevel feedback queue
   (b) SJF
   (c) HRN
9. Write short notes on the following.
   (a) Real-time process scheduling in Linux
   (b) Difference between multilevel queue and multilevel feedback queue scheduling

(c) Soft affinity *vs* hard affinity

(d) Dispatcher

(e) Scheduling approaches for multiprocessor scheduling

10. Consider a scheduling algorithm that prefers to schedule those processes first which have consumed the least amount of CPU time. How will this algorithm treat the I/O bound and CPU bound processes? Is there any chance of starvation?

11. Explain various methods used for evaluating performance of scheduling algorithms.

12. Describe scheduling in soft real-time systems.

Chapter 05

Process Synchronization

Learning Objectives

After reading this chapter, you will be able to:

- ☐ Understand the need of synchronization among processes
- ☐ Describe the critical-section problem
- ☐ Explain the Peterson solution for critical-section problem
- ☐ Explain the bakery algorithm
- ☐ Discuss the hardware-supported solutions for critical-section problem
- ☐ Define semaphores
- ☐ Discuss various classical synchronization problems and their solutions
- ☐ Understand the concept of monitors

5.1 INTRODUCTION

Operating systems that support multiprogramming allow multiple processes to execute concurrently in a system even with a single processor. These processes may share information with each other through shared memory locations or shared files. A process that share information with other processes is cooperating process. If cooperating processes are not executed in an ordered manner, data inconsistency may occur. Therefore, various mechanisms have been developed to ensure data consistency with concurrent execution of cooperating processes.

5.2 SYNCHRONIZATION

As mentioned above, unordered execution of cooperating processes may result in data inconsistency. To understand the concept, consider two cooperating processes P_1 and P_2 that update the balance of an account in a bank. The code segment for the processes is given in Table 5.1.

Table 5.1: Code Segment for Processes P_1 and P_2

Process P_1	Process P_2
Read Balance	Read Balance
Balance = Balance + 1000	Balance = Balance - 400

Suppose that the balance is initially 5000, then after the execution of both P_1 and P_2, it should be 5600. The correct result is achieved if P_1 and P_2 execute one by one in any order either P_1 followed by P_2 or P_2 followed by P_1. However, if the instructions of P_1 and P_2 are interleaved arbitrarily, the balance may not be 5600 after the execution of both P_1 and P_2. One possible interleaving sequence for the execution of instructions of P_1 and P_2 is given in Table 5.2.

Table 5.2: Possible Interleaved Sequence

Process P_1	Process P_2	Balance
Read Balance		5000
	Read Balance	5000
Balance = Balance + 1000		6000
	Balance = Balance - 400	4600

The above interleaved sequence results in an inconsistent balance, that is, 4600. If the order of last two instructions is interchanged, the balance would be 6000 (again, inconsistent). Note that a situation where several processes sharing some data execute concurrently and the result of execution depends on the order in which the shared data is accessed by the processes is called **race condition**.

To avoid race conditions or such inconsistent situations, some form of synchronization among the processes is required which ensures that only one process is manipulating the shared data at a time. One common way to synchronize the processes is signalling, in which the process generates signals to allow other processes to manipulate the shared data.

5.3 CRITICAL REGIONS

The portion of the code of a process in which it accesses or changes the shared data is known as its **critical region** (also called **critical section**). It is important for the system to ensure that the execution of critical sections by the cooperating processes is mutually exclusive. It means that no two processes are allowed to execute in their critical sections at one time.

5.3.1 Critical-Section Problem

The critical-section problem is to design a protocol that the processes can use to cooperate. Each process must request permission to enter its critical section and signal the entrance by setting the values of some variables. The process does this in the code just before the critical section. That part of code is called the **entry section**. After executing the critical section, the process again sets some variables to signal the exit from the critical section. The portion of code in which the process does this is called the **exit section**. A solution to critical-section problem must satisfy the mutual exclusion requirement in addition to the following two requirements.

- **Progress:** Suppose a process P_1 is executing in its critical section, then all other processes that wish to enter their critical sections have to wait. When P_1 finishes its execution in critical section, a decision as to which process will enter its critical section next is to be made. In the decision, only the waiting processes will participate and the decision should be made in a finite amount of time. A process that has exited from its critical section cannot prevent other processes from entering their critical sections.
- **Bounded waiting:** A process wishing to enter its critical section cannot be delayed indefinitely. There is an upper bound on the number of times that other processes are allowed to enter their critical sections after a process has made a request to enter its critical section and before the permission is granted.

A number of mechanisms have been developed to solve the critical-section problem. These mechanisms include software solutions, hardware supported solutions, operating system primitives and programming language constructs. In this section, we present two process and multiple process software solutions. Hardware-supported solutions, operating system primitives (semaphores) and programming language constructs (monitors) are discussed in *Sections 5.4, 5.5* and *5.7*, respectively.

Peterson's Algorithm: Two Process Solution

Peterson proposed an algorithm to solve the critical-section problem for two processes. The algorithm lets the two processes P_i and P_j to share the following two variables:

```
int turn;
boolean flag[2];
```

The value of variable `turn` is initialized to either `i` or `j` and both the elements of array `flag` are initialized to `false`. The general structure for the code segment of process, say P_i, is as follows:

```
do
{

    flag[i] = true;
    turn = j;
    while(flag[j] && turn==j)          ←——— Entry section
            doNothing();

    //critical section
```

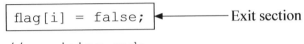

```
flag[i] = false;
```
←————————— Exit section

```
//remaining code
}while(1);
```

When any process, suppose P_i, wishes to enter its critical section, it first sets flag[i] to true and the value of turn to other number, that is, j. It then verifies the following two conditions:

1. Whether flag[j] is true
2. Whether turn equals j

If any of these conditions is false, the process P_i enters its critical section, otherwise, it waits. In case, only P_i wishes to enter the critical section, the first condition remains false. The process P_i then executes in its critical section and after that resets the flag[i] to false, indicating that P_i is not in its critical section.

Now, consider the case when both P_i and P_j wish to enter their critical sections at the same time. In this case, both the elements of the flag will be set to true and the value of turn will be set to i and j one by one (by P_i and P_j) but only one retains. Now, the first condition is true, thus, the value of turn decides which process enters its critical section first. The other process has to wait. It implies mutual exclusion is preserved.

To verify that the algorithm also satisfies the other two requirements, observe that a process P_i can be prevented from entering its critical section if flag[j] is true and turn is j. If P_j does not wish to enter its critical section, then P_i found flag[j] as false and can enter its critical section. However, when both processes wish to enter their critical section at the same time the variable turn plays its role and allowed one process to enter its critical section. Suppose turn is j, then P_j is allowed first and P_i is stuck in the loop. Now, when P_j exits from its critical section, it sets flag[j] to false to indicate that it is not in its critical section now. This allows P_i to enter its critical section. It means P_i enters its critical section after at most one entry by P_j, satisfying both progress and bounded-waiting requirements.

Bakery Algorithm: Multiple Process Solution

Lamport proposed an algorithm, known as the bakery algorithm, to solve the critical-section problem for N processes. The algorithm lets the processes to share the following two variables:

```
boolean choosing[N];
int number[N];
```

All the elements of the arrays, that is, choosing and number are initialized to false and 0, respectively.

The algorithm assigns a number to each process and serves the process with the lowest number first. The algorithm cannot ensure that two processes do not receive the same number. Thus, if two processes, say P_i and P_j, receive the same number, then P_i is served first if i<j. The general structure for the code segment of process, say P_i, is discussed further.

```
do
{
```

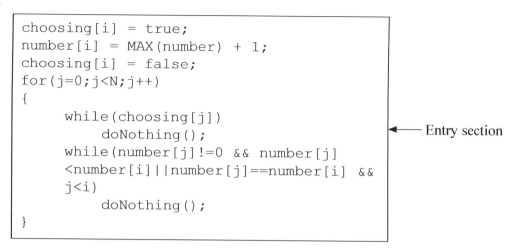

```
        choosing[i] = true;
        number[i] = MAX(number) + 1;
        choosing[i] = false;
        for(j=0;j<N;j++)
        {
                while(choosing[j])
                        doNothing();
                while(number[j]!=0 && number[j]
                <number[i]||number[j]==number[i] &&
                j<i)
                        doNothing();
        }
```

───── Entry section

```
        //critical section
```

```
        number[i] = 0;
```
◄────── Exit section

```
        //remaining code
}while(1);
```

> **Note:** For simplicity, the notation MAX(number) is used to retrieve the maximum element in the array number.

To verify that mutual exclusion is preserved, suppose a process P_0 is executing in its critical section and another process, say P_1, attempts to enter the critical section. For $j=0$, the process P_1 is not blocked in the first while loop because P_0 had set choosing[0] to false in the entry section. However, in the second while loop for $j=0$, P_1 finds the following:

- number[j]!=0, since P_0 is executing in the critical section after setting it to a non-zero number in the entry section
- number[j]<number[i], since P_1 is assigned a number after P_0. Though, P_1 may be assigned the same number as that of P_0 but in that case, P_1 finds j<i because 0<1.

Since, the result in the second while loop is true, P_1 is blocked in the while loop until P_0 finishes execution in its critical section, thus, preserving the mutual exclusion requirement. The algorithm not only preserves the mutual exclusion requirement, but also the progress and bounded-waiting requirements. To verify these requirements, observe that if two or more processes are waiting to enter the critical sections, then the process that had come first is allowed to enter the critical section first. The conditions in the second while statement ensures this. It means the processes are served on a first-come, first-serve basis and no process is delayed because of starvation.

5.4 SYNCHRONIZATION HARDWARE

The hardware-supported solutions developed for the critical-section problem make use of hardware instructions available on many systems, thus, are effective and efficient.

On a system with a single processor, only one process executes at a time. The other processes can gain control of processor through interrupts. Therefore, to solve the critical-section problem, it must be ensured that when a process is executing in its critical-section, interrupt should not occur. A process can achieve this by disabling interrupts before entering in its critical section. Note that the process must enable the interrupts after finishing execution in its critical section.

This method is simple, but it has certain disadvantages. First, it is feasible in a single-processor environment only because disabling interrupts in a multiprocessor environment takes time as message is passed to all the processors. This message passing delays processes from entering into their critical sections, thus, decreasing the system efficiency. Second, it may affect the scheduling goals, since the processor cannot be preempted from a process executing in its critical section.

Due to the disadvantages of the above method, many systems provide special hardware instructions to solve the critical-section problem. One special instruction is the TestAndSet instruction which can be defined as follows:

```
boolean TestAndSet (boolean &lock)
{
    if(lock)
        return lock;
    else
    {
        lock = true;
        return false;
    }
}
```

An important characteristic of the TestAndSet instruction is that it executes as an atomic action. It means that if two TestAndSet instructions are executed simultaneously (each on a different CPU) in a multiprocessor system, then one must complete before another one starts on another processor.

On systems that support the `TestAndSet` instruction, the mutual exclusion can be implemented by allowing the processes to share a Boolean variable, say `lock`, initialized to `false`. The general structure for the code segment of process, say P_i, is as follows:

```
do
{
```

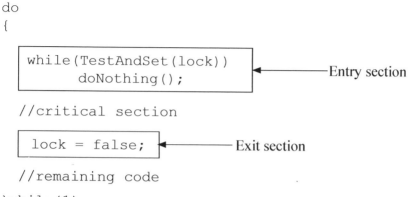

```
        while(TestAndSet(lock))
                doNothing();
```
Entry section

```
        //critical section
```

```
        lock = false;
```
Exit section

```
        //remaining code
}while(1);
```

The algorithm is easy and simple to understand. Any process that wishes to enter its critical section executes the `TestAndSet` instruction and passes the value of `lock` as a parameter to it. If the value of `lock` is `false` (means no process is in its critical section), the `TestAndSet` instruction sets the `lock` to `true` and returns `false`, which breaks the `while` loop and allows the process to enter its critical section. However, if the value of `lock` is `true`, the `TestAndSet` instruction returns `true`, thus, blocking the process in the loop. The algorithm satisfies the mutual exclusion requirement, but does not satisfy the bounded-waiting requirement.

Another special hardware instruction is the `Swap` instruction that operates on two Boolean variables. Like the `TestAndSet` instruction, the `Swap` instruction also executes as an atomic action. This instruction can be defined as follows:

```
void Swap(boolean &a, boolean &b)
{
        boolean temp = a;
        a = b;
        b = temp;
}
```

On systems that support the `Swap` instruction, the mutual exclusion can be implemented by allowing the processes to share a Boolean variable, say `lock`, initialized to `false`. In addition to this, each process uses a local Boolean variable, say `key`. The general structure for the code segment of process, say P_i, is as follows:

```
do
{
```

```
        key = true;
        while (key==true)
                Swap(lock, key);
```
Entry section

```
//critical section
```

```
lock = false;          ◄─────────── Exit section
```

```
//remaining code
```

```
}while(1);
```

The algorithm is again very easy and simple to understand. Initially, the value of `lock` is `false`, so the first process, say P_i, when executes the `Swap` instruction sets the `key` to `false` and `lock` to `true`. The `false` value for `key` allows the process to enter its critical section. Any other process, say P_j, that attempts to enter its critical section finds that the `lock` is `true` and when it is swapped with `key`, the `key` remains `true`. The `true` value for `key` blocks the process P_j in the `while` loop until the `lock` becomes `false`. Note that the `lock` becomes `false` when P_i exits from the critical section. This algorithm also satisfies only the mutual exclusion requirement and does not satisfy the bounded-waiting requirement.

To meet all the requirements of the solution for critical-section problem, another algorithm is developed that uses the `TestAndSet` instruction. The algorithm lets the processes to share the following two variables:

```
boolean lock;
boolean waiting[N];
```

The variable `lock` and all the elements of array `waiting` are initialized to `false`. Each process also has a local Boolean variable, say `key`. The general structure for the code segment of process, say P_i, is as follows:

```
do
{
```

```
waiting[i] = true;
key = true;
while(waiting[i] && key)           ◄──────── Entry section
      key = TestAndSet(lock);
waiting[i] = false;
```

```
//critical section
```

```
j = (i + 1) % N;
while(j!=i && waiting[next_ts]==false)
        j = (j + 1) mod N;
if (j==i)                          ◄──────── Exit section
        lock = false;
else
        waiting[j] = false;
```

```
    //remaining code
}while(1);
```

To verify that the mutual exclusion requirement is met, suppose a process P_i attempts to enter its critical section. It first sets the `waiting[i]` and `key` to `true`, and then reaches the `while` loop in the entry section. If P_i is the first process attempting to enter its critical section, it finds that both the conditions in the `while` loop are `true`. Then it executes the `TestAndSet` instruction which sets the `lock` to `true` and returns `false`, since `lock` is initially `false`. The returned value, that is `false`, is assigned to `key`, which allows the process P_i to exit from the loop and enter its critical section after resetting the `waiting[i]` to `false`.

Now, the value of `lock` is `true`, thus, any other process, say P_j, that attempts to enter its critical section when executes the `TestAndSet` instruction sets the `key` to `true` and is blocked in the `while` loop until either `key` or `waiting[j]` becomes `false`. Note that neither `key` nor `waiting[j]` becomes `false` until P_i is in its critical section. This maintains the mutual exclusion requirement.

To verify the progress requirement, observe in the exit section that P_i sets either `lock` or `waiting[j]` to `false`. Setting `lock` (on which the value of `key` depends) or `waiting[j]` to `false` allows any other waiting process to enter its critical section.

The algorithm also satisfies the bounded-waiting requirement. To verify this, observe that when any process, say P_i, exits from its critical section, it scans the `waiting` array in the cyclic order $(i+1, i+2,\ldots, N-1, 0, 1, \ldots, i-1)$ to locate the first process, say P_j, with `waiting[j]` equal to `true`. If no such process is found, P_i sets `lock` to `false`, so that any other process that now attempts to enter its critical section need not to wait. On the other hand, if such a process is found, it enters its critical section `next`, since P_i sets `waiting[j]` to `false`. In this way, each process gets its turn to enter its critical section after a maximum of $N-1$ processes.

CHECK YOUR PROGRESS

5. Critical-section problem can be solved disabling interrupts. What are the disadvantages of this method as a solution to critical-section problem?
6. Give `TestAndSet` instruction.
7. Executing the `Swap` instruction as an atomic action is not a requirement. (True or False)

5.5 SEMAPHORES

In 1965, Dijkstra suggested to use an abstract data type called **semaphore** for controlling synchronization. A semaphore `S` is an integer variable which is used to provide a general purpose solution to critical-section problem. In his proposal, two standard atomic operations are defined on `S`, namely, `wait` and `signal`, and after initialization, `S` is accessed only through these two operations. The definition of `wait` and `signal` operation in pseudocode is as follows:

```
wait(S)
{
      while(S<=0)
      doNothing();
      S--;
}
signal(S)
{
      S++;
}
```

The solution of critical-section problem for N processes is implemented by allowing the processes to share a semaphore S, which is initialized to 1. The general structure for the code segment of process, say P_i, is as follows:

```
do
{
```

```
//critical section
```

```
//remaining code
}while(1);
```

Note that all the solutions presented so far for the critical-section problem, including the solution using semaphore, require busy waiting. It means if a process is executing in its critical section, all other processes that attempt to enter their critical sections must loop continuously in the entry section. Executing a loop continuously wastes CPU cycles and is considered a major problem in multiprogramming systems with one processor.

To overcome the busy waiting problem, the definition of semaphore is modified to hold an integer value and a list of processes, and the wait and signal operations are also modified. In the modified wait operation, when a process finds that the value of the semaphore is negative, it blocks itself instead of busy waiting. Blocking a process means it is inserted in the queue associated with the semaphore and the state of the process is switched to the waiting state. The signal operation is modified to remove a process, if any, from the queue associated with the semaphore and restart it. The modified definition of semaphore, the wait operation and the signal operation is as follows:

```
struct semaphore
{
      int value;
      struct process *queue;
};
```

```
void wait(semaphore S)
{
      S.value--;
      if(S.value<0)
      {
            insert this process to queue associated with S
            block(); //suspend this process
      }
}
void signal(semaphore S)
{
      S.value++;
      if(S.value<=0)
      {
          remove a process P from the queue associated with S
          wakeup(P);//resume the execution of blocked process P
      }
}
```

Note: The `block()` operation and `wakeup()` operation are provided by the operating system as basic system calls.

An important requirement is that both the `wait` and `signal` operations must be treated as atomic instructions. It means no two processes can execute `wait` and `signal` operations on the same semaphore at the same time. We can view this as a critical-section problem, where the critical section consists of `wait` and `signal` operations. This problem can be solved by employing any of the solutions presented earlier.

In this way, though, we have not completely eliminated the busy waiting but limited the busy waiting to only the critical sections consisting of `wait` and `signal` operations. Since these two operations are very short, busy waiting occurs rarely and for a very short time only.

The semaphore presented above is known as **counting semaphore** or **general semaphore**, since its integer value can range over an unrestricted domain. Another type of semaphore is **binary semaphore** whose integer value can range only between 0 and 1. Binary semaphore is simpler to implement than general semaphore. The `wait` and `signal` operations for a binary semaphore S, initialized to 1, are as follows:

```
void wait(semaphore S)
{
    if(S.value==1)
        S.value = 0;
    else
        insert this process to queue associated with S
```

```
        block(); //suspend this process
}
void signal(semaphore S)
{
    if(emptyqueue()) //check if queue is empty
        S.value = 1;
    else
        remove a process P from the queue associated with S
        wakeup(P); //resume the execution of blocked process P
}
```

CHECK YOUR PROGRESS

9. Define semaphore.
10. The two standard atomic operations defined on semaphore are _____ and _____.
11. What is busy waiting?
12. The problem of busy waiting is eliminated completely with the use of semaphores. (True or False)
13. The type of semaphore whose integer value can range only between 0 and 1 is called _____ semaphore.

5.6 CLASSICAL PROBLEMS OF SYNCHRONIZATION

In the previous section, the use of semaphore to develop solution for critical-section problem is presented. Semaphore can also be used to solve various synchronization problems. In this section, we present some classical problems of synchronization and use semaphores for synchronization in the solutions of these problems. Note that these problems of synchronization are used for testing almost all the newly proposed synchronization scheme.

5.6.1 Bounded-Buffer Problem

The bounded-buffer problem was introduced in *Chapter 02* where a solution to this problem was presented using shared memory. Recall from *Chapter 02* that our solution allows at most `size-1` items to be in the buffer at the same time. One possible solution to eliminate this inadequacy is to have an integer variable `count`, initialized to 0, to keep track of the number of items in the buffer. The producer process increments the `count` every time it adds a new item to the buffer and the consumer process decrements the `count` every time it removes an item from the buffer. The modified code of the producer and consumer processes is as follows:

```
//producer process
while(1)
{
    item_produced = produce_item();
    while(count == size)
        doNothing();
```

```
    buffer[in] = item_produced;
    in = (in + 1) % size;
    count++;
}
//consumer process
while(1)
{
    while(count == 0)
        doNothing();
    item_consumed = buffer[out];
    out = (out + 1) % size;
    count--;
    consume_item(item_consumed);
}
```

The producer process first determines whether the value of count is equal to size. If it is, the producer waits, since the buffer is full. Otherwise, it adds an item to the buffer and increments the count. Similarly, the consumer process first determines whether the value of count is 0. If it is, the consumer waits, since the buffer is empty. Otherwise, it removes an item from the buffer and decrements the count.

Though, both producer and consumer processes are correct separately, but concurrent execution of these processes may lead to the race condition. To understand this, suppose the statement count++ is internally implemented as follows:

```
register₁ = count
register₁ = register₁ + 1
count = register₁
```

Here, $register_1$ is a local CPU register. In this implementation, the value of count is first read into a local CPU register. Then, the value in the register is incremented by one, which is finally assigned back to the variable count. Similarly, suppose the statement count-- is internally implemented as follows:

```
register₂ = count
register₂ = register₂ - 1
count = register₂
```

Further, suppose the value of count is currently 2, and the producer process reads this value in $register_1$ and then increments the value in $register_1$. The value in $register_1$ becomes 3. However, before the producer process assigns back the incremented value to count, the scheduler decides to temporarily suspend it and start running the consumer process. The consumer process reads the value of count (which is still 2) in $register_2$ and then decrements it. The value in $register_2$ becomes 1.

Now, the order in which count is updated by the producer and consumer processes decides the final value of count. It means, if first producer and then consumer updates count, its value becomes 1. On the other hand, if first consumer and then producer updates count, its value becomes 3. However, the correct value of count is 2, which now cannot be produced. The incorrect result is generated because access to the variable count is unconstrained and both the processes manipulate it concurrently.

To avoid the possibility of occurrence of race condition, we present a solution to the bounded-buffer problem using semaphores. The solution using semaphores not only avoids the race condition but also allows to have size items in the buffer at the same time, thus, eliminating the inadequacies of the solutions using shared memory. The following three semaphores are used in this solution.

- The mutex semaphore, initialized to 1, is used to provide the producer and consumer processes the mutually exclusive access to the buffer. This semaphore ensures that only one process, either producer or consumer, is accessing the buffer and the associated variables at a time.
- The full semaphore, initialized to 0, is used to count the number of full buffers. This semaphore ensures that the producer stops executing items when the buffer is full.
- The empty semaphore, initialized to the value of size, is used to count the number of empty buffers. This semaphore ensures that consumer stops executing when the buffer is empty.

The general structure for the code segment of producer process and consumer process is as follows:

```
//structure of producer process
do
{
    item_produced = produce_item();
    wait(empty);
    wait(mutex);
    buffer[in] = item_produced;
    in = (in + 1) % size;
    signal(mutex);
    signal(full);
}while(1);
//structure of consumer process
do
{
    wait(full);
    wait(mutex);
    item_consumed = buffer[out];
    out = (out + 1) % size;
    signal(mutex);
    signal(empty);
    consume_item(item_consumed);
}while(1);
```

5.6.2 The Readers-Writers Problem

Concurrently executing processes that are sharing a data object, such as a file or a variable, can be categorized into two groups: readers and writers. The processes in the readers group want only to read the contents of the shared object, whereas, the processes in writers group want to update (read and write) the value of shared object. There is no problem if multiple readers access the shared object simultaneously, however, if a writer and some other process (either a reader or a writer) access the shared object simultaneously, data may become inconsistent. We have illustrated such a problem in *Section 5.1*.

To ensure that such a problem does not arise, we must guarantee that when a writer is accessing the shared object, no reader or writer accesses that shared object. This synchronization problem is termed as **readers-writers** problem and it has many variations. The first readers-writers problem (the simplest one) requires the following.

- All readers and writers should wait if a writer is accessing the shared object. It means writers should get mutually exclusive access to the shared object.
- Readers should not wait unless a writer is accessing the shared object. It means if a reader is currently reading the shared object, and a writer and a reader make a request, then writer should wait, but reader should not wait just because of a writer is waiting.

To develop the solution to the first readers-writers problem, the readers are allowed to share two semaphores `read` and `write`, both initialized to 1, and an integer variable `count`, initialized to 0. The writers share the semaphore `write` with the readers. The functions of `read` and `write` semaphores and `count` variable are as follows:

- The `count` variable is used to count the number of readers currently reading the shared object. Each time a reader enters or exits the critical section, `count` is updated.
- The `read` semaphore is used to provide mutual-exclusion to readers when `count` is being updated.
- The `write` semaphore is used to provide mutual-exclusion to writers. It is accessed by all the writers and only the first or last reader that enters or exits its critical section.

The general structure for the code segment of a reader process and a writer process is as follows:

```
//structure of a reader process
        wait(read); //mutual-exclusion for readers before  updating
                    //count
        count++;
        if(count==1) //if it is the first reader
            wait(write);
        signal(read);
        ...
        reading contents of shared object
        ...
        wait(read);
        count--;
        if(count==0)   //if it is the only reader
```

```
        signal(write);
        signal(read);
//structure of a writer process
        wait(write);   //mutual-exclusion for writers
        ...
        updating the shared object
        ...
        signal(write);
```

5.6.3 The Dining-Philosophers Problem

To understand the dining-philosophers problem, consider five philosophers sitting around a circular table. There is a bowl of rice in the center of the table and five chopsticks—one in between each pair of philosophers (see Figure 5.1).

Figure 5.1: The Situation in Dining Philosophers

Initially, all the philosophers are in the thinking stage and while thinking they do not interact with each other. As time goes on, philosophers might feel hungry. When a philosopher feels hungry, he attempts to pick up the two chopsticks closest to him (that are in between him and his left and his right philosophers). If the philosophers on his left and right are not eating, he successfully gets the two chopsticks. With the two chopsticks in his hand, he starts eating. After eating is finished, he puts the chopsticks back on the table and starts thinking again. On the other hand, if the philosopher on his left or right is already eating, then he is unable to successfully grab the two chopsticks at the same time and thus, must wait. Note that this situation is similar to the one that occurs in the system to allocate resources among several processes. Each process should get required resources to finish its task without being deadlocked and starved.

A solution to this problem is to represent each chopstick as a semaphore and philosophers must grab or release chopsticks by executing `wait` operation or `signal` operation, respectively, on the appropriate semaphores. We use an array `chopstick` of size 5 where each element is initialized to 1. The general structure for the code segment of philosopher `i` is as follows:

```
do
{
    ...
    thinking
```

```
...
wait(chopstick[i]);
wait(chopstick[(i+1)%5];

...
eating
...

signal(chopstick[i]);
signal(chopstick[(i+1)%5];
...
thinking
...

}while(1);
```

This solution is simple and ensures that no two neighbours are eating at the same time. However, the solution is not free from deadlock. Suppose all the philosophers attempt to grab the chopsticks simultaneously and grab one chopstick successfully. Now, all the elements of chopstick will be 0. Thus, when each philosopher attempts to grab the second chopstick, he will go in waiting state forever.

A simple solution to avoid this deadlock is to ensure that a philosopher either picks up both chopsticks or no chopstick at all. It means he must pick chopsticks in a critical section. A deadlock free solution to dining-philosophers problem is presented in the next section with the use of monitors.

CHECK YOUR PROGRESS

14. What are the requirements of first readers-writers problem?
15. Give the general structure for the code segment of a reader process.
16. The use of semaphores in solving bounded-buffer problem eliminates the possibility of occurrence of the race condition. (True or False)
17. A solution to dining-philosophers problem is to represent each chopstick as a _____ .

5.7 MONITORS

A monitor is a programming language construct which is also used to provide mutually exclusive access to critical sections. The programmer defines monitor type which consists of declaration of shared data (or variables), procedures or functions that access these variables and initialization code. The general syntax of declaring a monitor type is as follows:

```
monitor <monitor-name>
{
    //shared data (or variable) declarations
    data type <variable-name>;
    ...
    //function (or procedure) declarations
    return_type <function-name>(parameters)
```

```
{
    //body of function
}
.
.
.
monitor-name()
{
    //initialization code
}
}
```

The variables defined inside a monitor can only be accessed by the functions defined within the monitor and no process is allowed to directly access these variables. Thus, processes can access these variables only through the execution of the functions defined inside the monitor. Further, the monitor construct ensures that only one process may be executing within the monitor at a time. If a process is executing within the monitor, then other requesting processes are blocked and placed on an entry queue.

Though, monitor construct ensures mutual exclusion for processes, but sometimes programmer may find them insufficient to represent some synchronization schemes. For such situations, programmer needs to define his own synchronization mechanisms. He can define his own mechanisms by defining variables of condition type on which only two operations can be invoked: wait and signal. Suppose, programmer defines a variable C of condition type, then execution of the operation C.wait() by a process, say P_i, suspends the execution of P_i and places it on a queue associated with the condition variable C. On the other hand, the execution of the operation C.signal() by a process, say P_i, resumes the execution of exactly one suspended process P_j, if any. It means that the execution of the signal operation by P_i allows other suspended process P_j to execute within the monitor. However, only one process is allowed to execute within the monitor at one time. Thus, monitor construct prevents P_j from resuming until P_i is executing in the monitor. There are following possibilities to handle this situation.

- The process P_i must be suspended to allow P_j to resume and wait until P_j leaves the monitor.
- The process P_j must remain suspended until P_i leaves the monitor.
- The process P_i must execute the signal operation as its last statement in the monitor so that P_j can resume immediately.

Now, we are in a situation to use the monitor to develop a deadlock-free solution to dining-philosophers problem. The following monitor controls the distribution of chopsticks to philosophers.

```
monitor diningPhilosophers
{
    enum{thinking, hungry, eating} state[5];
    condition self[5];
```

```
void getChopsticks(int i)
{
    int left, right;
    state[i] = hungry;
    left = (i+4)%5;
    right = (i+1)%5;
    if((state[left]==eating) || (state[right]==eating))
        self[i].wait();
    else
        state[i] = eating;
}
void putDownChopsticks(int i)
{
    int left, right;
    state[i] = thinking;
    left = (i+4)%5;
    right = (i+1)%5;
    verifyAndAllow(left);
    verifyAndAllow(right);
}
void verifyAndAllow(int i)
{
    int left, right;
    left = (i+4)%5;
    right = (i+1)%5;
    if(state[i]==hungry)
    {
        if((state[left]!=eating) && (state[right]!=eating))
        {
            state[i] = eating;
            self[i].signal();
        }
    }
}
}
void initial()
{
    int i;
    for(i=0; i<5; i++)
        state[i] = thinking;
}
}
```

Each philosopher that feels hungry must invoke the getchopsticks() operation before start eating and after eating is finished, he must invoke putDownchopsticks() operations and then may start thinking. Thus, the general structure for the code segment philosopher `i` is as follows:

```
...
diningPhilosophers.getChopsticks(i);
eating
diningPhilosophers.putDownChopsticks(i);
...
```

The `getChopsticks()` operation changes the state of philosopher process from thinking to hungry and then verifies whether philosopher on his left or right is in eating state. If either philosopher is in eating state, then the philosopher process is suspended and its state remains hungry. Otherwise, the state of philosopher process is changed to eating.

After eating has finished, each philosopher invokes `putDownChopsticks()` operation before start thinking. This operation changes the state of philosopher process to thinking and then invoke `verifyAndAllow()` operation for philosophers on his left and right side (one by one). The `verifyAndAllow()` operation verifies whether the philosopher feels hungry, and if so then allows him to eat in case philosophers on his left and right side are not eating.

CHECK YOUR PROGRESS

18. What is a monitor?
19. Programmer can define his own synchronization mechanisms. (True or False)
20. Monitor construct ensures that _____ may be executing within the monitor at a time.

Let Us Summarize

1. If cooperating processes are not executed in an ordered manner, data inconsistency may occur.
2. A situation where several processes sharing some data execute concurrently and the result of the execution depends on the order in which the shared data is accessed by the processes is called race condition.
3. To avoid race conditions, some form of synchronization among the processes is required which ensures that only one process is manipulating the share data at a time.
4. Critical section is the portion of code of a process in which it accesses or changes the shared data. No two processes are allowed to execute in their critical sections at one time.
5. The critical-section problem is to design a protocol that the processes can use to cooperate.
6. A solution to critical-section problem must me the mutual exclusion, progress and bounded-waiting requirements.
7. Peterson proposed an algorithm to solve the critical-section problem for two processes.
8. Lamport proposed an algorithm, known as bakery algorithm, to solve the critical-section problem for N processes.
9. The hardware-supported solutions developed for the critical-section problem that make use of hardware instruction available on many systems, thus, are effective and efficient.
10. On a system with single processor, the critical-section problem can be solved by disabling interrupts, but this solution is not feasible in multiprocessor environment.
11. Many systems provide special hardware instructions to solve the critical-section problem.
12. One special instruction is the `TestAndSet` instruction. An important characteristic of this instruction is that it executes as an atomic action.
13. Another special hardware instruction is the `Swap` instruction that operates on two Boolean variables. It also executes as an atomic action.

14. To meet all the requirement of the solution for critical-section problem, an algorithm is developed that uses the `TestAndSet` instruction.

15. A semaphore S is an integer variable which is used to provide a general-purpose solution to critical-section problem.

16. Two standard atomic operations are defined on S, namely, `wait` and `signal`, and after initialization, S is accessed only through these two operations.

17. The semaphore whose integer value can range over an unrestricted domain is known as counting semaphore or general semaphore. Another type of semaphore whose integer value can range only between 0 and 1 is known as binary semaphore.

18. Semaphore can also be used to solve various synchronization problems. Some classical problems of synchronization include bounded-buffer problem, readers-writes problem and dining-philosophers problem. These problems of synchronization are used for testing almost all the newly proposed synchronization scheme.

19. A monitor is a programming language construct which is also used to provide mutually exclusive access to critical sections.

20. Monitor construct ensures that only one process may be executing within the monitor at a time.

21. Programmer can define his own synchronization mechanisms by defining variables of `condition` type on which only two operations can be invoked: `wait` and `signal`.

22. Monitor is used to develop a deadlock-free solution to dining-philosophers problem.

 ## ANSWERS TO 'CHECK YOUR PROGRESS'

1. A situation where several processes sharing some data execute concurrently and the result of execution depends on the order in which the shared data is accessed by the processes is called race condition.

2. Data inconsistency

3. (d)

4. True

5. The general structure for the code segment of a process, say `Pi` is as follows:
```
do
{
```

```
    choosing[i] = true;
    number[i] = MAX(number) + 1;
    choosing[i] = false;
    for(j=0;j<N;j++)
    {
        while(choosing[j])
            doNothing();
        while(number[j]!=0 && number[j]
        <number[i] || number[j]==number[i] &&
        j<i)
            doNothing();
    }
```
⟵——— Entry section

```
    //critical section
```

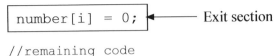
```
number[i] = 0;
```
Exit section

```
//remaining code
}while(1);
```

6. First, disabling interrupts is feasible in a single-processor environment only because doing this in a multiprocessor environment takes time as message is passed to all the processors. This message passing delays processes from entering into their critical sections, thus, decreasing the system efficiency. Second, it may affect the scheduling goals, since the processor cannot be preempted from a process executing in its critical section.

7. The `TestAndSet` instruction can be defined as follows:

```
boolean TestAndSet (boolean &lock)
{
    if(lock)
        return lock;
    else
    {
        lock = true;
        return false;
    }
}
```

8. False

9. A semaphore S is an integer variable which is used to provide a general-purpose solution to critical-section problem. Two standard atomic operations are defined on S, namely, `wait` and `signal`, and after initialization, S is accessed only through these two operations.

10. `wait` and `signal`

11. If a process is executing in its critical section, then all other processes that attempt to enter their critical sections loop continuously in the entry section. The time that the process spends executing a loop continuously is busy waiting. Executing a loop continuously wastes CPU cycles and is considered a major problem in multiprogramming systems with one processor.

12. False

13. Binary

14. The first readers-writers problem (the simplest one) requires the following.
    - All readers and writers should wait if a writer is accessing the shared object. It means writers should get mutually exclusive access to the shared object.
    - Readers should not wait unless a writer is accessing the shared object. It means if a reader is currently reading the shared object, and a writer and a reader make a request, then writer should wait, but reader should not wait just because of a writer is waiting.

15. The general structure for the code segment of a reader process is as follows:

```
//structure of a reader process
wait(read); //mutual-exclusion for readers before updating
            //count
count++;
if(count==1) //if it is the first reader
    wait(write);
signal(read);
...
```

```
reading contents of shared object
...
wait(read);
count--;
if(count==0)   //if it is the only reader
    signal(write);
signal(read);
```

16. True
17. Semaphore
18. A monitor is a programming language construct which is also used to provide mutually exclusive access to critical sections. The programmer defines monitor type which consists of declaration of shared data (or variables), procedures or functions that access these variables and initialization code.
19. True
20. Only one process

 ## TEST YOURSELF

1. Explain with example that why some form of synchronization among the processes is required.
2. Define critical-section problem. Also explain all the requirements that a solution to critical-section problem must met.
3. Describe bakery algorithm to solve critical-section problem.
4. Give `TestAndSet` instruction. Also give the algorithm that uses `TestAndSet` instruction to solve the critical-section problem and meets all the requirements of the solution for the critical-section problem.
5. Write short notes on the following:
   (a) Semaphore
   (b) `Swap` instruction
   (c) Entry and exit section
   (d) Critical section
6. What is busy waiting? How semaphore is used to overcome the busy waiting problem?
7. Explain the use of semaphore in developing a solution to bounded-buffer problem.
8. Describe the dining-philosophers problem. Give a solution to the dining-philosopher problem with the use of monitors.

Chapter 06

Deadlock

Learning Objectives

After reading this chapter, you will be able to:

- ☐ Define system model
- ☐ Discuss the features that characterize the deadlock
- ☐ Discuss the different methods of handling deadlock
- ☐ Explain how a deadlock can be prevented by eliminating one of the four conditions of a deadlock
- ☐ Understand the concept of safe and unsafe state
- ☐ Explain various deadlock avoidance algorithms
- ☐ Discuss different deadlock detection methodologies
- ☐ List the ways to recover from a deadlock

6.1 INTRODUCTION

Deadlock occurs when every process in a set of processes are in a simultaneous wait state and each of them is waiting for the release of a resource held exclusively by one of the waiting processes in the set. None of the processes can proceed until at least one of the waiting processes release the acquired resource. Deadlocks may occur on a single system or across several machines. This chapter discusses the different ways in which these deadlocks can be handled.

6.2 SYSTEM MODEL

A system consists of various types of resources, such as input/output devices, memory space, processors, disks, etc. For some resource types, several instances may be available. For example, a system may have two printers. When several instances of a resource type are available, any one of them can be used to satisfy the request for that resource type.

A process may need multiple resource types to accomplish its task. However, to use any resource type, it must follow some steps which are as follows:

1. Request for the required resource.
2. Use the allocated resource.
3. Release the resource after completing the task.

If the requested resource is not available, the requesting process enters a waiting state until it acquires the resource. Consider a system with a printer and a disk drive and two processes P_1 and P_2 are executing simultaneously on this system. During execution, the process P_1 requests for the printer and process P_2 requests for the disk drive and both the requests are granted. Further, the process P_2 requests for the printer held by process P_1 and process P_1 requests for the disk drive held by the process P_2. Here, both processes will enter a waiting state. Since each process is waiting for the release of resource held by other, they will remain in waiting state forever. This situation is called **deadlock**.

6.3 DEADLOCK CHARACTERIZATION

Before discussing the methods to handle a deadlock, we will discuss the conditions that cause a deadlock and how a deadlock can be depicted using resource allocation graph.

6.3.1 Deadlock Conditions

A deadlock occurs when all the following four conditions are satisfied at any given point of time.

1. **Mutual exclusion:** Only one process can acquire a given resource at any point of time. Any other process requesting for that resource has to wait for earlier process to release it.
2. **Hold and wait:** Process holding a resource allocated to it and waiting to acquire another resource held by other process.
3. **No preemption:** Resource allocated to a process cannot be forcibly revoked by the system, it can only be released voluntarily by the process holding it.
4. **Circular wait:** A set of processes waiting for allocation of resources held by other processes, forms a circular chain in which each process is waiting for the resource held by its successor process in chain.

In the absence of any one of these conditions, deadlock will not occur. We will discuss these conditions in detail in subsequent sections and see how they can be prevented.

6.3.2 Resource Allocation Graph

A deadlock can be depicted with the help of a directed graph known as **resource allocation graph**. The graph consists of two different types of nodes, namely, processes and resources. The processes are depicted as circles and resources as squares. A directed arc from a process to a resource (known as **request edge**) indicates that the process has requested for the resource and is waiting for it to be allocated. Whereas a directed arc from a resource to a process (known as **assignment edge**) indicates that the resource has been allocated to the process. For example, consider the resource allocation graph shown in Figure 6.1. Here, the process P_1 is holding resource R_2 and requesting for the resource R_1, which in turn is held by the process P_2. The process P_2 is requesting for the resource R_2 held by the process P_1. That means there is a deadlock.

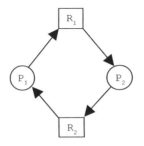

Figure 6.1: Resource Allocation Graph

It can be observed that this graph forms a cycle ($P_1 -> R_1 -> P_2 -> R_2 -> P_1$). A cycle in the resource allocation graph indicates that there is deadlock and the processes forming the part of the cycle are deadlocked. If there is no cycle in a graph, there is no deadlock. In this example, there is only one instance of each resource type. However, there can exist multiple instances of a resource type. The resource allocation graph for two instances (R_{21} and R_{22}) of resource type R_2 is shown in Figure 6.2.

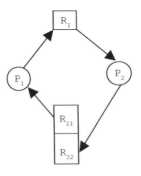

Figure 6.2: Resource Allocation Graph for Multiple Instances of a Resource Type

This resource allocation graph has the following indications.

1. Process P_1 is waiting for the allocation of resource R_1 held by the process P_2.
2. Process P_2 is waiting for the allocation of instance (R_{22}) of resource type R_2.
3. Process P_1 is holding an instance (R_{21}) of resource type R_2.

It can be observed that the graph forms a cycle but still processes are not deadlocked. The process P_2 can acquire the second instance (R_{22}) of the resource type R_2 and completes its execution. After completing the execution, it can release the resource R_1 that can be used by the process P_1. Since, no process is in waiting state, there is no deadlock.

From this discussion, it is clear that if each resource type has exactly one instance, cycle in resource allocation graph indicates a deadlock. If each resource type has several instances, cycle in resource allocation graph does not necessarily imply a deadlock. Thus, it can be concluded that if a graph contains no cycle, the set of processes are not deadlocked; however, if there is a cycle then deadlock may exist.

6.4 METHODS FOR HANDLING DEADLOCKS

A deadlock can be handled in four different ways which are as follows:

- Prevent the deadlock from occurring.
- Adopt methods for avoiding the deadlock.
- Allow the deadlock to occur, detect it and recover from it.
- Ignore the deadlock.

Deadlock prevention or **deadlock avoidance techniques** can be used to ensure that deadlocks never occur in a system. If any of these two techniques is not used, a deadlock may occur. In this case, an algorithm can be provided for detecting the deadlock and then using the algorithm to recover the system from the deadlock.

One or the other method must be provided to either prevent the deadlock from occurrence or detect the deadlock and takes an appropriate action if a deadlock occurs. However, if in a system, deadlock occurs less frequently (say, once in two years) then it is better to ignore the deadlocks instead of adopting expensive techniques for deadlock prevention, deadlock avoidance or deadlock detection and recovery.

6.5 DEADLOCK PREVENTION

As stated earlier, a deadlock occurs when all of the four conditions are satisfied at any point of time. The deadlock can be prevented by not allowing all four conditions to be satisfied simultaneously, that is, by making sure that at least one of the four conditions does not hold. Now let us analyse all four conditions one by one and see how their occurrence can be prevented.

6.5.1 Eliminating Mutual Exclusion

The mutual exclusion property does not hold for the resources that are sharable. For example, a file which is opened in read only mode can be shared among various processes. Hence, processes will never have to wait for the sharable resources. However, there are certain resources which can never be shared, such as printer can work for only one process at a time. It cannot print data being sent as output from more than one process simultaneously. Hence, the condition of mutual exclusion cannot be eliminated in case of all the resources.

6.5.2 Eliminating Hold and Wait Condition

This condition can be eliminated by not allowing any process to request for a resource until it releases the resources held by it, which is impractical as process may require the resources simultaneously. Another way to prevent hold and wait condition is by allocating all the required resources to the process before starting the execution of that process. The disadvantage associated with it is that a process may not know in advance about the resources that will be required during its execution. Even if it knows in advance, it may unnecessarily hold the resources which may be required at the end of its execution. Thus, the resources are not utilized optimally.

6.5.3 Eliminating No Preemption

The elimination of this condition means a process can release the resource held by it. If a process requests for a resource held by some other process then instead of making it wait, all the resources currently held by this process can be preempted. The process will be restarted only when it is allocated the requested as well as the preempted resources. Note that only those resources can be preempted whose current working state can be saved and can be later restored. For example, the resources, such as printer and disk drives cannot be preempted.

6.5.4 Eliminating Circular wait Condition

The circular wait condition can be eliminated by assigning a priority number to each available resource and a process can request resources only in increasing order. Whenever a process requests for a resource, the priority number of the required resource is compared with the priority numbers of the resources already held by it. If the priority number of a requested resource is greater than that of all the currently held resources, the request is granted. If the priority number of a requested resource is less than that of the currently held resources, all the resources with greater priority number must be released first, before acquiring the new resource.

CHECK YOUR PROGRESS

1. A deadlock can occur on a single system only. (True or False)
2. What are the steps performed by a process to use any resource type?
3. List the conditions necessary for a deadlock to occur.
4. If the requested resource is not available, the requesting process enters a _____ until it acquires the resource.
5. Which one of the following is not associated with the resource allocation graph to depict the deadlock?
   - (a) Request edge
   - (b) Claim edge
   - (c) Assignment edge
   - (d) None of these
6. List the various ways to handle a deadlock.

6.6 DEADLOCK AVOIDANCE

A deadlock can be prevented by eliminating any one of the four necessary conditions of the deadlock. Preventing deadlock using this method results the inefficient use of resources. Thus, instead of preventing deadlock, it can be avoided by never allowing allocation of a resource to a process if it leads to a deadlock. This can be achieved when some additional information is available about how the processes are going to request for resources in future. Information can be in the form of how many resources of each type will be requested by a process and in which order. On the basis of amount of information available, different algorithms can be used for deadlock avoidance.

One of the simplest algorithms requires each process to declare the maximum number of resources (of each type) required by it during its course of execution. This information is used to construct an algorithm that will prevent the system from entering a state of deadlock. This deadlock avoidance algorithm continuously examines the state of resource allocation ensuring that circular wait condition never exists in a system. The state of resource allocation can be either safe or unsafe.

A state is said to be **safe** if allocation of resources to processes does not lead to the deadlock. More precisely, a system is in safe state only if there is a safe sequence. A **safe sequence** is a sequence of process execution such that each and every process executes till its completion. For example, consider a sequence of processes $(P_1, P_2, P_3, \ldots, P_n)$ forming a safe sequence. In this sequence, first the process P_1 will be executed till its completion and then P_2 will be executed till its completion and so on. The number of resources required by any process can be allocated either from the available resources or from the resources held by previously executing process. When a process completes its execution, it releases all the resources held by it which then can be utilized by the next process in a sequence. That is, the request for the resources by the process P_n can be satisfied either from the available resources or from the resources held by the process P_m, where $m<n$. Since this sequence of process execution is safe, the system following this sequence is in the safe state. If no such sequence of process execution exists then the state of the system is said to be unsafe.

Figure 6.3: Relationship between Safe State, Unsafe State and Deadlock

For example, consider a system in which three processes P_1, P_2 and P_3 are executing and there are 10 instances of a resource type. The maximum number of resources required by each process, the number of resources already allocated and the total number of available resources are shown in Figure 6.4.

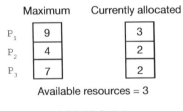

Available resources = 3

(a) Initial state

Available resources = 1

(b) Resource allocation to process P_2

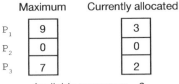

Available resources = 6

(c) State after completion of process P_2

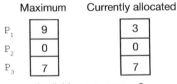

Available resources = 0

(d) Resource allocation to process P_3

Available resources = 7

(e) State after completion of process P_3

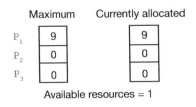

Available resources = 1

(f) Resource allocation to process P_1

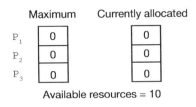

Available resources = 10

(g) State after completion of process P_1

Figure 6.4: Safe Sequence of Execution of Processes

On the basis of available information, it can be easily observed that the resource requirements of the process P_2 can be easily satisfied. Therefore, resources are allocated to the process P_2 and it is allowed to execute till its completion. After the execution of the process P_2, all the resources held by it are released. The number of the resources now available are not enough to be allocated to the process P_1, whereas, they are enough to be allocated to the process P_3. Therefore, resources are allocated to the process P_3 and it is allowed to execute till its completion. The number of resources available after the execution of process P_3 can now easily be allocated to the process P_1. Hence, the execution of the processes in sequence P_2, P_3, P_1 is safe.

Now consider a sequence P_2, P_1, P_3. In this sequence, after the execution of process P_2, the number of available resources is 6 and is allocated to the process P_1. Even after the allocation of all the available resources, the process P_1 is still short of one resource for its complete execution. As a result, the process P_1 enters a waiting state and waits for process P_3 to release the resource held by it, which in turn is waiting for the remaining resources to be allocated for its complete execution. Now the processes P_1 and P_3 are waiting for each other to release the resources, leading to the deadlock. Hence, this sequence of process execution is unsafe.

Note that a safe state is a deadlock free state, whereas all unsafe states may or may not result in a deadlock. That is, an unsafe state may lead to a deadlock but not always.

6.6.1 Resource Allocation Graph Algorithm

As discussed earlier, resource allocation graph consists of two types of edges: request edge and assignment edge. In addition to these edges, another edge known as **claim edge** can also be introduced in this graph, which helps in avoiding the deadlock. A claim edge from a process to the resource indicates that the process will request for that resource in near future. This edge is represented same as that of request edge but with dotted line. Whenever the process actually requests for that resource, the claim edge is converted to the request edge. Also, whenever a resource is released by any process, corresponding assignment edge is converted back to the claim edge. The prerequisite of this representation is that all the claim edges related to a process must be depicted in the graph before the process starts executing. However, a claim edge can be added at the later stage only if all the edges related to that process are claim edges.

Whenever the process requests for a resource, the claim edge is converted to request edge only if converting the corresponding request edge to assignment edge does not lead to the formation of a cycle in a graph, as cycle in a graph indicates the deadlock. For example, consider the resource allocation graph shown in Figure 6.5, the claim edge from process P_1 to the resource R_1 cannot be converted to the request edge as it will lead to the formation of cycle in the graph.

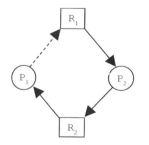

Figure 6.5: Resource Allocation Graph with Claim Edges

6.6.2 Banker's Algorithm

In case there are multiple instances of a resource type in a system, the deadlock cannot be avoided using resource allocation graph algorithm. This is because the presence of cycle in the resource allocation graph for multiple resources does not always imply the deadlock. An algorithm known as **banker's algorithm** is used in such a case. In this algorithm, any process entering the system must inform the maximum number of resources (less than the total number of available resources) required during its execution. If allocating this much number of resources to the process leaves the system in a safe state the resources are allocated. On the other hand, if allocation of resources leaves the system in unsafe state then the resources are not allocated and the process is forced to wait for some other processes to release enough resources. To implement the banker's algorithm certain data structures are required, which help in determining whether the system is in safe state or not. These data structures are as follows:

1. **Available resources, A:** A vector of size q stores information about the number of resources available of each type.
2. **Maximum, M:** A matrix of order p×q stores information about the maximum number of resources of each type required by each process (p number of processes). That is, M[i][j] indicates the maximum number of resources of type j required by the process i.
3. **Current allocation, C:** A matrix of order p×q stores information about the number of resources of each type allocated to each process. That is, C[i][j] indicates the number of resources of type j currently held by the process i.
4. **Required, R:** A matrix of order p×q stores information about the remaining number of resources of each type required by each process. That is, R[i][j] indicates the remaining number of resources of type j required by the process i. Note that this vector can be obtained by M–C, that is, R[i][j] =M[i][j]–C[i][j].

The values of these data structures keep on changing during the execution of processes. Note that the condition A<=B holds for the vectors A and B of size p, if and only if A[i]<=B[i] for all i=1, 2, 3, ..., p. For example, if A={2, 1} and B={3, 4}, then A<=B.

To understand the algorithm for determining whether a system is in safe state, consider a vector Complete of size p. Following are the steps of the algorithm.

1. Initialize Complete[i]=False for all i=1, 2, 3,..., p. Complete[i]=False indicates that the ith process is still not completed.
2. Search for an i, such that Complete[i]=False and (R<=A) that is, resources required by this process is less than the available resources. If no such process exists, then go to step 4.
3. Allocate the required resources and let the process finish its execution. Set A=A+C and Complete[i]=True for that process. Go to step 2.
4. If Complete[i]=True for all i, then the system is in safe state. Otherwise, it indicates that there exists a process for which Complete[i]=False and resources required by it are more than the available resources. Hence, it is in unending waiting state leading to an unsafe state.

Once it is confirmed that system is in safe state, an algorithm called **resource-request** algorithm is used for determining whether the request by a process can be satisfied or not. To understand this algorithm, let Req be a matrix of the order p×q, indicating the number of resources of each type requested by each process at any given point of time. That is, `Req[i][j]` indicates the number of resources of jth type requested by the ith process at any given point of time. Following are the steps of this algorithm.

1. If `Req[i][j]<=R[i][j]`, go to step 2, otherwise an error occurs as process is requesting for more resources than the maximum number of resources required by it.
2. If `Req[i][j]<=A[i][j]`, go to step 3, otherwise the process P_i must wait until the required resources are available.
3. Allocate the resources and make the following changes in the data structures.

```
A = A - Req
C = C + Req
R = R - Req
```

For example, consider a system with three processes (P_1, P_2 and P_3) andw three resource types (X, Y and Z). There are 10 instances of resource type X, 6 of Y and 7 of Z. The matrix M for maximum number of resources required by the process, matrix C for the number of resources currently allocated to each process and vector A for maximum available resources are shown in Figure 6.6.

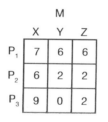

M

	X	Y	Z
P_1	7	6	6
P_2	6	2	2
P_3	9	0	2

(a) Maximum matrix

C

	X	Y	Z
P_1	0	1	0
P_2	2	0	0
P_3	3	0	2

(b) Current Allocation matrix

A

X	Y	Z
6	4	6

(c) Available resources vector

R

	X	Y	Z
P_1	7	4	6
P_2	3	2	2
P_3	6	0	0

(d) Required matrix

Figure 6.6: Initial State of System

Now, the matrix R representing the number of remaining resources required by each process can be obtained by the formula M−C, which is shown in Figure 6.6.

It can be observed that currently the system is in safe state and safe sequence of execution of processes is (P_2, P_3, P_1). Now suppose that process P_2 requests one more resource of each type, that is, the request vector for process P_2 is (1, 1, 1). First, it is checked whether this request vector is less than or equal to its corresponding required vector (3, 2, 2). If the process has requested for less number of resources than the declared maximum number of resources of each type by it at initial stage, then it is checked whether these much number of resources of each type are available. If it is then it is assumed that the request is granted and the changes will be made in the corresponding matrices shown in Figure 6.7.

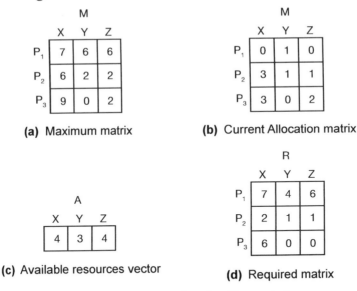

(a) Maximum matrix   **(b)** Current Allocation matrix

(c) Available resources vector   **(d)** Required matrix

Figure 6.7: State after Granting Request of P_2

This new state of system must be checked whether it is safe. For this an algorithm to check the safe state of the system is executed and it is determined that the sequence (P_2, P_3, P_1) is a safe sequence. Thus, the request of process P_2 is granted immediately.

Consider another state of a system shown in Figure 6.8. Now, a request for $(1, 2, 2)$ from process P_2 arrives. If this request is granted, the resulting state is unsafe. This is because after the complete execution of process P_2, the resultant vector A is $(6, 4, 6)$. Clearly, the resource requirement of processes P_1 and P_3 cannot be satisfied. Thus, even though the system has resources, request cannot be granted.

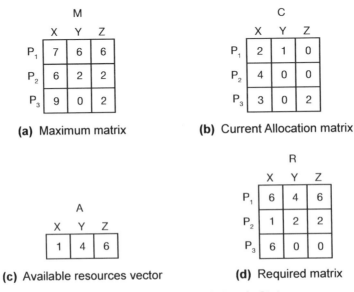

(a) Maximum matrix   **(b)** Current Allocation matrix

(c) Available resources vector   **(d)** Required matrix

Figure 6.8: An Example of Unsafe State

6.7 DEADLOCK DETECTION

There is a possibility of deadlock if neither the deadlock prevention nor deadlock avoidance method is applied in a system. In such a situation, an algorithm must be provided for detecting the occurrence of deadlock in a system. Once the deadlock is detected, a methodology must be provided for the recovery of the system from the deadlock. In this section, we will discuss some of the ways by which deadlock can be detected.

6.7.1 Single Instance of Each Resource Type

When only single resource of each type is available, the deadlock can be detected by using variation of resource allocation graph. In this variation, the nodes representing resources and corresponding edges are removed. This new variation of resource allocation graph is known as **wait-for graph**, which shows the dependency of a process on another process for the resource allocation. For example, an edge from the process P_i to P_j indicates that the process P_i is waiting for the process P_j to release the resources required by it. If there exists two edges $P_n -> R_i$ and $R_i -> P_m$ in resource allocation graph, then the corresponding edge in the wait-for graph will be $P_n -> P_m$ indicating that the process P_n is waiting for the process P_m for the release of the resources. A resource allocation graph involving 6 processes and 6 resources is shown in Figure 6.9 (a). The corresponding wait-for graph is shown in Figure 6.9 (b).

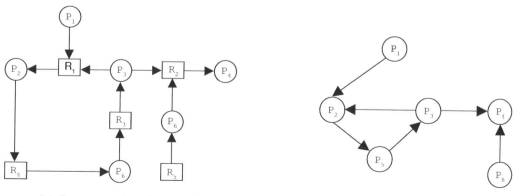

(a) Resource allocation graph   **(b)** Wait-for graph

Figure 6.9: Converting Resource Allocation Graph to Wait-for Graph

If there exists a cycle in wait-for graph, there is a deadlock in the system and the processes forming the part of cycle are blocked in the deadlock. In wait-for graph (see Figure 6.9), the processes P_2, P_3 and P_6 form the cycle and hence are blocked in the deadlock. To take appropriate action to recover from this situation, an algorithm needs to be called periodically to detect existence of cycle in wait-for graph.

6.7.2 Multiple Instances of a Resource Type

When multiple instances of a resource type exist, the wait-for graph becomes inefficient to detect the deadlock in the system. For such system, another algorithm which uses certain data structures similar to the ones used in banker's algorithm is applied. The data structures used are as follows:

1. **Available resources, A:** A vector of size q stores information about the number of available resources of each type.
2. **Current allocation, C:** A matrix of order p×q stores information about the number of resources of each type allocated to each process. That is, `C[i][j]` indicates the number of resources of type j currently held by the process i.
3. **Request, Req:** A matrix of order p×q stores information about the number of resources of each type currently requested by each process. That is, `R[i][j]`, indicates the number of resources of type j currently requested by the process i.

To understand the working of deadlock detection algorithm, consider a vector `Complete` of size p. Following are the steps to detect the deadlock.

1. Initialize `Complete[i]=False` for all i=1, 2, 3,...,p. `Complete[i]=False` indicates that the ith process is still not completed.
2. Search for an i, such that `Complete[i]=False` and (Req<=A), that is, resources currently requested by this process is less than the available resources. If no such process exists, then go to step 4.
3. Allocate the requested resources and let the process finish its execution. Set A=A+C and `Complete[i]=True` for that process. Go to step 2.
4. If `Complete[i]=False` for some i, then the system is in the state of deadlock and the ith process is deadlocked.

6.8 DEADLOCK RECOVERY

Once the system has detected deadlock in the system, some method is needed to recover the system from the deadlock and continue with the processing. The two different ways in which system can be recovered are—terminate one or more process to break the circular wait condition and preempt the resources from the processes involved in the deadlock.

6.8.1 Terminating the Processes

There are two methods that can be used for terminating the processes to recover from the deadlock. These two methods are discussed further.

- **Terminating one process at a time until the circular wait condition is eliminated.** It involves an overhead of invoking a deadlock detection algorithm after termination of each process to detect whether circular wait condition is eliminated or not, that is, whether any processes are still deadlocked.
- **Terminating all processes involved in the deadlock.** This method will definitely ensure the recovery of a system from the deadlock. The disadvantage of this method is that many processes may have executed for a long time; close to their completion. As a result, the computations performed till the time of termination are discarded.

In both the cases, all the resources which were acquired by the processes being terminated are returned to the system. While terminating any process, it must be ensured that it does not leave any part of the system in an inconsistent state. For example, a process might be in the middle of updating a disk file and termination of such a process may leave that file in an inconsistent state. Similarly, a printer might be in the middle of printing some document. In this case when system is recovered from the deadlock, the system must reset the printer to a correct state.

In case of partial termination, while selecting the process to be terminated, the choice of processes must be such that it incurs minimum cost to the system. The factors which can effect the selection of a process for termination are as follows:

- Number of remaining resources required by it to complete its task
- Number of processes required to be terminated
- Number and type of resources held by the process
- Duration of time for which process has already been executed
- Priority of the process

6.8.2 Preempting the Resources

An alternative method to recover system from the state of deadlock is to preempt the resources from the processes one by one and allocate them to other processes until the circular wait condition is eliminated. The steps involved in the preemption of resources from the process are as follows:

1. **Select a process for preemption:** The choice of resources and processes must be such that they incur minimum cost to the system. All the factors mentioned earlier must be considered while making choice.
2. **Rollback of the process:** After preempting the resources, the corresponding process must be rolled backed properly so that it does not leave the system in an inconsistent state. Since resources are preempted from the process, it cannot continue with the normal execution, hence must be brought to some safe state from where it can be restarted later. In case no such safe state can be achieved, the process must be totally rolled backed. However, partial rollback is always preferred over total rollback.
3. **Prevent starvation:** In case the selection of a process is based on the cost factor, it is quiet possible that same process is selected repeatedly for the rollback leading to the situation of starvation. This can be avoided by including the number of rollbacks of a given process in the cost factor.

CHECK YOUR PROGRESS

11. When only single resource of each type is available, the deadlock can be detected by using variation of resource allocation graph called _____ .
12. Which one of the following data structures is not used in algorithm for detecting deadlock in case of multiple instances of a resource type?
    (a) Available resources   (b) Current allocation
    (c) Request   (d) Maximum
13. In wait-for graph, only the processes are represented. (True or False)
14. Mention different ways by which a system can be recovered from a deadlock.

Let Us Summarize

1. Deadlock occurs when every process in a set of processes are in a simultaneous wait state and each of them is waiting for the release of a resource held exclusively by one of the waiting processes in the set.
2. A system consists of various types of resources, such as input/output devices, memory space, processors, disks, etc. For some resource types, several instances may be available. When several instances of a resource type are available, any one of them can be used to satisfy the request for that resource type.
3. Four necessary conditions for a deadlock are mutual exclusion, hold and wait, no preemption and circular wait.
4. A deadlock can be depicted with the help of a directed graph known as resource allocation graph.
5. In case there are multiple instances of a resource type in a system, the deadlock cannot be avoided using resource allocation graph algorithm. An algorithm known as banker's algorithm is used in such a case.
6. If each resource type has exactly one instance, cycle in resource allocation graph indicates a deadlock. If each resource type has several instances, cycle in resource allocation graph does not necessarily imply a deadlock.
7. Deadlock prevention or deadlock avoidance techniques can be used to ensure that deadlocks never occur in a system.
8. A deadlock can be prevented by not allowing all four conditions to be satisfied simultaneously, that is, by making sure that at least one of the four conditions does not hold.
9. A deadlock can be avoided by never allowing allocation of a resource to a process if it leads to a deadlock. This can be achieved when some additional information is available about how the processes are going to request for resources in future.
10. A state is said to be safe if allocation of resources to processes does not lead to the deadlock. More precisely, a system is in safe state only if there is a safe sequence. A safe sequence is a sequence of process execution such that each and every process executes till its completion. If no such sequence of process execution exists then the state of the system is said to be unsafe.
11. There is a possibility of deadlock if neither deadlock prevention nor deadlock avoidance method is applied in a system. In such a situation, an algorithm must be provided for detecting the occurrence of deadlock in a system.
12. When only single resource of each type is available, the deadlock can be detected by using variation of resource allocation graph known as wait-for graph.

13. When multiple instances of a resource type exist, the wait-for graph becomes inefficient to detect the deadlock in the system. For such system, another algorithm which uses certain data structures similar to the ones used in banker's algorithm is applied.

14. Once the deadlock is detected, a methodology must be provided for the recovery of the system from the deadlock.

15. The two different ways in which system can be recovered are—terminate one or more process to break the circular wait condition and preempt the resources from the processes involved in the deadlock.

 ## ANSWERS TO 'CHECK YOUR PROGRESS'

1. False

2. To use any resource, following steps must be performed.
   i)   Request for the required resource.
   ii) Use the allocated resource.
   iii) Release the resource after completing the task.

3. A deadlock occurs when all the following four conditions are satisfied.
   - Mutual exclusion
   - Hold and wait
   - No preemption
   - Circular wait

4. Waiting state

5. (b)

6. A deadlock can be handled in four different ways which are as follows:
   - Prevent the deadlock from occurring
   - Adopt methods for avoiding the deadlock
   - Allow the deadlock to occur, detect it and recover from it
   - Ignore the deadlock

7. A state is said to be safe if allocation of resources to processes does not lead to the deadlock. More precisely, a system is in safe state only if there is a safe sequence. If no such sequence of process execution exists then the state of the system is said to be unsafe.

8. False

9. Claim edge

10. (c)

11. Wait-for graph

12. (d)

13. True

14. The two different ways in which system can be recovered are—terminate one or more process to break the circular wait condition and preempt the resources from the processes involved in the deadlock.

TEST YOURSELF

1. Explain deadlock with an example.
2. What are the four conditions necessary for the deadlock? Explain them.

3. Consider a system having three instances of a resource type and two processes. Each process needs two resources to complete its execution. Can deadlock occur? Explain.

4. How can the circular wait condition be prevented?

5. Consider a system is in an unsafe state. Illustrate that the processes can complete their execution without entering a deadlock state.

6. Consider a system has six instances of a resource type and m processes. For which values of m, deadlock will not occur?

7. Consider a system consisting of four processes and a single resource. The current sate of the system is given here.

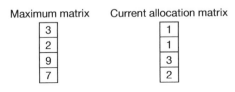

Maximum matrix   Current allocation matrix

Maximum matrix	Current allocation matrix
3	1
2	1
9	3
7	2

For this state to be safe, what should be the minimum number of instances of this resource?

8. Consider the following state of a system.

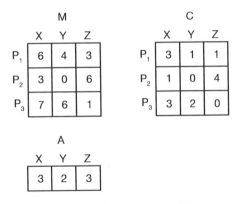

M

	X	Y	Z
P_1	6	4	3
P_2	3	0	6
P_3	7	6	1

C

	X	Y	Z
P_1	3	1	1
P_2	1	0	4
P_3	3	2	0

A

X	Y	Z
3	2	3

Answer the following questions using the banker's algorithm:

(a) What is the content of the matrix `Required`?

(b) Is the system in a safe state?

(c) If a request from a process P_2 arrives for (1, 0, 2), can the request be granted immediately.

Memory Management

7.1 INTRODUCTION

As we know that most of the systems allow multiple processes to reside in the main memory at the same time to increase the CPU utilization. It is the job of memory manager, a part of the operating system, to manage memory between these processes in an efficient way. For this, it keeps track of which part of the memory is occupied and which part is free, allocates and deallocates memory to the processes whenever required, etc. Moreover, it provides the protection mechanism to protect the memory allocated to each process from being accessed by the other processes. For managing the memory, the memory manager may use from a number of available memory management strategies which are discussed in this chapter.

7.2 BACKGROUND

Every byte in the memory has a specific address that may range from 0 to some maximum value as defined by the hardware. This address is known as **physical address**. Whenever a program is brought into main memory for execution, it occupies certain number of memory locations. The set of all physical addresses used by the program is known as **physical address space**. However, before a program can be executed, it must be compiled to produce the machine code. A program is compiled to run starting from some fixed address and accordingly all the variables and procedures used in the source program are assigned some specific address known as **logical address**. Thus, in machine code, all references to data or code are made by specifying the logical addresses and not by the variable or procedure names, etc. The range of addresses that user programs can use is system-defined and the set of all logical addresses used by a user program is known as its **logical address space**.

When a user program is brought into main memory for execution, its logical addresses must be mapped to physical addresses. The mapping from addresses associated with a program to memory addresses is known as **address binding**. The addresses binding can take place at one of the following times.

- **Compile time:** The address binding takes place at compile time if it is known at the compile time which addresses the program will occupy in the main memory. In this case, the program generates **absolute code** at the compile time only, that is, logical addresses are same as that of physical addresses.
- **Load time:** The address binding occurs at load time if it is not known at the compile time which addresses the program will occupy in the main memory. In this case, the program generates **relocatable code** at the compile time which is then converted into the absolute code at the load time.
- **Run time:** The address binding occurs at run time if the process is supposed to move from one memory segment to other during its execution. In this case also, the program generates relocatable code at compile time which is then converted into the absolute code at the run time.

> **Note:** The run time address binding is performed by the hardware device known as Memory Management Unit (MMU).

7.3 MEMORY MANAGEMENT STRATEGIES

To improve the utilization of the CPU and the speed of the computer's response to its users, the system keeps several processes in memory, that is, several processes share memory. Due to the sharing of memory, there is need of memory management. There are various strategies that are used to manage memory. All these strategies allocate memory to the processes using either of following two approaches.

- Contiguous memory allocation
- Non-contiguous memory allocation

Both these approaches are discussed in detail in the subsequent sections.

7.4 CONTIGUOUS MEMORY ALLOCATION

In contiguous memory allocation, each process is allocated a single contiguous part of the memory. The different memory management schemes that are based on this approach are single partition and multiple partitions.

7.4.1 Single Partition

One of the simplest ways to manage memory is to partition the main memory into two parts. One of them is permanently allocated to the operating system while the other part is allocated to the user process (see Figure 7.1). In this figure, the operating system is in lower part of the memory. However, it is not essential that operating system must reside at the bottom of memory; it can reside at the upper part of the memory also. In order to provide a contiguous area for the user process, it usually resides at one extreme end of memory. The factor that decides the location of the operating system in the memory is the location of the interrupt vector. The operating system is placed at the same end of the memory where the interrupt vector is located.

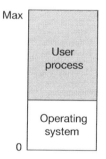

Figure 7.1: Memory Having Single Partition

In this scheme, only one process can execute at a time. Whenever a process is to be executed, the operating system loads it into the main memory for execution. After termination of that process, the operating system waits for another process. When another process arrives, the operating system loads it into the main memory, thus overwriting the first one.

This scheme is easy to implement. Generally, the operating system needs to keep track of the first and the last location allocated to the user processes. However, in this case, the first location is immediately following the operating system and the last location is determined by the capacity of the memory. It needs no hardware support except for protecting the operating system from the user process.

> **Note:** The memory management scheme having single partition is used by single process microcomputer operating systems, such as CP/M and PC-DOS.

7.4.2 Multiple Partitions

A single partition scheme restricts the system to have only one process in memory at a time that reduces utilization of the CPU as well as of memory. Thus, monoprogramming systems are rarely used. Most of the systems used today support multiprogramming which allows multiple processes to reside in the memory at the same time. The simple way to achieve multiprogramming is to divide main memory into a number of partitions which may be of fixed or variable size.

Fixed Partitions

In this technique, each partition is of fixed size and can contain only one process. There are two alternatives for this technique—equal-sized partitions or unequal sized partitions (see Figure 7.2). First, consider the case of equal-sized partitions where any process can be loaded into any partition. Whenever a partition is free, a process whose size is less than or equal to the partition size is selected from the input queue and loaded into this partition. When the process terminates, the partition becomes free to be allocated to another process. The implementation of this method does not require much effort since all partitions are of same size. The operating system is required to keep track only of the partition occupied by each process. For this, it maintains a table that keeps either the starting address of each process or the partition number occupied by each process.

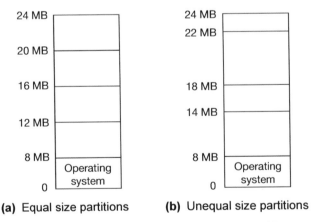

(a) Equal size partitions   **(b)** Unequal size partitions

Figure 7.2: Memory Having Multiple Fixed Partitions

There is one problem with this method that is the memory utilization is not efficient. Any process regardless of how small it is, occupies an entire partition which leads to the wastage of memory within the partition. This phenomenon which results in the wastage of memory within the partition is called **internal fragmentation**. For example, loading a process of size 4M-n bytes into a partition of size 4MB (where, MB stands for megabytes) would result in a wasted space of n bytes within the partition.

This problem cannot be resolved completely but can be reduced to some extent by using unequal-sized partition method where a separate input queue is maintained for each partition. Whenever a process arrives, it is placed into the input queue of the smallest partition large enough to hold it. When this partition becomes free, it is allocated to the process. For example, according to Figure 7.2(b), if a process of size 5MB arrives, it will be accommodated in the partition of size 6 MB. In this case also, some memory is wasted, that is, internal fragmentation still exists, but less than that of equal-sized partition method.

With this method, there may be possibility that the input queue for a large partition is empty but the queue for small partition is full (see Figure 7.3(a)). That is, the small jobs have to wait to get loaded into memory, though a large amount of memory is free. To prevent this, a single input queue can be maintained (see Figure 7.3(b)). Whenever a partition becomes free, the process that fits in it can be chosen from the input queue using some scheduling algorithm.

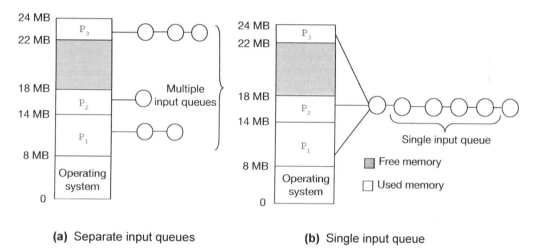

(a) Separate input queues   **(b)** Single input queue

Figure 7.3: Memory Allocation in Fixed Partitions

The fixed-partitioning technique is easy to implement and requires less overhead but has some disadvantages which are as follows:

- The number of processes in memory depends on the number of partitions. Thus, the degree of multiprogramming is limited.
- The memory cannot be used efficiently in case of processes of small sizes.

Note: The technique having fixed partitions is no longer in use.

Variable Partitions

To overcome the disadvantages of fixed partitions technique, a technique called **MVT (Multiprogramming with a Variable number of Tasks)** is used. It is the generalization of the fixed-partitions technique in which the partitions can vary in number and size. In this technique, the amount of memory allocated is exactly the amount of memory a process requires. To implement this, the table maintained by the operating system stores both the starting address and ending address of each process.

Initially, when there is no process in the memory, the whole memory is available for the allocation and is considered as a single large partition of available memory (a **hole**). Whenever a process requests for the memory, the hole large enough to accommodate that process is allocated. The rest of the memory is available to other processes. As soon as the process terminates, the memory occupied by it is deallocated and can be used for other processes. Due to subsequent memory allocations and deallocations, at a given time, some parts of memory will be in use while others will be free (see Figure 7.4 (a)). Now to make further allocations, the memory manager must keep track of the free space in memory. For this, the memory manager maintains a free-storage list that keeps track of the unused part (holes of variable sizes) of memory. The free-storage list is implemented as a linked list where each node contains the size of the hole and the address of the next available hole (see Figure 7.4 (b)).

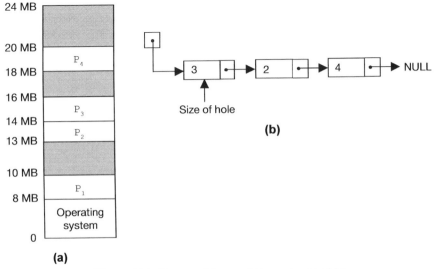

Figure 7.4: Memory Map and Free-storage List

In general, at a certain point of time, there will be a set of holes of various sizes dispersed in the memory. As a result, there may be possibility that the total available memory is large enough to accommodate the waiting process. However, it cannot be utilized as it is scattered. This wastage of the memory space is called **external fragmentation** (also known as **checkerboarding**), since the wasted memory is not a part of any partition. For example, if a request for a partition of size 5MB arrives, it cannot be granted because no single partition is available that is large enough to satisfy the request (see Figure 7.4). However, the combined free space is sufficient to satisfy the request.

To get rid of this problem, it is desirable to relocate (or shuffle) some or all portions of the memory in order to place all the free holes together at one end of memory to make one large hole. This technique of reforming the storage is termed as **compaction.** Compaction results in the memory partitioned into two contiguous blocks—one of used memory and another of free memory. Figure 7.5 shows the memory map after performing compaction. Compaction may take place at the moment any node frees some memory or when a request for allocating memory fails, provided the combined free space is enough to satisfy the request. Since it is expensive in terms of CPU time, it is rarely used.

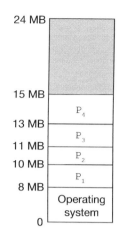

Figure 7.5: Memory After Compaction

Partition Selection Algorithms

Whenever a process arrives and there are various holes large enough to accommodate it, the operating system may use one of the following algorithms to select a partition for the process.

- **First fit:** In this algorithm, the operating system scans the free-storage list and allocates the first hole that is large enough to accommodate that process. This algorithm is fast because search is little as compared to other algorithms.
- **Best fit:** In this algorithm, the operating system scans the free-storage list and allocates the smallest hole whose size is larger than or equal to the size of the process. Unlike first fit algorithm, it allocates a partition that is close to the size required for that process. It is slower than the first fit algorithm as it has to search the entire list every time. Moreover, it leads to more wastage of memory as it results in the smallest leftover holes that cannot be used to satisfy the memory allocation request.
- **Worst fit:** In this algorithm, the operating system scans the free-storage list and allocates the largest hole to that process. Unlike best fit, this algorithm results in the largest leftover holes. However, simulation indicates that worst fit allocation is not very effective in reducing the wastage of memory.

Note: First fit and best fit are among the most popular algorithms for dynamic memory allocation.

Example 7.1:

Consider the memory map given in Figure 7.4, how would each of the first fit, best fit and worst fit algorithms allocate memory to a process P of size 2 MB.

Solution:

According to the different algorithms, memory will be allocated to the process P as shown in Figure 7.6.

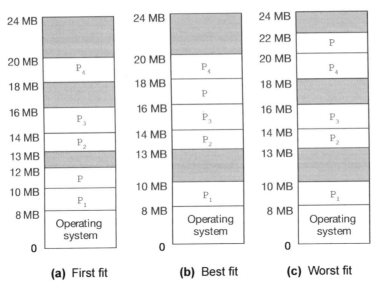

Figure 7.6: Memory Allocation Using Different Algorithms

Relocation and Protection

In multiprogramming environment, multiple processes are executed due to which two problems can arise which are relocation and protection.

Relocation

From the earlier discussion, it is clear that the different processes run at different partitions. Now, suppose a process contains an instruction that requires access to address location 50 in its logical address space. If this process is loaded into a partition at address 10 MB, this instruction will jump to absolute address 50 in physical memory which is inside the operating system. In this case, it is required to map the address location 50 in logical address space to the address location 10 MB + 50 in the physical memory. Similarly, if the process is loaded into some other partition, say at address 20 MB, then it should be mapped to address location 20 MB + 50. This problem is known as **relocation problem**. This relocation problem can be solved by equipping the system with a hardware register called **relocation register** which contains the starting address of the partition into which the process is to be loaded. Whenever an address is generated during the execution of a process, the memory management unit adds the content of the relocation register to the address resulting in physical memory address.

Example 7.2:

Consider the logical address of an instruction in a program is 7632 and the content of relocation register is 2500. To which location in the memory will this address be mapped?

Solution:

Here, Logical address = 7632,
        Content of relocation register = 2500
Since, Physical address = Logical address + Content of relocation register

Physical address $= 7632 + 2500 = 10132$

Thus, the logical address 7632 will be mapped to the location 10132 in memory.

Protection

Using relocation register, the problem of relocation can be solved but there is a possibility that a user process may access the memory address of other processes or the operating system. To protect the operating system from being accessed by other processes and the processes from one another, another hardware register called **limit register** is used. This register holds the range of logical addresses. Each logical address of a program is checked against this register to ensure that it does not attempt to access the memory address outside the allocated partition. Figure 7.7 shows relocation and protection mechanism using relocation and limit register.

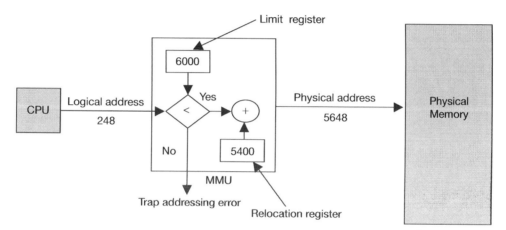

Figure 7.7: Relocation and Protection Using Relocation and Limit Register

CHECK YOUR PROGRESS

1. Distinguish physical address and the logical address.
2. The mapping from addresses associated with a program to memory addresses is known as _____.
3. The run time address binding performed by hardware device is known as _____.
4. At what time, the address binding occurs if the process is supposed to move from one memory segment to other during its execution.
   (a) Compile time   (b) Load time
   (c) Run time   (d) None of these
5. Differentiate internal and external fragmentation.
6. In first fit algorithm, a partition close to the size required for a process is allocated. (True or False)
7. To protect the operating system from access by other processes and the processes from one another, another hardware register called _____ is used.

7.5 NON-CONTIGUOUS MEMORY ALLOCATION

In non-contiguous allocation approach, parts of a single process can occupy non-contiguous physical addresses. In this section, we will discuss memory management schemes based on non-contiguous allocation.

7.5.1 Paging

In paging, the physical memory is divided into fixed sized blocks called **page frames** and logical memory is also divided into fixed size blocks called **pages** which are of same size as that of page frames. When a process is to be executed, its pages can be loaded into any unallocated frames (not necessarily contiguous) from the disk. Figure 7.8 shows two processes A and B with all their pages loaded into the memory. In this figure, the page size is of 4 KB. Nowadays, the pages sizes between 4 KB and 8 KB are used. However, some systems support even larger page sizes.

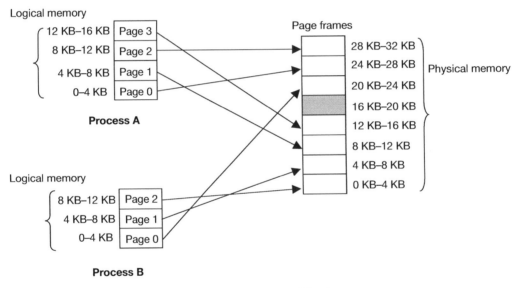

Figure 7.8: Concept of Paging

Note: Some systems, such as solaris support multiple page sizes (say 8 KB and 4 MB) depending on the data stored in the pages.

When the CPU generates a logical address, it is divided into two parts: a page number (p) [high-order bits] and a page offset (d) [low-order bits] where d specifies the address of the instruction within the page p. Since the logical address is a power of 2, the page size is always chosen as a power of 2 so that the logical address can be converted easily into page number and page offset. To understand this, consider the size of logical address space is 2^m. Now, if we choose a page size of 2^n (bytes or words), then n bits will specify the page offset and $m-n$ bits will specify the page number.

Example 7.3:

Consider a system that generates logical address of 16 bits and page size is 4 KB. How many bits would specify the page number and page offset?

Solution:

Here, the logical address is of 16 bits, that is, the size of logical address space is 2^{16} page size is 4KB, that is, 4×1024 bytes $= 2^{12}$ bytes

Thus, the page offset will be of 12 bits and page number will be of $(16 - 12) = 4$ bits.

Now let us see how a logical address is translated into a physical address. In paging, address translation is performed using a mapping table, called **page table**. The operating system maintains a page table for each process to keep track of which page frame is allocated to which page. It stores the frame number allocated to each page and the page number is used as index to the page table (see Figure 7.9).

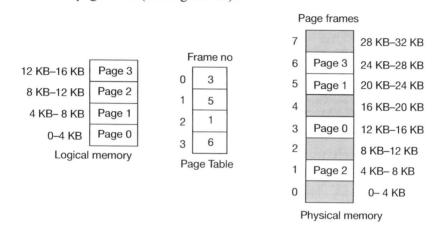

Figure 7.9: A Page Table

When CPU generates a logical address, that address is sent to MMU. The MMU uses the page number to find the corresponding page frame number in the page table. That page frame number is attached to the high-order end of the page offset to form the physical address that is sent to the memory. The mechanism of translation of logical address into physical address is shown in Figure 7.10.

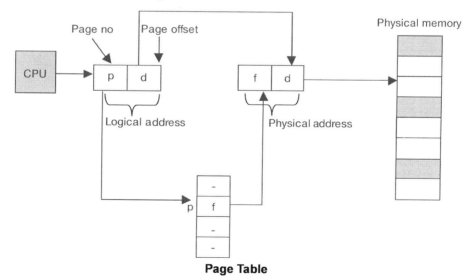

Page Table

Figure 7.10: Address Translation in Paging

> **Note:** Since both the page and page frames are of same size, the offset within them are identical and need not be mapped.

Example 7.4:

Consider a paged memory system with eight pages of 8 KB page size each and 16 page frames in memory. Using the following page table, compute the physical address for the logical address 18325.

7	1010
6	0100
5	0000
4	0111
3	1101
2	1011
1	1110
0	0101

Page Table

Solution:

Since, total number of pages = 8, that is, 2^3 and each page size = 8 KB, that is, 2^{13} bytes, the logical address will be of 16 bits. Out of these 16 bits, the three high-end order bits represent the page number and the thirteen low-end order bits represent offset within the page. In addition, there are 16, that is, 2^4 page frames in memory, thus, the physical address will be of 16 bits.

Given logical address = 18325 which is equivalent to 0100011110010101. In this address, page number = 010, that is, 2 and page offset = 0011110010101. From the page table it is clear that the page number 2 is in page frame 1011.

Therefore, the physical address = 1011001110010101, which is equivalent to 92053.

Advantages
- Since the memory allocated is always in fixed unit, any free frame can be allocated to a process. Thus, there is no external fragmentation.

Disadvantages
- There may be some internal fragmentation. To illustrate this, consider a page size is of 4KB and a process requires memory of 8195 bytes, that is 2 page + 3 bytes. In this case, for only 3 bytes, an entire frame is wasted resulting in internal fragmentation.

Hardware Implementation of Page Table

A page table can be implemented in several ways. The simplest way is to use registers to store the page table entries indexed by page number. Though this method is faster and does not require any memory reference, its disadvantage is that it is not feasible in case of large page table as registers are expensive. Moreover, at every context switch, the page table needs to be changed which in turn requires all the registers to be reloaded. This degrades the performance.

Another way is to keep the entire page table in main memory and the pointer to page table stored in a register called **Page Table Base Register (PTBR)**. Using this method, page table can be changed by reloading only one register, thus reduces context switch time to a great extent. The disadvantage of this scheme is that it requires two memory references to access a memory location; first to access page table using PTBR to find the page frame number and second to access the desired memory location. Thus, memory accessing is slowed down by a factor of two.

To overcome this problem, the system can be equipped with a special hardware device known as **Translation Look-aside Buffer (TLB)** (or **associative memory**). The TLB is inside MMU and contains a limited number of page table entries. When CPU generates a logical address and presents it to the MMU, it is compared with the page numbers present in the TLB. If a match is found in TLB (called **TLB hit**), the corresponding page frame number is used to access the physical memory. In case a match is not found in TLB (called **TLB miss**), memory is referenced for the page table. Further, this page number and the corresponding frame number are added to the TLB so that next time if this page is required, it can be referenced quickly. Since the size of TLB is limited so when it is full, one entry must be replaced. Figure 7.11 shows the mechanism of paging using TLB.

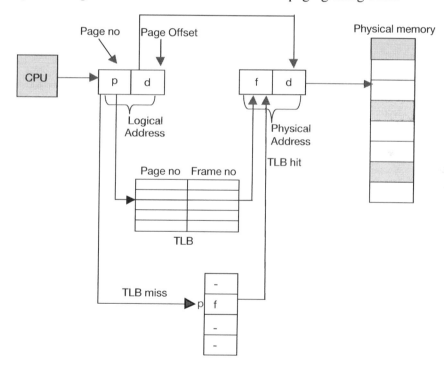

Figure 7.11: Paging with TLB

TLB can contain entries for more than one process at the same time, so there is a possibility that two processes map the same page number to different frames. To resolve this ambiguity, a process identifier (PID) can be added with each entry of TLB. For each memory access, the PID present in the TLB is matched with the value in a special register that holds the PID of the currently executing process. If it matches, the page number is searched to find the page frame number; otherwise, it is treated as a TLB miss.

7.5.2 Segmentation

A user views a program as a collection of segments, such as main program, routines, variables, etc. All of these segments are variable in size and their size may also vary during execution. Each segment is identified by a name (or segment number) and the elements within a segment are identified by their offset from the starting of the segment. Figure 7.12 shows the user view of a program.

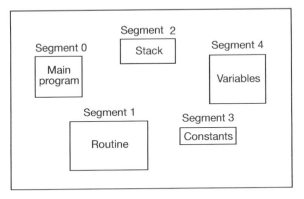

Figure 7.12: User View of a Program

Segmentation is a memory management scheme that implements the user view of a program. In this scheme, the entire logical address space is considered as a collection of segments with each segment having a number and a length. The length of a segment may range from 0 to some maximum value as specified by the hardware and may also change during the execution. The user specifies each logical address consisting of a segment number (s) and an offset (d). This differentiates segmentation from paging in which the division of logical address into page number and page offset is performed by the hardware.

To keep track of each segment, a **segment table** is maintained by the operating system (see Figure 7.13). Each entry in the segment table consists of two fields: segment base and segment limit. The **segment base** specifies the starting address of the segment in physical memory and the **segment limit** specifies the length of the segment. The segment number is used as an index to the segment table.

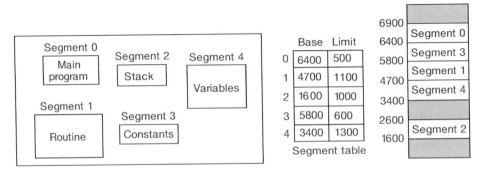

Figure 7.13: A Segment Table

When CPU generates a logical address, that address is sent to MMU. The MMU uses the segment number of logical address as an index to the segment table. The offset is compared with the segment limit and if it is greater, invalid address error is generated. Otherwise, the offset is added to the segment base to form the physical address that is sent to the memory. Figure 7.14 shows the hardware to translate logical address into physical address in segmentation.

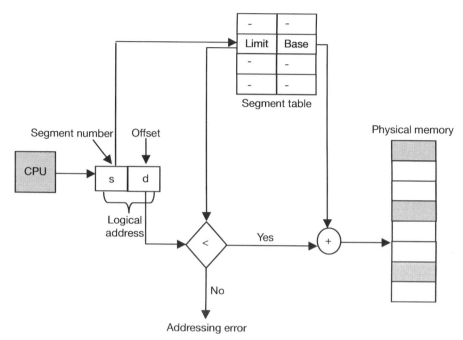

Figure 7.14: Segmentation Hardware

Advantages

- Since a segment contains one type of object, each segment can have different type of protection. For example, a procedure can be specified as execute only, whereas, a `char` type array can be specified as read only.
- It allows sharing of data or code between several processes. For example, a common function or shared library can be shared between various processes. Instead of having them in address space of every process, they can be put in a segment and that segment can be shared.

Example 7.5:

Using the following segment table, compute the physical address for the logical address consisting of segment and offset as given below.

	Base	**Limit**
0	5432	350
1	115	100
2	2200	780
3	4235	1100
4	1650	400

Segment Table

(a) Segment 2 and offset 247
(b) Segment 4 and offset 439

Solution:

(a) Here, offset = 247 and segment is 2
It is clear from the segment table that limit of segment 2 = 780 and
segment base = 2200
Since, the offset is less than the segment limit, physical address is computed as
physical address = offset + segment base = 247 + 2200 = 2447

(b) Here, offset = 439 and segment is 4
It is clear from the segment table that limit of segment 4 = 400 and
Segment base = 1650
Since, the offset is greater than the segment limit, invalid address error is generated.

7.5.3 Segmentation with Paging

The idea behind the segmentation with paging is to combine the advantages of both paging (such as uniform page size) and segmentation (such as protection and sharing) together into a single scheme. In this scheme, each segment is divided into a number of pages. To keep track of these pages, a page table is maintained for each segment. The segment offset in the logical address (comprising segment number and offset) is further divided into a page number and a page offset. Each entry of segment table contains the segment base, segment limit and one more entry that contains the address of the segment's page table.

The logical address consists of three parts: segment number (s), page number (p) and page offset (d). Whenever address translation is to be performed, firstly, the MMU uses the segment number as an index to segment table to find the address of page table. Then the page number of logical address is attached to the high-order end of the page table address and used as an index to page table to find the page table entry. Finally, the physical address is formed by attaching the frame number obtained from the page table entry to the high-order end of the page offset. Figure 7.15 shows the address translation in segmentation with paging scheme.

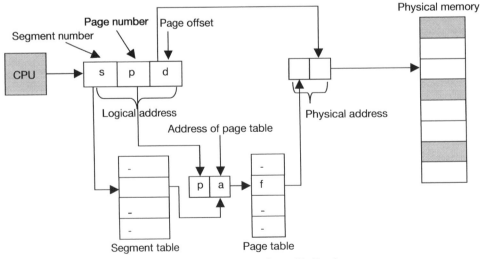

Figure 7.15: Segmentation with Paging

7.6 SWAPPING

In multiprogramming, a memory management scheme called swapping can be used to increase the CPU utilization. The process of bringing a process to memory and after running for a while, temporarily copying it to disk is known as **swapping**. Figure 7.16 shows the swapping process. The decision of which process is to swapped in and which process is to be swapped out is made by the CPU scheduler. For example, consider a multiprogramming environment with priority based scheduling algorithm. When a process of high priority enters the input queue, a process of low priority is swapped out so that the process of high priority can be loaded and executed. On the termination of this process, the process of low priority is swapped back in the memory to continue its execution.

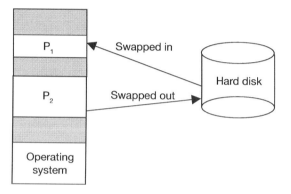

Figure 7.16: Swapping

CHECK YOUR PROGRESS

8. The division of logical memory into fixed size blocks is called _____.
9. In paging, the pages and the page frames may not be of same size. (True or False)
10. _____ is a hardware device which is situated in MMU used to implement page table.
11. What do you mean by segmentation?
12. The idea behind the segmentation with paging is to combine the advantages of both paging (such as uniform page size) and segmentation (such as protection and sharing) together into a single scheme. (True or False)
13. The process of bringing a process to memory and after running for a while, temporarily copying it to disk is known as _____.

Let Us Summarize

1. Most of the systems allow multiple processes to reside in the main memory at the same time to increase the CPU utilization. It is the job of memory manager, a part of the operating system, to manage memory between these processes in an efficient way.
2. Every byte in the memory has a specific address that may range from 0 to some maximum value as defined by the hardware. This address is known as physical address.

3. A program is compiled to run starting from some fixed address and accordingly all the variables and procedures used in the source program are assigned some specific address known as logical address.

4. The mapping from addresses associated with a program to memory addresses is known as address binding. The address binding can take place at complie time, load time or run time.

5. For managing the memory, the memory manager may use from a number of available memory management strategies.

6. All the memory management strategies allocate memory to the processes using either of two approaches: contiguous memory allocation or non-contiguous memory allocation.

7. In contiguous memory allocation, each process is allocated a single contiguous part of the memory. The different memory management schemes that are based on this approach are single partition and multiple partitions.

8. In single partition technique, main memory is partitioned into two parts. One of them is permanently allocated to the operating system while the other part is allocated to the user process.

9. There are two alternatives for multiple partition technique: equal-sized partitions or unequal-sized partitions.

10. In equal-sized partitions technique, any process can be loaded into any partition. Regardless of how small a process is, occupies an entire partition which leads to the wastage of memory within the partition. This phenomenon which results in the wastage of memory within the partition is called internal fragmentation.

11. In unequal-sized partition, whenever a process arrives, it is placed into the input queue of the smallest partition large enough to hold it. When this partition becomes free, it is allocated to the process.

12. MVT (Multiprogramming with a Variable number of Tasks) is the generalization of the fixed partitions technique in which the partitions can vary in number and size. In this technique, the amount of memory allocated is exactly the amount of memory a process requires.

13. In MVT, the wastage of the memory space is called external fragmentation (also known as checkerboarding), since the wasted memory is not a part of any partition.

14. Whenever a process arrives and there are various holes large enough to accommodate it, the operating system may use one of the algorithms to select a partition for the process: first fit, best fit and worst fit

15. In multiprogramming environment, multiple processes are executed due to which two problems can arise which are relocation and protection.

16. The relocation problem can be solved by equipping the system with a hardware register called relocation register which contains the starting address of the partition into which the process is to be loaded.

17. To protect the operating system from access by other processes and the processes from one another, another hardware register called limit register is used.

18. In non-contiguous allocation approach, parts of a single process can occupy non-contiguous physical addresses.

19. Paging and segmemtation are the memory management techniques based on the non-contiguous allocation approach.

20. In paging, the physical memory is divided into fixed sized blocks called page frames and logical memory is also divided into fixed size blocks called pages which are of same size as that of page frames. The address translation is performed using a mapping table, called page table.

21. Segmentation is a memory management scheme that implements the user view of a program. In this scheme, the entire logical address space is considered as a collection of segments with each segment having a number and a length. To keep track of each segment, a segment table is maintained by the operating system

22. The idea behind the segmentation with paging is to combine the advantages of both paging (such as uniform page size) and segmentation (such as protection and sharing) together into a single scheme. In this scheme, each segment is divided into a number of pages. To keep track of these pages, a page table is maintained for each segment.

23. A memory management scheme called swapping can be used to increase the CPU utilization. The process of bringing a process to memory and after running for a while, temporarily copying it to disk is known as swapping.

 ## ANSWERS TO 'CHECK YOUR PROGRESS'

1. **Physical address:** Every byte in the memory has a specific address that may range from 0 to some maximum value as defined by the hardware. This address is known as physical address. **Logical address:** A program is compiled to run starting from some fixed address and accordingly all the variables and procedures used in the source program are assigned some specific address known as logical address.
2. Address binding
3. MMU (Memory Management Unit)
4. (c)
5. The wastage of memory within the partition is known as internal fragmentation, whereas, the wastage of the memory space that is not a part of any partition called external fragmentation.
6. False
7. Limit register
8. Pages
9. False
10. Translation Look-aside Buffer (TLB)
11. Segmentation is a memory management scheme that implements the user view of a program.
12. True
13. Swapping

 ## TEST YOURSELF

1. What is address binding? At what times does it take place?
2. Consider the following memory map with a number of variable size partitions.

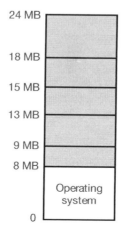

Assume that initially, all the partitions are empty. How would each of the first fit, best fit and the worst fit partition selection algorithms allocate memory to the following processes arriving one after another?

(a) P_1 of size 2 MB

(b) P_2 of size 2.9 MB

(c) P_3 of size 1.4 MB

(d) P_4 of size 5.4 MB

Does any of the algorithms result in a process waiting because of insufficient memory available? Also determine using which of the algorithms the memory is most efficiently used?

3. Which of the following memory management schemes suffer from internal or external fragmentation?

(a) Multiple fixed partition

(b) Multiple variable partition

(c) Paging

(d) Segmentation

4. Consider a paged memory system with 16 pages of 2048 bytes each in logical memory and 32 frames in physical memory. How many bits will each of the following comprise?

(a) Logical address

(b) Page number

(c) Page offset

(d) Physical address

5. Consider a paged memory system with 2^{16} bytes of physical memory, 256 pages of logical address space and a page size of 2^{10} bytes, how many bytes are in a page frame?

6. Can a process on a paged memory system access memory allocated to some other process? Why or why not?

7. What are the two major differences between segmentation and paging?

8. How does the segmentation scheme allow different processes to share data or code?

9. Using the following segment table, compute the physical address for the logical address consisting of segment and offset as given below.

	Base	Limit
0	5432	350
1	115	100
2	2200	780
3	4235	1100
4	1650	400

Segment Table

(a) Segment 0 and offset 193

(b) Segment 2 and offset 546

(c) Segment 3 and offset 1265

10. What is the idea behind combining segmentation with paging? When is it useful?

Chapter 08

Virtual Memory

Learning Objectives

After reading this chapter, you will be able to:

☐ Understand the concept of virtual memory
☐ Implement virtual memory using demand paging
☐ Discuss how process creation and execution can be made faster
☐ Explain various page replacement algorithms
☐ Discuss allocation of frames to processes
☐ Explain thrashing along with its causes and its prevention
☐ Understand how memory is managed in Linux

8.1 INTRODUCTION

In *Chapter 07*, we discussed various memory management strategies. All these strategies require the entire process to be in main memory before its execution. Thus, the size of the process is limited to the size of physical memory. To overcome this limitation, a memory management scheme called **overlaying** can be used, that allows a process to execute irrespective of the system having insufficient physical memory. The programmer splits a program into smaller parts called **overlays** in such a way that no two overlays are required to be in main memory at the same time. An overlay is loaded into memory only when it is needed. Initially, overlay 0 would run. When it is completed, it would call another overlay and so on until the process terminates. These overlays reside on the disk and swapped in and out of memory dynamically as needed, thereby, reducing the amount of memory needed by the process. The major disadvantage of this technique is that it requires a major involvement of the programmer. Moreover, splitting a program into smaller parts is time consuming.

This resulted in the formulation of another memory management technique known as **virtual memory**. Virtual memory gives the illusion that the system has much larger memory than actually available memory. The basic idea behind this technique is that the combined size of code, data and stack may exceed the amount of physical memory. Thus, virtual memory frees programs from the constraints of physical memory limitation. The virtual memory can be implemented by demand paging or demand segmentation. Out of these two ways, demand paging is commonly used as it is easier to implement.

8.2 BACKGROUND

Virtual memory is a technique that allows executing a program that is partially in memory. In this technique, the operating system loads only those parts of program in memory that are currently needed for the execution of the process. The rest part is kept on the disk and is loaded into the memory only when needed. For example, a 64MB program can run on a 32MB system by loading the 32MB in the memory at an instant; the parts of the program are swapped between memory and the disk as needed.

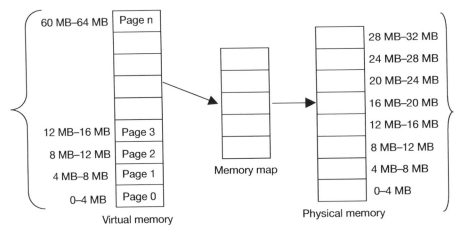

Figure 8.1: Virtual Memory and Physical Memory

Note: In virtual memory systems, the logical address is referred to as virtual address and logical address space is referred to as virtual address space.

8.3 DEMAND PAGING

In demand paging, a page is loaded into the memory only when it is needed during program execution. Pages that are never accessed are never loaded into the memory.

A demand paging system combines the features of paging with swapping. To facilitate swapping, the entire virtual address space of a process is stored contiguously on a secondary storage device (usually, a disk). Whenever a process is to be executed, an area on secondary storage device is allocated to it on which its pages are copied. The area is known as **swap space** of the process. During the execution of a process, whenever a page is required, it is loaded into the main memory from the swap space. Similarly, when a process is to be removed from main memory, it is written back into the swap space if it has been modified.

Other than swap space, some form of hardware support is also needed to differentiate the pages that are in memory from that are on disk. For this, an additional bit `valid` is maintained in each page table entry to indicate whether the page is in memory. If a page is valid (that is, it exists in the virtual address space of the process) and in memory, the associated `valid` bit is set to 1, otherwise it is set to 0. Figure 8.2 shows the page table in demand paging system.

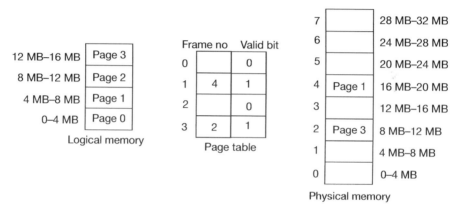

Figure 8.2: Page Table in Demand Paging System

Whenever a process requests for a page, the virtual address is sent to MMU. The MMU checks the `valid` bit in the page table entry of that page. If the `valid` bit is 1 (that is, the requested page is in memory), it is accessed as in paging (discussed in *Chapter 07*). Otherwise, the MMU raises an interrupt called **page fault** or a **missing page interrupt** and the control is passed to the page fault routine in the operating system.

To handle the page fault, the page fault routine first of all checks, whether the virtual address for the desired page is valid, from its PCB stored in the process table. If it is invalid, it terminates the process giving error. Otherwise, it takes the following steps.

1. Locates for a free page frame in memory and allocates it to the process.
2. Swaps the desired page into this allocated page frame.
3. Updates the process table and page table to indicate that the page is in memory.

After performing these steps, the CPU restarts from the instruction that it left off due to the page fault.

Note: In demand paging, the process of loading a page in memory is known as **page-in** operation instead of swap-in. It is because the whole process is not loaded; only some pages are loaded into the memory.

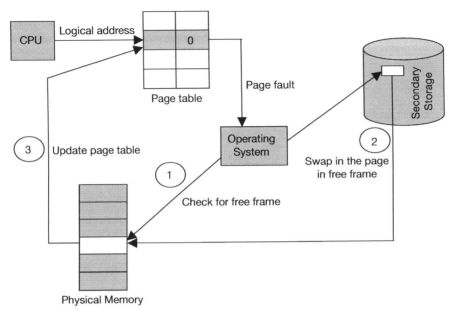

Figure 8.3: Handling a Page Fault

Advantages
- It reduces the swap time since only the required pages are swapped in instead of swapping the whole process.
- It increases the degree of multiprogramming by reducing the amount of physical memory required for a process.
- It minimizes the initial disk overhead as initially not all pages are to be read.
- It does not need extra hardware support.

8.4 PROCESS CREATION

Demand paging enables a process to start faster by just loading the page containing its first instruction in memory. Virtual memory provides two other techniques, namely, copy-on-write and memory-mapped files that make the process creation and execution faster.

8.4.1 Copy-on-Write

Recall from *Chapter 02*, a process may need to create several processes during its execution, and the parent and child processes have their own distinct address spaces. If the newly created process is the duplicate of the parent process, it will contain same pages in its address space as that of parent. However, if the newly created process need to load another program in its memory space, immediately after creation, then the copying of parent's address space may be unnecessary. To avoid copying, a technique made available by virtual memory called **copy-on-write** can be employed.

In this technique, initially, parent and child processes are allowed to share the same pages and these shared pages are marked as copy-on-write pages. Now, if either process attempts to write on a shared page, a copy of that page is created for that process. Note that only the pages that can be modified (for example, pages containing data) are marked as copy-on-write pages while the pages that cannot be modified (for example, pages containing executable code) are shared between parent and child processes.

To implement this, a bit is associated in page table entry of each shared page to indicate that it is a copy-on-write page. Whenever either process say, child process tries to modify a page, the operating system creates a copy of that page, maps it to the address space of the child process and turns off the copy-on-write bit. Now, the child process can modify the copied page without effecting the page of the parent process. Thus, copy-on-write technique makes the process creation faster and conserves the memory.

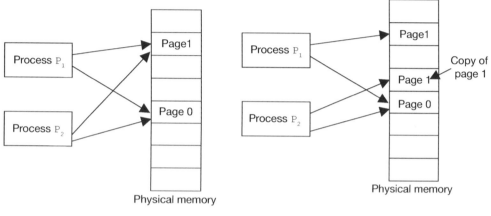

(a) Before process P_2 modifies page 1   **(b)** After process P_2 modifies page 1

Figure 8.4: Implementing Copy-on-Write

Note: A number of operating systems, including Windows XP, Linux and Solaris, support the use of copy-on-write technique.

8.4.2 Memory-mapped Files

Every time a process needs to access a file on disk, it needs to use a system call, such as read(), write() and then access the disk. This becomes very time consuming as disk access is much slower than the memory access. An alternative technique made available by virtual memory is **memory-mapped file** that allows treating disk access as memory access. The memory mapping of a file by a process means binding that file to a portion of virtual address space of the process. This binding takes place at the time process executes a memory map system call. A portion (equivalent to page size in memory) of the desired file is mapped to a page in the virtual memory of the process. After the file has been mapped, the process can access the file pages in the same way as it would access other pages in its address space, thereby, enhancing performance. Figure 8.5 shows the memory mapping of a file myfile by a process P.

Note that if the pages of process P that do not belong to mapped file myfile are to be paged-in or out of the physical memory, the virtual memory handler performs this job using

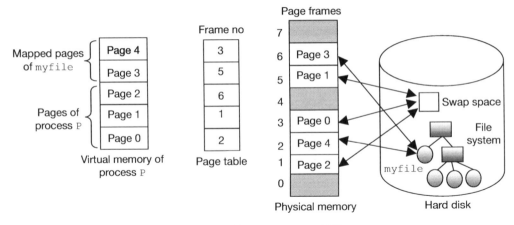

Figure 8.5: Memory-mapped File

the swap space of process P. On the other hand, in case of read/write to file `myfile`, the file system is used in combination with virtual memory handler.

Whenever the process, during execution, writes/modifies data in mapped pages of file, the new/modified data is not immediately written to the file on disk. In some systems, the file on disk is modified when the operating system periodically checks that any of the mapped pages of file has been modified; whereas other systems may choose to write to the physical file when the page frame containing the modified page needs to be evicted. Moreover, when the process executes a memory unmap system call, the pages of mapped file are removed from the virtual address space of the process and the modified data (if any) is written to the file on disk.

CHECK YOUR PROGRESS

1. Define overlays.
2. _____ is a technique that allows a program that is partially in memory to execute.
3. The basic idea behind virtual memory is that the combined size of code, data and stack cannot exceed the amount of physical memory. (True or False)
4. Which of the following memory management strategies combines the features of paging system with swapping?
   (a) Segmentation (b) Demand paging
   (c) Both of these (d) None of these
5. Whenever a process is to be executed, an area on secondary storage device is allocated to it on which its pages are copied. The area is known as _____ of the process.
6. What is a page fault?
7. The purpose of copy-on-write technique is to conserve memory by avoiding copying of parent's address space. (True or False)

8.5 PAGE REPLACEMENT

As stated earlier, when page fault occurs, page fault routine locates for a free page frame in memory and allocates it to the process. However, there is a possibility that the memory is full, that is, no free frame is available for allocation. In that case, the operating system has to evict a page from the memory to make space for the desired page to be swapped in. The page to be evicted will be written to the disk depending on whether it has been modified or not. If the page has been modified while in the memory, it is rewritten to the disk; otherwise no rewrite is needed.

To keep track whether the page has been modified, a **modified (M)** bit (also known as **dirty** bit) is added to each page table entry. This bit indicates whether the page has been modified. When a page is first loaded into the memory, this bit is cleared. It is set by the hardware when any word or byte in the page is written into. At the time of page replacement, if `dirty` bit for a selected page is cleared, it implies that the page has not been modified since it was loaded into the memory. The page frame is written back to the swap space only if `dirty` bit is set.

The system can select a page frame at random and replace it by the new page. However, if the replaced page is frequently accessed, then another page fault would occur when the replaced page is accessed again resulting in degradation of system performance. Thus, there must be some policy to select a page to be evicted. For this, there are various page replacement algorithms. These replacement algorithms can be evaluated by determining the number of page faults using a reference string. A **reference string** is an ordered list of memory references made by a process. It can be generated by a random number generator or recording the actual memory references made by an executing program. To illustrate the page replacement algorithms, consider the reference string as shown in Figure 8.6 for the memory with three page frames. For simplicity, instead of actual memory references, we have considered only the page numbers.

Figure 8.6: The Reference String

8.5.1 FIFO Page Replacement

The First-In First-Out (FIFO) is the simplest page replacement algorithm. As the name suggests, the first page loaded into the memory is the first page is to be replaced. That is, the page is replaced in the order in which it is loaded into the memory.

To illustrate the FIFO replacement algorithm, consider our example reference string shown in Figure 8.6. Assuming that initially, all the three frames are empty, the first two references made to page 5 and 0 and cause page faults. As a result, they are swapped in memory. The third reference made to page 5 does not cause page fault as it is already in memory. The next reference made to page 3 causes a page fault and that page is brought in memory. The reference to page 2 causes a page fault which results in the replacement of page 5 as it is the oldest page. Now, the oldest page is 0, so reference made to page 5 will replace page 0. This process continues until all the pages of reference string are accessed. It is clear from the Figure 8.7 that there are nine page faults.

To implement this algorithm, each page table entry includes the time (called **swap-in** time) when the page was swapped in the memory. When a page is to be replaced, the page with the earliest swap-in time is replaced. Alternatively, a FIFO queue can be created to

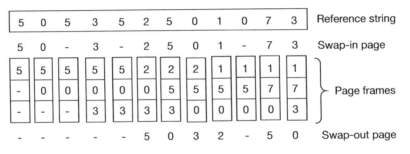

Figure 8.7: The FIFO Replacement Algorithm

keep track of all the pages in the memory with the earliest one at the front and the recent at the rear of the queue. At the time of page fault, the page at the front of the queue is removed and the newly arrived page is added to the rear of the queue.

The FIFO page replacement algorithm is easier to implement as compared to all other replacement algorithms. However, it is rarely used as it is not very efficient. Since it does not consider the pattern of the usage of a page, a frequently used may be replaced resulting in more page faults. Moreover, it suffers from **Belady's anomaly**—a situation in which increasing the number of page frames would result in more page faults. To illustrate this, consider the reference string containing five pages, numbered from 2 to 6 (see Figure 8.8). From this figure, it is clear that with three page frames, a total of nine page faults occur. On the other hand, with four page frames, a total of ten page faults occur.

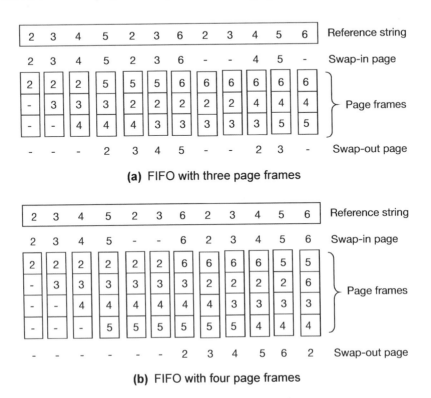

(a) FIFO with three page frames

(b) FIFO with four page frames

Figure 8.8: Belady's Anomaly

8.5.2 Optimal Page Replacement

The Optimal Page Replacement (OPT) algorithm is the best possible page replacement algorithm. The basic idea behind this algorithm is that whenever a page fault occurs, some pages are in memory; out of these pages, one will be referenced at the next instruction while other pages may not be referenced until the execution of certain number of instructions. In case of page replacement, the page that is referenced at last will be replaced. That is, the page to be referenced in the most distant future is replaced. For this, each page can be labelled in the memory with the number of instructions to be executed before that page is referenced for the first time. The page with the highest label is replaced from the memory.

To illustrate this algorithm, consider our example reference string (see Figure 8.6). Like FIFO, the first two references made to page 5 and 0 cause page faults. As a result, they are swapped into the memory. The third reference made to page 5 does not cause page fault as it is already in memory. The reference made to page 3 causes a page fault and thus is swapped into memory. However, the reference made to page 2 replaces page 3 because page 3 is required at the last instruction, whereas, pages 5 and 0 are required at next instructions. The page faults and the pages swapped-in and swapped-out for all the page references are shown in Figure 8.9. This algorithm causes seven page faults.

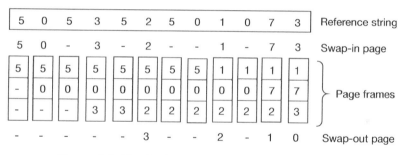

Figure 8.9: The Optimal Page Replacement Algorithm

The advantage of this algorithm is that it causes the lowest number of page faults as compared to other algorithms. The disadvantage of this algorithm is that its implementation requires prior knowledge of which page will be referenced next. Though this algorithm is not used in systems practically, it is used as the basis for comparing performance of other algorithms.

Note: To implement OPT, a program can be executed on a simulator and all the page references are recorded. Using the page reference records obtained during first run, it can be implemented at second run.

8.5.3 LRU Page Replacement

The Least Recently Used (LRU) algorithm is an approximation to the optimal algorithm. Unlike optimal algorithm, it uses the recent past behaviour of the program to predict the near future. It is based on the assumption that the page that has been used in the last few instructions will probably be referenced in the next few instructions. Thus, it replaces the page that has not been referenced for the longest time.

Consider our example reference string (see Figure 8.6). As a result of this algorithm, the page faults and the pages swapped-in and swapped-out for all the page references are shown in Figure 8.10. Upto five references, page faults are same as that of optimal algorithm. When a reference is made to page 2, page 0 is replaced as it was least recently used. However, after page 5, it is being used again leading to a page fault. Regardless of this, the number of page faults is eight which is less than in case of FIFO.

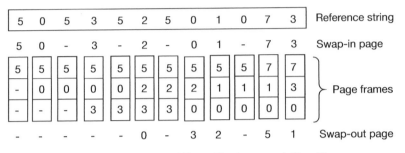

Figure 8.10: The LRU Page Replacement Algorithm

One way to implement LRU is maintaining a linked list of all the pages in the memory; the most recently used page is at the head and the least recently used page is at the tail of the list. Whenever a page is to be replaced, it is deleted from the tail of the linked list and the new page is inserted at the head of the linked list. The problem with this implementation is that it requires updating the list at every page reference despite of whether page fault occurs or not. It is because whenever a page in memory is referenced, being the most recent page, it is removed from its current position and inserted at the head of the linked list. This results in extra overhead.

Alternatively, the hardware can be equipped with a counter. This counter is incremented by one after each instruction. The page table has a field to store the value of the counter. Whenever a page is referenced, the current value of the counter is copied to that field in the page table entry for that page. Whenever a page is to be replaced, this algorithm searches the page table for the entry having the lowest counter value (means the least recently used page) and replaces that page.

Clearly, it has less page faults as compared to FIFO algorithm. Moreover, it does not suffer from the Belady's anomaly. Thus, it is better than FIFO algorithm and is used in many systems. The disadvantage of this algorithm is that it is time consuming when implemented using linked list. Otherwise, it needs extra hardware support for its implementation.

Note: Both the optimal and LRU algorithms belong to a special class of page replacement algorithms called **stack algorithms** that never exhibit Belady's anomaly.

8.5.4 The Second Chance Page Replacement

The second chance page replacement algorithm (sometimes also referred to as **clock** algorithm) is a refinement over FIFO algorithm. It replaces the page that is both the oldest as well as unused instead of the oldest page that may be heavily used. To keep track of the usage of the page, it uses the `reference` (R) bit which is associated with each page. This bit indicates whether the reference has been made to the page while it is in memory. It is set whenever a page is accessed for either reading or writing. If this bit is clear for a page that means this page is not being used.

Whenever, a page is to be replaced, this algorithm uses the FIFO algorithm to find the oldest page and inspects its `reference` bit. If this bit is clear, the page is both the oldest and unused and thus, replaced. Otherwise, the second chance is given to this page and the `reference` bit of this page is cleared and its load time is set to the current time. Then the algorithm moves to the next oldest page using FIFO algorithm. This process continues until a page is found whose `reference` bit is clear. If the `reference` bit of all the pages is set (that is, all the pages are referenced), then this algorithm will proceed as pure FIFO.

This algorithm is implemented using a circular linked list and a pointer that points to the next victim page. Whenever a page is to be replaced, the list is traversed until a page whose `reference` bit is clear is found. While traversing, the `reference` bit of each examined page is cleared. When a page whose `reference` bit is clear is found, that page is replaced with the new page and pointer is advanced to the next page. For example, consider our example reference string with `reference` bits shown in Figure 8.11. The algorithm starts with the page 5, say at time $t = 18$. Since, the `reference` bit of this page is set, its `reference` bit is cleared and time is reset to the current system time as though it has just arrived in the memory. The pointer is advanced to the next page that is page 0. The reference bit of this page is clear, so it is replaced by the new page. The pointer is advanced to the page 3 which will be the starting point for next invocation of this algorithm.

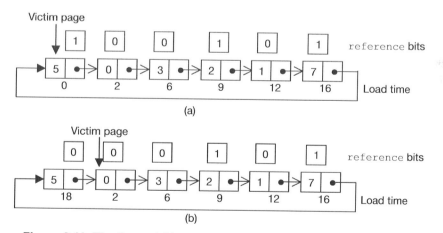

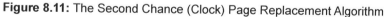

Figure 8.11: The Second Chance (Clock) Page Replacement Algorithm

8.5.5 Counting-Based Page Replacement Algorithm

Other than the page replacement algorithms discussed earlier, there are several other algorithms. Some of them keep record of how often each page has been referenced by associating a counter with each page. Initially, the value of this counter is 0, which is incremented every time when a reference to that page is made. That is, the counter counts the number of references that have been made to each page. A page with the highest value of the counter is heavily used while for a page with the lowest value of counter, there are following interpretations.

- That page is least frequently used.
- That page has just brought in and has yet to be used.

The algorithm based on the first interpretation is known as **Least Frequently Used (LFU)** page replacement algorithm. In this algorithm, when a page is to be replaced, the page with lowest value of counter is chosen for replacement. Clearly, the page that is heavily used is not replaced. The problem with this algorithm arises when there is a page that was used heavily initially, but afterwards never used again. For example, in a multipass compiler, some pages are used heavily during pass 1; after that pass, they may not be required. Still, these pages will not be replaced as they have high value of counter. Thus, this algorithm may replace useful pages instead of pages that are not in use. The algorithm that is based on the second interpretation is called the **Most Frequently Used (MFU)** page replacement algorithm.

Both these algorithms are not commonly used, as their implementation is expensive. Moreover, they do not approximate the OPT page replacement algorithm.

CHECK YOUR PROGRESS

8. A _____ is an ordered list of memory references made by a process.
9. How does the system keep track of whether the page has been modified?
10. Which of the following algorithms suffer from Belady's anomaly?
    (a) Optimal page replacement   (b) FIFO page replacement
    (c) LRU page replacement   (d) None of these
11. Which algorithm is used as the basis for comparing performance of other algorithms?
12. The LRU page replacement algorithm is also referred to as clock algorithm. (True or False)
13. The algorithm based on the interpretation that page has just brought in and has yet to be used is _____ .

8.6 ALLOCATION OF FRAMES

As we know the physical memory is divided into frames and at a time, there can be limited number of frames for allocation. In a single-user system, the memory allocation is simple as all free frames can be allocated to a single process. However, in multiprogramming systems where a number of processes may reside in main memory at the same time, the free frames must be divided among the competing processes. Thus, a decision is to be made on the number of frames that should be allocated to each process.

A common approach for allocating frames to processes is to use an algorithm. We can use several allocation algorithms; all algorithms are constrained in the following ways:

- Each process must be allocated at least some minimum number of frames, which is defined by the computer architecture.
- The maximum number of frames to be allocated to the runnable processes cannot exceed the total number of free frames.

8.6.1 Allocation Algorithms

Two common algorithms used to divide free frames among competing processes are as follows:

- **Equal allocation:** This algorithm allocates available frames to processes in such a way that each runnable process gets an equal share of frames. For example, if p frames are to be distributed among q processes, then each process will get p/q frames. Though, this algorithm seems to be fair, it does not work well in all situations. For example, let us consider we have two processes P_1 and P_2 and the memory requirement of P_1 is much higher than P_2. Now, allocating equal number of frames to both P_1 and P_2 does not make any sense; it would result in wastage of frames. This is because the process P_2 might be allocated more number of frames than it actually needs.
- **Proportional allocation:** This algorithm allocates frames to each process in proportion to its total size. To understand this algorithm, let us consider F be the total number of available frames and v_i is the amount of virtual memory required by a process P_i. Therefore, the overall virtual memory, V, required by all the running process and the number of frames (n_i) that should be allocated to a process P_i can be calculated as:

$$V = \sum v_i$$

$$n_i = \frac{v_i}{V} \times F$$

> **Note:** The value of n_i should be adjusted to an integer greater than minimum number of frames and the sum of all n_i should not exceed F.

Example 8.1:

Consider a system with 2 KB frame size and 48 free frames. If there are two runnable processes P_1 and P_2 of sizes 20 KB and 160 KB, respectively, then how many frames would be allocated to each process in case of:

a) Equal allocation algorithm
b) Proportional allocation algorithm

Solution:

As frame size is 2 KB, P_1 requires 10 frames and P_2 requires 80 frames. Thus, a total of 90 frames are required to run both P_1 and P_2. As the total number of free frames is 48, then

a) According to equal allocation algorithm, both P_1 and P_2 will be allocated 24 frames each.
b) According to proportional allocation algorithm, P_1 will be allocated $5 \left(\frac{10}{90} \times 48 \right)$ frames and P_2 will be allocated $42 \left(\frac{80}{90} \times 48 \right)$ frames.

8.6.2 Global *vs* Local Allocation

The allocation of frames to processes is greatly affected by page replacement algorithm. Recall from *Section 8.5*, a page replacement algorithm is used to replace a page from the set of allocated frames, in case of page fault. The algorithm used for page replacement may belong to either of two categories, namely, global replacement and local replacement. In **global replacement algorithm**, the victim page is selected from the set of frames allocated to any of the multiple running processes. Thus, global algorithm allows a process to take frames from any other process that means the number of frames allocated to a process may change from time to time.

On the other hand, **local replacement algorithm** allows selecting the victim page from the set of frames allocated to the faulty process (that caused page fault) only. Thus, the number of frames allocated to a process does not change.

8.7 THRASHING

When a process has not been allocated as much frames as it needs to support its pages in active use, it causes a page fault. To handle this page fault, some of its page is to be replaced. But since all its pages are being actively used, the replaced page will soon be referenced again, thereby, causing another page fault. Eventually, page faults would occur very frequently, replacing pages that would soon be required to be brought back into memory. As a result, the system would be mostly busy in performing paging (page-out, page-in) rather than executing the processes. This high paging activity is known as **thrashing**. It results in poor system performance as no productive work is being performed during thrashing.

The system can detect thrashing by evaluating CPU utilization against the degree of multiprogramming. Generally, as we increase the degree of multiprogramming, the CPU utilization increases. However, this does not always hold true. To illustrate this, consider the graph shown in Figure 8.12 that depicts the behaviour of paging systems. Initially, the CPU utilization increases with increase in degree of multiprogramming. It continues to increase until it reaches maximum. Now, if the number of running processes is still increased, the CPU utilization drops sharply. To increase the CPU utilization at this point, the degree of multiprogramming must be decreased.

To understand why it happens, consider a paging system with few processes running on it; and the system uses global page replacement algorithm. The operating system continuously

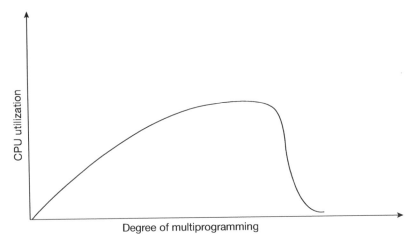

Figure 8.12: Behaviour of Paging Systems

observes the system's CPU utilization. After it observes a low CPU utilization, it attempts to improve it by increasing the degree of multiprogramming, that is, by starting new processes. Now suppose a running process requires more frames to continue its execution and thus, causes a page fault. If all in-memory pages of the faulty process are in active use, the page replacement algorithm selects the page to be replaced from the set of frames allocated to other processes. When these processes require the replaced pages, they also cause page fault, taking frames from other processes.

Thus, at a time, most processes are waiting for their pages to be brought in memory and as a result, CPU utilization drops. To increase the still-decreasing CPU utilization, the operating system again increases the degree of multiprogramming. The new processes are started by freeing frames from already running processes, thereby, resulting in more page faults. The operating system still tries to improve utilization by increasing degree of multiprogramming. Consequently, thrashing sets in the system, decreasing the CPU utilization and in turn, system throughput. Now, at this point, the system must reduce the degree of multiprogramming in order to eliminate thrashing and improve CPU utilization.

Locality

Thrashing can be prevented if each process is allocated as much memory (frames) as it requires. But now the issue arises how the operating system knows the memory requirement (number of frames required) of a process. The solution to this problem is influenced by two opposite factors: over-commitment and under-commitment of memory. If a process is allocated more number of frames (over-commitment) than it requires, less page faults would occur. The process performance would be good; however, degree of multiprogramming would be low. As a result, CPU utilization and system performance would be poor. In contrast, under-commitment of memory to a process causes high pagefault rate (as discussed earlier) which would result in poor process performance. Thus, for better system performance, it is necessary to allocate appropriate number of frames to each process.

A clue about the number of frames needed by a process can be obtained using the locality model of a process execution. The locality model states that while a process executes, it moves from locality to locality. **Locality** is defined as the set of pages that are actively used together.

Note:	Localities of a process may coincide partially or wholly.

The principle of locality ensures that not too many page faults would occur, if the pages in the current locality of a process are present in memory. However, it does not imply the absence of page faults. Once all pages in the current locality of a process are in memory, page fault would not occur until the process changes locality. On the other hand, if a process has not been allocated enough frames to accommodate its current locality, thrashing would result.

8.7.1 Working Set Model

Working set model is an approach used to prevent thrashing and is based on the assumption of locality. It uses a parameter (say, n) to define the **working set** of a process, which is the set of pages that a process has referenced in the latest n page references. The notion of working set helps the operating system to decide how many frames should be allocated to a process.

Since the locality of process changes from time to time, so as the working set. At a particular instant of time, a page in active use is included in the working set while a page that was referenced before the most recent n references is not included. Note that the performance of working set strategy depends to a greater extent on the value of n. A too large value of n would result in over-commitment of memory to a process. The working set may contain those pages which are not supposed to be referenced. In contrast, a too small value of n would cause under-commitment of memory, which in turn results in high page fault rate and consequently thrashing. Thus, the value of n must be carefully chosen for the accuracy of working set strategy.

The most important property of working set is its size, as it indicates the number of frames required by a process. The knowledge of working set size of each process helps to compute the total number of frames required by all the running processes. For example, if WSS_i denotes the working set size of a process P_i at time t, then the total number of frames required (say, V) at time t can be calculated as:

$$V = \Sigma WSS_i$$

Now, thrashing can be prevented by ensuring V <= F where F denotes the total number of available frames in memory at time t.

The idea behind the working set strategy is to have the working set of processes in memory at all times in order to prevent thrashing. For this, the operating system continuously monitors the working set of each running process and allocates enough frames to accommodate its working set size. If still some frames are remaining, the operating system may decide to increase the degree of multiprogramming by starting a new process. On the other hand, if at any instant the operating system finds V > F, it selects some process and suspends its execution, thereby, decreasing the degree of multiprogramming. In totality, the degree of multiprogramming is kept as high as possible and thus, working set strategy results in optimum CPU utilization.

8.7.2 Page Fault Frequency (PFF)

PFF is another approach to prevent thrashing that takes into account the page fault rate of a process. As we know that a process with high page fault rate means there are no enough frames allocated to the process and thus, more frames should be allocated. On the other hand, low page fault rate means the process has been allocated excess number of frames and thus, some frames can be removed. The PFF approach provides an idea of when to increase or decrease the frame allocation.

Figure 8.13 depicts the desirable page fault characteristic, which is a graph of page fault rate against the number of frames allocated to the process. It is clear from the figure that the page-fault rate decreases monotonically as we increase the number of frames. To control the page fault, the PFF approach establishes an upper and lower limit on the page fault rate of the processes (see Figure 8.13). If a process during its execution crosses the upper limit, more frames are allocated to it. If there are no free frames, the operating system must select some process and suspend its execution. The freed frames are then distributed among the

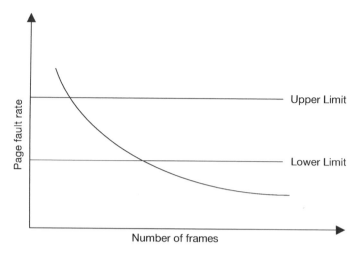

Figure 8.13: Page Fault Frequency

processes with high page fault rates. Conversely, if the page fault rate of a process goes down the lower limit, some frames are removed from it. This way the page fault rate of the processes can be controlled and as a result, thrashing can be prevented.

8.8 CASE STUDY: MEMORY MANAGEMENT IN LINUX

As we know memory management is not only concerned with the allocation of physical memory to the requesting processes but with managing virtual memory also. So, whenever we talk about memory management of any operating system, we need to consider both physical memory and virtual memory.

8.8.1 Physical Memory Management

In Linux, due to several hardware limitations, different regions of physical memory cannot be dealt in the similar manner. Thus, Linux divides the physical memory into three different zones, which are as follows:

- **ZONE_DMA:** refer to physical memory regions used for Direct Memory Access DMA purposes.
- **ZONE_NORMAL:** refer to physical memory regions used for satisfying routine memory space request. This area is mapped to the address space of CPU.
- **ZONE_HIGHMEM:** refer to physical memory regions used for pages with high-memory address. This area is not mapped into the address space of kernel.

Note: The layout of the memory zones depends upon the architecture of the system.

For each zone, the kernel maintains a separate **page allocator** to manage memory individually. In order to keep track of free pages in physical memory, the page allocator uses the **buddy algorithm**. In this algorithm, if a memory request for a small chunk cannot be fulfilled by the smallest available chunk, then the available chunk is divided into two buddies of equal size. If the resulting chunks are still too large to accommodate the request, one of them is further subdivided into two equal size buddies. This process continues until a chunk of the desired size is obtained. Note that the buddy algorithm always allocates memory in the power of 2 units. For example, a process of 5 KB will always be allocated an 8 KB block of memory.

To understand the buddy algorithm, suppose the smallest available memory block is of 32 KB and a request for 4 KB arrives. To fulfill this request, the block of 32 KB is divided into two blocks of 16 KB each. Since 16 KB is still larger, one block of 16 KB is further subdivided into two blocks of 8 KB each. This process continues until the smallest block enough to accommodate the request (in our case 4 KB) is available. This whole process is depicted in Figure 8.14.

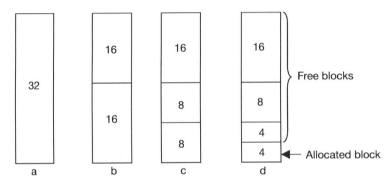

Figure 8.14: Buddy Algorithm

The allocator would then allocate one of the 4 KB blocks to the requesting process and keep the rest of the block of 4 KB, 8 KB and 16 KB on the free block list. Though this algorithm is simple, it results in internal fragmentation; each memory request is rounded up to a power of 2, which generally leads to wastage of large amount of memory.

8.8.2 Virtual Memory Management

The virtual memory is responsible for creating virtual pages and managing the transfer of those pages from disk to memory and vice versa. In Linux, virtual memory is considered from two different views, namely, logical view and physical view.

- **Logical view:** According to this view, the virtual address space of a process comprises a set of homogeneous, contiguous, page aligned areas or regions. Each area is described by `vm_area_struct` structure. Each entry in this structure lists the properties of that area, such as read/write permission.
- **Physical view:** According to this view, the virtual address space consists of a set of pages. The information related to pages is stored in a page table. Using the page table, the location of each page of virtual memory can be determined.

Creating Virtual Address Space

A new virtual address space is created by the kernel when either an entirely new code is executed by a process using the `exec()` system call or a process spawns a child process using the `fork()` system call. Whenever a process is created using `exec()` system call, a new virtual address space is assigned to that process. On the other hand, whenever a process is created using `fork()` system call, a new virtual address space is created but it is an exact replica of that of parent process. The parent's process `vm_area_struct` descriptors are copied and a new set of page tables are created for the child process. In child's page table, the page table of parent's is copied directly, thereby, allowing both parent and child process to share the same physical pages in their virtual address space.

Paging

The earlier versions of UNIX were based on swapping; when all the active processes could not be kept in memory, some of them were moved to the disk in their entirety. This implies, at a particular moment, the whole process would either be in memory or on disk. However, the modern UNIX versions are based on paging in which the transfer between memory and disk are always done in units of pages. Similar to UNIX, Linux also rely on paging.

The page replacement in Linux is performed using a variation of the clock algorithm discussed in *Section 8.5.4*. Each page is associated with `age` that indicates how frequently the page is accessed. Obviously, the pages which are accessed frequently will have higher value of `age` as compared to that of less frequently accessed pages. During each pass of clock, the `age` of a page is either increased or decreased depending on its frequency of usage. Whenever a page is to be replaced, the page replacement algorithm chooses the page with the least value of `age`.

CHECK YOUR PROGRESS

14. Name two algorithms used for allocating physical frames to processes.
15. Each process must be allocated at least some minimum number of frames, which is defined by the memory manager. (True or False)
16. What does the logical view of virtual memory in Linux describes?
17. In Linux, the page allocator uses the _____ to keep track of free pages in physical memory.

Let Us Summarize

1. Overlaying allows a process to execute irrespective of the system having insufficient physical memory. The programmer splits a program into smaller parts called overlays in such a way that no two overlays are required to be in main memory at the same time. An overlay is loaded into memory only when it is needed.
2. Virtual memory is a technique that allows a program that is partially in memory to execute. The virtual memory can be implemented by demand paging or demand segmentation.
3. In demand paging, a page is loaded into the memory only when it is needed during program execution. Pages that are never accessed are never loaded into the memory.
4. Whenever a process requests for a page and that page is not in memory then MMU raises an interrupt called page fault or a missing page interrupt.
5. A reference string is an ordered list of memory references made by a process.
6. A technique made available by virtual memory called copy-on-write makes the process creation faster and conserves memory.

7. The First-In, First-Out (FIFO) is the simplest page replacement algorithm. As the name suggests, the first page loaded into the memory is the first page is to be replaced.

8. The Optimal Page Replacement (OPT) algorithm is the best possible page replacement algorithm in which the page to be referenced in the most distant future is replaced.

9. The Least Recently Used (LRU) algorithm is an approximation to the optimal algorithm in which the page that has not been referenced for the longest time is replaced.

10. The second chance page replacement algorithm (sometimes also referred to as clock algorithm) is a refinement over FIFO algorithm which replaces the page that is both the oldest as well as unused instead of the oldest page that may be heavily used.

11. The Least Frequently Used (LFU) algorithm replaces the page that is least frequently used.

12. The Most Frequently Used (MFU) algorithm replaces the page that has just brought in and has yet to be used.

13. In multiprogramming systems where a number of processes may reside in main memory at the same time, the free frames must be divided among the competing processes. Thus, a decision is to be made on the number of frames that should be allocated to each process.

14. Two common algorithms used to divide free frames among competing processes include equal allocation and proportional allocation algorithm.

15. Equal allocation algorithm allocates available frames to processes in such a way that each runnable process gets an equal share of frames while proportional allocation algorithm allocates frames to each process in proportion to its total size.

16. A situation when the system is mostly busy in performing paging (page-out, page-in) rather than executing the processes is known as thrashing. It results in poor system performance as no productive work is being performed during thrashing.

17. A clue about the number of frames needed by a process can be obtained using the locality model of a process execution. The locality model states that while a process executes, it moves from locality to locality. Locality is defined as the set of pages that are actively used together.

18. Working set model is an approach used to prevent thrashing and is based on the assumption of locality. It uses a parameter (say, n) to define the working set of a process, which is the set of pages that a process has referenced in the latest n page references.

19. PFF is another approach to prevent thrashing that takes into account the page fault rate of a process. This approach provides an idea of when to increase or decrease the frame allocation.

20. In Linux, due to several hardware limitations, the physical memory regions cannot be dealt in the similar manner. So, Linux divides the physical memory into three different zones, which are ZONE_DMA, ZONE_NORMAL and ZONE_HIGHMEM.

21. The virtual memory is responsible for creating virtual pages and managing the transfer of those pages from disk to memory and vice versa.

ANSWERS TO 'CHECK YOUR PROGRESS'

1. The splitting of a program into smaller parts to execute a process whose size is larger than that of physical memory is called overlaying and the smaller parts are known as overlays.

2. Virtual memory

3. False

4. (b)

5. Swap space

6. Whenever a process requests for a page, the virtual address is sent to MMU. The MMU checks the valid bit in the page table entry of that page. If the valid bit is 1 (that is, the requested page

is in memory), it is accessed as in paging. Otherwise, the MMU raises an interrupt called page fault.
7. True
8. Reference string
9. The system keeps track of whether the page has been modified by adding a modified (M) bit to each page table entry. If this bit is set, that means the page has been modified.
10. (d)
11. The optimal page replacement algorithm is used as the basis for comparing performance of other algorithms.
12. False
13. Most frequently used
14. The physical frames can be allocated to processes using the equal allocation algorithm or proportional allocation algorithm.
15. False
16. According to logical view, the virtual address space of a process comprises a set of homogeneous, contiguous, page aligned areas or regions. Each area is described by `vm_area_struct` structure. Each entry in this structure lists the properties of that area like read/write permission.
17. Buddy algorithm

TEST YOURSELF

1. Explain the concept of virtual memory.
2. When does a page fault occur? Mention the steps that are taken to handle the page fault.
3. What is demand paging? List some of its advantages.
4. Discuss the hardware support for demand paging.
5. Copy-on-write technique makes the creation of process faster and conserves memory. Explain.
6. What is Belady's anomaly? Does LRU replacement algorithm suffer from this anomaly? Justify your answer with an example.
7. Consider the following reference string consisting of 7 pages from 0 to 6.

0	1	2	3	1	0	4	5	1	0	1	2	6	5	2	1	0	1

Determine how many page faults would occur in case of the following algorithms:
(a) FIFO replacement
(b) Optimal replacement
(c) LRU replacement assuming one, two, three and four frames.
8. Consider Figure 8.11 (b) and suppose that R bits for the pages are 111001. Which page will be replaced using second chance replacement algorithm?
9. What will be the effect of setting the value of parameter n (in working set model) either too low or too high on the page fault rate?
10. What is thrashing? Explain the approaches that can be used to prevent thrashing.
11. Suppose we have a block of 512 KB available in physical memory. How would the buddy system of Linux serve the following memory requests coming in the shown order?
(a) 120 KB
(b) 60 KB
(c) 30 KB
(d) 80 KB
Illustrate the memory allocations diagrammatically.

Chapter 09

File System Interface

Learning Objectives

After reading this chapter, you will be able to:

- ☐ Understand the concept of file
- ☐ Discuss the aspects related to file system
- ☐ Explain different file access methods
- ☐ Discuss various types of directory structures
- ☐ Explain file system mounting and unmounting
- ☐ Explore the protection mechanism

9.1 INTRODUCTION

Computer applications require large amount of data to be stored, so that it can be used as and when required. For this, secondary storage devices, such as floppy disk, magnetic disk, magnetic tape and hard disk, are used. The storage of data on the secondary storage devices makes the data persistent, that is, the data is permanently stored and can survive system failures and reboots. In addition, a user can access the data on these devices as per his requirement.

To store and retrieve files on the disk, the operating system provides a mechanism called the **file system**. The file system is a part of the operating system that is primarily responsible for the management and organization of various files in a system. In this chapter, we will discuss various aspects related to the file system.

9.2 FILE CONCEPT

As stated earlier, a system stores data on various storage devices. The operating system, however, for the convenience of use of data on these devices provides a uniform logical view of the data storage to the users. The operating system abstracts from the physical properties of its storage devices and defines a logical storage unit known as a **file**. This allows user to directly access the data (on physical devices) without knowing where the data is actually stored.

A file is a collection of related data stored as a named unit on the secondary storage. It can store different types of data, such as text, graphic, database, executable code, sound, videos, etc., and on the basis of the data stored, a file can be categorized as a data file, graphic file, database file, executable file, sound file, video file, etc.

Moreover, the structure of a file is based on the type of the file. For example, a graphic file is an organized collection of pixels, a database file is a collection of tables and records, and a batch file is a collection of commands.

> **Note:** From users' view, it is not possible to write data directly to storage device until it is within a file.

9.2.1 File Attributes

A file in a system is identified by its name. The file name helps a user to locate a specific file in the system. Different operating systems follow different file naming conventions. However, most operating systems accept a file name as a string of characters or numbers or some special symbols as well. For instance, names, such as `alice`, `tom`, `3546`, `!hello` and `table2-1`, are all valid file names. Note that some operating systems distinguish the uppercase and lowercase characters in the file names. For instance, in UNIX the file names `Alice`, `alice`, `ALICE` refer to three different files, whereas, in DOS and Windows they refer to the same file.

Apart from the file name, some additional information (also known as **file attributes**) is also associated with each file. This information helps the file system to manage a file within the system. The file attributes related to a file may vary in different operating systems. Some of the common file attributes are as follows:

- **Name:** Helps to identify and locate a file in a system.
- **Size:** Stores information about the current size of the file (in bytes, words or blocks).
- **Type:** Helps the operating system to recognize and use the recommended program to open a particular file type. For instance, to open an `mpeg` (multimedia) file, operating system uses a media player.
- **Identifier:** A unique tag, usually a number that helps the file system to recognize the file within the file system.

- **Location:** A pointer that points to the device and to the location of the file on that device.
- **Date and Time:** Stores information related to a file, such as creation, last modification and last use. Such information may be useful in case of protection, security and monitoring, etc.
- **Protection:** Stores information about the access permissions (read, write, execute) for different users. For example, it may specify who can access the file and which operations can be performed on a file by a user.

Figure 9.1 shows the list of some attributes that MS-DOS attach to a file.

Date	Time	Size	Name and Type
01/30/2009	03:33 PM	323	EXC.CPP
12/18/2008	01:40 PM	22,058,104	antivir_workstation_winu_en_h.exe
02/03/2009	01:21 PM	3	src.txt

Figure 9.1: File Attributes of MS-DOS

The information related to a file is stored as a directory entry in the directory structure. The directory entry includes the file's name and the unique identifier. The identifier in turn locates the other file attributes (discussed in detail in *chapter 10*).

9.2.2 File Operations

File operations are the functions that can be performed on a file. Operating system handles the file operations through the use of system calls. The various operations that can be performed on a file are create, write, read, seek, delete, open, append, rename and close a file.

- **Create a file:** To bring a file into existence, the `create` system call is used. When this system call is used, the operating system searches for the free space in the file system and allocates it to the file. In addition, the operating system makes a directory entry to record the name, location and other information about the file.
- **Open file:** To open a file, the `open` system call is used which accepts the file name and the access mode (read, write, execute) as parameters and returns a pointer to the entry in the **open file table** (a table in the main memory that stores information about the files that are opened at a particular time). The operating system searches the directory entry table for the file name and checks if the access permission in directory entry matches the request. If that access mode is allowed, it then copies the directory entry of the file to the open file table.
- **Write to a file:** To store data into a file, the `write` system call is used which accepts the file name and the data to be written to the file as parameters. The operating system searches the directory entry to locate the file and writes data to the specified position in the file and also updates the `write` pointer to the location the where next `write` operation is to take place.
- **Read a file:** To retrieve data from a file, the `read` system call is used which accepts the file name, amount of data to be read and a `read` pointer to point to the position from where the data is to be read as parameters. The operating system searches the specified

file using the directory entry, performs the read operation and updates the pointer to the new location. Note that since a process may be only reading or writing a file at a time, a single pointer called **current position pointer** can be used for both reading and writing. Every time a read or write operation is performed, this pointer must be updated.

- **Seek file:** To position the pointer to a specific position in a file, the `seek` system call is used. Once the pointer is positioned, data can be read from and written to that position.
- **Close file:** When all the operations on a file are completed, it must be closed using the `close` system call. The operating system searches and erases the file entry from the open file table to make the space for new file entries. Some systems automatically close a file when the process, that has opened the file, terminates.
- **Delete file:** When a file is not required, the `delete` system call is used. The operating system searches the file name in the directory listing. Having found the associated entry, it releases all space allocated to the file (that can be reused by other files) by erasing its corresponding directory entry.
- **Append file:** To add data at the end of an existing file, `append` system call is used. This system call works similar to the `write` system call, except that it positions the pointer to the end of file and then performs the write operation.
- **Rename file:** To change the name of an existing file, `rename` system call is used. This system call changes the existing entry for the file name in the directory to a new file name.

9.2.3 File Types

As stated earlier, files can be of different types. The operating system can handle a file in a reasonable way only if it recognizes and supports that file type. A user request to open an executable file with a text editor will produce garbage if the operating system has not been told that it is an executable file.

The most common technique to implement a file type is by providing extension to a file. The file name is divided into two parts, with the two parts separated by a period ('.') symbol, where the first part is the name and the second part after the period is the **file extension**. A file extension is generally one to three characters long. It indicates the type of the file and the operations (read, write, execute) that can be performed on that file. For example, in the file name `Itlesl.doc`, `Itlesl` is the name and `.doc` is the file extension. The extension `.doc` indicates that `Itlesl.doc` is a document file and should be opened with an editor. Similarly, a file with `.exe` or `.com` extension is an executable file. Table 9.1 lists various file types, extension and their meaning.

Table 9.1: File Types and Extensions

File Type	Extension	Meaning
Archive	arc, zip, tar	related files compressed and grouped together into single file for storage
Batch	bat, sh	an executable file stores a series of commands that can be executed with a single command

Backup file	bak, bkf	stores a copy of the data on the disk, used for recovering system crash
Executable	exe, com, bin	used to run various programs on a computer
Library	lib, a, so, dll,	stores libraries of routines for programmers
Image	bmp, jpeg, gif, jfif, dib	stores images and graphics
Multimedia	mpeg, mp2, mpa, mpe	stores audio and video information
Object	obj, o	machine language file, precompiled, used for generating output
System file	inf, ini, drv	stores system information for loading and managing different applications
Text	txt, doc	stores textual data, documents
Word processor	wp, txt, rrf, doc	stores various word processor formats

File extensions helps the operating system to know about the application program that has created the file. For instance, the file with .txt extension will be opened with a text editor and the file with .mp3 extension will be opened with a music player supporting the .mp3 files. Note that the operating system automatically opens the application program (for the known file types) whenever a user double clicks the file icon.

Some operating systems, such as UNIX, support the use of double extension to a file name. For example, the file name file1.c.z is a valid file name, where .c reveals that file1 is a C language file and .z reveals that the file is compressed using some zip program. A file extension can be system defined or user defined.

Another way to implement the file type is the use of **magic number**. A magic number is a sequence of bits, placed at the starting of a file to indicate roughly the type of file. The UNIX system makes use of magic number to recognize the file type. However, not all its files have magic numbers. To help its user to determine the type of contents of the file, it allows file-name-extension hints.

9.2.4 File Structure

The file structure refers to the internal structure of the file, that is, how a file is internally stored in the system. The most common file structures recognized and enforced by different operating systems are as follows:

● **Byte sequence:** In this file structure, each file is made up of sequence of 8-bit bytes (see Figure 9.2(a)) having no fixed structure. The operating system does not attach any meaning to the file. It is the responsibility of the application program to include code to interpret the input file into an appropriate structure. This type of file structure provides flexibility to the user programs as they can store any type of data in the files and name these files in any way as per their convenience. UNIX operating systems support this type of file structure.

● **Record sequence:** In this file structure, a file consists of a sequence of fixed length records where, arbitrary number of records can be read from or written to a file. The records cannot be inserted or deleted in the middle of a file. In this system, the read operation returns one record and the write operation appends or overwrites one record. CP/M (Control Program for Microcomputers) operating system supports this type of scheme.

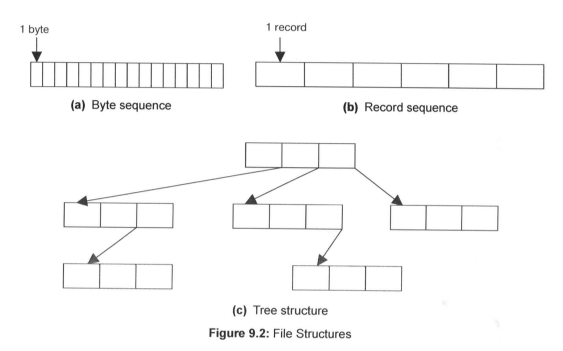

(a) Byte sequence

(b) Record sequence

(c) Tree structure

Figure 9.2: File Structures

● **Tree structure:** In this file structure, a file consists of a tree of disk blocks where, each block holds a number of records of varied lengths. Each record contains a key field at a fixed position. The records are searched on key value and new records can be inserted anywhere in the file structure. This type of file structure is used on mainframe system where, it is called **ISAM (Indexed Sequential Access Method)**.

Regardless of the file structure used, all disk I/O take place in terms of blocks (physical records), where all blocks are of equal size and the size of a block is generally determined by the size of the sector. Since the disk space to a file is allocated in number of blocks, some portion of the last block in a file is generally wasted. For instance, if each block is of 512 bytes, then a file of 3150 bytes would be allocated seven blocks and the last 434 bytes will be wasted. The wastage of bytes to keep everything in units of blocks (instead of bytes) is internal fragmentation. Note that all file systems face internal fragmentation and with larger block sizes, there is more internal fragmentation.

9.3 ACCESS METHODS

The information stored in the file can be accessed in one of the two ways: sequential access or direct access.

9.3.1 Sequential Access

When the information in the file is accessed in order, one record after the other, it is called **sequential access**. It is the easiest file access method. Compilers, multimedia applications, sound files and editors are the most common examples of the programs using sequential access.

The most frequent and common operations performed on a file are read and write operations. In case of read operation, the record at the location pointed by the file pointer is read and the file pointer is then advanced to the next record. Similarly, in case of write operation, the record is written to the end of the file and pointer is advanced to the end of new record.

9.3.2 Direct Access

With the advent of disks as a storage media, large amount of data can be stored on it. Sequential access of this data would be very lengthy and slow process. To overcome this problem, the data on the disk is stored as blocks of data with index numbers which helps to read and write data on the disk in any order (known as **random** or **direct access**).

Under direct access, a file is viewed as a sequence of blocks (or records) which are numbered. The records of a file can be read or written in any order using this number. For instance, it is possible to read block 20, then write block 4 and then read block 13. The block number is a number given by the user. This number is relative to the beginning of the file. This relative number internally has an actual absolute disk address. For example, the record number 10 can have the actual address 12546 and block number 11 can have the actual address 3450. The relative address is internally mapped to the absolute disk address by the file system. The user gives relative block number for accessing the data without knowing the actual disk address. Depending on the system, this relative number starts with either 0 or 1 for a file.

In direct access, the system calls for read and write operations are modified to include the block number as a parameter. For instance, to perform the read or write operation on a file, user gives `read n` or `write n` (n is the block number) rather than `read next` or `write next` system calls used in sequential access.

Most applications with large databases require direct access method for immediate access to large amounts of information. For example, in a railway reservation system, if a customer requests to check the status for reservation of the ticket, the system must be able to access the record of that customer directly without having the need to access all other customers' records.

Note that an operating system may support either sequential access or direct access or both for accessing the files. Some systems require a file to be defined as sequential or direct when it is created, so that it can be accessed in the way it is declared.

9.4 DIRECTORY STRUCTURE

As stated earlier, a computer stores numerous data on disk. To manage this data, the disk is divided into one or more partitions (also known as **volumes**) and each partition contains information about the files stored in it. This information is stored in a **directory** (also known as **device directory**). Figure 9.3 shows different file system organization.

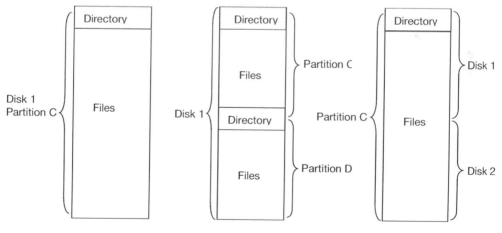

(a) Single disk single partition   (b) Single disk multi partition   (c) Multi disk single partition

Figure 9.3: Various File System Organization Schemes

Note: It is possible to have more than one operating system on a single disk, where a user can boot any of the operating system according to the need.

Different operations that can be performed on a directory are as follows:

- **Create a file:** New files can be created and added to a directory by adding a directory entry in it.
- **Search a file:** Whenever a file is required to be searched, its corresponding entry is searched in the directory.
- **List a directory:** All the files along with their contents in the directory entry are listed.
- **Rename a file:** A file can be renamed. A user might need to rename the file with the change in its content. When a file is renamed its position within the directory may also change.
- **Delete a file:** When a file is no longer required, it can be deleted from the directory.
- **Traverse the file system:** Every directory and every file within a directory structure can be accessed.

Note: A directory is a flat file that stores information about files and subdirectories.

There are various schemes to define the structure of a directory. The most commonly used schemes are as follows:

- Single-level directory
- Two-level directory
- Hierarchical directory

All these schemes are discussed in subsequent sections.

9.4.1 Single-Level Directory

Single-level directory is the simplest directory structure. There is only one directory that holds all the files. Sometimes this directory is referred to as **root directory**. Figure 9.4 shows a single-level directory structure having five files. In this figure, box represents directory and circles represent files.

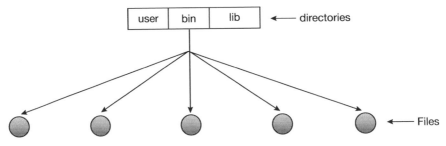

Figure 9.4: Single-level Directory Structure

The main drawback of this system is that no two files can have the same name. For instance, if one user (say, `jojo`) creates a file with name `file1` and then another user (say, `abc`) also creates a file with the same name, the file created by the user `abc` will overwrite the file created by the user `jojo`. Thus, all the files must have unique names in a single-level directory structure. With the increase in number of files and users on a system, it becomes very difficult to have unique names for all the files. This problem can be resolved by introduction of two-level directory.

9.4.2 Two-Level Directory

In a two-level directory structure, a separate directory known as **User File Directory (UFD)** is created for each user. Whenever a new UFD is created, an entry is added to the **Master File Directory (MFD)** which is at the highest level in this structure (see Figure 9.5). When a user refers to a particular file, first, the MFD is searched for the UFD entry of that user and then the file is searched in the UFD.

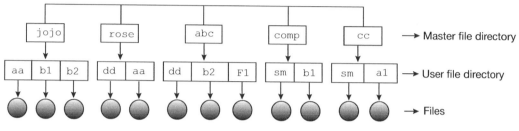

Figure 9.5: Two-Level Directory Structure

Unlike, single-level directory structure, only the file names in a directory should be unique. That is, there may be files with same name in different directories. Thus, there will not be the problem of name collision in this directory structure but the disadvantage is that the users in this directory structure are not allowed to access files of other users. If a user wants to access a file of other user, he needs special permissions from the administrator. In addition, to access other user's file, the user must know the **path name** (that includes the user name and the file name). Note that different systems use different syntax for file naming in directories. For instance, in MS-DOS, to access the file in the sm directory, the user gives //comp/sm, where // refers to root, comp is the user name, sm is the directory.

In some situations, a user might need to access files other than their own file. One such situation might occur with system files. The user might want to use system programs, such as compilers, assembler, loaders or other utility programs. In such a case, to copy all the files in every user directory would require a lot of space and thus, would not be feasible. One possible solution to this is to make a special user directory and copy system files into it. Now, whenever a filename is given, it is first search in the local UFD and if not found then the file is searched in the special user directory that contains system files.

9.4.3 Hierarchical Directory

The hierarchical directory, also known as **tree of directory** or **tree-structured directory**, allows users to have subdirectories under their directories, thus making the file system more logical and organized for the user. For instance, a user may have directory furniture, which stores files related to types of furniture, say wooden, steel, cane, etc. Further, he wants to define a subdirectory which states the kind of furniture available under each type, say sofa, bed, table, chair, etc. Under this system, the user has the flexibility to define, group and organize directories and subdirectories according to his requirements.

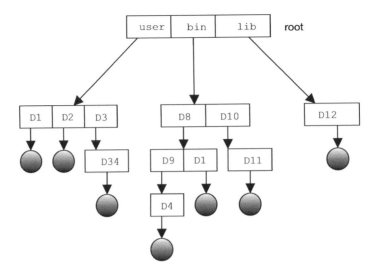

Figure 9.6: Hierarchical Directory Structure

The hierarchical directory structure has the root directory at the highest level, which is the **parent** directory for all directories and subdirectories. The root directory generally consists of system library files. All files or directories at the lower levels are called **child** directories and a directory with no files or subdirectory is called a **leaf**. Every file in the system has a unique path name. A path name is the path from the root, through all the subdirectories, to a specified file. Figure 9.6 shows the hierarchical directory structure having different level of directories, subdirectories and related files.

The user under hierarchical directory system can access files of other users in addition to his own files. To access the files the user can specify either absolute path name or relative path name. The **absolute path name** begins at the root and follows a path down to the specified file or using the **relative path name** that defines a path from the current working directory. For instance, to access a file under directory D1, using absolute path name, the user will give the path \\bin\D8\D1\filename. On the other hand, if the user's current working directory is \\bin\D8, the relative path name will be D1\filename.

In this structure, the major concern is the deletion of the files. If a directory is empty it can simply be deleted, however, if the directory contains subdirectories and files, they need to be handled first. Some systems, for example, MS-DOS requires a directory to be completely empty before a delete operation can be performed on it. The user needs to delete all the files, subdirectories, files in subdirectories before performing the delete operation on a directory. Whereas, some systems, for example, UNIX is flexible as it allows user to delete a complete directory structure containing files and subdirectory with a single rm command. Though it is easy for a user to handle delete operation on directory under the UNIX system, but it increases the chances of accidental deletion of files.

Note: MS-DOS, Windows and UNIX are some of the examples of systems using hierarchical directory structure.

9.5 FILE SYSTEM MOUNTING

A disk is partitioned into many logical disks (partitions) and on each partition, there exists a file system. To access files of a file system, it is required to mount the file system. Mounting a file system means attaching the file system to the directory structure of the system.

To implement mounting, it is required to specify the root of the file system to be mounted and the mount point to the operating system. Mount point specifies the location within the file structure at which the file system is to be attached. Typically, mount points are empty files in the file system hierarchy which are meant for mounting purpose only. The mount operation is carried out on the file system by command mount file system name (`<Filesystem_name>`), `<mount_point_name>`). Once the file system is mounted, a file (say, `myfile`) with its relative directory (say, `mypath`) in directory `Filesystem_name` can be accessed using the pathname `<mount_point_name>/mypath/myfile`.

To understand the file system mounting, let us consider the file system shown in Figure 9.7. Here, Figure 9.7(a) shows the file system before mounting and Figure 9.7(b) shows the file system after the mount operation `mount(department, company/manager)` has been performed. Now, the `employee` file can be accessed through the pathname `company/manager/marketing/employee`.

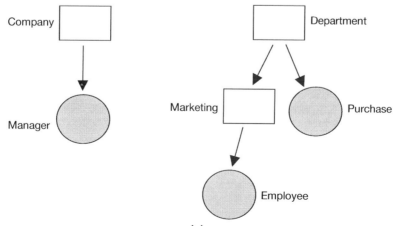

(a)

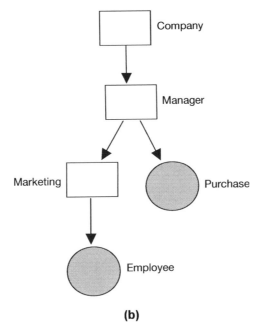

(b)

Figure 9.7: Mounting of a File System

The affect of mounting lasts until the file system is unmounted. Unmounting a file system means detaching a file system from the system's directory structure. The unmount operation is carried out by command unmount(<filesystem_name>, <mount_point_name>). For example, if the unmount operation unmount(department, company/manager) is performed on the file system shown in Figure 9.7(b), the file system will be restored to the file system shown in Figure 9.7(a). Note that the files of the mounted file system must be closed in order to carry out the unmount operation successfully.

Note: A file system is unmounted automatically whenever a system is rebooted.

9.6 PROTECTION

The information stored in a system requires to be protected from the physical damage and unauthorized access. A file system can be damaged due to various reasons, such as a system breakdown, theft, fire, lightning or any other extreme condition that is unavoidable and uncertain. It is very difficult to restore the data back in such conditions. In some cases, when the physical damage is irreversible, the data can be lost permanently. Though, physical damage to a system is unavoidable, measures can be taken to safeguard and protect the data.

In a single-user system, protection can be provided by storing a copy of information on the disk to the disk itself or to some other removable storage media, such as magnetic tapes and compact disc. If the original data on the disk is accidentally erased or overwritten or becomes inaccessible because of its malfunctioning, the backup copy can be used to restore the lost or damaged data. Apart, from protecting the files from physical damage, the files in a system also needs a protection mechanism to control improper access.

9.6.1 Types of Access

In a single-user system or in a system where users are not allowed to access the files of other users, there is no need for a protection mechanism. However, in a multi-user system where one user can access files of other users and the system is prone to improper access, a protection mechanism is required. The access rights define the type of operation that a user is allowed to perform on a file. The different access rights that can be assigned to a particular user for a particular a file are as follows:

- **Read:** Allows reading from the file.
- **Write:** Allows writing or rewriting the file.
- **Execute:** Allows running the program or application.
- **Append:** Allows writing new information at the end of the file.
- **Copy**: Allows creating a new copy of the file.
- **Rename:** Allows renaming a file.
- **Edit:** Allows adding and deleting information from the file.
- **Delete:** Allows deleting the file and releasing the space.

There are many protection mechanisms, each having some advantages and disadvantages. However, the kind of protection mechanism used depends on the need and size of the organization. A smaller organization needs a different protection mechanism while a larger organization with large number of people accessing the files needs a different protection mechanism.

9.6.2 Access Control

To protect the files from improper access, the access control mechanism can follow either of the two approaches.

- **Password:** A password can be assigned to each file and only a user knowing the password can access the file. This scheme protects the file from unauthorized access. The main drawback of this approach is the large number of passwords which are practically very difficult to remember (for each files separately). However, if only one password is used for accessing all the files, then if once the password is known, all the files become accessible. To balance the number of passwords in a system, some systems follow a scheme, where a user can associate a password with a subdirectory. This scheme allows a user to access all the files under a subdirectory with a single password. This scheme is also not very much safe. To overcome the drawbacks of these schemes, the protection must be provided at a more detailed level by using multiple passwords.
- **Access control list:** In this approach, access to a file is provided on the basis of identity of the user. An **Access Control List (ACL)** is associated with each file and directory, it stores user names and the type of access allowed to each user. When a user tries to access a file, the ACL is searched for that particular file. If that user is listed for the requested access, the access is allowed. Otherwise, the user is denied to access the file. This system of access control is effective but, in case if all users want to read a file, the ACL for this file should list all users with read permission.

The main drawback of this system is that, making such a list would be a tedious job when number of users is not known. Moreover, the list need to be dynamic in nature as the number of users will keep on changing, thus resulting in complicated space management.

To resolve the problems associated with ACL, a restricted version of the access list can be used in which the length of the access list is shortened by classifying the users of the system into the following three categories.

- **Owner:** The user who created the file.
- **Group:** A set of users who need similar access permission for sharing the file is a group, or work group.
- **Universe:** All the other users in the system form the universe.

Based on the category of a user, access permissions are assigned. The owner of the file has full access to a file and can perform all file operations (read, write and execute), whereas, a group user can read and write a file but cannot execute or delete a file. However, the member of the universe group can only read a file and are not allowed to perform any other operations on a file.

The above method of classifying users in groups will not work, when one user wants to access file of other user (for performing a specific file operation). For example, say, a user comp wants to access the file abc of other user comp1, for reading its content. To provide file-specific permissions to a user, in addition to the user groups, an access control list is attached to a file. This list stores the user names and permissions in a specific format.

The UNIX operating system uses this method of access control, where the users are divided into three groups and access permissions for each file is set with the help of three fields. Each field is a collection of bits where, three bits are used for setting protection information and an additional bit is kept for a file owner, for the file's group and for all other users. The bits are set as -rwx where r controls read access, w controls write access and x controls execution. When all three bits are set to -rwx, it means a user has full permission on a file, whereas, if only -r-- field is set, it means a user can only read from a file and when -rw- bits are set, it means user can read and write but cannot execute a file. The scheme requires total nine bits, to store the protection information. The permissions for a file can be set either by an administrator or a file owner.

CHECK YOUR PROGRESS

10. What do you mean by file system mounting? Why it is required?
11. The information in a computer needs to be protected from _____ and _____.
12. Which of these results in permanent information loss?
    (a) Unauthorized access   (b) Theft
    (c) Fire   (d) Illegal shut down
13. What is the use of an access control list?
14. In a single-user system, there is no need for a protection mechanism. (True or False)

Let Us Summarize

1. Computer applications require large amount of data to be stored, so that it can be used as and when required.
2. The storage of data on the secondary storage devices makes the data persistent that is, the data is permanently stored and can survive system failures and reboots.
3. To store and retrieve files on the disk, the operating system provides a mechanism called the file system.
4. The file system is primarily responsible for the management and organization of various files in a system.
5. A file is a collection of related data stored as a named unit on the secondary storage.
6. The additional information known as file attributes are associated with each file. This information helps the file system to manage a file within the system.
7. The common file attributes are name, size, type, identifier, location, date and time, and protection.
8. File operations are the functions that can be performed on a file. Operating system handles the file operations through the use of system calls.
9. The various operations that can be performed on a file are create, write, read, seek, delete, open, append, rename and close.
10. The most common technique to implement a file type is by providing extension to a file. The file name is divided into two parts, with the two parts separated by a period ('.') symbol, where the first part is the name and the second part after the period is the file extension.
11. Another way to implement the file type is the use of magic number. A magic number is a sequence of bits, placed at the starting of a file to indicate roughly the type of file.
12. The file structure refers to the internal structure of the file, that is, how a file is internally stored in the system.
13. The most common file structures recognized and enforced by different operating systems are byte sequence, record sequence and tree structure.
14. Regardless of the file structure used, all disk I/O takes place in terms of blocks (physical records).
15. The information stored in the file can be accessed in one of the two ways: sequential access or direct access.
16. When the information in the file is accessed in order, one record after the other, it is called sequential access.
17. When a file is viewed as a sequence of blocks (or records) which are numbered and can be read or written in any order using this number, it is called direct access.
18. The various schemes to define the structure of a directory are, single-level directory, two-level directory and hierarchical directory.
19. Mounting a file system means attaching the file system to the directory structure of the system. The affect of mounting lasts until the file system is unmounted. Unmounting a file system means detaching a file system from the system's directory structure.
20. The information stored in a system requires to be protected from the physical damage and unauthorized access.
21. To protect the files from improper access, the access control mechanism can make use of passwords and Access Control List (ACL).

ANSWERS TO 'CHECK YOUR PROGRESS'

1. True
2. File attributes
3. False
4. UNIX
5. (b)
6. (a) and (c)
7. Index number
8. True
9. Absolute path name begins at the root and follow a path down to the specified file, whereas, the relative path name defines a path from the current working directory.
10. Mounting a file system means attaching the file system to the directory structure of the system. It is required because the files of a file system cannot be accessed until the file system is mounted.
11. Unauthorized access, physical damage
12. (b) and (c)
13. An access control list stores the user names and the type of access allowed to each user. When a user tries to access a file, the ACL is searched for that particular file. If that user is listed for the requested access, the access is allowed. Otherwise, the user is denied access to the file.
14. True

TEST YOURSELF

1. Explain the need of storing data on secondary storage devices?
2. Define the role of file system in organizing and managing different files in a system?
3. 'The operating system gives a logical view of the data to its user.' Justify this statement?
4. When a user double clicks on a file listed in Windows Explorer, a program is run and gives that file as parameter. List two different ways the operating system could know which program to run?
5. Some systems simply associate a stream of bytes as a structure for a file's data, while others associate many types of structure for a file's data. What are the related advantages and disadvantages of each system?
6. Explain with example why some systems face more internal fragmentation as compared to others?
7. A program has just read the seventh record; it next wants to read the fifteenth record. How many records must the program read to input the fifteenth record?
   (a) With direct access
   (b) With sequential access
8. Give an example of an application in which data in a file is accessed in the following order:
   (a) Sequentially
   (b) Randomly
9. What do you mean by file system mounting? How it is performed?
10. Explain the relative merits and demerits of using hierarchical directory structure over single-level and two-level directory structures?
11. Define the following terms
    (a) Path name
    (b) Magic number

Chapter 10

File System Implementation

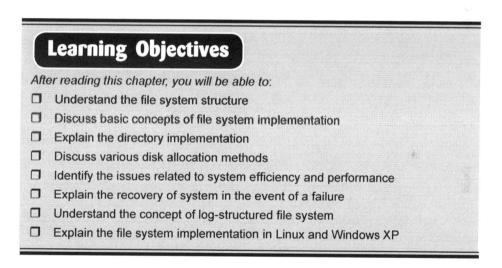

Learning Objectives

After reading this chapter, you will be able to:

☐ Understand the file system structure
☐ Discuss basic concepts of file system implementation
☐ Explain the directory implementation
☐ Discuss various disk allocation methods
☐ Identify the issues related to system efficiency and performance
☐ Explain the recovery of system in the event of a failure
☐ Understand the concept of log-structured file system
☐ Explain the file system implementation in Linux and Windows XP

10.1 INTRODUCTION

In the previous chapter, we have discussed the basic file concepts, such as how files are named, what operations are allowed on files, what the directory tree looks like and the other similar issues which help users to understand the file system. In this chapter, we discuss various issues related to file system implementation in which the file system designers are interested. This involves how files and directories are implemented and stored, how the available disk space is managed, and how file system can be made efficient and reliable.

10.2 FILE SYSTEM STRUCTURE

Every operating system imposes a file system that helps to organize, manage and retrieve data on the disk. The file system resides permanently on the disk. The design of the file system involves two key issues. The first issue includes defining a file and its attributes, operations that can be performed on a file, and the directory structure. The second issue includes creating data structures and algorithms for mapping the logical file system onto the secondary storage devices.

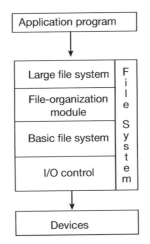

Figure 10.1: File System Layers

Figure 10.1 shows that the file system is made up of different layers, where each layer represents a level. Each level uses the features of the lower levels to create new features that are used by higher levels. When the user interacts with the file system (through system commands), the I/O request occurs on a device. The device driver in turn generates an interrupt to transfer information between the disk drive and the main memory. Input to device driver consists of high-level commands and its output is low-level hardware specific instructions. The device driver also writes specific bit pattern to special locations in the I/O controller's memory which tell the controller on which device location to act and what actions to take.

The next component in the file system is the **basic file system** that issues generic (general) commands to the appropriate device driver to read and write physical blocks on the disk. The physical blocks are referred by the numeric disk address (for example, drive 1, cylinder 43, track 4, sector 16).

The component at the next level of the file system is the **file-organization module** that organizes the files. It knows the physical block address (the actual address) and logical block address (the relative address), allocation method, and location of a file. Using this information, it translates the logical address into physical address and helps basic file system to transfer files. The other function of the file-organization module is to keep track of the free space and provide this space for allocation when needed.

The **logical file system** at the next level manages all the information about a file except the actual data (content of the file). It manages the directory structure to provide the necessary information to the file-organization module when the file name is given. It maintains file structure using the **File Control Block (FCB)** that stores information about a file, such as ownership, permissions and location of the file content. Protection and security is also taken care by the logical file system.

Apart from the physical disk drive, there are other removable devices, such as CD-ROM, floppy disk, pen drives and other storage devices attached to a system. Each of these devices has a standard file system structure imposed by its manufactures. For instance, most CD-ROMs are written in High Sierra Format (HSF), which is a standard format agreed upon by CD-ROM manufacturers. The standard file system for the removable media makes them interoperable and portable for use on different systems. Apart from the file systems for removable devices each operating system has one (or more) disk based file system. UNIX system uses the UNIX File System (UFS) as a base. Windows NT supports disk file system formats such as FAT, FAT32 and NTFS (or Windows NT File System), along with CD-ROM, DVD and floppy disk file system formats.

10.2.1 File System Implementation

There are several **on-disk** and **in-memory** structures that are used to implement a file system. Depending on the operating system and the file system, these may vary, but the general principles remain same. Many of the structures that are used by most of the operating system are discussed here. The on-disk structures include:

- **Boot control block:** It contains enough information that the system needs to boot the operating system from that partition. Though, not all the partitions in a disk contain a bootable operating system, every partition starts with a boot block. Having one block in each partition reserved for a boot block is a good idea because any partition can have operating system in the future. If the partition does not contain any operating system this block can be empty. In Unix File System (UFS), this block is called the **boot block** and in Windows (NTFS), it is called the **partition boot sector**.
- **Partition control block:** It is a table that stores key information related to partition, number and size of blocks in the partition, free block count and free block pointers, and FCB pointers and free FCB count. In UFS this is called **superblock**, in NTFS, it is **Master File Table**.

Further, each partition has a directory structure, with root directory at the top. The directory structure helps to manage and organize the files in the file system. On creation of a new file, a new FCB is allocated that stores information, such as file permissions, ownership, size and location of the data blocks. In UFS this is called the **i-node** (an

| Boot block | Super block | Free space management | i-nodes | Root directory | Files and Directories |

Figure 10.2: Structure of a partition

array of data structures, one for each file). In NTFS, this information is kept within the Master File Table, which uses a relational database structure, where each row stores information about a file. Figure 10.2 shows the structure of a partition on UNIX file system.

The in-memory structure helps in improving performance of the file system. The in-memory structures include:

- **In-memory partition table:** It stores information about each mounted partition.
- **In-memory directory structure:** It stores the information about the recently accessed directories.
- **System-wide open-file table:** It contains a copy of the FCB of each open file and a count of the number of processes that have the file open.
- **Per-process open-file table:** It contains a pointer to the corresponding entry in the system-wide open-file table along with some related information.

When the `open` call passes a file name to the file system, the directory structure is searched for the given file name. When the file is found, its FCB is copied into the system-wide open-file table and the count is incremented.

After updating the system-wide open-file table, an entry is made in the per-process open-file table. This entry includes a pointer to the appropriate entry in the system-wide open-file table, a pointer to the position in the file where the next read or write will occur and the mode in which the file is open. The `open` call returns a pointer to the appropriate entry in the per-process file system table. This pointer is used to perform all the operations as long as the file is open. It means that until a file is closed, all the operations are carried out on the open-file table.

When a process closes the file, the corresponding entry from the per-process open-file table is removed and the system-wide entry's open `count` is decremented. The value in the `count` indicates the number of users who have opened the file currently. Thus, when this value becomes 0, the updated file information is copied back to the disk based structures and the entry is removed from the system-wide open-file table.

CHECK YOUR PROGRESS

1. Name the component of the file system that is responsible for transfer of information between the disk drive and the main memory.
2. Which of these are component of a file system?
   - (a) Logical file system
   - (b) Basic file system
   - (c) File-organization module
   - (d) All of these
3. The user interacts with the system by using the system calls. (True/False)
4. A _____ stores all the information related to a file.

10.3 DIRECTORY IMPLEMENTATION

The efficiency, performance and reliability of a file system are directly related to the directory-management and directory-allocation algorithms selected for a file system. The most commonly used directory-management algorithms are linear list and hash table.

10.3.1 Linear List

The linear list method organizes a directory as a collection of fixed size entries, where each entry contains a (fixed length) file name, a fixed structure to store the file attributes and pointers to the data blocks (see Figure 10.3). The linear list method stores all attributes of a file at one place as a single directory entry and uses a linear search for searching a directory entry from the list of entries. It means to search or find out an entry in the list of entries, each entry (starting from the first entry in the directory) is examined one by one until the desired entry is found. This is simple to program, however, with extremely large directories the search becomes very slow, which is a major disadvantage of this method. MS-DOS and Windows operating system use this approach for implementing directories.

Directory

Itlesl	attributes
Language	attributes
Magazine	attributes
Sports	attributes
Computer	attributes

Figure 10.3: An Example of Linear List Directory Entry (in MS-DOS and Windows)

Some systems follow a variation of linear list method for recording the file information. For example, in UNIX, the directory entry consists of two fields: the file name and the i-node (Index-Node) number. The **i-node number** contains the disk address of the i-node structure that stores the file attributes and the address of the file's data blocks (see Figure 10.4). With this approach, the size of the directory entry is very small and the approach has certain advantages over the linear list of directory.

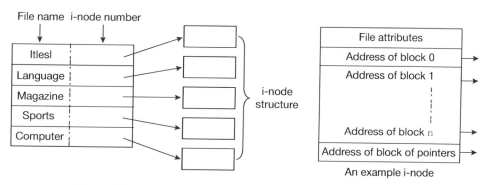

Figure 10.4: An Example of Linear List Directory Entry (in UNIX)

In both cases, when the user sends a request to create a new file, the directory is searched to check whether any other file has the same name or not. If no other file has the same name, the memory will be allocated and an entry for the same would be added at the end of the directory. To delete a file, the directory is searched for the file name and if the file is found, the space allocated to it is released. The delete operation results in free space that can be reused. To reuse this space, it can be marked with a used-unused bit, a special name can be assigned to it, such as all-zeros or it can be linked to a list of free directory entries.

When performing the file operations, one thing is common, that is, searching the directory for a particular file. The search technique applied, greatly influences the time taken to make the search, and in turn the performance and efficiency of the file system. As discussed, with long directories, a linear search becomes very slow and takes O(n) comparisons to locate a given entry, where n is the number of all entries in a directory. To decrease the search time, the list can be sorted and a binary search can be applied. Applying binary search reduces the average search time but keeping the list sorted is a bit difficult and time consuming, as directory entries have to be moved with every creation and deletion of file.

10.3.2 Hash Table

A major concern while implementing directories is the search time required to locate a directory entry corresponding to a file. To considerably reduce the search time, a more complex data structure known as a hash table along with the linear list of directory entry is used.

A hash table is a data structure, with 0 to n-1 table entries, where n is the total number of entries in the table (see Figure 10.5). It uses a hash function to compute a hash value (a number between 0 to n-1) based on the file name. For instance, file name is converted into integers from 0 to n-1 and this number is divided by n to get the remainder. Then, the table entry corresponding to the hash value (value of remainder) is checked. If the entry space is unused, then a pointer to the file entry (in the directory) is placed there. However, if the entry is already in use, we say a **collision** has occurred. In such a situation, a linked list of entries that hash to the same value is created and the table entry is made to point to the header of the linked list.

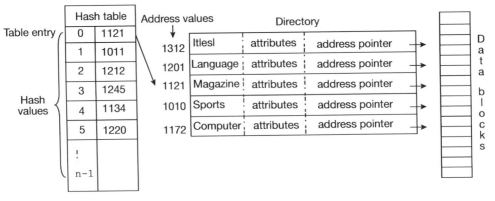

Figure 10.5: A Hash Table Linked to a Directory

To search a file, the same process is followed. The file name is hashed to locate the hash table entry and then all the entries on the chain are checked to see if the file name exists. If the name is not found in the chain, the file is not present in the directory.

The main disadvantage of this approach is the creation of long overflow chains if the hash function is not distributing the values uniformly. Now, in order to search an entry, a linear search in the long overflow chain may be required, which increases the access time. In addition, the administration of hash table becomes a complex process. Some system copies the directory entries for frequently accessed files in the cache memory. This saves the time required to reread information from the disk, thus, making the file access fast.

CHECK YOUR PROGRESS

5. The _____ and _____ are the two most commonly used directory-management algorithms.
6. Which of these statements are true in context to i-node numbers?
   (a) It stores directory information.
   (b) It is the disk address that points to an i-node structure used to store the file attributes.
   (c) MS-DOS and Windows operating system support i-node number.
   (d) All of these
7. A linear search requires $O(n)$ comparisons. (True/False)

10.4 ALLOCATION METHODS

An important function of the file system is to manage the space on the secondary storage. It includes keeping track of the number of disk blocks allocated to files and the free blocks available for allocation.

The two main issues related to disk space allocation are:

- Optimum utilization of the available disk space.
- Fast accessing of files.

The widely used methods for allocation of disk space are: contiguous, linked and indexed. For discussing these different allocation strategies, a file is considered to be a sequence of blocks and all I/O operations on a disk occurs in terms of blocks.

10.4.1 Contiguous Allocation

In contiguous allocation, each file is allocated contiguous blocks on the disk, that is, one after the other (see Figure 10.6). Assuming only one job is accessing the disk, once the first block, say b, is accessed, accessing block b+1 requires no head movement normally. Head movement is required only when the head is currently at the last sector of a cylinder and moves to the first sector of the next cylinder; the head movement is only one track. Therefore, number of seeks and thus, seek time in accessing contiguously allocated files is minimal. This improves the overall file system performance.

It is relatively simple to implement the file system using contiguous allocation method. The directory entry for each file contains the file name, the disk address of the first block and the total size of the file.

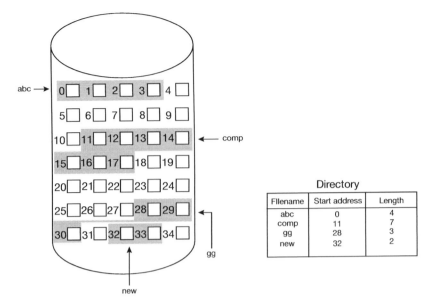

Figure 10.6: An Example of Contiguous Allocation

Contiguous allocation supports both sequential and direct access to a file. For sequential access, the file system remembers the disk address of the last block referenced and when required, reads the next block. For direct access to block b of a file that starts at location L, the block L+b can be accessed immediately.

Contiguous allocation has a significant problem of external fragmentation. Initially, the disk is free and each new file can be allocated contiguous blocks starting from the block where the previous file ends. When a file is deleted, it leaves behind some free blocks in the disk. This is not a problem until we have contiguous blocks to allocate to a new file at the end of disk. However, with time, the disk will become full and at that time the free blocks are fragmented throughout the disk. One solution to this problem is **compaction**, which involves moving the blocks on the disk to make all free space into one contiguous space. Compaction is expensive in terms of time as it may take hours to compact a large hard disk that uses contiguous allocation. Moreover, normal operations are not permitted generally during compaction.

An alternative to expensive compaction is to reuse the space. For this, we need to maintain a list of holes (an unallocated segment of contiguous blocks). In addition, we must know the final size of a file at the time of its creation so that a sufficiently large hole can be allocated to it. However, determining the file size in advance is generally difficult and allocating either too little or too more space to a file is a problem. If we allocate more space than that it needs, we end up in wasting costly memory. On the other hand, if we allocate too little space than that it needs, we may not extend the file, since the blocks on both sides of the file may be allocated to some other files. One possibility to extend the space is to terminate the user program and then the user must restart it with more space. However, restarting the user program repeatedly may again be costly. Alternatively, system may find the larger hole, copy the contents of the file to the new space and release the previous space.

This can be done repeatedly as long as required space is available contiguously in the disk. Moreover, the user program need not be restarted and the user is also not informed about this. However, the task is again time consuming.

10.4.2 Linked Allocation

The file size generally tends to change (grow and shrink) over time. The contiguous allocation of such files results in the several problems. Linked allocation method overcomes all the problems of contiguous allocation method.

In the linked allocation method, each file is stored as a linked list of disk blocks. The disk blocks are generally scattered throughout the disk and each disk block stores the address of the next block. The directory entry contains the file name, and the address of the first and last blocks of the file (see Figure 10.7).

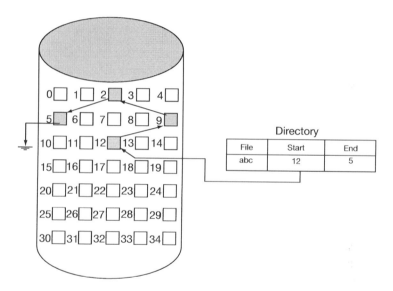

Figure 10.7: An Example of Linked Allocation

This figure shows the linked allocation for a file. A total of four disk blocks are allocated to the file. The directory entry indicates that the file starts at block 12. It then continues at block 9, block 2 and finally ends at block 5.

The simplicity and straightforwardness of this method makes it easy to implement. The linked allocation results in optimum utilization of disk space as even a single free block between the used blocks can be linked and allocated to a file. This method does not come across with the problem of external fragmentation, thus, compaction is never required.

The main disadvantages of using linked allocation are the slow access speed, disk space utilization by pointers and low reliability of the system. As this method provides only sequential access to files, therefore, to find out the nth block of a file, the search starts at the beginning of the file and follows the pointer until the nth block is found. For a very large file, the average turn around time is high.

In linked allocation, maintaining pointers in each block requires some disk space. The total disk space required by all the pointers in a file becomes substantial, which results in more space required by each file. The space required to store pointers can otherwise be used to store the information. To overcome this problem, contiguous blocks are grouped together as a **cluster** and allocation to files takes place as clusters rather than blocks. Clusters allocated to a file are then linked together. Having a pointer per cluster rather than per block reduces the total space needed by all the pointers. This approach also improves the disk throughput as fewer disk seeks are required. However, this approach may increase internal fragmentation because having a partially full cluster wastes more space than having a partially full block.

The linked allocation is also not very reliable. Since disk blocks are linked together by pointers, a single damaged pointer may prevent us from accessing the file blocks that follows the damaged link. Some operating systems deal with this problem by creating special files for storing redundant copies of pointers. One copy of file is placed in main memory to provide faster access to disk blocks. Other redundant pointers files helps in safer recovery.

10.4.3 Indexed Allocation

There is one thing common to both linked and indexed allocation, that is, non-contiguous allocation of disk blocks to the files. However, they follow different approaches to access the information on the disk. Linked allocation supports sequential access, whereas, indexed allocation supports sequential as well as direct access.

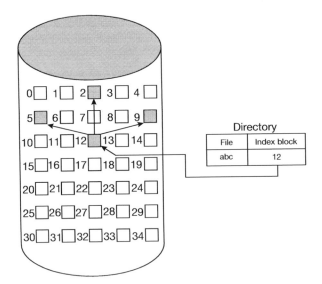

Figure 10.8: An Example of Indexed allocation

In indexed allocation, the blocks of a file are scattered all over the disk in the same manner as they are in linked allocation. However, here the pointers to the blocks are brought together at one location known as the **index block**. Each file has an index block (see Figure 10.8), which is an array of disk block pointers (addresses). The kth entry in the index block points to the kth disk block of the file. To read the kth disk block of a file, the pointer in the kth index block entry is used to find and read the desired block. The index block serves the same purpose as a page map table does in the paged memory systems.

The main advantage of indexed allocation is the absence of external fragmentation, since, any free blocks on the disk may be allocated to fulfill a demand for more space. Moreover, the index can be used to access the blocks in a random manner.

When compared to linked allocation, the pointer overhead in indexed allocation is comparatively more. This is because with linked allocation, a file of only two blocks uses a total of 8 bytes for storing pointers (assuming each pointer require 4 bytes of space). However, with indexed allocation, the system must allocate one block (512 bytes) of disk space for storing pointers. This results in wastage of 504 bytes of the index block as only 8 bytes are used for storing the two pointers.

Clearly, deciding the size of index block is a major issue because too large block may result in wastage of memory and too small index block limits the size of largest file in the system. If 4 bytes are used to store a pointer to a block, then a block of size 512 bytes can store up to 128 pointers, thus, the largest file in that system can have 65536 bytes (512×128) of information. However, we may have a file which exceeds the size limit of 65536 bytes. To solve this problem, **multi-level indexes**, with two, three or four levels of indexes may be used. The two level indexes, with 128×128 addressing is capable of supporting file sizes up to 8 MB and the three level indexes with $128 \times 128 \times 128$ addressing can support file size of up to 1 GB.

The performance of the file system can be greatly enhanced by placing the frequently accessed index blocks in cache memory. This reduces the number of disk accesses required to retrieve the address of the target block.

CHECK YOUR PROGRESS

8. List the two important issues related to disk space allocation?
9. The widely used methods for disk allocation are _____ , _____ and _____ .
10. A cluster is defined as group of _____ .
    (h) Non-contiguous blocks   (b) Contiguous blocks
    (c) Free blocks   (d) Used blocks

10.5 FREE SPACE MANAGEMENT

Whenever a new file is created, it is allocated some space from the available free space on the disk. The free space can be either the space on the disk that is never used for allocation or the space left by the deleted files. The file system maintains a **free-space list** that indicates the free blocks on the disk. To create a file, the free-space list is searched for the required amount of space, and the space is then allocated to the new file. The newly allocated space is removed from the free-space list. Similarly, when a file is deleted, its space is added to the free-space list. The various methods used to implement free-space list are bit vector, linked list, grouping and counting.

10.5.1 Bit Vector

Bit vector also known as **bit map** is widely used to keep track of the free blocks on a disk. To track all the free and used blocks on a disk with total n blocks, a bit map having n bits is required. Each bit in a bit map represents a disk block where, a 0 in a bit represents an allocated block and a 1 in a bit represent a free block. Figure 10.9 shows bit map representation of a disk.

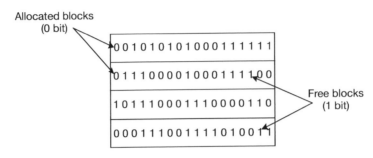

Figure 10.9: A Bit map

The bit map method for free-space list implementation is simple. For instance, if a file requires four free blocks using contiguous allocation method, free blocks 12, 13, 14 and 15 (the first four free blocks on the disk that are adjacent to each other) may be allocated. However, for the same file using linked or indexed allocation, the file system may use free blocks 2, 4, 6 and 8 for allocation to the file.

The bit map is usually kept in main memory to optimize the search for free blocks. However, for systems with larger disks, keeping the complete bit map in main memory becomes difficult. For a 2 GB disk with 512 byte blocks, a bit map of 512 KB would be needed.

10.5.2 Linked List

The linked list method for free-space management creates a linked list of all the free blocks on the disk. A pointer to the first free block is kept in a special location on the disk and is cached in the memory. This first block contains a pointer to next free block, which contains a pointer to next free block and so on. Figure 10.10 shows the linked list implementation of free blocks, where block 2 is the first free block on the disk, which points to block 4, which points to block 5, which points to block 8, which points to block 9 and so on.

Linked list implementation for managing free-space list requires additional space. This is because a single entry in linked list requires more disk space to store a pointer as compared to 1 bit in bit map method. In addition, traversing the free-list requires substantial I/O operations as we have to read each and every block, which takes a lot of time.

10.5.3 Grouping

Grouping is a modification to the free-list approach in the sense that instead of having a pointer in each free block to the next free block, we have pointers for first n free blocks in the first free block. The first $n-1$ blocks are then actually free. The nth block contains

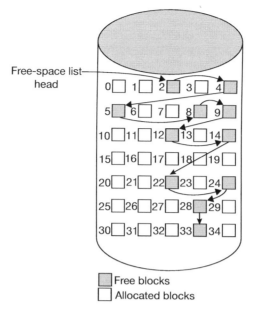

Figure 10.10: Free-space Management through Linked List

the address of next n free blocks and so on. A major advantage of this approach is that the addresses of many free disk blocks can be found with only one disk access.

10.5.4 Counting

When contiguous or clustering approach is used, creation or deletion of a file allocates or deallocates multiple contiguous blocks. Therefore, instead of having addresses of all the free blocks, as in grouping, we can have a pointer to the first free block and a count of contiguous free blocks that follow the first free block. With this approach, the size of each entry in the free-space list increases because an entry now consists of a disk address and a count, rather than just a disk address. However, the overall list will be shorter, as count is usually greater than 1.

10.6 EFFICIENCY AND PERFORMANCE

The allocation methods and directory management techniques discussed so far greatly affects the disk performance and efficiency.

10.6.1 Efficiency

The optimum utilization of disk space to store the data in an organized manner defines the efficiency of a file system. A careful selection of the disk-allocation and directory-management algorithms is most important to improve the efficiency of a disk.

To improve the disk efficiency, the UNIX file system preallocates (allocation in advance) the i-nodes on a disk partition. The i-nodes are spread throughout the partition. The allocation and free-space algorithms then attempt to keep file's data blocks near its i-node block. This reduces the seek time to access file's data and thus improves the disk as well as system's performance.

UNIX also makes use of clustering (discussed in *Section 10.4*) to improve its file system performance. The size of clusters depends on the file size. For large files, large clusters are used and for small files, small clusters are used. This reduces the internal fragmentation that otherwise occurs when normal clustering takes place.

The amount and nature of information kept in the file's directory (i-node) influences the efficiency of the file system. A file's directory that stores detailed information about a file is informative but at the same time it requires more disk read/write for keeping the information up to date. Therefore, while designing the file system, due consideration must be given to the data that should be kept in the directory.

Other consideration that must be kept in mind while designing the file system is determining the size of the pointers (to access data from files). Most systems use either 16 bit or 32 bit pointers. These pointer sizes limit the file sizes to either 2^{16} (64 KB) or 2^{32} bytes (4 GB). A system that requires larger files to store data can implement a 64 bit pointer. This pointer size supports file of 2^{64} bytes. However, the greater the size of the pointer, the more the disk space is required to store it. This in turn makes allocation and free-space management algorithms (linked list, indexes and so on) to use more disk space.

For better efficiency and performance of a system, the various factors, such as pointer size, length of directory entry and table size, etc., need to be considered while designing the operating system.

10.6.2 Performance

The system's read and write operations with memory are much faster as compared to the read and write operations with the disk. To reduce this time difference between disk and memory access, various disk optimization techniques, such as caching, free-behind and read-ahead are used.

To reduce the disk accesses and improve the system performance, blocks of data from secondary storage are selectively brought into main memory (or cache memory) for faster accesses. This is termed as **caching** of disk data.

When a user sends a read request, file system searches the cache to locate the required block. If the block is found then the request will be satisfied with no need for a disk access. However, if the block is not in the cache, it is first brought into the cache and then copied to the process which requires it. All the successive requests for the same block can then be satisfied from the cache.

When a request to read a block from disk occurs, a disk access is required to transfer the block from disk to the main memory. With the assumption that the block may be used again in future, it is kept in a separate section of the main memory. This technique of caching disk blocks in memory is called **block cache**. In some other systems, file data is cached as pages (using virtual-memory techniques) rather then as file system oriented blocks. This technique is called **page cache**. Caching file data using virtual addresses is more efficient as compared to caching through physical disk blocks. Therefore, some systems use page cache to cache both process pages and file data. This is called as **unified virtual memory**.

Now, consider the two alternatives to access a file from disk: memory mapped I/O and standard system calls, such as `read` and `write`. Without a unified buffer cache, the standard system calls have to go through the buffer cache, whereas, the memory mapped I/O has to use the two caches, the page cache and the buffer cache (see Figure 10.11). Memory mapped I/O requires **double caching**. First the disk blocks are read from the file system into the buffer cache and then the contents in the buffer cache are transferred to the page cache. This is because virtual memory system cannot interface with the buffer cache. Double caching has several disadvantages. First, it wastes memory in storing copy of data in both the caches. Second, each time the data is updated in the page cache, the data in the buffer cache must also be updated to keep the two caches consistent. This extra movement of data within the memory results in the wastage of CPU and I/O time.

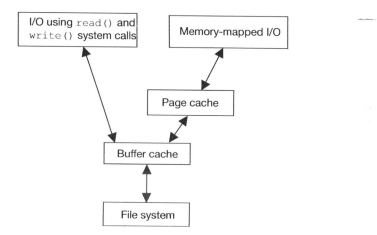

Figure 10.11: Input/Output without a Unified Buffer Cache

However, with a unified buffer cache, both memory mapped I/O, and the `read` and `write` system calls can use the same page cache (see Figure 10.12). This saves the system resources which are otherwise required for double caching.

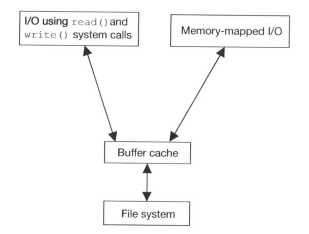

Figure 10.12: Input/Output using a Unified Buffer Cache

The cache memory has a limited space, therefore, once it is full, bringing new pages in cache requires some existing pages to be replaced. A replacement algorithm is applied to remove a page (and rewrite to the disk if it has been modified since being brought in) and then load the new page in the buffer cache. The most widely used replacement algorithms are Least Recently Used (LRU), First-In First-Out (FIFO) and second chance (discussed in *Chapter 8*). Out of these, LRU is the general-purpose algorithm for replacing pages. However, LRU must be avoided with the sequential access files, since the most recently used pages will be used last or may be never again. Instead, sequential access can be optimized by techniques known as free-behind and read-ahead.

The **free-behind** technique removes (free) a page from the buffer as soon as the next page is requested. The pages that are used once are not likely to be used again and they are only wasting buffer space, thus, they are chosen for replacement. Another technique is **read-ahead** in which when a request to read a page arises, the requested page and the several subsequent pages are also read and cached in advance. This is because they are likely to be accessed after the processing of the current page. Bringing the data from the disk in one transfer and caching it saves a considerable amount of time.

CHECK YOUR PROGRESS

11. A _____ stores addresses of all the blocks which are free for allocation.
12. Which of these methods requires minimal memory for storing free blocks information?
    (a) Grouping   (b) Linked list
    (c) Bit vector   (d) Counting
13. The amount and nature of information kept in the directory influences the efficiency and performance of the file system. (True/False)
14. Define the term caching.

10.7 RECOVERY

As discussed earlier, a computer stores data in the form of files and directories on the disk and in the main memory. This data is important for the users who have created it and also for other users who are using it or might use it in future. However, a system failure (or crash) may result in loss of data and in data inconsistency. This section discusses how a system can be recovered to a previous consistent state prior to its failure. The data recovery includes creating full and incremental backups of data to restore the system to a previous working state and checking data consistency using consistency checker.

10.7.1 Backup and Restore

Creating a backup includes recording both file data and control data to some other storage devices, such as floppy disk, magnetic tape or optical disc. The frequency of backup depends on the type and nature of the data. If the system is used to store critical data then backups can be created on a daily basis, otherwise, the backup can be created after a fixed interval of time for instance, after every seven or fifteen days.

However, creating full backups daily would lead to significant copying overhead. To avoid recopying complete information, organizations take incremental backups in between the two full backups. An incremental backup includes copying only the changed information (based on the date and time of last backup) to another storage device. Figure 10.13 shows an example of full and incremental backups between two distinct system states. Note that from day n, the cycle of taking incremental backups starts again.

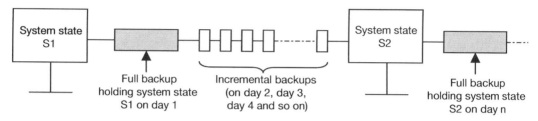

Figure 10.13: Full and Incremental Backups between Two Distinct System States

Consider a situation where a system failure leads to some data loss. To recover this data, the last saved full backup is restored on the system first. Following this, all the incremental backups are restored one by one in the reverse order. However, there may be some processes that are executed in the time between the last incremental backup and the system failure. These processes are re-executed following the recovery to update the system to the last working state (that is the state at the time of system crash).

10.7.2 Consistency Checking

Consider a situation, where due to some reasons (such as, power failure or system crash) the system goes down abruptly and leaves the system in an inconsistent state. The system is said to be in the inconsistent state when there is a difference between the directory information and the actual data on the disk.

The main reason behind the system's inconsistent state is the use of main memory to store directory information. As soon as a file operation occurs, corresponding information in directory is updated in the main memory. However, directory information on disk does not necessarily updated at the same time.

To overcome this problem, most systems use a special program called **consistency checker** which runs at the time of system boot. It compares the data in the directory structure with the data blocks on the disk and tries to fix any inconsistency it finds.

10.8 LOG-STRUCTURED FILE SYSTEM

Recall *Section 10.6.2* where we have discussed various techniques to optimize the disk access operations. These techniques work well in case of read operations where data can be read directly from the caches rather than the disk. However, if majority of operations are write, these techniques no longer gain much performance. This is because most of the time is spent in disk head movement rather than actually performing the writes. To reduce the disk head movements, a new kind of file system known as log-structured file system was introduced.

The log-structured file system maintains a log file that contains the metadata and data of all the files in the file system. Whenever the data is modified or new data is written in a file, this new data is recorded at the end of the log file. The file system also maintains an index block corresponding to each file in the log file. An index block contains the pointers to the disk blocks containing the file data in the log file.

Using the log structured file system, writing data to the file requires little disk head movement as the data is written at the end of the log file. On the other hand, during read operation the disk head movement depends on whether data to be read is written recently or is the older data. It is obvious that if the data is written recently, reading that data will require little disk head movement, while if the data is the older one, more disk head movements are required.

To understand log-structured file system, consider the Figure 10.14. Here, we assume that log file contains data of a single file. Corresponding to this file, there is an index block that points to the data blocks of the file. Further, assume that some modifications are made to the block 1 and block 4, and the new data is written to the new blocks, say block 5 and block 6, respectively. Now, the file system will create a new index block in which the pointer to block 1 and pointer to block 4 will point to block 5 and block 6, respectively. After the modifications have been made, the old index block, block 1 and block 4 become free.

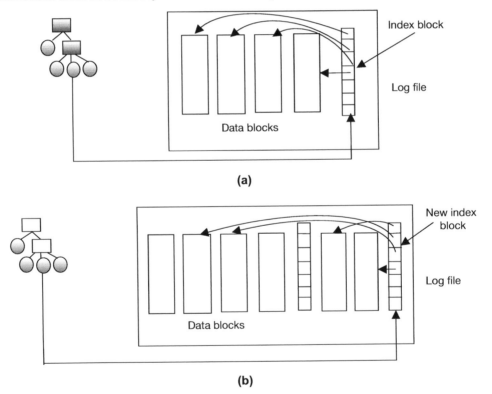

Figure 10.14: File Updating Process in Log-structured File System

10.9 CASE STUDY: FILE SYSTEM IN LINUX

The earliest file system used in Linux was the Minix file system. It was restricted by short filenames up to 14 characters and maximum file size of 64 MB. Therefore, after five years, a new improved file system, known as **extended file system (extfs)**, was developed. This file system supported larger filenames and greater file size but it was slower than the Minix file system. So, the extfs was redesigned to add the missing features and improve the performance of the file system and it gave rise to the **ext2** file system ext2fs also called **second extended file system**. The ext2fs has now become the standard file system of Linux. Apart from ext2fs, Linux offers a variety of other file systems also.

Linux also supports multiple disk partitions with each partition having the same or different file system on it. In order to facilitate the processes and applications to interact with different file systems at the same time, Linux offers a Virtual File System (VFS)—a layer of software between the process and file system—that hides the differences among the various file systems from the processes and applications. Thus, a user can use a file system of his/her choice irrespective of the file system implementation.

The Virtual File System

The virtual file system is an abstraction that supports a generic file model. It defines four types of objects, including inode, file, superblock and dentry, and each object type is associated with a set of operations. The description of VFS object types is as follows:

- **i-node:** An i-node (a shortened form of index node) object describes a specific file. VFS defines an i-node object corresponding to each file in the file system. Since devices and directories in Linux are also treated as files, they have corresponding i-nodes also. An i-node is maintained on the physical disk as a data structure that contains pointers to the disk blocks storing the actual file contents.
- **File:** The file object describes an open file associated with a process. Before accessing the contents of an i-node object, a process needs to obtain the file object which points to the i-node. The file object also keeps track of the current position in file where the read/write operation is being performed. Note that there can be multiple file objects corresponding a single i-node object with each file object belonging to a single process.
- **Superblock:** The superblock object describes a set of linked files that constitute an independent file system. The main task of superblock object is to provide access to the i-nodes. Each i-node is identified in VFS by a unique pair of file system and i-node number. Whenever, an i-node is to be accessed, the VFS passes the request to the superblock object which then returns the i-node with that number.
- **Dentry:** The dentry object describes a directory entry which may comprise the actual filename or the name of the directory in pathname of the file. For example, for a file with the pathname `/bin/include/conio.h`, there will be four dentry objects corresponding to four directory entries `/`, `bin`, `include` and `conio.h`.

10.9.1 The Linux ext2 File System

The Linux ext2fs is the most popular on-disk file system in use. It uses the same mechanism for storing the pointers to data blocks and finding the data blocks corresponding to a file as used in UNIX BSD Fast File System (FFS). In this file system, the i-nodes have a fixed size and can accommodate only a fixed number of pointer entries. An i-node holds only thirteen pointers out of which, first ten pointers are 'direct' pointers and remaining three pointers are 'indirect' pointers. Direct pointers point directly to the data blocks, whereas, indirect pointers point to index blocks which further point to data blocks.

Though in Linux the directory files are treated as normal files, they are interpreted in a different manner. Each data block of a directory file contains a linked list. Each entry of linked list stores the file name, i-node number of the i-node associated with that file, length of entry and the information about the group of blocks allocated to the file. The major thing that distinguishes ext2fs and FFS is the disk allocation policies. The ext2fs performs allocations in small units; block sizes of 1 KB, 2 KB or 4 KB, in contrast to FFS file system, where allocation is performed in large blocks of 8 KB each.

10.9.2 The Linux ext3 File System

The Linux ext2 file system improved the performance of the file system by allocating blocks of small size, but in case of sudden system failures and breakdowns, its performance was not satisfactory. The inefficiencies in the Linux ext2 file system gave rise to ext3 file system which uses the concept of journaling. The **journaling** refers to the process of maintaining a log (journal) in which the changes made to the file system are recorded in a sequential order. The changes written sequentially help in reducing the overheads due to disk head movements at the time of random disk accesses as already explained in log-structured file systems.

10.9.3 The Linux proc File System

The Linux proc (process) file system does not store files persistently, instead the files are read and used when required by the user. The basic idea is that for each individual process in system, a directory is created in the proc file system. The name of this directory is the decimal number corresponding to process's PID, such as `/proc/345`. Inside this directory are the virtual files (not actually stored on the disk) that seem to store process related information, such as its signal masks, command line, etc. When a user needs to read these virtual files, the system retrieves the desired information from the actual process at that time and returns it.

10.10 CASE STUDY: FILE SYSTEM IN WINDOWS XP

On a system running Windows XP, one of three file systems, namely, FAT16, FAT32 and NTFS (New Technology File System) can be used. However, NTFS supersedes the FAT file systems and has become the standard file system of Windows XP because of several improvements. Some of the major improvements in NTFS over FAT file systems are as follows:

- It includes features, such as data recovery, file compression, large files and file systems, encryption, etc.
- It provides greater control over security and access of data within the file system.
- It supports large drives or partitions.
- It provides improved performance, reliability and efficient storage using advanced data structure.

Note: Despite of the improvements in NTFS, Windows XP continues to use FAT16 and FAT32 to read removable media, such as floppy disks and for interoperability of media with Windows 95/98 systems, respectively.

NTFS Physical Structure

The basic entity of NTFS is volume. An **NTFS volume** can be a logical partition of the disk or the entire disk. It is organized as a sequence of clusters where a cluster is a collection of contiguous disk sectors; the number of disk sectors in a cluster is a power of 2. It is the smallest unit of disk space that can be allocated to a file. The size of a cluster for a volume varies from 512 bytes to 64 KB depending on the size of volume. For example, the default cluster size for a 2 GB volume is 2 KB. Each cluster starting from the beginning of the disk to the end is assigned a number known as **Logical Cluster Number** (**LCN**). NTFS uses these logical cluster numbers instead of actual disk addresses while allocating space to files.

In NTFS, a file is considered to be a structured object consisting of a set of attributes which are nothing but independent byte streams. Some standard attributes, such as name, timestamp and the date of creation are defined for all the files. Note that user data is also considered as an attribute and is stored in data attributes.

In order to keep track of information regarding each file on volume, NTFS maintains a Master File Table (MFT). It is created in addition to the boot sector and some system files when a volume is formatted using NTFS. The **MFT** is itself a file that contains at least one record for each file. Each MFT record consists of a sequence of (attribute header, value) pairs. The attribute header identifies the attribute and indicates the length of the value. If the value of attribute is short enough to fit in the MFT record, it is stored in the MFT record and is called **resident attribute**. On the other hand, if the value of attribute is too long, it is placed on one or more contiguous extents on the volume and a pointer to each extent is stored in the MFT record. Such attribute is known as **non-resident attribute**. Note that there may be a case when a file is extremely large or it has many attributes. In such case, two or more MFT records are required; the first one is known as **base record** that points to the other MFT records. Some of the attributes along with their description are listed in Table 10.1.

Table 10.1: Some Attributes in MFT Records

Attribute	Description
Standard information	Contains information like flag bits, timestamp.
File name	Contains the file name in Unicode.
Attribute list	Lists the location of additional MFT records.
Object ID	Represents the file identifier unique to the volume.
Volume name	Contains the name of the volume; used in $Volume metadata file
Volume information	Contains the version of the volume; used in $Volume metadata file
Index root	Used to implement directories.
Index allocation	Used to implement very large directories.
Data	Contains stream data.

NTFS associates each file with a unique ID known as **file reference**. It is of 64 bits where first 48 bit and last 16 bits represent the file number and the sequence number, respectively. The **file number** represents the record number in the MFT containing that file's entry and the **sequence number** shows the number of times that MFT entry has been used.

Metadata Files

In NTFS, the internal information about the data for a volume is stored in special system files known as metadata files. The MFT is also one of the metadata files; it not only stores information about itself but also about other metadata files. The first 16 MFT records are reserved for metadata files, the first one being the record for MFT itself. The second record is mirror copy of MFT that contains first 16 entries of original MFT file. It is used for recovery in case the original MFT file gets corrupted.

Metadata files are represented in the MFT using a dollar sign ($) at the beginning of the filename. Some of the metadata files other than MFT along with their file names and description are listed in Table 10.2.

Table 10.2: Some Metadata Files in MFT

System File	Filename	Description
Log file	$LogFile	Contains metadata updates to restore the data during recovery after a system failure.
Volume	$Volume	Contains information about the volume like the volume label and the volume version.
Attribute definitions	$AttrDef	Lists attribute names used in the volume and the operations that can be performed on them.
Boot sector	$Boot	Contains the BIOS parameter that stores the information about the volume like name, size, etc. and boot code to load the operating system if the volume is bootable.
Cluster bitmap	$Bitmap	Indicates the free clusters on the volume.
Root file name index	.	The root folder.
Security file	$Secure	Contains unique security descriptors for all files within a volume.
Bad cluster file	$BadClus	Indicates the bad clusters on a volume.

Directory Implementation

Like in MS DOS and UNIX, the file system is organized as a hierarchy of directories, a directory can contain other directories. NTFS implements each directory using a data structure called B$^+$ tree; an index of the filenames of that directory is stored in B$^+$ tree. B$^+$ tree not only makes insertion of new names in the directory at appropriate place easier but also facilitates efficient search of a file in a directory. This is because, in B$^+$ tree, the length of each path from the root of the tree to a leaf is same.

CHECK YOUR PROGRESS

15. A _____ may result in data loss or data inconsistency.
16. Which technique is most commonly used to recover the lost data?
17. The log-structured file system maintains a log file that contains the _____ and data of all the files in the file system.
18. Linux ext2 file system was restricted by the short filenames up to 14 characters and maximum file size of 64 MB. (True or False)
19. What does the file object in Linux VFS describe?
20. In NTFS, each cluster starting from the beginning of the disk to the end is assigned a number known as _____.

Let Us Summarize

1. Every operating system imposes a file system that helps to organize, manage and retrieve data on the disk.
2. The design of file system involves two key issues. The first issue involves defining a file and its attributes, operations that can be performed on a file, and the directory structure for organizing files. The second issue involves creating algorithms and data structures to map the logical file system onto the physical secondary storage devices.
3. The file system is made up of different layers, where each layer represents a level.
4. The various file system components are the I/O controller, basic file system, file-organization module and logical file system.
5. The file control block stores information about a file, such as ownership, permissions and location of the file content.
6. Several on-disk and in-memory structures are used to implement a file system.
7. The key issue related to directory implementation is the management of directories to locate files in a file system.
8. The most commonly used directory-management algorithms are linear list and hash table.
9. The linear list method organizes a directory as a collection of fixed size entries, where each entry contains a (fixed-length) filename, a fixed structure to store the file attributes and pointers to the data blocks
10. The hash table is a complex data structure with 0 to $n-1$ table entries, where n is the total number of entries. It uses a hash function to compute a hash value (a number between 0 to $n-1$) based on a file attribute.
11. The hash table is used along with the linear list of directory to reduce the search time.
12. The two main issue related to disk allocation are optimum utilization of the available disk space and the fast access to files.
13. The different allocation methods used for allocating disk space to files are contiguous, linked and indexed.
14. In contiguous allocation, each file is allocated contiguous blocks on the disk, that is, one after the other.
15. In the linked allocation method, each file is stored as a linked list of disk blocks. The disk blocks are generally scattered throughout the disk and each disk block stores the address of the next block.
16. In indexed allocation, the blocks of a file are scattered all over the disk in the same manner as they are in linked allocation. However, here the pointers to the blocks are brought together at one location known as the index block.
17. The free-space list that indicates the free blocks on the disk.
18. The different methods that are used to implement free-space list are bit vector, linked list, grouping and counting.
19. A careful selection of the disk-allocation and directory-management algorithms is most important to improve the efficiency of a disk.
20. Data recovery includes creating full and incremental backups of data to restore the system to a previous working state and checking data consistency using consistency checker.
21. The log-structured file system was introduced to reduce the disk head movements while accessing the disk. It maintains a log file that contains the metadata and data of all the files in the file system. Whenever the data is modified or new data is written in a file, this new data is recorded at the end of the log file.

22. Linux supports a variety of file systems, including ext2fs, ext3fs and proc file system. In order to facilitate the processes and applications to interact with these different file systems at the same time, Linux offers a Virtual File System (VFS)—a layer of software between the process and file system—that hides the differences among the various file systems from the processes and applications.

23. On a system running Windows XP, one of three file systems, namely, FAT16, FAT32 and NTFS (New Technology File System) can be used. However, NTFS supersedes the FAT file systems and has become the standard file system of Windows XP.

ANSWERS TO 'CHECK YOUR PROGRESS'

1. Device driver
2. (d)
3. False
4. File control block
5. Linear list, hash table
6. (b)
7. True
8. The two important issues related to disk space allocation are optimum utilization of the available disk space and fast accessing of files
9. Contiguous, linked, indexed
10. (b)
11. free-space list
12. (c)
13. True
14. When blocks of data from secondary storage are selectively brought into main memory (or cache memory) for faster accesses to reduce the disk accesses and improve the system performance. It is known as caching of disk data.
15. System failure (crash)
16. Backup and restore
17. Metadata
18. False
19. The file object describes an open file associated with a process. Before accessing the contents of an i-node object, a process needs to obtain the file object which points to the i-node. The file object also keeps track of the current position in file where the read/write operation is being performed.
20. Logical cluster number

TEST YOURSELF

1. Explain the role of the each layer in a file system?
2. Both linked and indexed allocation schemes uses non-contiguous allocation of disk blocks to files but follows different approaches to access the information on the disk? Explain why?
3. Explain the need for having a standard file system structure attached to various devices in a system?

4. Explain the various on-disk and in-memory structures that are used for implementing a file system?

5. List the advantage of using linked list and index allocation over linear list allocation method?

6. Give an example to show that the pointer overhead in indexed allocation is more as compared to linked allocation.

7. Compare the advantages of various schemes used for free space management.

8. Discuss the various methods used in UNIX improving the efficiency and performance of the system?

9. What is the difference between caching with and without the unified buffer cache?

10. Explain how data on a system can be recovered to a previous working state without any data inconsistency after a system failure?

11. Write short note on the following:
    (a) Linux ext2 file system
    (b) Metadata files in NTFS
    (c) Linux virtual file system

12. How does the log-structured file system reduce the disk head movements?

I/O Systems

Learning Objectives

After reading this chapter, you will be able to:

☐ Understand the basics of I/O hardware
☐ Explain how various I/O services are embodied in the application I/O interface
☐ Discuss the services provided by the kernel I/O subsystem
☐ Describe the UNIX System V STREAMS mechanism
☐ Understand different factors affecting the performance of I/O

11.1 INTRODUCTION

A computer system contains many I/O devices and usually, most of the computer time is spent in performing I/O. Thus, controlling and managing the I/O devices and the I/O operations is one of the main responsibilities of an operating system. The operating system must issue commands to the devices to work, provide a device-independent interface between devices and the rest of the system, handle errors or exceptions, catch interrupts, etc.

Since a variety of I/O devices are attached to the system, providing a device-independent interface is a major challenge among operating system designers. To meet this challenge, designers use a combination of hardware and software techniques. Most I/O devices are connected to ports, buses or device controllers. To hide the details of different devices, operating system designers let the kernel to use device-driver modules. Note that, device drivers present a uniform device-access interface.

11.2 I/O HARDWARE

Computer communicates with a variety of I/O devices ranging from mouse, keyboard and disk to highly specialized devices, such as fighter plane steering. However, one needs to digest only a few concepts to understand how the operating systems facilitate device-independent communication with I/O devices.

A device is attached with the computer system via a connection point known as **port** (such as serial or parallel port). After being attached, the device communicates with the computer by sending signals over a bus. A **bus** is a group of wires that specifies a set of messages that can be sent over it. Recall Figure 1.2 of *Chapter 01* that shows the interconnection of various components to the computer system via a bus. Note that connection of some devices to the common bus is shown via device controller. A **device controller** (or **adapter**) is an electronic component that can control one or more identical devices depending on the type of device controller. For example, a **serial port controller** is simple and controls the signals sent to the serial port. On the other hand, **SCSI controller** is complex and can control multiple devices.

Each device controller includes one or more registers that play an important role in communication with processor. Processor writes data in these registers to let the device take some action and reads data from these registers to know the status of the device. There are two approaches to let the communication between processor and controller occur.

- In the first approach, special I/O instructions are used, which specify the read or write signal, I/O port address and CPU register. The I/O port address helps in the selection of correct device.
- The second approach is memory-mapped I/O. In this, registers of device are mapped into the address space of the processor and standard data-transfer instructions are used to perform read/write operation with the device.

There are basically three different ways to perform I/O operations, including programmed I/O (polling), interrupt-driven I/O and Direct Memory Access (DMA). All these ways are discussed in this section.

11.2.1 Polling

A complete interaction between a host and a controller may be complex, but the basic abstract model of interaction can be understood by a simple example. Suppose that a host wishes to interact with a controller and write some data through an I/O port. It is quite possible that controller is busy in performing some other task, hence, the host has to wait before starting an interaction with a controller. When a host is in this waiting state, we say the host is **busy-waiting** or **polling**.

> **Note:**   Controllers are programmed to indicate something or understand some indications. For example, every controller sets a busy bit when busy and clears it when gets free.

To start the interaction, the host continues to check the busy bit until the bit becomes clear. When a host finds that the busy bit has become clear, it writes a byte in the data-out register and sets the write bit to indicate the write operation. It also sets the command-ready bit to let the controller take action. When controller notices that the ready bit is set, it sets the busy bit and starts interpreting the command. As it identifies that write bit is set, it starts reading the data-out register to get the byte and writes it to the device. After this, the controller clears the ready bit and busy bit to indicate that it is ready to take the next instruction. In addition, controller also clears an error bit (in the status register) to indicate the successful completion of I/O operation.

11.2.2 Interrupt-driven I/O

The above scheme for performing interaction between host and controller is not always feasible, since it requires busy-waiting for host. When either controller or device is slow, this waiting time may be long. In that scenario, host must switch to another task. However, if host switches to another task and stops checking the busy bit, then how would it come to know that the controller has become free.

One solution to this problem is that the host must check the busy bit periodically and determine the status of controller. This solution, however, is not feasible because in many cases host must service the device continuously, otherwise the data may be lost.

Another solution is to arrange the hardware with which a controller can inform the CPU that it has finished the work given to it. This mechanism of informing the CPU about completion of a task (rather than CPU inquires the completion of task) is called **interrupt**. The interrupt mechanism eliminates the need of busy-waiting of processor and hence, considered more efficient than the previous one.

Now let us understand, how interrupt mechanism works. The CPU hardware has an interrupt-request line, which the controllers use to raise an interrupt. Controller asserts a signal on this line when I/O device becomes free after completing the assigned task. As CPU senses the interrupt-request line after executing every instruction, it frequently comes to know that an interrupt has occurred. To handle the interrupt, CPU performs the following steps:

1. It saves the state of current task (at least the program counter) so that the task can be restarted (later) from where it has been stopped.
2. It switches to the interrupt-handling routine (at some fixed address in memory) for servicing the interrupt. The interrupt handler determines the cause of interrupt, does the necessary processing and causes the CPU to return to the state prior to the interrupt.

The above discussed interrupt-handling mechanism is the ideal one. However, in modern operating systems, the interrupt-handling mechanism must accommodate the following features:

- High-priority interrupts must be identified and serviced before low-priority interrupts. If two interrupts occur at the same time, the interrupt with high-priority must be identified and serviced first. Also, if one interrupt is being serviced and another high-priority interrupt occurs, the high-priority interrupt must be serviced immediately by pre-empting the low-priority interrupt.

- CPU must be able to disable the occurrence of interrupts. This is useful when CPU is going to execute those instructions of a process that must not be interrupted (like instructions in the critical section of a process). However, disabling all the interrupts is not a right decision. This is because the interrupts not only indicate the completion of task by a device but many exceptions also, such as an attempt to access non-existent memory address, divide by zero error, etc. To resolve this, most CPUs have two interrupt-request lines: maskable and non-maskable interrupts. **Maskable interrupts** are used by device controllers and can be disabled by CPU whenever required but **non-maskable interrupts** handle exceptions and should not be disabled.

11.2.3 Direct Memory Access (DMA)

Devices, such as disk drives, are frequently involved in transferring large amount of data. To keep the CPU busy in transferring the data one byte at a time from such devices is clearly wastage of CPU's precious time. To avoid this, a scheme called Direct Memory Access (DMA) is often used in systems. Note that for using DMA, the hardware must have a DMA controller, which most systems have. In DMA, the CPU assigns the task of transferring data to DMA controller and continues with other tasks. The DMA controller can access the system bus independent of CPU so it transfers the data on its own. After the data has been transferred, it interrupts the CPU to inform that transfer is completed.

> **Note:**   Some systems have a separate DMA controller for each device, whereas, some systems have a single DMA controller for multiple devices.

DMA works as follows. The CPU tells the DMA controller the source of data, destination of data and the **byte count** (the number of bytes to transfer) by setting up several registers of DMA controller. The DMA controller then issues the command to the disk controller to read the data into its internal buffer and verifies that no read error has occurred. After this, DMA controller starts transferring data by placing the address on the bus and issuing read request to disk controller. Since the destination memory address is on the address lines of bus, the disk controller reads data from its buffer and writes to the destination address. After the data has been written, the disk controller acknowledges DMA controller by sending signal over the bus. The DMA controller then increments the memory address to use and decrements the byte count. If byte count is still greater than 0, the incremented memory address is placed over the bus address lines and read request is issued to the disk controller. The process continues until byte count becomes 0. Once the transfer has been complete, DMA controller generates an interrupt to the CPU. The entire process is illustrated in Figure 11.1.

Note that when DMA controller acquires the bus for transferring data, CPU has to wait for accessing bus and main memory, though it can access cache. This mechanism is called

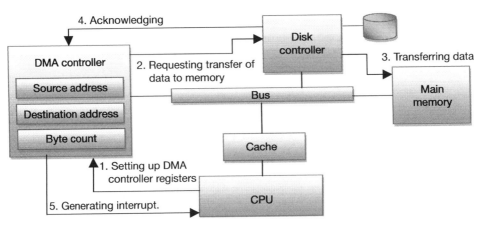

Figure 11.1 Transferring Data using DMA

cycle stealing and it can slightly slow down the CPU. However, it is much important to note that large amount of data gets transferred with negligible task by CPU. Hence, DMA seems to be a very good approach of utilizing CPU for multiple tasks.

11.3 APPLICATION I/O INTERFACE

As stated earlier, there is a variety of I/O devices that can be attached with the computer system and the operating system has to deal with all these devices. However, it is almost impossible that operating system developer would write separate code to handle every distinct I/O device. Because then manufacturing of each new device would lead to changing or adding some code in operating system. Clearly, this is not a feasible solution. Instead, I/O devices are grouped under a few general kinds. For each general kind, a standardized set of functions (called **interface**) is designed through which the device can be accessed. The differences among the I/O devices are encapsulated into the kernel modules called **device drivers**. Note that a device driver is specific to each device and each device driver exports one of the several standard interfaces. Figure 11.2 shows the several software layers in the kernel I/O structure.

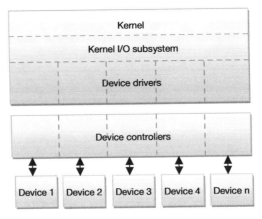

Figure 11.2 Layers in the Kernel I/O Structure

With this structure implemented, the I/O subsystem becomes independent of the hardware. Thus, the device can be accessed through one of the standard interfaces and independent of the device itself. Also, when hardware vendors manufactures new device, they either make it compatible with one of the several available device drivers or write the new device driver exporting one of the several standard interfaces.

Block and Character Devices

All I/O devices can be roughly divided into two classes: block and character devices. A **block device** stores data in fixed size blocks with each block having a specific address. The data transfer to/from a block device is performed in units of blocks. An important characteristic of block devices is that they allow each block to be accessed independently regardless of other blocks. Some commonly used block devices include hard disks, USB memory sticks and CD-ROMs. Applications can interact with the block devices through the **block-device interface**, which supports the following basic system calls.

- **read()**: To read from the device
- **write()**: To write to the device
- **seek()**: To specify the next block to be accessed

On the other hand, a **character device** is the one that accepts and produces a stream of characters. Unlike block devices, character devices are not addressable. The data transfer to/from them is performed in units of bytes. Some commonly used character devices include keyboards, mice and printers. Applications can interact with a character device through the **character-stream interface**, which supports the following basic system calls.

- **get()**: To read a character from the device
- **put()**: To write a character to the device

In addition to block and character devices, there are certain devices that do not fit under any of these categories. For example, clocks and timers are such devices. They are neither block addressable nor they accept or produce character streams, rather they are only used to generate interrupts after some specified interval.

> **Note:** Though block devices allow random access, some applications (for example, DBMS) may access the block device as a sequential array of blocks. This type of access is referred to as raw I/O.

Blocking and Non-blocking I/O

An operating system may use blocking or non-blocking I/O system calls for application interface. The blocking I/O system call causes the invoking process to remain blocked until the call is completed. The process is removed from the run queue and placed into the wait queue. Once the call has been completed, it is put back into the run queue and the results returned by the system call are communicated to it.

On the other hand, the non-blocking I/O system calls do not suspend the execution of the invoking process for a long period, rather they return quickly with a return value which indicates the number of bytes that have been transferred. An alternative to non-blocking I/O is **asynchronous I/O** where the invoking process need not wait for I/O completion, rather it can continue its execution. When the system call is completed, some signal or interrupt is generated and the results returned by the system call are provided to the process.

Note: Most operating systems prefer to use blocking system calls as their code is comparatively easier to use and understand.

CHECK YOUR PROGRESS

1. A device is attached with the computer system via a connection point known as _____.
2. Which of the following involves busy-waiting?
   (a) Interrupt-driven I/O   (b) DMA
   (c) Programmed I/O   (d) None of these
3. DMA stands for _____.
4. Maskable interrupts are used by device controllers and can be disabled by the CPU whenever required. (True or False)
5. Applications can interact with the block and character devices through the _____ and _____, respectively.
6. What is asynchronous I/O?

11.4 KERNEL I/O SUBSYSTEM

The main concern of operating system designers is the control of devices attached to the computer. A wide variety of methods are used to control these devices. These methods altogether form the I/O subsystem of kernel. The kernel I/O subsystem is responsible for providing various I/O related services, which include scheduling, buffering, caching and so on. In this section, we will discuss some of these services.

11.4.1 I/O Scheduling

I/O scheduling means deciding the order in which the I/O requests should be executed. Like process scheduling, I/O scheduling also tends to improve the overall system performance. Thus, the I/O requests from different processes should be scheduled in such a manner that each process should get a fair share of an I/O device and has to wait for the least possible time for I/O completion.

To implement I/O scheduling, a wait-queue mechanism is used. As we have already studied in *Chapter 02*, for each I/O device in the system, a queue is maintained. Whenever a process invokes a blocking I/O system call, it is kept into the queue of that specific I/O device. Now, depending on the application, the I/O scheduler may use an appropriate scheduling algorithm to select the request from the queue. For instance, it may use a priority based algorithm to serve I/O requests from a critical application on a priority basis as compared to less critical applications. Note that the I/O scheduler can also rearrange the I/O requests in the queue for improving the system's performance.

11.4.2 Buffering

A buffer is a region of memory used for holding streams of data during data transfer between an application and a device or between two devices. Buffering serves the following purposes in a system.

- The speed of producer and consumer of data streams may differ. If the producer can produce items at a faster speed than the consumer can consume or vice versa, the producer or consumer would be in waiting state for most of the time, respectively. To cover up this speed mismatch between producer and consumer, buffering may be used. Both producer and consumer share a common buffer. The producer produces an item, places it in the buffer and continues to produce the next item without having to wait for the consumer. Similarly, the consumer can consume the items without having to wait for the producer. However, due to fixed size of buffer, the producer and consumer still have to wait in case of full and empty buffer, respectively. To resolve this, **double buffering** may be used which allows to share two buffers between producer and consumer, thereby, relaxing the timing requirements between them.
- The sender and receiver may have different data transfer sizes. To cope with such disparities, buffers are used. At the sender's side, large data is fragmented into small packets, which are then sent to the receiver. At the receiver's side, these packets are placed into a reassembly buffer to produce the source data.
- Another common use of buffering is to support copy semantics for application I/O. To understand the meaning of copy semantics, consider an application invokes the `write()` system call for data in the buffer associated with it to be written to the disk. Further suppose that meanwhile the system call returns, the application changes the contents of buffer. As a result, the version of data meant to be written to disk is lost. But with copy semantics, the system can ensure that the appropriate version of data would be written to the disk. To ensure this, a buffer is maintained in the kernel. At the time, the application invokes `write()` system call, the data is copied to the kernel buffer. Thus, any subsequent changes in the application buffer would have no effect.

11.4.3 Caching

A cache is an area of very high speed memory, which is used for holding copies of data. It provides a faster and an efficient means of accessing data. It is different from the buffer in the sense that a buffer may store the only existing copy of data (that does not reside anywhere else) while a cache may store a copy of data that does reside elsewhere.

Though caching and buffering serve different purposes, sometimes an area of memory is used for both purposes. For example, the operating system may maintain a buffer in main memory to store disk data for efficient disk I/O and at the same time can use this buffer as cache to store the file blocks which are being accessed frequently.

11.4.4 Spooling

SPOOL is an acronym for Simultaneous Peripheral Operation On-Line. **Spooling** refers to storing jobs in a buffer so that CPU can be efficiently utilized. Spooling is useful because devices access data at different rates. The buffer provides a waiting station where data can rest while the slower device catches up. The most common spooling application is print spooling. In print spooling, documents are loaded into a buffer and then the printer pulls them off from the buffer at its own rate. Meanwhile, a user can perform other operations on the computer while the printing takes place in the background. Spooling also lets a user place a number of print jobs on a queue instead of waiting for each one to finish before specifying the next one. The operating system manages all requests to read or write data from hard disk through spooling.

11.4.5 Error Handling

Many kinds of hardware and application errors may occur in the system during operation. For example, a device may stop working or some I/O transfer call may fail. The failures may be either due to transient reasons (such as overloaded network) or permanent (such as disk controller failure). The kernel I/O subsystem protects against transient failures so that a system failure would not result. For instance, an I/O system call returns one bit that indicates the success or failure of the operation.

11.5 STREAMS

STREAMS is a UNIX System V mechanism that enables asynchronous I/O between a user and a device. It provides a full duplex (two-way communication) connection between a user process and the device driver of the I/O device. A STREAM consists of a stream head, driver end and stream modules (zero or more). The **stream head** acts as an interface to the user process and the **driver end** controls the device. Between the stream head and the driver end, are the **stream modules** that provide the functionality of STREAMS processing. Each of the stream head, driver end and stream modules is associated with two queues: read queue and write queue. The **read queue** is used to store the requests for reading from device while the **write queue** is used to store the requests for writing to the device. Each queue can communicate with its neighbouring queue via message passing. Figure 11.3 shows the structure of STREAMS.

Whenever a user process invokes a `write()` system call for output to a device, the stream head prepares a message, copies the data into it and passes the message to the write queue of the adjacent stream module. The message continues to pass down through the write queues until it reaches to the write queue of driver end and finally, to the device. Similarly, the user process can read from the stream head by invoking a `read()` system call, however, this time the communication takes place via read queues.

Though streams facilitate non-blocking I/O, the user process wishing to write to device blocks if the write queue of stream head is full and remains blocked until there is space in the write queue. Similarly, while reading from the device, the user process remains blocked until some data becomes available in the read queue.

STREAMS offer various benefits, which are as follows:

- It provides a framework to modular and incremental approach for writing network protocols and device drivers.

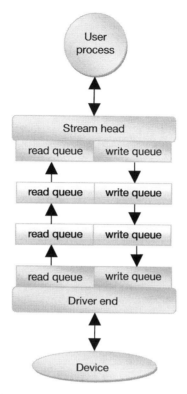

Figure 11.3: Structure of STREAMS

- Different STREAMS (or different devices) may utilize the same set of stream modules, thereby, resulting in reusability of device drivers.
- Most implementations of UNIX provide support for STREAMS and favour this method to write protocols and device drivers.

11.6 PERFORMANCE

The system performance is greatly affected by I/O. As we know that an I/O system call invoked by an application has to pass through a number of software layers, such as kernel, device driver and device controller, before reaching to the physical device. This demands more CPU time and therefore, performing I/O is costly in terms of CPU cycles. Moreover, the layers between the application and the physical device imply overhead of:

- Context switching while crossing the kernel's protection boundary
- Interrupt-handling and signal-handling in the kernel to serve the I/O device
- Load on the CPU and memory bus while copying data between device controller and physical memory, and between kernel buffers and application space

One cause behind context switches is the occurrence of interrupts. Whenever an interrupt occurs, the system performs a state change, executes the appropriate interrupt handler and then restores the state. Though modern computers are able to deal with several thousands of interrupts per second, handling an interrupt is a quite expensive task.

Another reason that causes high context-switch rate is the network traffic. To understand how it happens, suppose that a process on one machine wants to login on a remote machine connected via network. Now, the following sequence of steps takes place for transferring each character from local machine to the remote machine.

1. A character is typed on the local machine causing a keyboard (hardware) interrupt. The system state is saved and the control is passed to the appropriate interrupt handler.
2. After the interrupt has been handled, the character is passed to the device driver and from there to the kernel. Finally, the character is passed from the kernel to the user process. A context switch occurs as the kernel switches form kernel mode to user mode.
3. The user process invokes a network I/O system call to pass the character through the network. A context switch occurs and the character flows into the local kernel.
4. The character passes through network layers that prepare a network packet which is transferred to the network device driver and then to the network controller.
5. The network controller transfers the packet onto the network and causes an interrupt. The system's state is saved and the interrupt is handled.
6. After the interrupt has been handled, a context switch occurs to indicate the completion of network I/O system call.
7. At the receiving side, the network packet is received by the network hardware and an interrupt occurs which causes the state save.
8. The character is unpacked and is passed to the device driver and from there to the kernel. A context switch occurs and the character is passed to the appropriate network daemon.
9. The network daemon determines which login session involved and passes the character to the network subdaemon via kernel, thereby, resulting in two context switches.

Thus, it is clear that passing data through the network involves a lot of interrupts, state switches, and context switches. Moreover, if the receiver has to echo the character back to the sender, the work doubles.

In general, the efficiency of I/O in a system can be improved by:

- reducing the number of context switches
- reducing the frequency of interrupt generation by employing large data transfers, smart controllers and polling
- reducing the frequency of copying data in memory during data transfer between application and device
- balancing the load of memory bus, CPU and I/O
- employing DMA knowledgeable controllers for increasing concurrency.

11.7 CASE STUDY: I/O IN LINUX

In Linux, all the I/O devices can be treated as files and can be accessed through the same system calls (`read()` and `write()`) as used for ordinary files. In order to enable applications to access I/O devices, Linux integrates I/O devices into a file system as what are called **special files**. Each of the I/O devices is assigned a pathname, normally under the directory `/dev`. For example, a printer might be accessed as `/dev/lp`. An important characteristic of special files is that they can be accessed like regular files and no special system calls are required to open, read or write these files.

Linux splits special files into two classes: block special files and character special files. A **block special file** corresponds to a block device (such as hard disk, floppy disk, CD-ROM, DVD, etc.) and comprises a sequence of fixed size numbered blocks. It allows random access, that is, each block in a block special file can be accessed individually. On the other hand, a **character special file** corresponds to a character device that reads/writes stream of characters, such as mouse, keyboard, printer, etc. The character special files do not support all the functionality provided by regular files and even they don't need to.

Each I/O device in Linux is uniquely identified by the combination of major device number and minor device number. The **major device number** is used to identify the driver associated with that device while the **minor device number** is used to identify the individual device in case the driver supports multiple devices. Linux also maintains a separate hash table for character and block I/O devices. Both the hash tables store data structures containing pointers to the procedures for opening, reading or writing to the device. Whenever an application accesses any special file, the file system checks whether the accessed file is a block special file or character special file. Then, it identifies the major and minor device numbers associated with that file. The major device number is used to index into the appropriate internal hash table (block or character) and the minor device number is used as a parameter.

> **Note:** Adding a new I/O device to Linux requires adding an entry into the appropriate internal hash table as well as providing corresponding procedures to deal with different operations on device.

11.7.1 Handling Block I/O Devices

Block devices provide the main interface to all the disk devices in a system. Therefore, the part of I/O system that handles block devices aims to minimize:

- the number of disk accesses while disk I/O
- the latency of repetitive disk head movements.

The former objective is achieved by employing a **cache** between the disk drivers and the file system that stores a large number of most recently accessed disk blocks. Whenever a disk block is to be read, the file system searches the cache to locate the desired block. If the block is found then there is no need for a disk access, which results in better system performance. However, if the block is not in the cache, it is read from the disk, copied to the cache and then copied to wherever it is required. All the successive requests for the same block can now be satisfied from the cache. The cache works well in case of disk writes also. Whenever it is required to write to disk blocks, it also goes to cache and not to the disk. At the time cache grows above its specified limit, all the dirty blocks (modified disk blocks) are transferred to the disk. Note that to avoid any inconsistency, dirty blocks are transferred after every 30 seconds.

To achieve the latter objective of I/O system handling block devices, scheduling of I/O operations is required. The disk I/O requests should be scheduled in an order that optimizes the disk access. The basic scheduler of Linux is **Linus Elevator** that exploits the order in which I/O requests are added or removed from each device queue. A list is maintained to store the disk I/O requests with the requests arranged in an increasing order of the address of desired sectors (sorted list). New I/O requests are added to the list in a sorted order, thereby, avoiding repetitive disk head movements. However, this scheduler may lead to starvation of requests (towards the end of list) in case more and more requests are added in between the sorted list. Therefore, modern versions of Linux use a different scheduler named **deadline scheduler**.

The deadline scheduler works in the same way as elevator scheduler, however, it avoids starvation by associating a deadline with each request. It maintains two additional lists: one for read requests and other for write requests both of which are ordered by deadline. Each I/O request is inserted in the sorted list as well as in one of the read list (in case of read request) and write list (in case of write request). Normally, the requests are scheduled from the sorted list but in case the deadline of any request from read or write list expires, the requests are scheduled from the list containing the expired request. Thus, the deadline scheduling guarantees to complete all the requests within their specified deadlines.

11.7.2 Handling Character I/O Devices

Handling character devices is relatively simple. As character devices input or output a stream of characters, the character device drivers do not allow for random access to fixed size blocks and even it does not make any sense. For instance, is it is not meaningful (even not possible) to access a specified block (say, 230) on a mouse. However, an exception to this is the set of character device drivers associated with terminal devices.

Each character device driver implementing a terminal device is represented in the kernel with the help of a `tty_struct` data structure. Furthermore, each terminal device is associated with a **line discipline**—an interpreter for the data exchanged with that terminal device. The `tty_struct` structure provides buffering for the data stream from the terminal device and feeds that data to the line discipline. The most common line discipline for the terminal devices is the `tty` discipline. This line discipline enables the user processes to directly interact with the terminal by attaching the terminal's input/output with the standard input/output streams of the user process.

CHECK YOUR PROGRESS

7. _____ means deciding the order in which the I/O requests should be executed.
8. List two common uses of buffering.
9. Define spooling.
10. A stream consists of a _____, _____ and _____.
11. An area of memory cannot be used for both buffering and caching. (True of False)
12. Each I/O device in Linux is uniquely identified by a combination of _____ and _____.
13. Deadline scheduler is the basic scheduler of Linux. (True or False)

Let Us Summarize

1. Controlling and managing the I/O devices and the I/O operations is one of the main responsibilities of an operating system. The operating system must issue commands to the devices to work, provide a device-independent interface between devices and the rest of the system, handle errors or exceptions, catch interrupts and so on.

2. A device is attached with the computer system via a connection point known as port (such as serial or parallel port). After being attached, the device communicates with the computer by sending signals over a bus. A bus is a group of wires that specifies a set of messages that can be sent over it.

3. A device controller (or adapter) is an electronic component that can control one or more identical devices depending on the type of device controller.

4. There are basically three different ways to perform I/O operations, including programmed I/O (polling), interrupt-driven I/O and Direct Memory Access (DMA).

5. During programmed I/O, the host may have to wait continuously while the controller is busy in performing some other task. This behaviour is often called busy-waiting or polling.

6. In interrupt-driven I/O, the CPU is informed about the completion of a task (rather than CPU inquires the completion of task) by means of interrupts. The interrupt mechanism eliminates the need of busy-waiting of processor and hence considered more efficient than programmed I/O.

7. In DMA, the DMA controller interacts with the device without the CPU being bothered. As a result, the CPU can be utilized for multiple tasks.

8. All I/O devices are grouped under a few general kinds. For each general kind, a standardized set of functions (called interface) is designed through which the device can be accessed. The differences among the I/O devices are encapsulated into the kernel modules called device drivers.

9. All I/O devices can be roughly divided into two classes: block and character devices. A block device stores data in fixed size blocks with each block having a specific address. A character device is the one that accepts and produces a stream of characters. Unlike block devices, character devices are not addressable.

10. An operating system may use blocking or non-blocking I/O system calls for application interface. The blocking I/O system call causes the invoking process to block until the call is completed. On the other hand, the non-blocking I/O system calls do not suspend the execution of the invoking process for a long period; rather they return quickly with a return value which indicates the number of bytes that have been transferred.

11. A wide variety of methods are used to control the devices attached to the computer system. These methods altogether form the I/O subsystem of kernel. The kernel I/O subsystem is responsible for providing various I/O-related services, which include scheduling, buffering, caching and so on.

12. STREAMS is a UNIX System V mechanism that enables asynchronous (non-blocking) I/O between a user and a device. It provides a full duplex (two-way communication) connection between a user process and the device driver of the I/O device.

13. In Linux, all the I/O devices can be treated as files and can be accessed through the same system calls (`read()` and `write()`) as used for ordinary files.

14. In order to enable applications to access I/O devices, Linux integrates I/O devices into a file system as what are called special files. Linux splits these special files into two classes: block special files and character special files.

15. Each block special file corresponds to a block device (such as hard disk, floppy disk, CD-ROM, DVD, etc.) and comprises a sequence of fixed-sized numbered blocks. On the other hand, a character special file corresponds to a character device that reads/writes stream of characters, such as mouse, keyboard, printer, etc.

 ## ANSWERS TO 'CHECK YOUR PROGRESS'

1. Port
2. (c)
3. Direct memory access
4. True
5. Block-device interface, Character-stream interface
6. In asynchronous I/O, the invoking process needs not wait for I/O completion; rather it can continue its execution. When the system call is completed, some signal or interrupt is generated and the results returned by the system call are provided to the process.
7. I/O scheduling
8. Buffering may be used for:
   - Covering up the speed mismatch between the producer and consumer
   - Supporting copy semantics for application I/O.
9. Spooling refers to storing jobs in a buffer so that CPU can be efficiently utilized. Spooling is useful because devices access data at different rates.
10. Stream head, Driver end, Stream modules
11. False
12. Major device number, Minor device number
13. False

 ## TEST YOURSELF

1. State the difference between blocking and non-blocking I/O.
2. Describe some services provided by the I/O subsystem of kernel.
3. How can the efficiency of I/O be improved in a system?
4. How does DMA result in increased system concurrency?
5. Differentiate between STREAMS driver and STREAMS module.
6. Explain how I/O is handled in Linux.
7. Write a short note on the following:
   (a) Interrupt-driven I/O
   (b) Block and character devices
   (c) Kernel I/O structure

Chapter 12

Mass-Storage Structure

Learning Objectives

After reading this chapter, you will be able to:

- ☐ Understand the physical structure of magnetic disk
- ☐ Describe disk scheduling and various algorithms that are used to optimize disk performance
- ☐ Explain disk management including formatting of disk and management of boot and damaged blocks
- ☐ Discuss swap-space management
- ☐ Explain RAID and its levels
- ☐ Describe disk attachment
- ☐ Explore stable storage and tertiary storage

12.1 INTRODUCTION

As discussed in the previous chapter, a computer system consists of several devices (such as mouse, keyboard, disk, monitor, CD-ROM) that deal with different I/O activities. Among all these I/O devices, disk (or some kind of disk) is considered as an essential requirement for almost all the computers. Other devices, such as mouse, CD-ROM or even keyboard and monitor, are optional for some systems, such as servers. This is because servers are usually accessed by other resources (say clients) on the network. Therefore, this chapter mainly focuses on disk related issues, such as its physical structure, algorithms used to optimize its performance, its management and reliability.

12.2 DISK STRUCTURE

A magnetic disk is the most commonly used secondary storage medium. It offers high storage capacity and reliability. Whenever the data stored on the disk needs to be accessed by CPU, it is first moved to the main memory and then the required operation is performed. Once the operation has been performed, the modified data must be copied back to the disk. The system is responsible for transferring the data between the disk and the main memory as and when required. Data on the disk survives power failures and system crash. There is a chance that disk may sometimes fail itself and destroy the data, however, such failures occur rarely.

Data is represented as magnetized spots on a disk. A magnetized spot represents 1 and the absence of a magnetized spot represents 0. To read the data, the magnetized spots on the disk are converted into electrical impulses, which are then transferred to the processor. Writing data onto the disk is accomplished by converting the electrical impulses received from the processor into magnetized spots on the disk. The data in a magnetic disk can be erased and reused virtually infinitely. The disk is designed to reside in a protective case or cartridge to shield it from the dust and other external interference

12.2.1 Organization of Magnetic Disks

A magnetic disk consists of **plate/platter**, which is made up of metal or glass material and its surface is covered with magnetic material to store data on its surface. If the data can be stored on only one side of the platter, the disk is **single-sided disk** and if both sides are used to hold the data, the disk is **double-sided disk**. When the disk is in use, the spindle motor rotates the platters at a constant high speed. Usually the speed at which they rotate is 60, 90 or 120 revolutions per second.

Disk surface of a platter is divided into imaginary tracks and sectors. **Tracks** are concentric circles where the data is stored and are numbered from the outermost to the innermost ring, starting with zero. There are about 50,000 to 100,000 tracks per platter and a disk generally has 1 to 5 platters. Tracks are further subdivided into sectors (or track sectors). A **sector** is just like an arc that forms an angle at the center. It is the smallest unit of information that can be transferred to/from the disk. There are about hundreds of sectors per track and the sector size is typically 512 bytes. The inner tracks are of smaller length than the outer tracks, thus, there are about 500 sectors per track in the inner tracks and about 1000 sectors per track towards the boundary. In general, the disk containing large number of tracks on each surface of platter and more sectors per track has higher storage capacity.

A disk contains one **read/write head** for each surface of a platter, which is used to store and retrieve data from the surface of platter. Information is magnetically stored on a sector by the read/write head. The head moves across the surface of platter to access different tracks. All the heads are attached to a single assembly called a **disk arm**. Thus, all the heads of different platters move together. The disk platters mounted on a **spindle** together with the heads mounted on a disk arm is known as **head-disk assemblies**. All the read/write heads are on the equal diameter track on different platters at one time. The tracks of equal diameter on different platters form a **cylinder**. Accessing data of one cylinder is much faster than accessing data that is distributed among different cylinders. A close look at the internal structure of magnetic disk is shown in Figure 12.1.

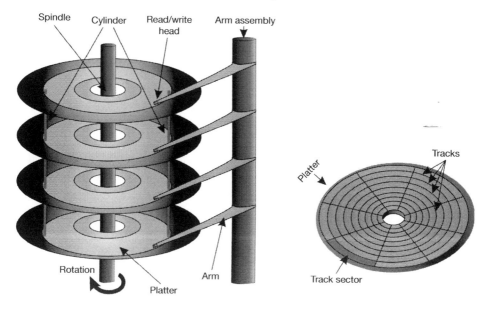

Figure 12.1: Moving Head Disk Mechanism

> **Note:** Some disks have one read/write head for each track of platter. These disks are termed as **fixed-head** disks, since one head is fixed on each track and is not moveable. On the other hand, disks in which the head moves along the platter surface are termed as **moveable-head** disks.

12.2.2 Accessing Data from Magnetic Disk

Data in a magnetic disk is recorded on the surface of the circular tracks with the help of read/write head, which is mounted on the arm assembly. These heads can be multiple in numbers to access the adjacent tracks simultaneously and thus, making a disk access faster. The transfer of data between memory and disk drive is handled by a **disk controller**, which interfaces the disk drive to the computer system.

Some common interfaces used for disk drives on personal computers and workstations are **SCSI (Small Computer System Interface**; pronounced 'scuzzy'), **ATA (AT Attachment)** and **SATA (Serial ATA)**. In latest technology, disk controller is implemented within the disk drive. The controller accepts high-level I/O commands (to read or write sector) and start positioning the disk arm over the right track in order to read or write the data. Disk controller computes an error-correcting code for the data to be written on the sector and attach it with the sector. When the sector is to be read, the controller again computes the code from the sector data and compares it with stored code. If there is any difference between them, the controller signals a read failure.

Remapping of bad sectors is another major task performed by the disk controllers. During initial formatting of the disk, if the controller detects a bad (or damaged) sector, it logically maps the bad sector to another physical location. Disk is notified for the remapping and any further operation is carried out on the new location. Management of bad sectors is discussed in *Section 12.4.2*.

The process of accessing data comprises three steps:

1. **Seek:** As soon as the disk unit receives the read/write command, the read/write heads are positioned on specific track on the disk platter. The time taken in doing so is known as seek time. It is average time required to move the heads from one track to some other desired track on the disk. Seek times of modern disk may range between 6–15 milliseconds.
2. **Rotate:** Once the heads are positioned on the desired track, the head of the specific platter is activated. Since the disk is rotated constantly, the head has to wait for the required sector or cluster (desired data) to come under it. This delay is known as rotational delay time or latency of the disk. The average rotational latencies range from 4.2 to 6.7 ms.
3. **Data Transfer:** After waiting for the desired data location, the read/write head transfers the data to or from the disk to primary memory. The rate at which the data is read from or written to the disk is known as data transfer rate. It is measured in kilobits per second (kbps). Some of the latest hard disks have a data transfer rate of 66 MB/second. The data transfer rate depends upon the rotational speed of the disk. If the disk has a rotational speed of 6000 rpm (rotations per minute), having 125 sectors and 512 bytes/sector, the data transfer rate per revolution will be $125 \times 512 = 64,000$ bytes. Hence, the total transfer rate per second will be $64000 \times 6000/60 = 6,400,000$ bytes/second or 6.4 MB/second.

The combined time (seek time, latency time and data transfer time) is known as the **access time**. Specifically, it can be described as the period of time that elapses between a request for information from disk or memory and the information arriving at the requesting device. Memory access time refers to the time it takes to transfer a character from memory to or from the processor, while disk access time refers to the time it takes to place the read/write heads over the requested data. RAM may have an access time of 9–70 nanoseconds, while hard disk access time could be 10–40 milliseconds.

The **reliability** of the disk is measured in terms of the **Mean Time To Failure (MTTF)**. It is the amount of time for which the system can run continuously without any failure. Manufacturers claim that the mean time to failure of disks ranges between 1,000,000 hours (about 116 years) to 1,500,000 hours (about 174 years). Although, various research studies conclude that failure rates are, in some cases, 13 times greater than what manufacturer claims. Generally, expected life span of most disks is about 4 to 5 years. However, disks have a high rate of failure when they become a few years old.

12.3 DISK SCHEDULING

As discussed, accessing data from disk requires seek, rotational delay and data transfer. Among these three, seek time is the one that dominates the entire access time. Recall, it is the time in which the read/write heads are positioned on specific track on the disk platter.

Whenever, a disk access request arrives, the head is moved to place on the specific track. In case, only one request comes in at one time, all the requests are serviced as and when they arrive; nothing can be done to reduce seek time. However, there is always a possibility that new requests arrive when the system is servicing any one. In this case, new requests are placed in the queue of pending requests. Thus, after completing the current request, the operating system has a choice of which request from the queue is to be serviced next. Several algorithms have been developed that serve this purpose for operating system, some of them are discussed here. We will see that selecting requests in an appropriate order can reduce the seek time significantly.

12.3.1 First-Come First-Served (FCFS) Algorithm

In this algorithm, the request at the front of queue is always selected to be serviced next. That is, the requests are served on First-Come First-Serve basis. To understand the concept, consider a disk with 100 cylinders and a queue of pending requests to access blocks at cylinders

$$15, 96, 35, 27, 73, 42, 39, 55$$

Further, suppose that the head is resting at cylinder 40 when the requests arrive. First, the head is moved to cylinder 15, since it is at the front of the queue. After servicing the request at cylinder 15, the head is moved to 96, then on 35, 27, 73 and so on (see Figure 12.2). It is clear that servicing all the requests results in total head movement of 271 cylinders.

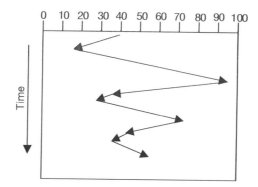

Figure 12.2: FCFS Algorithm

Though it is the simplest algorithm to select a request from the queue, it does not optimize the disk performance. It is clear that head movement from cylinder 15 to cylinder 96 and then back again to cylinder 35 constitutes the major portion of the total head movement of 271 cylinders. If the request for cylinder 96 would be scheduled after the requests for cylinders 35 and 27 then, the total head movement could be reduced noticeably from 271 to 179 cylinders.

12.3.2 Shortest Seek Time First (SSTF) Algorithm

As just discussed, scheduling request for cylinder that are far away from the current head position after the request for closest cylinder can reduce the total head movement significantly. This is what SSTF algorithm attempts to do. This algorithm suggests operating system to select the request for cylinder which is closest to the current head position. To understand this, consider once again the same pending request queue as in previous section with head initially at cylinder 40. The request for cylinder 39 is closest to the current head position, so it will move to cylinder 39. After servicing request at cylinder 39, the head will move to cylinder 42 and then to service requests at cylinders 35, 27 and 15. Now, the request for cylinder 55 is closest, so head will move to cylinder 55. Next closest request is for cylinder 73, so the head will move to cylinder 73 and finally to cylinder 96 (see Figure 12.3).

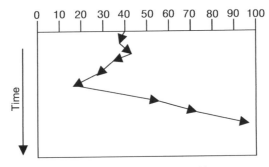

Figure 12.3: SSTF Algorithm

This algorithm requires a total head movement of 112 cylinders, a major improvement over FCFS. However, this algorithm can cause some request to wait indefinitely—a problem called **starvation**. Suppose, when the request for cylinder 15 is being serviced, new request arrives for cylinder 17. Clearly, this algorithm makes the head to move to cylinder 17. Further, suppose while the request at cylinder 17 is being serviced new requests arrive for cylinders 14 and 22. In fact, if requests close to the current head position arrive continuously, then requests for cylinders that are far away will have to wait indefinitely.

12.3.3 SCAN Algorithm

In this algorithm, the head starts at one end of the disk and moves toward the other end, with servicing the requests at cylinders that comes in the way. Upon reaching the other end, the head reverses its movement and continues servicing the requests in the way. This process of moving head across the disk continues.

To understand this concept, consider the above example again. Here, in addition to request queue and current head position, we must know the direction in which the head is moving. Suppose, the head is moving toward the cylinder 100; it will service the requests at cylinders 42, 55, 73 and 96 in the same order. Then, upon reaching the end, that is, at cylinder 100, the head reverses its movement and service the requests at cylinders 39, 35, 27 and 15 (see Figure 12.4).

The algorithm is simple and almost avoids the starvation problem. However, all the requests that are behind the head will have to wait (no matter how close they are to the head) until head reaches the end of disk, reverses its direction and comes back to them.

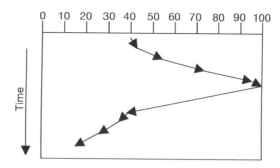

Figure 12.4: SCAN Algorithm

Whereas, a new request that is in front of head will be serviced almost immediately (no matter when it enters the queue).

12.3.4 LOOK Algorithm

A little modification of SCAN algorithm is LOOK algorithm. In this algorithm, the head starts at one end and scans toward the other end with servicing the requests in the way, just like the SCAN algorithm. However, here, the head does not necessarily reach the end of disk, instead when there are no more requests in the direction in which the head is moving it reverses its direction. Figure 12.5 illustrates LOOK algorithm for our example queue of pending requests. In this example, the head reverses its direction after servicing the request for cylinder 96.

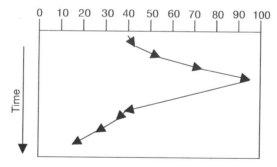

Figure 12.5: LOOK Algorithm

12.3.5 C-SCAN and C-LOOK Algorithms

The C-SCAN (Circular SCAN) and C-LOOK (Circular LOOK) are the variants of SCAN and LOOK algorithms, respectively, which are designed to provide a more uniform wait time. In these algorithms, though the head scans through the disk in both directions, but services the requests in one direction only. That is, when the head reaches at the other hand, it immediately returns to starting end without servicing any requests. Figure 12.6 illustrates the C-SCAN and C-LOOK algorithm for our example queue of requests.

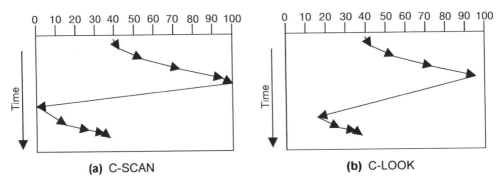

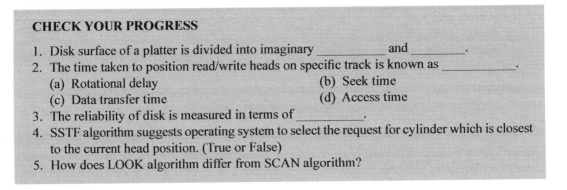

(a) C-SCAN   **(b)** C-LOOK

Figure 12.6: C-SCAN and C-LOOK Algorithms

CHECK YOUR PROGRESS

1. Disk surface of a platter is divided into imaginary _____ and _____.
2. The time taken to position read/write heads on specific track is known as _____.
   (a) Rotational delay   (b) Seek time
   (c) Data transfer time   (d) Access time
3. The reliability of disk is measured in terms of _____.
4. SSTF algorithm suggests operating system to select the request for cylinder which is closest to the current head position. (True or False)
5. How does LOOK algorithm differ from SCAN algorithm?

12.4 DISK MANAGEMENT

Providing disk management services also come under the operating systems responsibilities. In this section, we will discuss disk formatting and recovery from bad sectors.

12.4.1 Disk Formatting

When a disk is manufactured, it is just a stack of some platters of magnetic material on which data can be stored. At that time, there is no information on the disk. Before the disk can be used for storing data, all the platters of the disk must be divided into sectors (that disk controller can read and write) using some software. This process is called **low-level** (or **physical**) **formatting**, which is usually performed by manufacturer.

During this process, a special data structure for each sector is written to the disk, which typically consists of a preamble, a data portion and an Error Correcting Code (ECC). The preamble begins with a certain bit pattern to indicate the start of a new sector and also contain information, such as sector number, cylinder number, etc. The size of data portion determines the maximum amount of data that each sector can hold. It is possible to choose the size of data portion among 256, 512 and 1024 bytes, but usually this size is 512 bytes. The ECC plays its role during each read and write. When some data is written to a sector by the disk controller, it calculates a code from all the bytes of data being written to the sector and updates the ECC with that code. Now, whenever that sector is read, the disk controller recalculates the code from the data that is read from the sector and compares it with the code stored in ECC. Any mismatch in the values indicates that the data of the sector is destroyed. ECC not only helps in detecting that some bits are destroyed, in fact in case only a few bits are destroyed, it enables disk controller to identify the destroyed bits and calculate their correct values.

After low-level formatting, the disk is partitioned into one or more groups of cylinders. The operating system treats each partition as a logically separate disk. On most computers, some boot code and a partition table is stored in sector 0. The partition table tells the starting sector and the size of each partition on the disk.

The last step is **logical** (or **high-level) formatting** of each partition of the disk. During this step, the operating system stores initial file system data structures and a boot block on the disk. The file system data structures include an empty directory, storage space administration (free list or bitmap), etc. After logical formatting, the disk can be used to boot the system and store the data.

12.4.2 Management of Bad Sectors

Due to manufacturing defects, some sectors of a disk drive may be found defective or bad during low-level formatting. Some sectors may also become bad during read or write operations with the disk. This is because the read/write head moves just at a distance of few microinches from the surface of disk platters and if the head becomes misaligned or a tiny dust particle comes between the surface and the head, it may touch or even scratch the surface. This is termed as **head crash** and it may make one or more sectors defective. For these reasons, disk drives are manufactured with some spare sectors that are used to replace bad sectors.

There are several ways of handling bad sectors. On some simple disks, bad sectors need to be handled manually by using, for instance, format command or chkdsk command of MS-DOS. However, in modern disks with advanced disk controller, other schemes are also possible.

A simplest scheme is logical replacement of bad sector with one of the spare sectors in the disk. This scheme is known as **sector sparing** or **forwarding**. To understand this, suppose that the disk controller reads a sector and finds a mismatch in calculated and stored ECC. It reports the operating system that the sector is bad. Next time when the system is rebooted, the disk controller is asked to replace the sector with any spare sector. From now, whenever a request for that sector arrives, the disk controller translates the request into the address of spare sector chosen for replacement. To manage multiple bad sectors using this scheme, the disk controller maintains a list of bad sectors and translates the requests to access bad sectors into the address of corresponding spare sector. This list is usually initialized during low-level formatting and is updated regularly throughout the life of disk.

> **Note:** Usually, the data of bad sector is lost, thus, replacement of bad sector is not totally automatic process. It requires the data to be restored manually from backup media.

Though the above discussed scheme is simple, but the disk scheduling algorithm followed by the operating system for optimization may become less efficient or even worse. To understand this concept, suppose that the sector 29 becomes bad and the disk controller finds the first spare sector following the sector 278. Now, every request to access the sector 29 is redirected to the sector that follows 278 by the disk controller. If the operating system schedules the request to access the sectors 29, 35 and 275 in the order when the disk head is at sector 27, then the disk head first moves to corresponding spare sector, then to sector 35 and finally goes back to access sector 275. Though operating system schedules the requests for disk optimization with a total head movement of 252, but actually the total head movement is 736. To overcome this problem, most disks are manufactured with a few spare sectors in each cylinder and the disk controller attempts to replace a bad sector with a spare sector in the same cylinder.

There is an alternative scheme to sector sparing scheme known as **sector slipping**. In this scheme, instead of logically replacing the bad sector with a spare sector, all the sectors following the bad sector are shifted down one place, making the sector following the bad sector free. The contents of the bad sector are then copied to this free sector, leaving the bad sector unused. For example, considering the same case as discussed above, sector 278 is copied into the spare sector, then 277 is copied into 278 and so on until the sector 30 (following the bad sector) is copied to sector 31. After that, sector 29 (bad sector) is mapped into the space freed by sector 30.

12.5 SWAP-SPACE MANAGEMENT

As discussed in *Chapter 08*, virtual memory uses some amount of disk space known as **swap-space** as an extension of main memory. Swap-space is used in different ways by different operating systems depending upon the memory management algorithms. For example, operating system may use this space to:

- hold the image of a process (including its code and data segments) in case of systems implementing swapping.
- hold the pages swapped out of the main memory in case of paging systems.

Therefore, the amount of disk space required to serve as swap-space may vary from a few megabytes to gigabytes. Though, swap-space enables operating system to use more memory than that of available, but significant use of swap-space degrades system performance. This is because accessing disk is much slower than accessing main memory. Therefore, the swap-space should be designed and implemented in such a way that it provides best throughput for virtual memory systems.

Swap-space can reside with a normal file system and in this case it is simply a large file within the file system. Thus, file system routines can be used to create it, name it and to allocate its space. This is a simple approach to implement swap-space but inefficient as it requires extra disk accesses while navigating through the directory structure and disk-allocation structures.

As an alternative, swap-space can reside on a separate disk partition on which no file system or directory structure is placed. A swap-space storage manager is used to allocate and deallocate the swap space. Since data in swap-space resides for much lesser amount of time and swap-space is accessed much more frequently, the storage manager mainly focuses on the speed rather than storage efficiency. The problem with this approach is that a fixed amount of swap-space is created during disk partitioning and increasing the swap-space requires repartitioning of the disk resulting in deletion of other file system partitions. These partitions then need to be restored from other backup media.

12.6 RAID

The technology of semiconductor memory has been advancing at a much higher rate than the technology of secondary storage. The performance and capacity of semiconductor memory is much superior to secondary storage. To match this growth in semiconductor memory, a significant development is required in the technology of secondary storage. A major advancement in secondary storage technology is represented by the development of **RAID (Redundant Arrays of Independent Disks)**. The basic idea behind RAID is to have a large array of small independent disks. Presence of multiple disks in the system improves the overall transfer rates, if the disks are operated in parallel. Parallelising the operation of multiple disks allow multiple I/O to be serviced in parallel. This setup also offers opportunities for improving the reliability of data storage, because data can be stored redundantly on multiple disks. Thus, failure of one disk does not lead to loss of data. In other words, this large array of independent disks acts as a single logical disk with improved performance and reliability.

> **Note:** Originally RAID stands for Redundant Array of Inexpensive Disks, since array of cheap smaller capacity disk was used as an alternative to large expensive disk. Those days the cost per bit of data of smaller disk was less than that of larger disk.

12.6.1 Improving Performance and Reliability

In order to improve the performance of disk, a concept called **data striping** is used which utilizes parallelism. Data striping distributes the data transparently among N disks, which make them appear as a single large, fast disk. Striping of data across multiple disks improves the transfer rate as well, since operations are carried out in parallel. Data striping also balances the load among multiple disks.

In the simplest form, data striping splits each byte of data into bits and stores them across different disks. This splitting of each byte into bits is known as **bit-level data striping**. Having 8 bits per byte, an array of eight disks (or either a factor or multiple of eight) is treated as one large logical disk. In general, bit i of each byte is written to i^{th} disk. However, if an array of only two disks is used, all odd numbered bits go to first disk and even numbered bits to second disk. Since each I/O request is accomplished with the use of all disks in the array, transfer rate of I/O requests goes to N times, where N represents the number of disks in the array.

Alternatively, blocks of a file can be striped across multiple disks. This is known as **block-level striping**. Logical blocks of a file are assigned to multiple disks. Large requests for accessing multiple blocks can be carried out in parallel, thus improving data transfer rate. However, transfer rate for the request of a single block is same as it is in case of one disk. Note that the disks that are not participating in the request are free to carry out other operations.

Having an array of N disks in a system improves the system performance, however, lowers the overall storage system reliability. The chance of failure of at least one disk out of total N disks is much higher than that of a specific single disk. Assume that the Mean Time To Failure (MTTF) of a disk is about 1,50,000 hours (slightly over 16 years). Then, for an array of 100 disks, the MTTF of some disk is only 150,000/100 = 1500 hours (about 62 days). With such short MTTF of a disk, maintaining one copy of data in an array of N disks might result in loss of significant information. Thus, some solutions must be employed to increase the reliability of such storage system. The most acceptable solution is to have **redundant** information. Normally, the redundant information is not needed; however, in case of disk failure it can be used to restore the lost information of failed disk.

One simple technique to keep redundant information is **mirroring** (also termed as **shadowing**). In this technique, the data is redundantly stored on two physical disks. In this way every disk is duplicated and all the data has two copies. Thus, every write operation is carried on both the disks. During read operation, the data can be retrieved from any disk. In case of failure of one disk, second disk can be used until the first disk gets repaired. If second disk also fails before the repairing of first disk is completed, the data is lost. However, occurrence of such event is very rare. The mean time to failure of mirrored disk depends on two factors.

1. **Mean time to failure** of independent disks and,
2. **Mean time to repair** a disk. It is the time taken, on an average, to restore the failed disk or to replace it, if required.

Suppose failure of two disks is independent of each other. Further, assume that the mean time to repair of a disk is 15 hours and mean time to failure of single disk is 150,000 hours, then mean time to data loss in mirrored disk system is $(150,000)^2/(2 \times 15) = 7.5 \times 10^8$ hours or about 85,616 years.

Alternate solution to increase the reliability is storing error-correcting codes, such as parity bits and hamming codes. Such additional information is needed only in case of recovering the data of failed disk. Error-correcting codes are maintained in a separate disk called **check disk**. The parity bits corresponding to each bit of N disks are stored in check disk.

12.6.2 RAID Levels

Data striping and mirroring techniques improve the performance and reliability of a disk, respectively. However, mirroring is expensive and striping does not improve reliability. Thus, several RAID organizations, referred to as **RAID levels**, have been proposed which aims at providing redundancy at lower cost by using the combination of these two techniques. These levels have different cost–performance trade-offs. The RAID levels are classified into seven levels (from level 0 to level 6), as shown in Figure 12.7 and are discussed here. To understand all the RAID levels consider a disk array consisting of four disks.

- **RAID level 0:** RAID level 0 uses block-level data striping but does not maintain any redundant information. Thus, the write operation has the best performance with level 0, as only one copy of data is maintained and no redundant information needs to be updated. However, RAID level 0 does not have the best read performance among all the RAID levels, since systems with redundant information can schedule disk access based on shortest expected seek time and rotational delay. In addition, RAID level 0 is not fault tolerant because failure of just one drive will result in loss of data. However, absence of redundant information ensures 100 percent space utilization for RAID level 0 systems.

- **RAID level 1:** RAID level 1 is the most expensive system, as this level maintains duplicate or redundant copy of data using mirroring. Thus, two identical copies of the data are maintained on two different disks. Every write operation needs to update both the disks, thus, the performance of RAID level 1 system degrades while writing. However, performance while read operation is improved by scheduling request to the disk with the shortest expected access time and rotational delay. With two identical copies of data, RAID level 1 system ensures only 50 percent space utilization.

- **RAID level 2:** RAID level 2 is known as **Error Correcting Code (ECC)** organization. Two most popular error detecting and correcting codes are parity bits and Hamming codes. In memory system, each byte is associated with a parity bit. The parity bit is set to 0 if the number of bits in the byte that are set to 1 is even, otherwise the parity bit is set to 1. If any one bit in the byte gets changed, then parity of that byte will not match with the stored parity bit. In this way, use of parity bit detects all 1-bit errors in the memory system. Hamming code has the ability to detect the damaged bit. It stores two or more extra bits to find the damaged bit and by complementing the value of damaged bit, the original data can be recovered. RAID level 2 requires three redundant disks to store error detecting and correcting information for four original disks. Thus, effective space utilization is about 57 percent in this case. However, space utilization increases with the number of data disks because check disks grow logarithmically with the number of data disks.

- **RAID level 3:** As discussed, RAID level 2 uses check disks to hold information to detect the failed disk. However, disk controllers can easily detect the failed disk and hence, check disks need not to contain information to detect the failed disk. RAID level 3 maintains only single check disk with parity bit information for error correction as well as for detection. This level is also named as **bit-interleaved parity organization**.

    Performance of RAID level 2 and RAID level 3 are very similar but RAID level 3 has lowest possible overheads for reliability. So, in practice, level 2 is not used. In addition, level 3 has two benefits over level 1. Level 1 maintains one mirror disk for every disk, whereas, level 3 requires only one parity disk for multiple disks, thus, increasing effective space utilization. In addition, level 3 distributes the data over multiple disks, with N-way striping of data, which makes the transfer rate for reading or writing a single block by N times faster than level 1. Since every disk has to participate in every I/O operation, RAID level 3 supports lower number of I/O operations per second than RAID level 1.

- **RAID level 4:** Like RAID level 0, RAID level 4 uses block-level striping. It maintains parity block on a separate disk for each corresponding block from N other disks. This level is also named as **block-interleaved parity organization**. To restore the block of the failed disk, blocks from other disks and corresponding parity block is used. Requests to retrieve data from one block are processed with only one disk, leaving remaining disks free to handle other requests. Writing a single block involves one data disk and check disk. The parity block is required to be updated with each write operation, thus, only one write operation can be processed at a particular point of time.

With four data disks, RAID level 4 requires just one check disk. Effective space utilization for our example of four data disk is 80 percent. As always one check disk is required to hold parity information, effective space utilization increases with the number of data disks.

- **RAID level 5:** Instead of placing data across N disks and parity information in one separate disk, this level distributes the block-interleaved parity and data among all the N+1 disks. Such distribution has advantage in processing read/write requests. All disks can participate in processing read request, unlike RAID level 4, where dedicated check disks never participates in read request. So level 5 can satisfy more number of read requests in given amount of time. Since bottleneck of single check disk has been eliminated, several write request could also be processed in parallel. RAID level 5 has the best performance among all the RAID levels with redundancy. In our example of 4 actual disks, RAID level 5 system has five disks overall, thus, effective space utilization for level 5 is same as in level 3 and level 4.

- **RAID level 6:** RAID level 6 is an extension of RAID level 5 and applies P + Q redundancy scheme using Reed-Solomon codes. **Reed-Solomon codes** enable RAID level 6 to recover from up to two simultaneous disk failures. RAID level 6 requires two check disks, however, like RAID level 5, redundant information is distributed across all disks using block-level striping.

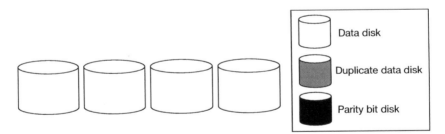

RAID level 0: Non-redundant

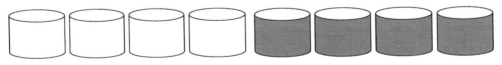

RAID level 1: Mirrored

RAID level 2: Memory-style error correcting code

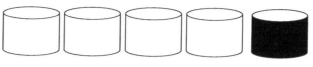

RAID level 3: Bit-interleaved parity

RAID level 4: Block-interleaved parity

RAID level 5: Block-interleaved distributed parity

RAID level 6: P+Q redundancy

Figure 12.7 Representing RAID Levels

CHECK YOUR PROGRESS

6. After physical formatting, the disk can be used to boot the system and store the data. (True or False)

7. _____ involves logical replacement of bad sector with one of the spare sectors in the disk.

8. In which ways, the swap-space can be used by the operating system?

9. In order to improve the performance of disk, a concept called _____ is used which utilizes parallelism.

10. Which of the following RAID level uses block-level stripping?
    (a) Level 0   (b) Level 1
    (c) Level 3   (d) Level 6

11. In RAID, one simple technique to keep redundant information is _____.

12.7 DISK ATTACHMENT

The disk can be attached with the computer system either through local I/O ports on the host computer or through a network connection. In the former case, disk storage is referred to as host-attached storage while in the latter case it is referred to as network-attached storage.

12.7.1 Host-attached Storage

A host-attached storage system is connected directly to the network server. This storage is accessed only through local I/O ports, which are available in many technologies. Normal desktop systems often use IDE or ATA bus architecture, whereas, the high technology systems, such as servers work on SCSI and Fiber Channel (FC) architectures.

In **SCSI bus architecture**, a ribbon cable consisting of large number of conductors serves as the physical medium. The SCSI protocol has the capacity to support up to16 devices, including one controller card and 15 storage devices. The controller card in the host is **SCSI initiator** and rest devices are **SCSI targets**. The SCSI protocol can address up to eight logical units in each SCSI target.

Fiber Channel (**FC**) architecture uses the optical fiber as its physical medium and thus, provides high speed data transfer between storage devices. It defines a high speed protocol which was originally developed for high-end workstations, large storage media and high performance desktop applications. Two variants of this architecture include a **switched fabric** that provides 24 bit address space and an **arbitrated loop** (**FC-AL**) that can address 126 devices. The fibre channel allows maximum flexibility in I/O communications with large address space and storage devices.

> **Note:** Various storage devices which are in use as host-attached storage, include hard disks, CD, DVD, optical disk, magnetic disk and pen drive.

12.7.2 Network-attached Storage

A Network-Attached Storage (NAS) describes a storage system designed to separate storage resources from network and application servers, in order to simplify storage management and improve the reliability, performance and efficiency of the network. It commonly supports NFS (Network File System) and CIFS (Common Internet File System). NAS is ideal for storing local databases and for keeping the backup of workstation data.

NAS facilitates all the computers in the network to access the storage with the same ease as in case of local host-attached storage. However, it is less efficient and results in lower system performance as compared to host-attached storage.

12.8 STABLE STORAGE

As discussed earlier, disks sometimes may make errors that result in disrupting good sectors or even the entire drive may fail. Though RAID, to some extent, provides protection against good sectors becoming bad or against drives failure, but it cannot provide protection against system crash during disk writes, which results in inconsistency on disk.

Ideally, a disk should always work without producing any errors. However, practically, it cannot be achieved. The only achievable thing is a disk subsystem called **stable storage** which ensures whenever a write is performed to the disk; it is performed either completely or not at all. To ensure this, the stable storage system maintains two physical blocks per each logical block and a write operation is performed in the following steps.

1. Data is written to the first physical block.
2. After the write to first physical block has been performed successfully, data is written in the second physical block.
3. After the write to second physical block has been performed successfully, the operation is declared to be complete.

During recovery, the recovery procedure checks both the physical blocks and the following likelihoods may result.

- Both blocks contain no detectable error. In this case, no further action is required.
- One of the two blocks contains a detectable error. In this case, the contents of the erroneous block are replaced with that of other block.
- Neither of two blocks contains a detectable error but they differ in their content. In this case, the contents of first block are replaced with that of second block.

In this way, the recovery procedure guarantees the write operation on stable storage either to be performed successfully or not to be performed.

12.9 TERTIARY STORAGE

Tertiary storage, also known as **tertiary memory**, is built from inexpensive disks and tape drives that use removable media. Due to relatively low speed of tertiary storage systems, they are primarily used for storing data that is to be accessed less frequently. In this section we will discuss various tertiary storage devices.

12.9.1 Removable Disks

Removable disks are one kind of tertiary storage. An example of removable magnetic disk is floppy disk. A **floppy disk** is a round, flat piece of Mylar plastic coated with ferric oxide (a rust like substance containing tiny particles capable of holding a magnetic field) and encased in a protective plastic cover (disk jacket). Common floppy disks can hold only about 1 MB of data. Due to limited storage capacity, the floppy disks have become outdates. Nowadays, other kinds of removable disks, including optical disks and magneto-optical disks, are in use.

Optical Disks

An optical disk is a flat, circular, plastic disk coated with material on which bits may be stored in the form of highly reflective areas and significantly less reflective areas, from which the stored data may be read when illuminated with a narrow-beam source, such as a laser diode. The optical disk storage system consists of a rotating disk coated with a thin layer of metal (aluminium, gold, or silver) that acts as a reflective surface and a laser beam, which is used as a read/write head for recording data onto the disk. Compact Disk (CD) and Digital Versatile Disk (DVD) are the two forms of optical disks.

Compact Disk (CD)

A CD is a shiny, silver colour metal disk of 12 cm in diameter. It is available in various formats: *CD-ROM* (*Compact Disk-Read Only Memory*), *CD-R* (*Compact Disk-Recordable*) and *CD-RW* (*Compact Disk-ReWritable*) disks. A CD-ROM disk comes with prerecorded data by the manufactures and can be read but cannot be altered. CD-R is a type of WORM (Write Once-Read Many) disk that allows you to record your own data. Once written, the data on the CD-R can be read but cannot be altered. A CD-RW disk is rewritable version of CD-R that means, it allows writing, erasing and rewriting of data several times.

A **CD** is made up of three coatings, namely, polycarbonate plastic, aluminium and an acrylic coating to protect the disk from external scratches and dust. The polycarbonate plastic is stamped with millions of tiny indentations (pits). A light is beamed from a semi-conductor laser through the bottom of the polycarbonate layer and aluminium coating monitors the light being reflected. Since the CD is read through the bottom of the disk, each pit appears as an elevated bump to the reading light beam. Light striking the land areas (the areas without bumps) is reflected normally and detected by a photodiode. As the disk rotates at speed between 200 and 500 rpm, the light bounces off the pits causing the frequency of the light to change. The reflected light then passes through a prism and onto a photo sensor. Light reflected from a pit is 180 degrees out of phase with the light from the lands and the differences in intensity are measured by the photoelectric cells, which converts into a corresponding electrical pulse.

On a new **CD-R** disk, the entire surface of the disk is reflective; the laser can shine through the dye and reflect off the gold layer. Hence, for a CD-R disk to work there must be a way for a laser to create a non-reflective area on the disk. A CD-R disk, therefore, has an extra layer that the laser can modify. This extra layer is a greenish dye. When you write data to a CD-R, the writing laser (which is much more powerful than the reading laser) heats up the dye layer and changes its transparency. The change in the dye creates the equivalent of a non-reflective bump. The decomposition of the dye in the pit area through the heat of the laser is irreversible (permanent). Therefore, once a section of a CD-R is written, it cannot be erased or rewritten. However, both CD and CD-R drives can read the modified dye as a bump later on.

In contrast to CD-R disk, **CD-RW** disk is erasable and rewritable because it uses phase-changing material on its recording layer usually alloy of silver, tellurium, indium and antimony metals. Phase-changing material changes its state when heated to a high temperature (above its melting point) and can be converted back to its original state when heated at a temperature slightly below its melting point.

In CD-RW disk, the recording layer has polycrystalline structure initially. While writing to the disk, the laser heats up the selected areas to a very high temperature (above the melting point), which melts the crystals into non-crystalline amorphous phase. These areas have lower reflectance than the remaining crystalline areas. This difference in reflectance helps in reading the recorded data as in the case of CD-R disk.

To erase data on a CD-RW disk, a process called **annealing** is used. During this process, area on the layer that has been changed to the amorphous phase (during writing) is converted back to its original crystalline state by heating it to a temperature slightly below the melting point of phase changing material.

Digital Versatile Disk (DVD)

DVD, initially called **Digital Video Disk**, is a high capacity data storage medium. At first glance, a DVD can easily be mistaken for a CD as both are plastic disks 120 mm in diameter and 1.2 mm thick and both rely on lasers to read data. However, the DVD's seven-fold increase in data capacity over the CD has been largely achieved by tightening up the tolerances throughout the predecessor system. Like CDs, DVDs are also available in different formats: DVD-ROM, DVD-R and DVD-RW.

In DVD, the tracks are placed closer together, thereby, allowing more tracks per disk. The DVD's track pitch (the distance between each) is reduced to 0.74 micron, less than half of CD's 1.6 micron. The pits, in which the data is stored, are also a lot smaller, thus allowing more pits per track. The minimum pit length of a single layer DVD is 0.4 micron as compared to 0.834 micron for a CD. With the number of pits having a direct bearing on capacity levels, DVD's reduced track pitch and pit size alone give DVDs four times the storage capacity of CDs.

Magneto-optical Disk

As implied by the name, these disks use a hybrid of magnetic and optical technologies. A magneto-optical disk writes magnetically (with thermal assist) and reads optically using the laser beam. A magneto-optical disk drive is so designed that an inserted disk will be exposed to a magnet on the label side and to the light (laser beam) on the opposite side. The disks, which come in $3\frac{1}{2}$ inch and $5\frac{1}{4}$ inch formats, have a special alloy layer that has the property of reflecting laser light at slightly different angles depending on which way it is magnetized and data can be stored on it as north and south magnetic spots, just like on a hard disk.

While a hard disk can be magnetized at any temperature, the magnetic coating used on magneto-optical media is designed to be extremely stable at room temperature, making the data unchangeable unless the disk is heated to above a temperature level called the **Curie point** (usually around 200° C). Instead of heating the whole disk, magneto-optical drives use a laser to target and heat specific regions of magnetic particles. This accurate technique enables magneto-optical media to pack in a lot more information than other magnetic devices. Once heated, the magnetic particles can easily have their direction changed by a magnetic field generated by the read/write head. Information is read using a less powerful laser, making use of the **Kerr effect**, where the polarity of the reflected light is altered depending on the orientation of the magnetic particles. Where the laser/magnetic head has not touched the disk, the spot represents a '0' and the spots where the disk has been heated up and magnetically written will be seen as data '1'. However, this is a 'two-pass' process, which, coupled with the tendency for magneto-optical heads to be heavy, resulted in early implementations being relatively slow. Nevertheless, magneto-optical disks can offer very high capacity and cheap media as well as top archival properties, often being rated with an average life of 30 years, which is far longer than any magnetic media.

12.9.2 Magnetic Tape

Magnetic tape appears similar to the tape used in music cassettes. It is a plastic tape with magnetic coating on it. The data is stored in the form of tiny segments of magnetized and demagnetized portions on the surface of the material. Magnetized portion of the surface refers to the bit value '1', whereas, the demagnetized portion refers to the bit value '0'. Magnetic tapes are available in different sizes, but the major difference between different magnetic tape units is the speed at which the tape is moved past the read/write head and the tape's recording density. The amount of data or the number of binary digits that can be stored on a linear inch of tape is the recording density of the tape.

Magnetic tapes are very durable and can be erased as well as reused. They are the cheap and reliable storage medium for organizing archives and taking backups. However, they are not suitable for data files that need to be revised or updated often because data on them is stored in a sequential manner. Every time the user needs to advance or rewind the tape to the position where the requested data starts. Tapes are also slow due to the nature of the media. If the tape stretches too much, then it will render it unusable for data storage and may result in data loss. The tape now has a limited role because disk has proved to be a superior storage medium than it. Today, the primary role of the tape drive is limited to backing up or duplicating the data stored on the hard disk to protect the system against loss of data during power failures or computer malfunctions.

CHECK YOUR PROGRESS

12. A _____ storage system is connected directly to the network server.
13. The controller card in the host is SCSI initiator and rest devices are SCSI targets. (True or False)
14. Which of the following is not a tertiary storage device?
    (a) Magnetic tape   (b) Optical disk
    (c) Floppy disk   (d) Hard disk
15. Define stable storage.

Let Us Summarize

1. A magnetic disk is the most commonly used secondary storage medium. It offers high storage capacity and reliability. Data is represented as magnetized spots on a disk. A magnetized spot represents 1 and the absence of a magnetized spot represents 0.
2. A magnetic disk consists of plate/platter, which is made up of metal or glass material and its surface is covered with magnetic material to store data on its surface.
3. Disk surface of a platter is divided into imaginary tracks and sectors. Tracks are concentric circles where the data is stored and are numbered from the outermost to the innermost ring, starting with zero. A sector is just like an arc that forms an angle at the center. It is the smallest unit of information that can be transferred to/from the disk.
4. A disk contains one read/write head for each surface of a platter, which is used to store and retrieve data from the surface of platter. All the heads are attached to a single assembly called a disk arm.
5. The transfer of data between memory and disk drive is handled by a disk controller, which interfaces the disk drive to the computer system. Some common interfaces used for disk drives on personal computers and workstations are SCSI (Small-Computer-System-Interface; pronounced 'scuzzy'), ATA (AT Attachment) and SATA (Serial ATA).
6. The process of accessing data comprises three steps, namely, seek, rotate and data transfer. The combined time (seek time, latency time and data transfer time) is known as the access time of disk. Specifically, it can be described as the period of time that elapses between a

request for information from disk or memory and the information arriving at the requesting device.

7. The reliability of the disk is measured in terms of the Mean Time To Failure (MTTF). It is the amount of time for which the system can run continuously without any failure.

8. Several algorithms have been developed for disk scheduling, which are First-Come First-Serve (FCFS), Shortest Seek Time First (SSTF), SCAN, LOOK, C-SCAN and C-LOOK algorithms.

9. Before the disk can be used for storing data, all the platters of the disk must be divided into sectors (that disk controller can read and write) using some software. This process is called low-level (or physical) formatting, which is usually performed by manufacturer.

10. After physical formatting, logical (or high-level) formatting of each partition of the disk is to be performed. During logical formatting, the operating system stores initial file system data structures and a boot block on the disk. After logical formatting, the disk can be used to boot the system and store the data.

11. Due to manufacturing defects, some sectors of a disk drive may be found defective or bad during low-level formatting. Some sectors may also become bad during read or write operations with the disk due to head crash.

12. There are several ways of handling bad sectors. On some simple disks, bad sectors need to be handled manually by using, for instance, format command or chkdsk command of MS-DOS. However, in modern disks with advanced disk controller, other schemes, including sector sparing and sector slipping can be used.

13. Swap-space is used in different ways by different operating systems depending upon the memory management algorithms. The amount of disk space required to serve as swap-space may vary from a few megabytes to gigabytes.

14. A major advancement in secondary storage technology is represented by the development of RAID (Redundant Arrays of Independent Disks). The basic idea behind RAID is to have a large array of small independent disks. Presence of multiple disks in the system improves the overall transfer rates, if the disks are operated in parallel.

15. In order to improve the performance of disk, a concept called data striping is used which utilizes parallelizm. Data striping distributes the data transparently among N disks, which make them appear as a single large, fast disk.

16. Several RAID organizations, referred to as RAID levels, have been proposed which aims at providing redundancy at lower cost. These levels have different cost–performance trade-offs. The RAID levels are classified into seven levels (from level 0 to level 6).

17. The disk of a computer system contains bulk of data which can be accessed by the system either directly through I/O ports (host-attached storage) or through a remote system connected via network (network-attached storage).

18. Ideally, a disk should always work without producing any errors. However, practically, it cannot be achieved. The only achievable thing is a disk subsystem called stable storage which ensures whenever a write is performed to the disk; it is performed either completely or not at all.

19. Tertiary storage, also known as tertiary memory, is built from inexpensive disks and tape drives that use removable media. Due to relatively low speed of tertiary storage systems, they are primarily used for storing data that is to be accessed less frequently. Some examples of tertiary storage devices, include floppy disk, optical disk, magneto-optical disk and magnetic tape.

ANSWERS TO 'CHECK YOUR PROGRESS'

1. Tracks, Sectors
2. (b)
3. Mean time to failure
4. True
5. In LOOK algorithm, the head does not necessarily reach the end of disk, instead when there are no more requests in the direction in which the head is moving it reverses its direction.
6. False
7. Sector sparing
8. An operating system may use the swap-space to:
   - hold the image of a process (including its code and data segments) in case of systems implementing swapping.
   - hold the pages swapped out of the main memory in case of paging systems.
9. Data striping
10. (a)
11. Mirroring
12. Host-attached
13. True
14. (d)
15. Stable storage is a disk subsystem which ensures whenever a write is performed to the disk; it is performed either completely or not at all.

TEST YOURSELF

1. Give hardware description and various features of magnetic disk. How do you measure its performance?
2. Explain why SSTF scheduling tends to favour middle cylinders over the innermost and outermost cylinders.
3. Consider a disk drive having 200 cylinders, numbered form 0 to 199. The head is currently positioned at cylinder 53 and moving towards the cylinder 199. The queue of pending I/O requests is:
   98, 183, 37, 122, 14, 124, 65, 67.
   Starting from the current head position, what is the total head movement (in cylinders) to service the pending requests for each of the following disk-scheduling algorithms?
   (a) FCFS
   (b) SSTF
   (c) SCAN
   (d) LOOK
   (e) C-SCAN
   (f) C-LOOK
4. Compare and contrast the sector sparing and sector slipping techniques for managing bad sectors.

5. Define the following:
   (a) Disk latency
   (b) Seek time
   (c) Head crash
   (d) MTTF
6. Define RAID. What is the need of having RAID technology?
7. How can the reliability and performance of disk be improved using RAID? Explain different RAID levels.
8. How does the stable storage ensure consistency on disk during a failure?
9. Write a short note on the following:
   (a) Tertiary storage
   (b) Swap-space management
   (c) Disk formatting

University Solved Question Papers

Anna University

BE/BTech DEGREE EXAMINATION, MAY/JUNE 2009

FIFTH SEMESTER
INFORMATION TECHNOLOGY
CS 1252 OPERATING SYSTEMS
(Regulation 2004)

Answer ALL Questions

♦♦♦

PART A — (10 × 2 = 20 marks)

Q.1. Write pros and cons of hard real-time system and soft real-time system.

Ans: In hard real-time systems, a process must be accomplished within the specified deadlines; otherwise, undesirable results may be produced. A process serviced after its deadline does not make any sense. Due to such rigid time constraints, these systems can be used in industrial control and robotics. However, the strict deadlines restrict the facilities available in hard real-time systems. For example, secondary storage devices, such as hard disk, which are slow in speed, are generally missing or limited in such systems. The data is written onto short term memory (which are volatile in nature) or Read Only Memory (ROM). Moreover, some advanced operating system facilities, such as virtual memory are also absent in hard real-time systems. Due to these reasons, these systems cannot be mixed with other type of systems, such as time-sharing system.

On the other hand, in soft real-time systems, the requirements are less strict; it is not mandatory to meet the deadline. A real-time process always gets the priority over other tasks and retains the priority until its completion. If the deadline could not be met due to any reason, then it is possible to reschedule the task and complete it. These systems support almost all advanced features of operating system and hence, can be mixed with other types of systems.

The main disadvantage of soft real-time systems is that since they do not have rigid timelines, it is risky to use them for industrial control and robotics. However, they can be used in several other areas, such as multimedia, virtual reality and advanced scientific applications, such as undersea exploration.

Q.2. What are cooperating processes? Give an example.

Ans: The processes that need to exchange data or information with each other are known as cooperating (or interacting) processes. In other words, we can say a cooperating process is the one that can affect or be affected by the actions of other concurrent processes. The producer-consumer problem is the most common example of cooperating processes. In this problem, there are two processes, one is `producer` that produces the items and other is `consumer` that consumes the items produced by the `producer`. These two processes need to run concurrently, thereby, requiring communication with each other. One possible solution to this problem can be provided through shared memory. Both the `producer` and `consumer` processes are made to share a common buffer between them. The `producer` fills the buffer by placing the produced items in it and the `consumer` vacates the buffer by consuming these items.

Q.3. State the resources that are used when a thread is created? How do they differ from those used when a process is created?

Ans: Since a thread is smaller than a process, thread creation typically requires fewer resources than the process creation. Whenever a thread (user-level or kernel-level) is created, the operating system allocates to it a data structure that holds a set of registers, stack and priority of the thread. When a process is created, a Process Control Block (PCB) is allocated, which is a large data structure. The PCB includes a memory map, list of open files and environment variables. Allocating and managing the memory map is typically the most time consuming activity.

Q.4. State why a swapping scheme is implemented in a medium term scheduler?

Ans: Sometimes, it may happen that during its execution, a process becomes suspended for an I/O activity or after issuing a system call. Since that process cannot be further executed until the related suspending condition is over, it is better to remove it from the memory to make space for other process. Once the suspending condition is over, that process needs to be reloaded into the memory for further execution. This task of temporarily switching a process in and out of main memory is known as swapping. It is the responsibility of medium-term scheduler to swap-out the suspended process and later swap-in the process for its execution. Hence, it is also known as swapper. That is why a swapping scheme is implemented in a medium-term scheduler.

Q.5. Mention the necessary conditions for deadlock occurrence?

Ans: A deadlock occurs when all the following four conditions are satisfied at any given point of time.

1. **Mutual exclusion:** Only one process can acquire a given resource at any point of time. Any other process requesting for that resource has to wait for earlier process to release it.
2. **Hold and wait:** Process holding a resource allocated to it and waiting to acquire another resource held by other process.
3. **No pre-emption:** Resource allocated to a process cannot be forcibly revoked by the system, it can only be released voluntarily by the process holding it.
4. **Circular wait:** A set of processes waiting for allocation of resources held by other processes forms a circular chain in which each process is waiting for the resource held by its successor process in chain.

Q.6. If a computer system has 16 bit address line and supports 1 KB page size what will be the maximum page number supported by the system?

Ans: A computer system has 16 bit address lines implies that the logical address is of 16 bits. Therefore, the size of logical address space is 2^{16} and page size is 1 KB, that is, 1×1024 bytes $= 2^{10}$ bytes.

Thus, the page offset will be of 10 bits and page number will be of $(16 - 10) = 6$ bits.

Therefore, the maximum page number supported by this system is 111111.

Q.7. How does the system detect thrashing? Briefly state.

Ans: The system can detect thrashing by evaluating CPU utilization against the degree of multiprogramming. Generally, as we increase the degree of multiprogramming, the CPU utilization increases. However, this does not always hold true. To illustrate this, consider the graph shown in the following figure that depicts the behaviour of paging systems. Initially, the CPU utilization increases with increase in degree of

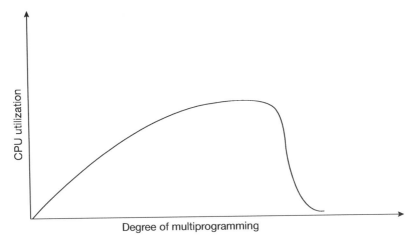

Behaviour of Paging Systems

multiprogramming. It continues to increase until it reaches maximum. Now, if the number of running processes is still increased, the CPU utilization drops sharply. To increase the CPU utilization at this point, the degree of multiprogramming must be decreased.

Q.8. What are immutable shared files?

Ans: An immutable shared file is a file that is once declared as shared by its creator cannot be modified. The two key properties of an immutable shared file are that once it is created, neither its name can be reused nor its contents can be changed. Thus, unlike a general file which contains variable information, an immutable file contains fixed information.

Q.9. State the major goal for the design and implementation of a swap space.

Ans: The major goal for the design and implementation of a swap space is to facilitate swapping of pages of the executing process. During the execution of a process, whenever a page is required, it is loaded into the main memory (swap-in) from the swap space. Similarly, when a process is to be removed (swap-out) from main memory, it is written back into the swap space if it has been modified.

Q.10. List the components of on-disk structure of a file system.

Ans: The on-disk structures include:

- **Boot control block:** It contains enough information that the system needs to boot the operating system from that partition. If the partition does not contain any operating system this block can be empty. In Unix File System (UFS), this block is called the boot block and in Windows (NTFS), it is called the partition boot sector.
- **Partition control block:** It is a table that stores key information related to partition, number and size of blocks in the partition, free block count and free block pointers, and FCB pointers and free FCB count. In UFS this is called superblock, in NTFS, it is Master File Table.

   Further, each partition has a directory structure, with root directory at the top. The directory structure helps to manage and organize the files in the file system. On creation of a new file, a new FCB is allocated that stores information, such as file permissions, ownership, size and location of the data blocks. In UFS this is called the i-node (an array of data structures, one for each file). In NTFS, this information is kept within the Master File Table, which uses a relational database structure, where each row stores information about a file.

PART B – (5 × 16 = 80 marks)

Q.11. (a) Explain the message passing interprocess communication and the various methods for logically implementing them.

Ans: In message passing interprocess communication, the cooperating processes communicate by sending and receiving messages from each other. The communication using message passing is very time consuming because it is implemented with the help of operating system calls and thus, it requires a major involvement of kernel.

In message passing systems, two system calls, `send()` and `receive()` are used. The sender process (say, P_1) sends the message to the operating system by invoking the `send()` system call. The operating system stores this message in the buffer area until the `receive()` system call is invoked by the receiver process (say, P_2). After that the operating system delivers this message to P_2. In case there is no message available for P_2 when it invokes the `receive()` system call, the operating system blocks it until some message arrives for it. On the other hand, if a number of messages arrive for P_2, the operating system puts them in a queue and delivers them in FIFO order upon the invocation of `receive()` call (one for each process) by P_2. The figure given below shows the message passing communication model.

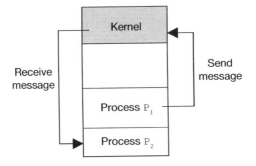

Message Passing Communication Model

In message passing, it is not necessary for the communicating processes to reside on the same computer rather they may reside on different computers connected via network (a distributed environment). Therefore, whenever two processes want to communicate, a communication link must be established between them. There are several ways of implementing a communication link. The physical implementation of the communication link can be achieved via shared variables or bus or the network, etc. On the other hand, the logical implementation of the link and the `send()` and `receive()` operations can be achieved using any of these methods:

Direct or Indirect Communication

In direct communication, processes address each other by their `PID` assigned to them by the operating system. For example, if a process P_1 wants to send a message to process P_2, then the system calls `send()` and `receive()` will be defined as follows:

- `send(PID₂, message)`
- `receive(PID₁, message)`

Since, both sender and receiver process need to know each other's `PID`, this type of communication is known as symmetric direct communication. However, asymmetry in addressing can be represented by making only the sender process to address the receiver process by its `PID` but the receiver process need not know the

PID of the sender process. In case of asymmetric direct communication, the calls send() and receive() will be defined as follows:

- send(PID$_2$, message)
- receive(id, message)

Now, when operating system delivers a message to process P$_2$ upon the invocation of receive() call by it, the parameter id is replaced with the PID of the sender process.

In indirect communication, messages are sent and received via mailbox (also known as port)—a repository of interprocess messages. A mailbox, as the name implies, is just like a post box into which messages sent by the processes can be stored and removed by other processes. The different characteristics of a mailbox are as follows:

- Each mailbox has a unique ID and the processes communicate with each other through a number of mailboxes.
- The process that creates the mailbox is the owner of mailbox and only this process can receive messages from it. Other processes can only send messages to it. In other words, there can be multiple senders but a single recipient for a mailbox.
- The process that knows the ID of a mailbox can send messages to it.
- Besides a user process, the operating system may also own a mailbox. In this case, the operating system may allow the processes to create or delete a mailbox, send and receive messages via mailbox. The process that creates the mailbox becomes the owner of that mailbox and may receive messages through this mailbox. However, with time, other processes can also be made to receive messages through this mailbox by passing ownership to them.

The system calls to send a message to a mailbox (say, X) and receive a message from a mailbox will be defined as follows:

- send(X, message)
- receive(X, message)

The communication link exhibits different properties in direct and indirect communication, which are listed in the table given below.

Comparison of Direct and Indirect Communication

Direct Communication	Indirect Communication
• There exists only one link between each pair of communicating processes.	• There may be multiple links between each pair of communicating processes, where each link corresponds to exactly one mailbox.
• A link is associated with just two processes.	• A link may be associated with more than two processes.
• The link is established automatically between the communicating processes, provided the sender process knows the PID of the receiver process.	• The communication link can be established between two processes only if both the communicating processes share a mailbox with each other.

Synchronous or Asynchronous Communication

Messages can be sent or received either synchronously or asynchronously, also called blocking or non-blocking, respectively. Various design options for implementing `send()` and `receive()` calls are as follows:

- **Blocking send:** If a process (say, P_1) invokes `send()` call to send a message to another process (say, P_2) or to a mailbox, the operating system blocks P_1 until the message is received by P_2 or by the mailbox.
- **Blocking receive:** If there is no message available for P_2 when it invokes the `receive()` system call, the operating system blocks it until some message arrives for it.
- **Non-blocking send:** P_1 sends the message and continues to perform its operation without waiting for the message delivery by P_2 or by mailbox.
- **Non-blocking receive:** When P_2 invokes a `receive()` call, it either gets a valid message if some message is available for it or NULL if there is no message available for it.

Automatic or Explicit Buffering

The messages sent by a process are temporarily stored in a temporary queue (called buffer) by the operating system before delivering them to the recipient. This buffer can be implemented in a variety of ways, which are as follows:

- **No buffering:** The capacity of buffer is zero, that is, no messages may wait in the queue. This implies the sender process has to wait until the message is received by the receiver process.
- **Bounded buffer:** The capacity of the buffer is fixed, say m, that is, at most m processes may wait in the queue at a time. When there are less than m messages waiting in the queue and a new message arrives, it is added in the queue. The sender process need not wait and it can resume its operation. However, if the queue is full, the sender process is blocked until some space becomes available in the queue.
- **Unbounded buffer:** The buffer has an unlimited capacity, that is, an infinite number of messages can be stored in the queue. In this case, the sender process gets never blocked.

Or

Q.11. (b) (i) What is the need for system calls? How system calls are used? Explain with an example.

Ans: System calls allow user programs to request services of the operating system. These calls are similar to a procedure call except that it switches the mode of execution from user mode to kernel mode and invokes the operating system. The operating system then determines what the user program actually asks or wants, performs the system call and returns the control back to the instruction following the system call. The user program now again proceeds in the user mode.

To understand how system calls are used, let us take an example of a program that opens a file and writes some data in it. Suppose the file name and the data to be written on it is provided by the user during the execution of the program. This program performs a sequence of system call during its execution. First, it makes a system call to prompt a message on screen to ask the user to provide the filename and the data to be written on the file. Then, the user provides the filename and the data by typing it through keyboard and reading this from keyboard again needs a system call. With having the filename, the program attempts to open the required file, for which another system call needs to be made. Once the file is opened, the data is written to the file (requires a system call) and the file is closed (another system call). Finally, a system call is performed to prompt the user with a message to inform that task is completed successfully.

The above discussion explains the use of system calls during normal operation; however, error could occur during any operation. For instance, when the program attempts to open the file, an error, such as file not found, hardware failure, file protection violation, etc., could occur. In this situation, the program cannot proceed with its normal behaviour, instead, it should prompt an appropriate message on the screen (a system call needed) and then terminate abnormally (another system call).

As now, it is clear that even the simple programs make heavy use of operating system services through system calls. In general, the services offered by these calls include creation and termination (or deletion) of processes, creation, deletion, reading, writing, opening and closing files, management of directories, and carrying out input and output. In fact, the set of services that are offered through system calls determines a significant part of the operating systems responsibilities. Here note that each system call may have same or different name in different operating systems.

Q.11. (b) (ii) Explain the process state diagram.

Ans: Each process in the operating system is tagged with a 'state' variable—an integer value that helps the operating system to decide what to do with the process. It also indicates the nature of the current activity in a process. A process may be in one of the following states depending on the current activity of the process.

- **New:** A process is said to be in 'new' state if it is being created.
- **Ready:** A process is said to be in 'ready' state if it is ready for the execution and waiting for the CPU to be allocated to it.
- **Running:** A process is said to be in 'running' state if CPU has been allocated to it and it is being executed.
- **Waiting:** A process is said to be in 'waiting' state (also called 'blocked' state) if it has been blocked by some event. Unless that event occurs, the process cannot continue its execution. Examples of such blocking events are completion of some I/O operation, reception of a signal, etc. Note that a process in waiting state is unable to run even if the CPU is available.
- **Terminated:** A process is said to be in 'terminated' state if it has completed its execution normally or it has been terminated abnormally by the operating system because of some error or killed by some other process.

Each process undergoes changes in states during its lifetime. The change in state of a process is known as state transition of a process. By and large, it is caused by the occurrence of some event in the system. There are many possible state transitions that may crop up along with their possible causes are as follows:

- **New → Ready:** This transition takes place if a new process has been loaded into the main memory and it is waiting for the CPU to be allocated to it.
- **Ready → Running:** This transition takes place if the CPU has been allocated to a ready process and it has started its execution.
- **Running → Ready:** This transition may occur if
  - the time slice of the currently running process has expired
  - some higher priority process gets ready for execution, etc.
  In this case, the CPU is pre-empted from the currently executing process and allocated to some another ready process.
- **Running → Waiting:** This transition may take place if the currently running process
  - needs to perform some I/O operation
  - has to wait for a message or some action from another process
  - requests for some other resource

In this case, the CPU gets freed by the process and can be allocated to some another ready process.

- **Running → Terminated:** This transition takes place if the currently running process
  - has completed its task and requests to the operating system for its termination
  - is terminated by its parent in case the function performed by it is no longer required
  - is terminated by the kernel because it has exceeded its resource usage limit or involved in a deadlock
  In this case, the CPU is pre-empted from the currently running process and allocated to some another ready process.
- **Waiting → Ready:** This transition takes place if an event (for example, I/O completion, signal reception, synchronization operation, etc.) for which the process was waiting, has occurred.

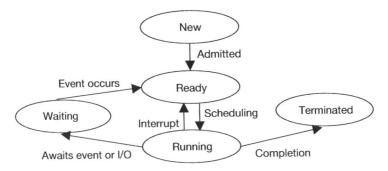

Process State Transition Diagram

Q.12. (a) (i) Write the C implementation of semaphores and the operations on it.

Ans: In 1965, Dijkstra suggested using an abstract data type called a semaphore for controlling synchronization. A semaphore S is an integer variable which is used to provide a general purpose solution to critical-section problem. In his proposal, two standard atomic operations are defined on S, namely, `wait` and `signal` and after initialization, S is accessed only through these two operations. The definition of `wait` and `signal` operation in pseudocode is as follows:

```
wait(S)
{
    while(S<=0)
        doNothing();
    S--;
}
signal(S)
{
    S++;
}
```

The solution of critical-section problem for N processes is implemented by allowing the processes to share a semaphore S, which is initialized to 1. The general structure for the code segment of process, say P_i, is as follows:

```
do
{
```

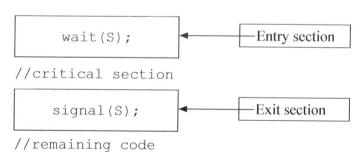

```
    //critical section
```

```
    //remaining code
}while(1);
```

Semaphores can be used to solve various synchronization problems, such as bounded-buffer problem, readers-writers problem and dining philosophers problem. Here, we present a solution to the bounded-buffer problem using semaphores. In bounded-buffer problem, there are two processes, one is `producer` that produces the items and other is `consumer` that consumes the items produced by the `producer`. Both the `producer` and `consumer` processes are made to share a common buffer between them. The `producer` fills the buffer by placing the produced items in it and the `consumer` vacates the buffer by consuming these items.

The following three semaphores are used in this solution.

- The `mutex` semaphore, initialized to 1, is used to provide the producer and consumer processes the mutually exclusive access to the buffer. This semaphore ensures that only one process, either producer or consumer, is accessing the buffer and the associated variables at a time.

- The `full` semaphore, initialized to 0, is used to count the number of full buffers. This semaphore ensures that the producer stops executing items when the buffer is full.
- The `empty` semaphore, initialized to the value of size, is used to count the number of empty buffers. This semaphore ensures that consumer stops executing when the buffer is empty.

The general structure for the code segment of producer process and consumer process is as follows:

```
//structure of a producer process
do
{
    item_produced = produce_item();
    wait(empty);
    wait(mutex);
    buffer[in] = item_produced;
    in = (in + 1) % size;
    signal(mutex);
    signal(full);
}while(1);
//structure of consumer process
do
{
    wait(full);
    wait(mutex);
    item_consumed = buffer[out];
    out = (out + 1) % size;
    signal(mutex);
    signal(empty);
    consume_item(item_consumed);
}while(1);
```

Q.12. (a) (ii) Define the critical section problem and discuss the three requirements that a solution to the critical section problem must satisfy.

Ans: The portion of the code of a process in which it accesses or changes the shared data is known as its critical region (also called critical section). The critical-section problem is to design a protocol that the processes can use to cooperate. Each process must request permission to enter its critical section and signal the entrance by setting the values of some variables. The process does this in the code just before the critical section. That part of code is called the entry section. After executing the critical section, the process again sets some variables to signal the exit from the critical section. The portion of code in which the process does this is called the exit section. A solution to critical-section problem must satisfy the following three requirements.

- **Mutual exclusion:** The system must ensure that the execution of critical sections by the cooperating processes is mutually exclusive. It means that no two processes are allowed to execute in their critical sections at one time.
- **Progress:** Suppose a process P_1 is executing in its critical section, then all other processes that wish to enter their critical sections have to wait. When P_1 finishes its execution in critical section, a decision as to which process will enter its critical section next is to be made. In the decision, only the waiting processes will participate, and the decision should be made in a finite amount of time. A process that has exited from its critical section cannot prevent other processes from entering their critical sections.
- **Bounded waiting:** A process wishing to enter its critical section cannot be delayed indefinitely. There is an upper bound on the number of times that other processes are allowed to enter their critical sections after a process has made a request to enter its critical section and before the permission is granted.

Or

Q.12. (b) (i) What are the advantages of threads? Describe the multi-threaded problems.

Ans: The major advantage that threads provide over processes is the low overhead during switching (as discussed in the previous section). In addition, threads offer some other advantages, which are as follows:

- **Computational speedup:** On a uniprocessor system, a process can be executed speedily by creating multiple threads in the process and executing them in a quasi-parallel manner (that is, by rapidly switching the CPU among multiple threads).
- **Economy:** Thread creation is more economical than the process creation. Every time a process is created, some memory and resources are required to be allocated to it. On the other hand, threads share the resources of the process to which they belong, so there is no need to allocate memory and resource at the time of thread creation.
- **Efficient communication:** As different threads of a process share the same address space, communication among them can be made via the shared memory. There is no need to execute system calls, which cause extra overhead.
- **Proper utilization of multiprocessor architecture:** In multiprocessor systems, threads prove more useful than processes. Multiple threads of a single process can be made to run on different CPUs at the same time, thereby, achieving real parallelism. In contrast, a single process can run only on one CPU regardless of the number of available CPUs.
- **Responsiveness:** In case of interactive processes, the major performance criteria is the response time. If such a process is multithreaded, a part of the process (thread) is able to run even if some other part of the process is blocked. As a result, responsiveness of the process to the user is increased.

Multi-threaded Models

Two types of thread can be created in a process, which are user-level and kernel-level. There may exist different types of relationship between user-level and kernel-level threads, each resulting in a specific multithreading model. Three common multithreading models are as follows:

- **Many-to-one (M:1) model:** In this model, the kernel creates only one kernel-level thread in each process and the multiple user-level threads (created by thread library) of the process are associated with this kernel-level thread. As the threads are managed in the user space, this model produces a similar effect as that of user-level threads. An example of a thread library that employs this model is Green threads available for Solaris 2.

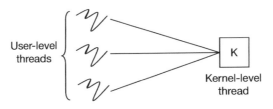

Many-to-One (M:1) Model

This model incurs a low switching overhead as kernel is not involved while switching between threads. But if one user-level thread issues a blocking system call, the kernel blocks the whole parent process. Moreover, as the kernel-level thread can be accessed by only one user-level thread at a time, multiple user-level threads cannot run in parallel on multiple CPUs, thereby, resulting in low concurrency.

- **One-to-one (1:1) model:** In this model, each user-level thread is associated with a kernel-level thread. The threads are managed by the kernel, therefore, this model provides an effect similar to kernel-level threads. Many modern operating systems, such as Windows 2000 and Windows NT, employ this model.

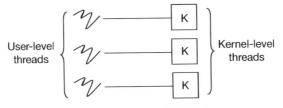

One-to-One (1:1) Model

In this model, multiple threads can run in parallel on multiple CPUs in a multiprocessor environment and thus, greater concurrency is achieved. As each user-level thread is mapped into a different kernel-level thread, blocking of one user-level thread does not cause other user-level threads to block. However, it results in high switching overhead due to involvement of kernel in switching. Also, most implementations of this model restrict on the number of threads that can be created in a process. This is because whenever a user-level thread is created in a process, a corresponding kernel-level thread is also required to be created. The creation of many kernel-level threads incurs an overhead to the system, thereby, degrading the performance.

- **Many-to-many (M:M) model:** In this model, many user-level threads are associated with many kernel-level threads with the number of kernel-level threads being equal to or less than that of user-level threads. This implies that more than one user-level threads may be associated with same kernel-level thread. This model overcomes the limitations of both many-to-one and one-to-one models. The operating systems, including Solaris 2 and Tru64 UNIX, employ this model.

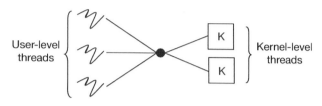

Many-to-Many (M:M) Model

In this model, many user-level threads can be made to run in parallel on different CPUs by mapping each user-level thread to a different kernel-level thread. Blocking of one user-level thread does not result in the blockage of other user-level threads that are mapped into different kernel-level threads. In addition, switching between user-level threads associated with same kernel-level thread does not incur much overhead. There is no restriction on the number of user-level threads that can be created in a process; as many user-level threads as required can be created. However, the implementation of this model is very complex.

Q.12. (b) (ii) What is the advantage of having different time-quantum sizes at different levels of a Multilevel Feedback Queue (MFQ) based scheduling?

Ans: The multilevel feedback queue scheduling also known as multilevel adaptive scheduling is an improved version of multilevel queue scheduling algorithm. In this scheduling algorithm, processes are not permanently assigned to queues; instead they are allowed to move between the queues. The decision to move a process between queues is based on the time taken by it in execution so far and its waiting time. If a process has already used too much CPU time, it is moved to a lower priority queue. Similarly, a process that has been waiting for too long in a lower priority queue is moved to a higher priority queue in order to avoid starvation.

To understand this algorithm, consider a multilevel feedback queue scheduler with three queues, namely, Q_1, Q_2 and Q_3. Further, assume that the queues Q_1 and Q_2 employ round robin scheduling algorithm with time quantum of 5 ms and 10 ms, respectively while in queue Q_3, the processes are scheduled in FCFS order. The scheduler first executes all processes in Q_1. When Q_1 is empty, the scheduler executes the processes in Q_2. Finally, when both Q_1 and Q_2 are empty, the processes in Q_3 are executed. While executing processes in Q_2, if a new process arrives in Q_1, the currently executing process is pre-empted and the new process starts executing. Similarly, a process arriving in Q_2 pre-empts a process executing in Q_3. Initially, when a process enters into ready queue; it is placed in Q_1 where it is allocated the CPU for 5 ms. If the process finishes its execution within 5 ms, it exits from the queue. Otherwise, it is pre-empted and placed at the end of Q_2. Here, it is allocated the CPU for 10 ms (if Q_1 is empty) and still if it does not finish, it is pre-empted and placed at the end of Q_3.

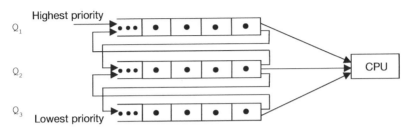

Multilevel Feedback Queue Scheduling

The main advantage of having different time-quantum sizes at different levels is that the I/O bound and interactive processes can be put in a queue with a small time-quantum, whereas, the CPU bound processes can be put in a queue with a larger quantum. This makes more efficient use of the computer.

Q.13. (a) Explain the difference between External Fragmentation and Internal Fragmentation. How to solve the fragmentation problem using paging?

Ans: Most of the systems used today support multiprogramming which allows multiple processes to reside in the memory at the same time. The simple way to achieve multiprogramming is to divide main memory into a number of partitions which may be of fixed or variable size. In fixed-partitions technique, each partition is of fixed size and can contain only one process. Whenever a partition is free, a process whose size is less than or equal to the partition size is selected from the input queue and loaded into this partition. When the process terminates, the partition becomes free to be allocated to another process.

In fixed-partitions technique, memory utilization is not efficient. Any process regardless of how small it is, occupies an entire partition which may lead to wastage of memory within the partition. This phenomenon which results in the wastage of memory within the partition is called internal fragmentation. For example, loading a process of size 3.9 KB into a partition of size 4 KB (where, KB stands for KiloBytes) would result in a wasted space of approximately 100 bytes within the partition.

To overcome the problem of fixed-partitions technique, a technique called MVT (Multiprogramming with a Variable number of Tasks) is used. It is the generalization of the fixed partitions technique in which the partitions can vary in number and size. In this technique, the amount of memory allocated is exactly the amount of memory a process requires. To implement this, the table maintained by the operating system stores both the starting address and ending address of each process.

Initially, when there is no process in the memory, the whole memory is available for the allocation and is considered as a single large partition of available memory (a hole). Whenever a process requests for the memory, the hole large enough to accommodate that process is allocated. The rest of the memory is available for other processes. As soon as the process terminates, the memory occupied by it is deallocated and can be used for other processes. Thus, at a given point of time, some parts of memory may be in use while other may be free. Due to a sequence of allocations and deallocations, there will be a set of holes of various sizes dispersed in the memory at a certain point of time. As a result, there may be possibility that the total available memory is large enough to accommodate the waiting process. However, it cannot be utilized as it is scattered. This wastage of the memory space is called external fragmentation since the wasted memory is not a part of any partition.

The main difference between internal fragmentation and external fragmentation is that in internal fragmentation the system cannot use the free memory space within the partition for any other process until that process is terminated and release the partition. However, in external fragmentation the scattered free space can be used by the system by relocating (or shuffling) some or all portions of the memory in order to place all the free holes together at one end of memory to make one large hole. This technique of reforming the storage is termed as compaction.

The problem of external fragmentation can be resolved using a technique called paging. In this technique, the physical memory is divided into fixed sized blocks called page frames and logical memory is also divided into fixed size blocks called pages which are of same size as that of page frames. When a process is to be executed, its pages can be loaded into any unallocated frames (not necessarily contiguous) from the disk. The figure given below shows two processes A and B with all their pages loaded into the memory. In this figure, the page size is of 4 KB.

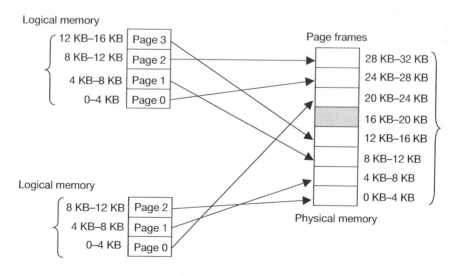

Concept of Paging

Since the memory allocated is always in fixed unit, any free frame can be allocated to a process. Thus, there is no external fragmentation. However, there may be some internal fragmentation because memory is allocated in terms of integral of number of page frames and if the size of a given process does not come out to be a multiple of page size, the last frame allocated to the process may not be completely used. Thus, internal fragmentation cannot be resolved completely.

Or

Q.13. (b) (i) Explain Banker's algorithm for deadlock avoidance.

Ans: The Banker's algorithm is used to ensure the deadlock avoidance. To implement this algorithm, certain data structures are required, which help in determining whether the system is in safe state or not. These data structures are as follows:

1. **Available resources, A:** A vector of size q stores information about the number of resources available of each type.
2. **Maximum, M**: A matrix of order p×q stores information about the maximum number of resources of each type required by each process (p number of processes). That is, M[i][j] indicates the maximum number of resources of type j required by the process i.
3. **Current allocation, C:** A matrix of order p×q stores information about the number of resources of each type allocated to each process. That is, C[i][j] indicates the number of resources of type j currently held by the process i.
4. **Required, R:** A matrix of order pxq stores information about the remaining number of resources of each type required by each process. That is, R[i][j] indicates the remaining number of resources of type j required by the process i. Note that this vector can be obtained by M−C, that is,

$$R[i][j] = M[i][j] - C[i][j]$$

To understand the algorithm for determining whether a system is in safe state, consider a vector Complete of size p. Following are the steps of the algorithm.

1. Initialize   Complete[i]=False   for   all   i=1,   2,   3,...,   p. Complete[i] =False indicates that the ith process is still not completed.
2. Search for an i, such that Complete[i]=False and (R<=A) that is, resources required by this process is less than the available resources. If no such process exists, then go to step 4.
3. Let the process finish its execution. Set A = A + C and Complete[i]=True. Go to step 2.
4. If Complete[i]=True for all i, then the system is in safe state. Otherwise, it indicates that there exists a process for which Complete[i] =False and resources required by it are more than the available resources. Hence, it is in unending waiting state leading to an unsafe state.

Once it is confirmed that system is in safe state, an algorithm called resource request algorithm is used for determining whether the request by a process can be satisfied or not. To understand this algorithm, let Req be a matrix of the order pxq, indicating the number of resources of each type requested by each process at any given point of time. That is, Req[i][j] indicates the number of resources of jth type requested by the ith process at any given point of time. Following are the steps of this algorithm.

1. If `Req[i][j] <=R[i][j]`, go to step 2, otherwise an error occurs as process is requesting for more resources than the maximum number of resources required by it.
2. If `Req[i][j] <=A[i][j]`, go to step 3, otherwise the process P_i must wait until the required resources are available.
3. Allocate the resources and make the following changes in the data structures.

```
A = A - Req
C = C + Req
R = R - Req
```

Now, if the resulting system state is safe, then the request can be granted immediately. Otherwise, the requesting process must wait and the old system state is restored.

Q.13. (b) (ii) With relevant diagrams and examples discuss the advantages and disadvantages of continuous memory allocation schemes.

Ans: In contiguous memory allocation, each process is allocated a single contiguous part of the memory. The different memory management schemes that are based on this approach are single partition and multiple partitions.

Single Partition

In single partition scheme, the main memory is partitioned into two parts—one of them is permanently allocated to the operating system while the other part is allocated to the user process.

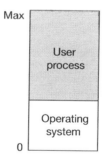

Memory having Single Partition

In this scheme, only one process can execute at a time. Whenever a process is to be executed, the operating system loads it into the main memory for execution. After termination of that process, the operating system waits for another process. When another process arrives, the operating system loads it into the main memory, thus overwriting the first one.

Advantages

- This scheme is easy to implement. Generally, the operating system needs to keep track of the first and the last location allocated to the user processes.

- It needs no hardware support except for protecting the operating system from the user process.

Disadvantages

- A single partition scheme restricts the system to have only one process in memory at a time that reduces utilization of the CPU as well as of memory.
- It does not support multiprogramming.

Multiple Partitions

Most of the systems used today support multiprogramming which allows multiple processes to reside in the memory at the same time. The simple way to achieve multiprogramming is to divide main memory into a number of partitions which may be of fixed or variable size.

In fixed partitions technique, each partition is of fixed size and can contain only one process. Whenever a partition is free, a process whose size is less than or equal to the partition size is selected from the input queue and loaded into this partition. When the process terminates, the partition becomes free to be allocated to another process.

Advantages

- The fixed partitioning technique is easy to implement and requires less overhead.
- It supports multiprogramming, which results in effective utilization of CPU as well as memory.

Disadvantages

- Any process regardless of how small it is, occupies an entire partition which leads to the wastage of memory within the partition. This phenomenon which results in the wastage of memory within the partition is called internal fragmentation. For example, loading a process of size 3.9 KB into a partition of size 4 KB (where, KB stands for KiloBytes) would result in a wasted space of approximately 100 bytes within the partition.
- The number of processes in memory depends on the number of partitions. Thus, the degree of multiprogramming is limited.
- The memory cannot be used efficiently in case most processes are of small sizes compared to partition sizes.

To overcome the problem of fixed partitions technique, a technique called MVT (Multiprogramming with a Variable number of Tasks) is used. It is the generalization of the fixed partitions technique in which the partitions can vary in number and size. In this technique, the amount of memory allocated is exactly the amount of memory a process requires. To implement this, the table maintained by the operating system stores both the starting address and ending address of each process.

Initially, when there is no process in the memory, the whole memory is available for the allocation and is considered as a single large partition of available memory (a hole). Whenever a process requests for the memory, the hole large enough to accommodate that process is allocated. The rest of the memory is available for other processes. As soon as the process terminates, the memory occupied by it is deallocated and can be used for other processes. Thus, at a given point of time, some parts of memory may be in use while others may be free.

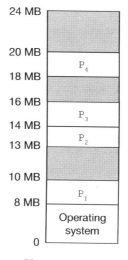

Memory Map

Due to a sequence of allocations and deallocations, there will be a set of holes of various sizes dispersed in the memory at a certain point of time. As a result, there may be possibility that the total available memory is large enough to accommodate the waiting process. However, it cannot be utilized as it is scattered. This wastage of the memory space is called external fragmentation since, the wasted memory is not a part of any partition. For example, if a request for a partition of size 5 MB arrives, it cannot be granted because no single partition is available that is large enough to satisfy the request (see the figure given below). However, the combined free space is sufficient to satisfy the request.

To get rid of this problem, it is desirable to relocate (or shuffle) some or all portions of the memory in order to place the free holes together at one end of memory to make one large hole. This technique of reforming the storage is termed as compaction. Compaction results in the memory partitioned into two contiguous blocks—one of used memory and another of free memory. The figure given below shows the memory map after performing compaction. Compaction may take place at the moment any node frees some memory or when a request for allocating memory fails, provided the combined free space is enough to satisfy the request. Since it is expensive in terms of CPU time, it is rarely used.

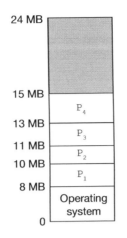

24 MB

15 MB

P_4

13 MB

P_3

11 MB

P_2

10 MB

P_1

8 MB

Operating system

0

Memory after Compaction

Q.14. (a) What are the causes of thrashing? Explain working-set model with an example.

Ans: Thrashing is caused due to underallocation of memory to a process. When a process has not been allocated as much frames as it needs to support its pages in active use, it causes a page fault. To handle this page fault, some of its page is to be replaced. But since all its pages are being actively used, the replaced page will soon be referenced again, thereby, causing another page fault. Eventually, page faults would occur very frequently, replacing pages that would soon be required to be brought back into memory. As a result, the system would be mostly busy in performing paging (page-out, page-in) rather than executing the processes. Thrashing results in poor system performance as no productive work is being performed during thrashing.

Working-set Model

Working set model is an approach used to prevent thrashing and is based on the assumption of locality. Locality is defined as the set of pages that are actively used together. Working-set model uses a parameter (say, n) to define the **working set** of a process, which is the set of pages that a process has referenced in the latest n page references. The notion of working set helps the operating system to decide how many frames should be allocated to a process.

Since the locality of process changes from time to time, so as the working set. At a particular instant of time, a page in active use is included in the working set while a page that was referenced before the most recent n references is not included. For example, consider the sequence of memory references given in the figure.

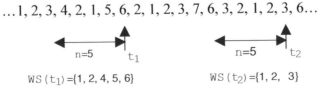

...1, 2, 3, 4, 2, 1, 5, 6, 2, 1, 2, 3, 7, 6, 3, 2, 1, 2, 3, 6...

n=5 t_1 n=5 t_2

WS(t_1) = {1, 2, 4, 5, 6}   WS(t_2) = {1, 2, 3}

Working-set Model

If the value of n is 5, then the working set at time t_1 is {1, 2, 4, 5, 6}. At time t_2 the working set would be {1, 2, 3}.

Note that the performance of working set strategy depends to a greater extent on the value of n. A too large value of n would result in over commitment of memory to a process. The working set may contain those pages which are not supposed to be referenced. In contrast, a too small value of n would cause under commitment of memory, which in turn results in high page fault rate and consequently thrashing. Thus, the value of n must be carefully chosen for the accuracy of working set strategy.

The most important property of working-set is its size, as it indicates the number of frames required by a process. The knowledge of working set size of each process helps to compute the total number of frames required by all the running processes. For example, if WSS_i denotes the working set size of a process P_i at time t, then the total number of frames required (say, V) at time t can be calculated as:

$$V = \sum_i WSS_i$$

Now, thrashing can be prevented by ensuring $V <= F$ where F denotes the total number of available frames in memory at time t.

The idea behind the working set strategy is to have the working set of processes in memory at all times in order to prevent thrashing. For this, the operating system continuously monitors the working set of each running process and allocates enough frames to accommodate its working set size. If still some frames are remaining, the operating system may decide to increase the degree of multiprogramming by starting a new process. On the other hand, if at any instant the operating system finds $V > F$, it selects some process and suspends its execution, thereby, decreasing the degree of multiprogramming. In totality, the degree of multiprogramming is kept as high as possible and thus, working set strategy results in optimum CPU utilization.

Or

Q.14. (b) Consider the following page reference string:

1, 2, 3, 4, 2, 1, 5, 6, 2, 1, 2, 3, 7, 6, 3, 2, 1, 2, 3, 6

How many page faults would occur for the following replacement algorithms, assuming one, two, three and four frames?

(i)   LRU replacement
(ii) FIFO replacement
(iii) Optimal replacement

Remember that all frames are initially empty, so your first unique pages will all cost one fault each.

Ans: In case of one page frame, each page reference causes a page fault. As a result, there will be 20 page faults for all the three replacement algorithms.

Page frames $= 2$

LRU replacement causes 18 page faults as shown in figure given below.

Reference string	1	2	3	4	2	1	5	6	2	1	2	3	7	6	3	2	1	2	3	6
Swap-in page	1	2	3	4	2	1	5	6	2	1	-	3	7	6	3	2	1	-	3	6
Page frames	1	1	3	3	2	2	5	5	2	2	2	2	7	7	3	3	1	1	3	3
Page frames	-	2	2	4	4	1	1	6	6	1	1	3	3	6	6	2	2	2	2	6
Swap-out page	-	-	1	2	3	4	2	1	5	6	-	1	2	3	7	6	3	-	1	2

FIFO replacement also causes 18 page faults (see the figure given below).

Reference string	1	2	3	4	2	1	5	6	2	1	2	3	7	6	3	2	1	2	3	6
Swap-in page	1	2	3	4	2	1	5	6	2	1	-	3	7	6	3	2	1	-	3	6
Page frames	1	1	3	3	2	2	5	5	2	2	2	3	3	6	6	2	2	2	3	3
Page frames	-	2	2	4	4	1	1	6	6	1	1	1	7	7	3	3	1	1	1	6
Swap-out page	-	-	1	2	3	4	2	1	5	6	-	2	1	3	7	6	3	-	2	1

Optimal replacement, on the other hand, causes only 15 page faults (see the figure given below).

Reference string	1	2	3	4	2	1	5	6	2	1	2	3	7	6	3	2	1	2	3	6
Swap-in page	1	2	3	4	-	1	5	6	-	1	-	3	7	6	-	2	1	-	3	6
Page frames	1	1	3	4	4	1	5	6	6	1	1	3	3	3	3	1	1	1	6	6
Page frames	-	2	2	2	2	2	2	2	2	2	2	7	6	6	2	2	2	3	3	3
Swap-out page	-	-	1	3	3	4	1	5	-	6	-	1	2	7	-	6	3	-	2	1

Page frames = 3

LRU replacement causes 15 page faults as shown in figure given below.

Reference string	1	2	3	4	2	1	5	6	2	1	2	3	7	6	3	2	1	2	3	6
Swap-in page	1	2	3	4	-	1	5	6	2	1	-	3	7	6	-	2	1	-	-	6
Page frames	1	1	1	4	4	4	5	5	5	1	1	1	7	7	7	2	2	2	2	2
Page frames	-	2	2	2	2	2	6	6	6	6	3	3	3	3	3	3	3	3	3	3
Page frames	-	-	3	3	3	1	1	1	2	2	2	2	2	6	6	6	1	1	1	6
Swap-out page	-	-	-	1	-	3	4	2	1	5	-	6	1	2	-	7	6	-	-	1

FIFO replacement causes 16 page faults as shown in figure given below).

Reference string	1	2	3	4	2	1	5	6	2	1	2	3	7	6	3	2	1	2	3	6
Swap-in page	1	2	3	4	-	1	5	6	2	1	-	3	7	6	-	2	1	-	3	6
Page frames	1	1	1	4	4	4	4	6	6	6	6	3	3	3	3	2	2	2	2	6
Page frames	-	2	2	2	2	1	1	1	2	2	2	2	7	7	7	7	1	1	1	1
Page frames	-	-	3	3	3	3	5	5	5	1	1	1	1	6	6	6	6	6	3	3
Swap-out page	-	-	-	1	-	2	3	4	1	5	-	6	2	1	-	3	7	-	6	2

Optimal replacement causes 11 page faults as shown in figure given below.

Reference string	1	2	3	4	2	1	5	6	2	1	2	3	7	6	3	2	1	2	3	6
Swap-in page	1	2	3	4	-	-	5	6	-	-	-	3	7	-	-	2	1	-	-	6
Page frames	1	1	1	1	1	1	1	1	1	1	1	3	3	3	3	3	3	3	3	6
	-	2	2	2	2	2	2	2	2	2	2	2	7	7	7	2	2	2	2	2
	-	-	3	4	4	4	5	6	6	6	6	6	6	6	6	6	1	1	1	1
Swap-out page	-	-	-	3	-	-	4	5	-	-	-	1	2	-	-	7	6	-	-	3

Page frames = 4

LRU replacement causes 10 page faults as shown in figure given below.

Reference string	1	2	3	4	2	1	5	6	2	1	2	3	7	6	3	2	1	2	3	6
Swap-in page	1	2	3	4	-	-	5	6	-	-	-	3	7	6	-	-	1	-	-	-
Page frames	1	1	1	1	1	1	1	1	1	1	1	1	1	6	6	6	6	6	6	6
	-	2	2	2	2	2	2	2	2	2	2	2	2	2	2	2	2	2	2	2
	-	-	3	3	3	3	5	5	5	5	5	3	3	3	3	3	3	3	3	3
	-	-	-	4	4	4	4	6	6	6	6	6	7	7	7	7	1	1	1	1
Swap-out page	-	-	-	-	-	-	3	4	-	-	-	5	6	1	-	-	7	-	-	-

FIFO replacement causes 14 page faults as shown in figure given below.

Reference string	1	2	3	4	2	1	5	6	2	1	2	3	7	6	3	2	1	2	3	6
Swap-in page	1	2	3	4	-	-	5	6	2	1	-	3	7	6	-	2	1	-	3	-
Page frames	1	1	1	1	1	1	5	5	5	5	5	3	3	3	3	3	1	1	1	1
	-	2	2	2	2	2	2	6	6	6	6	6	7	7	7	7	7	7	3	3
	-	-	3	3	3	3	3	3	2	2	2	2	2	6	6	6	6	6	6	6
	-	-	-	4	4	4	4	4	4	1	1	1	1	1	1	2	2	2	2	2
Swap-out page	-	-	-	-	-	-	1	2	3	4	-	5	6	2	-	1	3	-	7	-

Optimal replacement causes 8 page faults as shown in figure given below.

Reference string	1	2	3	4	2	1	5	6	2	1	2	3	7	6	3	2	1	2	3	6
Swap-in page	1	2	3	4	-	-	5	6	-	-	-	-	7	-	-	-	1	-	-	-
Page frames	1	1	1	1	1	1	1	1	1	1	1	1	7	7	7	7	1	1	1	1
	-	2	2	2	2	2	2	2	2	2	2	2	2	2	2	2	2	2	2	2
	-	-	3	3	3	3	3	3	3	3	3	3	3	3	3	3	3	3	3	3
	-	-	-	4	4	4	5	6	6	6	6	6	6	6	6	6	6	6	6	6
Swap-out page	-	-	-	-	-	-	4	6	-	6	-	-	1	7	-	-	7	-	-	-

Q.15. (a)(i) Explain the linked allocation and indexed allocation methods used in file systems. (8)

Ans: **Linked Allocation**

The file size generally tends to change (grow and shrink) over time. The contiguous allocation of such files results in the several problems. Linked allocation method overcomes the problems of contiguous allocation method.

In the linked allocation method, each file is stored as a linked list of disk blocks. The disk blocks are generally scattered throughout the disk and each disk block stores the address of the next block. The directory entry contains the filename and the address of the first and last blocks of the file as shown in the following figure.

This figure shows the linked allocation for a file. A total of four disk blocks are allocated to the file. The directory entry indicates that the file starts at block 12. It then continues at block 9, block 2 and finally ends at block 5.

The simplicity and straightforwardness of this method makes it easy to implement. The linked allocation results in optimum utilization of disk space as even a single free block between the used blocks can be linked and allocated to a file. This method does not come across with the problem of external fragmentation.

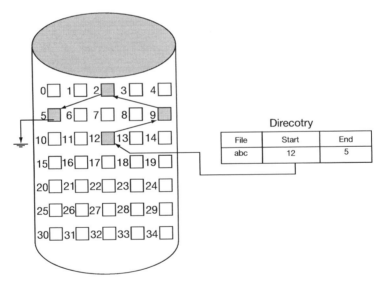

An Example of Linked Allocation

The main disadvantages of using linked allocation are the slow access speed, disk space utilization by pointers and low-reliability of the system. As this method provides only sequential access to files, therefore, to find out the nth block of a file, the search starts at the beginning of the file and follows the pointer until the nth block is found. For a very large file, the average turn around time is high.

In linked allocation, maintaining pointers in each block requires some disk space. The total disk space required by all the pointers in a file becomes substantial, which results in more space required by each file. The space required to store pointers can otherwise be used to store the information. The linked allocation is also not very reliable. Since disk blocks are linked together by pointers, a single damaged pointer may prevent us from accessing the file blocks that follows the damaged link.

Indexed Allocation

There is one thing common to both linked and indexed allocation, that is, non-contiguous allocation of disk blocks to the files. However, they follow different approaches to access the information on the disk. Linked allocation supports sequential access, whereas, indexed allocation supports sequential as well as direct access.

In indexed allocation, the blocks of a file are scattered all over the disk in the same manner as they are in linked allocation. However, here the pointers to the blocks are brought together at one location known as the index block. Each file has an index block, which is an array of disk-block pointers (addresses). The kth entry in the index block points to the kth disk block of the file. To read the kth disk block of a file, the pointer in the kth index block entry is used to find and read the desired block. The index block serves the same purpose as a page map table does in the paged memory systems.

The main advantage of indexed allocation is the absence of external fragmentation, since, any free blocks on the disk may be allocated to fulfill a demand for more space. Moreover, the index can be used to access the blocks in a random manner. When compared to linked allocation, the pointer overhead in indexed allocation is comparatively more. This is because with linked allocation, a file of only two blocks uses a total of 8 bytes for storing pointers (assuming each pointer require 4 bytes of space). However, with indexed allocation, the system must allocate one block (512 bytes) of disk space for storing pointers. This results in wastage of 504 bytes of the index block as only 8 bytes are used for storing the two pointers.

Q.15. (a)(ii) Compare and contrast 'free-space management' and 'swap space management'. (8)

Ans: Free space on the disk implies the space that has not been allocated to any file or directory. The file system maintains a free space list to keep track of the free blocks on the disk. To create a file, the free space list is searched for the required amount of space, and the space is then allocated to the new file. The newly allocated space is removed from the free space list. Similarly, when a file is deleted, its space is added to the free space list.

Swap space is the portion of disk that is used as an extension to main memory. It is used to hold either the image of a process (including its code and data segments) in case of systems implementing swapping or to hold the pages swapped out of the main memory in case of paging systems. Whenever a process is to be executed, swap space area on secondary storage device is allocated to it. During the execution of a process, whenever a page is required, it is loaded into the main memory from the swap space. Similarly, when a process is to be removed from main memory, it is written back into the swap space if it has been modified.

Some main differences between the swap space management and free space management are listed in the following table.

Swap Space Management	Free Space Management
• The amount of swap space on the disk may vary depending on the size of physical memory, virtual memory it is backing, and the way virtual memory is being used.	• The amount of free space on the disk is not concerned with the amount of physical memory.
• A swap-space storage manager is used to allocate and deallocate the swap space.	• Free-space manager is responsible for keeping track of unallocated blocks, allocating them, and adding the space freed by deletion of files to the free list.
• Adding more space to swap space requires repartitioning of the disk in case swap space resides in a raw partition.	• No disk repartitioning is required while adding more space to free space.
• Swap space is reinitialized each time the system is started.	• Free-space is not reinitialized at the time of system boot.

Or

Q.15. (b) Discuss the various techniques through which files can be allocated space on disk. Give relevant example and diagrammatic illustration. (16)

Ans: The widely used methods for allocation of disk space are, contiguous, linked and indexed. For discussing these different allocation strategies, a file is considered to be a sequence of blocks and all I/O operations on a disk occurs in terms of blocks.

Contiguous Allocation

In contiguous allocation, each file is allocated contiguous blocks on the disk, that is, one after the other. The directory entry for each file contains the filename, the disk address of the first block and the total size of the file. Assuming only one job is accessing the disk, once the first block, say b, is accessed, accessing block $b+1$ requires no head movement normally. Head movement is required only when the head is currently at the last sector of a cylinder and moves to the first sector of the next cylinder; the head movement is only one track. Therefore, number of seeks and thus, seek time in accessing contiguously allocated files is minimal. This improves the overall file system performance.

Contiguous allocation supports both sequential and direct access to a file. For sequential access, the file system remembers the disk address of the last block referenced and when required, reads the next block. For direct access to block b of a file that starts at location L, the block $L+b$ can be accessed immediately.

Though it is relatively simple to implement the file system using contiguous allocation method, it has a significant problem of external fragmentation.

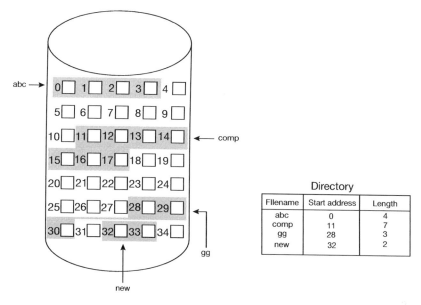

An Example of Contiguous Allocation

Linked Allocation

The file size generally tends to change (grow and shrink) over time. The contiguous allocation of such files results in the several problems. Linked allocation method overcomes the problems of contiguous allocation method.

In the linked allocation method, each file is stored as a linked list of disk blocks. The disk blocks are generally scattered throughout the disk and each disk block stores the address of the next block. The directory entry contains the filename and the address of the first and last blocks of the file as shown in the following figure.

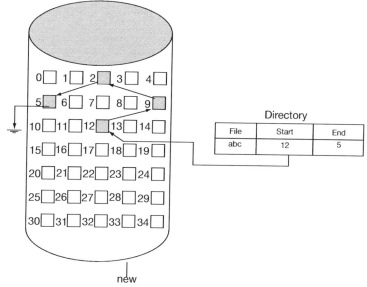

An Example of Linked Allocation

This figure shows the linked allocation for a file. A total of four disk blocks are allocated to the file. The directory entry indicates that the file starts at block 12. It then continues at block 9, block 2 and finally ends at block 5.

The simplicity and straightforwardness of this method makes it easy to implement. The linked allocation results in optimum utilization of disk space as even a single free block between the used blocks can be linked and allocated to a file. This method does not come across with the problem of external fragmentation.

The main disadvantages of using linked allocation are the slow access speed, disk space utilization by pointers and low-reliability of the system. As this method provides only sequential access to files, therefore, to find out the nth block of a file, the search starts at the beginning of the file and follows the pointer until the nth block is found. For a very large file, the average turn around time is high.

In linked allocation, maintaining pointers in each block requires some disk space. The total disk space required by all the pointers in a file becomes substantial, which results in more space required by each file. The space required to store pointers can otherwise be used to store the information. The linked allocation is also not very reliable. Since disk blocks are linked together by pointers, a single damaged pointer may prevent us from accessing the file blocks that follows the damaged link.

Indexed Allocation

There is one thing common to both linked and indexed allocation, that is, non-contiguous allocation of disk blocks to the files. However, they follow different approaches to access the information on the disk. Linked allocation supports sequential access, whereas, indexed allocation supports sequential as well as direct access.

In indexed allocation, the blocks of a file are scattered all over the disk in the same manner as they are in linked allocation. However, here the pointers to the blocks are brought together at one location known as the index block. Each file has an index block, which is an array of disk-block pointers (addresses). The kth entry in the index block points to the kth disk block of the file. To read the kth disk block of a file, the pointer in the kth index block entry is used to find and read the desired block. The index block serves the same purpose as a page map table does in the paged memory systems.

The main advantage of indexed allocation is the absence of external fragmentation, since, any free blocks on the disk may be allocated to fulfill a demand for more space. Moreover, the index can be used to access the blocks in a random manner. When compared to linked allocation, the pointer overhead in indexed allocation is comparatively more. This is because with linked allocation, a file of only two blocks uses a total of 8 bytes for storing pointers (assuming each pointer require 4 bytes of space). However, with indexed allocation, the system must allocate one block (512 bytes) of disk space for storing pointers. This results in wastage of 504 bytes of the index block as only 8 bytes are used for storing the two pointers.

Anna University

BE/BTech DEGREE EXAMINATION, NOV/DEC 2009

FOURTH SEMESTER
COMPUTER SCIENCE AND ENGINEERING
CS 1252 OPERATING SYSTEMS
(Regulation 2004)
(Common to BE (Part-time) Third Semester
Computer Science and Engineering Regulation 2005)

Answer ALL Questions

◆◆◆

PART A – (10 × 2 = 20 marks)

Q.1. What is the difference between OS for mainframe and desktop systems?

Ans: The design goals of OS for mainframe systems are much different from that of desktop systems. Due to less cost of PCs, the main focus in desktop systems is to provide improved usability and increased user interface functionality; efficient resource utilization is not the major issue. Contrastive to this, mainframe systems are quite expensive. Therefore, the main goal in such systems is to achieve maximum resource utilization even at the cost of ease of use.

Q.2. Differentiate long term scheduler from short term scheduler.

Ans: The long term scheduler works with the job queue. It selects the next process to be executed from the job queue and loads it into the main memory for execution. It is generally invoked only when a process exits from the system. On the other hand, the short term scheduler selects a process from the ready queue and allocates CPU to it. It is required to be invoked frequently as compared to long term scheduler.

Q.3. Define critical region.

Ans: The portion of the code of a process in which it accesses or changes the shared data is known as its critical region, also known as critical section. Among all the cooperating processes, only one process at a time can be in its critical region.

Q.4. What is meant by monitors?

Ans: A monitor is a programming language construct which is used to provide mutually exclusive access to critical sections. The programmer defines monitor type which consists of declaration of shared data (or variables), procedures or functions that access these variables and initialization code. The general syntax of declaring a monitor type is as follows:

```
monitor <monitor-name>
{
    //shared data (or variable) declarations
    data type <variable-name>;
    ...
    //function (or procedure) declarations
    return_type <function-name>(parameters)
    {
        //body of function
    }
    .
    .
    .
    monitor-name()
    {
        //initialization code
    }
}
```

Q.5. What is a safe state? Give the use of safe state in deadlock avoidance.

Ans: A system at any instant can be in either safe or unsafe state. The safe state means the allocation of resources to processes does not lead to the deadlock in the system. More precisely, a system is in safe state only if there is a safe sequence. A safe sequence is a sequence of process execution such that each and every process executes till its completion.

During deadlock avoidance, the safety algorithm is used to determine whether the system is in safe or unsafe state. A request from a process for the allocation of resources is granted only if granting the request leaves the system in safe state; otherwise, request is not granted. As a result, deadlock is avoided.

Q.6. Why is paging used?

Ans: Paging is a memory management scheme for multiprogramming systems. It allows the parts of a single process to occupy non-contiguous locations in the physical memory. It also avoids external fragmentation.

Q.7. What is meant by demand paging?

Ans: Demand paging is a memory management technique in which a page of program is loaded into memory only when it is needed, that is, only on demand. The pages that are never accessed are never loaded into the memory.

Q.8. Define thrashing.

Ans: The situation where most of the time of the system is being spent in performing page-out, page-in operations rather than executing processes is termed as thrashing.

A process is said to be thrashing if it causes page faults very frequently. Thrashing results in poor system performance as no productive work is being performed during thrashing.

Q.9. What is the importance of shells in Linux?

Ans: In Linux, shell is built outside the kernel and is written as a user process. It acts as an interface between the user and the operating system. It is the command line interpreter that enables the Linux users to invoke system commands. Every time a user logs on, the system invokes a copy of shell for that user. The users can use the shell in the following ways.

- **Interactive mode:** The user types a single command (a short string of words), the shell interprets the command and invokes the corresponding system call to carry out the desired action.
- **Shell scripts:** The users can create command files that contain few lines of code or an entire program and execute them as shell scripts.

Q.10. Differentiate worms from virus.

Ans: Both worms and virus are malicious programs designed to generate threats to the system, such as modification or destruction of files, system crash, etc. However, there is a certain difference between the two. Worm is a self-replicating program, which is self-contained and does not require a host program. The program creates a copy and causes it to execute; no user intervention is required. Worms commonly utilize network services to propagate to other host systems. On the other hand, virus is a small segment of code which replicates by attaching copies of itself to existing executables files. The new copy of the virus is executed when a user executes the new host program.

PART B – (5 × 16 = 80 marks)

Q.11. (a) Describe in detail the activities involved in sharing of information between two processes.   (16)

Ans: The processes running on a system often need to share information with each other. Two basic models used for providing communication between processes include message passing systems and shared memory systems. The communication using message passing is very time consuming because the message passing system is implemented with the help of operating system calls and thus, requires a major involvement of the kernel. On the other hand, in shared memory systems, system calls are used only to set up the shared memory area. Once the shared area is set up, no further kernel intervention is required.

Message Passing Systems

In message passing systems, processes communicate by sending and receiving messages from each other. The processes residing on the same computer communicate using `send()` and `receive()` system calls.

1. The sender process invokes get `processid()` system call to retrieve the `PID` of the receiver process. If the receiver process resides on some other computer connected via network, the sender process also executes get `hostid()` system call to obtain the IP address (hostid) of that system.
2. The sender process invokes `open connection()` system call, passing it the `PID` and `hostid` as parameters.
3. The receiver process executes `accept connection()` system call to accept the connection and give its permission for this communication.
4. Having permission from receiver process, the sender process sends the message to the operating system by invoking the `write message()` system call.
5. The operating system stores this message in the buffer area until the `read message()` system call is invoked by the receiver process.
6. Upon invocation of `read message()` system call by the receiver process, the operating system delivers this message to it. In case, there is no message for receiver process when it invokes the `read message()` system call, the operating system blocks it until some message arrives for it.
7. After sending all the messages, the sender process invokes the `close connection()` system call to terminate the connection.

Note that if a number of messages arrive for receiving process, the operating system puts them in a queue and delivers them in FIFO order upon the invocation of a sequence of `read message()` system call.

The following figure shows the message passing communication model.

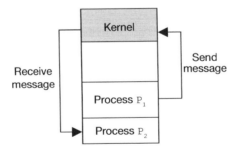

Message Passing Communication Model

Shared Memory Systems

In shared memory systems, a part of memory is shared among the communicating processes. The processes that need to exchange data or information can do so by writing to and reading from this shared memory. The process that needs to communicate with other processes creates a shared memory segment in its own address space. Other processes can communicate with this process by attaching its shared memory segment along with their address space. They can do so by invoking `map memory()` system calls. Once the memory region is mapped, processes can read or write data through this shared area. Note that the communicating processes must be synchronized so that no two processes should be able to access the shared area simultaneously. The following figure shows a shared memory communication model.

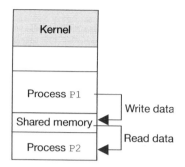

Shared Memory Communication Model

Or

Q.11. (b) Write short notes on: (10 + 6)

    (i) Virtual machines

    (ii) Hardware protection

Ans: (i) Virtual machines

Virtual machine is nothing but the identical copy of the bare hardware, including CPU, disks, I/O devices, interrupts, etc. It allows each user to run operating system or software packages of his own choice on a single machine, thereby, creating an illusion that each user has its own machine.

    The Virtual Machine Operating System (VMOS) creates several virtual machines by partitioning the resources of the real machine. The operating system uses the CPU scheduling and virtual memory concept to create an appearance that each running process has its own processor as well as own virtual memory (see following figure). The spooling and file system are used to create illusion of each user having own card reader and line printer.

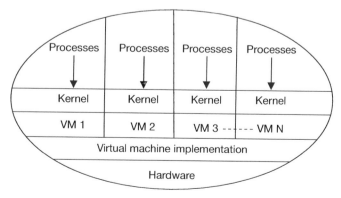

Virtual Machine Structure

The virtual memory approach provides the following benefits.

- Using virtual machines does not result in any extra overhead and performance degradation as each virtual machine has same architecture as that of real machine.
- Generally, while developing the operating system, the normal functioning of the current system is to be halted. However, by using virtual machine system, each system programmer can be provided with his own virtual machine for system development. Thus, there is no need to interrupt the normal system operation.
- The VMOS keeps the virtual machines isolated from one another. This results in protection of system resources.

(ii) Hardware protection

In case of single-user systems, an error in a currently running program can cause problems for that program only as it is the only active program at that point of time. However, when the resources are shared among several programs, then an error in one program can adversely affect the execution of other programs. It may also happen that an erroneous program modifies another program, or data of another program or the operating system itself. Without the protection from such type of errors, only one process must be allowed to execute at a time. However, to improve the resource utilization, it is necessary to allow resource sharing among several processes simultaneously. Therefore, to handle such environment, the operating system must be designed in such a way that it should ensure that an incorrect program does not affect the execution of other programs or the operating system itself.

- **Dual-mode operation:** In order to ensure the proper functioning of the computer system, the operating system, and all other programs and their data must be protected against the incorrect programs. To achieve this protection, two modes of operations, namely, user mode and monitor mode (also known as supervisor mode, system mode, kernel mode or privileged mode) are specified. A mode bit is associated with the computer hardware to indicate the current mode of operation. The value '1' indicates user mode and '0' indicates the monitor mode. When the mode bit is 1, it implies that the execution is done on behalf of the user and when it is 0, it implies that the execution is done on behalf of the operating system. This dual mode of operation helps in protecting the operating system and the other programs, from malicious programs.
- **I/O protection:** In order to protect the I/O devices from the illegal operations performed by the users, the I/O instructions are designated as privileged instructions, which can only be executed in the monitor mode. If the users want to issue I/O instructions, then they must do with the help of operating system. Whenever a user program needs to perform an I/O operation, it executes a system call to request the operating system to perform the I/O on its behalf. The system call transfers the control to the operating system, which is running in the monitor mode. The operating system then performs a validity check on the request. If the request is valid, it performs the desired I/O operation. The operating system then passes the control to the user program.

- **Memory protection:** In case of multiprogramming environment, multiple programs reside simultaneously in the main memory along with the operating system. Thus, it is necessary to protect the operating system from the access by user programs and to protect user programs from one another. That is, it is necessary to separate the memory space occupied by the operating system and other programs. This can be achieved by defining a range of legal address that a program can access. For this, two registers, namely, base register and limit register are used. The base register contains the smallest legal physical memory address and the limit register contains the size of the range. For example, if the base register contains the value 340 and the limit register contains the value 400, then the valid addresses that the program can access range from 340 to 740. If a program attempts to access the addresses outside the specified range, it results in a trap to the operating system. This mechanism of protection prevents the user programs from modifying the code and data structures for the operating system or another user programs.

- **CPU protection:** When a process starts executing, then it is quite possible that it gets stuck in an infinite loop and never returns the control to the operating system. Therefore, it is necessary to prevent a user program from gaining the control of the system for an infinite time. For this, a timer is maintained, which should interrupt the system after a specified period. This period can be fixed or variable. It is the responsibility of the operating system to set the timer; however, it is decremented with every clock tick. Whenever the value of timer reaches 0, an interrupt occurs. As the timer interrupts, the operating system gets the control of the system and then it takes the decision whether to abort the current user program or give it some more time to continue its execution. Note that the instructions that modify the operations of the timer are also defined as privileged instructions.

Q.12. (a) Discuss how the dining philosopher's problem can be solved by monitors. (16)

Ans: To understand the dining philosopher's problem, consider five philosophers sitting around a circular table. There is a bowl of rice in the center of the table and five chopsticks—one in between each pair of philosophers.

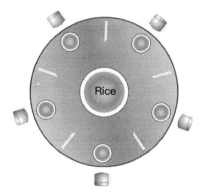

The Situation in Dining Philosophers

Initially, all the philosophers are in the thinking stage and while thinking they do not interact with each other. As time goes on, philosophers might feel hungry. When a philosopher feels hungry, he attempts to pick up the two chopsticks closest to him (that are in between him and his left and his right philosophers). If the philosophers on his left and right are not eating, he successfully gets the two chopsticks. With the two chopsticks in his hand, he starts eating. After eating is finished, he puts the chopsticks back on the table and starts thinking again. On the other hand, if the philosopher on his left or right is already eating, then he is unable to successfully grab the two chopsticks at the same time and thus, must wait. Thus, the dining philosopher problem is to distribute chopsticks among philosophers in a deadlock-free and starvation-free manner.

Using monitors, a deadlock-free solution to dining philosopher's problem can be developed. The following monitor controls the distribution of chopsticks to philosophers.

```
monitor diningPhilosophers
{
    enum {thinking, hungry, eating} state[5];
    condition self[5];

    void getChopsticks(int i)
    {
        int left, right;
        state[i] = hungry;
        left = (i+4)%5;
        right = (i+1)%5;
        if((state[left]==eating)||(state[right]==eating))
            self[i].wait();
        else
            state[i] = eating;
    }

    void putDownChopsticks(int i)
    {
        int left, right;
        state[i] = thinking;
        left = (i+4)%5;
        right = (i+1)%5;
        verifyAndAllow(left);
        verifyAndAllow(right);
    }

    void verifyAndAllow(int i)
    {
        int left, right;
        left = (i+4)%5;
        right = (i+1)%5;
```

```
        if(state[i]==hungry)
        {
            if((state[left]!=eating)&&(state[right]!
            =eating))
            {
                state[i] = eating;
                self[i].signal();
            }
        }
    }
    void initial()
    {
        int i;
        for(i=0; i<5; i++)
                state[i] = thinking;
    }
}
```

Each philosopher that feels hungry must invoke the `getChopsticks()` operation before start eating and after eating is finished, he must invoke `putDownChopsticks()` operation and then may start thinking. Thus, the general structure for the code segment philosopher `i` is as follows:

```
...
diningPhilosophers.getChopsticks(i);
eating
diningPhilosophers.putDownChopsticks(i);
...
```

The `getChopsticks()` operation changes the state of philosopher process from thinking to hungry and then verifies whether philosopher on his left or right is in eating state. If either philosopher is in eating state, then the philosopher process is suspended and its state remains hungry. Otherwise, the state of philosopher process is changed to eating.

After eating is finished, each philosopher invokes `putDownChopsticks()` operation before start thinking. This operation changes the state of philosopher process to thinking and then invoke `verifyAndAllow()` operation for philosophers on his left and right side (one by one). The `verifyAndAllow()` operation verifies whether the philosopher feels hungry and if so then allows him to eat in case philosophers on his left and right side are not eating.

Or

Q.12. (b) Explain the various process scheduling algorithms with example.   (16)

Ans: A wide variety of algorithms are used for process scheduling. Some of these algorithms are discussed below.

First-Come First-Served (FCFS) Scheduling

FCFS is one of the simplest scheduling algorithms. As the name implies, the processes are executed in the order of their arrival in the ready queue, which means the process that enters the ready queue first gets the CPU first. FCFS is a non-preemptive scheduling algorithm. Therefore, once a process gets the CPU, it retains the control of CPU until it blocks or terminates.

To understand FCFS scheduling algorithm, consider four processes P_1, P_2, P_3 and P_4 with their arrival times and required CPU burst (in milliseconds) as shown in the following table.

Process	P_1	P_2	P_3	P_4
Arrival time	0	2	3	5
CPU burst (ms)	15	6	7	5

According to FCFS scheduling algorithm, the processes will be scheduled as depicted in the following Gantt chart.

P_1	P_2	P_3	P_4

0   15   21   28   33

Waiting time for P_1 = 0 ms as P_1 starts immediately
Waiting time for P_2 = (15 − 2) = 13 ms as P_2 enters at t = 2 and starts at t = 15
Waiting time for P_3 = (21 − 3) = 18 ms as P_3 enters at t = 3 and starts at t = 21
Waiting time for P_4 = (28 − 5) = 23 ms as P_4 enters at t = 5 and starts at t = 28

Average waiting time = (0 + 13 + 18 + 23)/4 = 13.5 ms

Turnaround time for P_1 = (15 − 0) = 15 ms as P_1 enters at t = 0 and exits at t = 15
Turnaround time for P_2 = (21 − 2) = 19 ms as P_2 enters at t = 2 and exits at t = 21
Turnaround time for P_3 = (28 − 3) = 25 ms as P_3 enters at t = 3 and exits at t = 28
Turnaround time for P_4 = (33 − 5) = 28 ms as P_4 enters at t = 5 and exits at t = 33

Average turnaround time = (15 + 19 + 25 + 28)/4 = 21.75 ms

Shortest Job First (SJF) Scheduling

The shortest job first also known as Shortest Process Next (SPN) or Shortest Request Next (SRN) is a non-preemptive scheduling algorithm that schedules the processes according to the length of CPU burst they require. At any point of time, among all the ready processes, the one having the shortest CPU burst is scheduled first. Thus, a process has to wait until all the processes shorter than it have been executed. In case two processes have the same CPU burst, they are scheduled in the FCFS order.

To understand SJF scheduling algorithm, consider four processes P_1, P_2, P_3 and P_4 with their arrival times and required CPU burst (in milliseconds) as shown in the following table.

Process	P_1	P_2	P_3	P_4
Arrival time	0	1	3	4
CPU burst (ms)	7	5	2	3

According to SJF scheduling algorithm, the processes will be scheduled as depicted in the following Gantt chart.

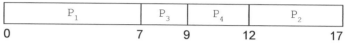

Waiting time for P_1 = 0 ms as P_1 starts immediately
Waiting time for P_2 = $(12 - 1)$ = 11 ms as P_2 enters at t = 1 and starts at t = 12
Waiting time for P_3 = $(7 - 3)$ = 4 ms as P_3 enters at t = 3 and starts at t = 7
Waiting time for P_4 = $(9 - 4)$ = 5 ms as P_4 enters at t = 4 and starts at t = 9

Average waiting time = $(0 + 11 + 4 + 5)/4$ = 5 ms

Turnaround time for P_1 = $(7 - 0)$ = 7 ms as P_1 enters at t = 0 and exits at t = 7
Turnaround time for P_2 = $(17 - 1)$ = 16 ms as P_2 enters at t = 1 and exits at t = 17
Turnaround time for P_3 = $(9 - 3)$ = 6 ms as P_3 enters at t = 3 and exits at t = 9
Turnaround time for P_4 = $(12 - 4)$ = 8 ms as P_4 enters at t = 4 and exits at t = 12

Average turnaround time = $(7 + 16 + 6 + 8)/4$ = 9.25 ms

Shortest Remaining Time Next (SRTN) Scheduling

The shortest remaining time next also known as Shortest Time to Go (STG) is a pre-emptive version of the SJF scheduling algorithm. It takes into account the length of remaining CPU burst of the processes rather than the whole length in order to schedule them. The scheduler always chooses the process for execution that has the shortest remaining processing time. While a process is being executed, the CPU can be taken back from it and assigned to some newly arrived process if the CPU burst of the new process is shorter than its remaining CPU burst. Notice that if at any point of time, the remaining CPU burst of two processes becomes equal; they are scheduled in the FCFS order.

To understand SRTN scheduling, consider the same set of processes, their arrival times and CPU burst as in case of SJF scheduling. According to SRTN scheduling, the processes will be scheduled as depicted in the following Gantt chart.

Waiting time for P_1 = $(11 - 1)$ = 10 ms as P_1 enters at t = 0, executes for 1 ms, pre-empts at t = 1, and then resumes at t = 11

Waiting time for $P_2 = (5 - 2 - 1) = 2$ ms as P_2 enters at $t = 1$, executes for 2 ms, pre-empts at $t = 3$, and then resumes at $t = 5$

Waiting time for $P_3 = 0$ ms as P_3 enters at $t = 3$, starts immediately and executes completely

Waiting time for $P_4 = (8 - 4) = 4$ ms as P_4 enters at $t = 4$, starts at $t = 8$ and executes completely

Average waiting time $= (10 + 2 + 0 + 4)/4 = 4$ ms

Turnaround time for $P_1 = (17 - 0) = 17$ ms as P_1 enters at $t = 0$ and exits at $t = 17$
Turnaround time for $P_2 = (8 - 1) = 7$ ms as P_2 enters at $t = 1$ and exits at $t = 8$
Turnaround time for $P_3 = (5 - 3) = 2$ ms as P_3 enters at $t = 3$ and exits at $t = 5$
Turnaround time for $P_4 = (11 - 4) = 7$ ms as P_4 enters at $t = 4$ and exits at $t = 11$

Average turnaround time $= (17 + 7 + 2 + 7)/4 = 8.25$ ms

Priority Based Scheduling

In priority based scheduling algorithm, each process is assigned a priority and the higher priority processes are scheduled before the lower priority processes. At any point of time, the process having the highest priority among all the ready processes is scheduled first. In case two processes are having the same priority, they are executed in the FCFS order.

The priority scheduling may be either pre-emptive or non-preemptive. The choice is made whenever a new process enters the ready queue while some process is executing. If the newly arrived process has the higher priority than the currently running process, the pre-emptive priority scheduling algorithm pre-empts the currently running process and allocates CPU to the new process. On the other hand, the non-preemptive scheduling algorithm allows the currently running process to complete its execution and the new process has to wait for the CPU.

To understand priority scheduling algorithm, consider four processes P_1, P_2, P_3 and P_4 with their arrival times, required CPU burst (in milliseconds) and priorities as shown in the following table.

Process	P_1	P_2	P_3	P_4
Arrival time	0	1	3	4
CPU burst (ms)	7	4	3	2
Priority	4	3	1	2

Assuming that the lower priority number means the higher priority, according to non-preemptive priority scheduling algorithm, the processes will be scheduled as depicted in the following Gantt chart.

Waiting time for $P_1 = 0$ ms as P_1 starts immediately
Waiting time for $P_2 = (12 - 1) = 11$ ms as P_2 enters at $t = 1$ and starts at $t = 12$

Waiting time for $P_3 = (7 - 3) = 4$ ms as P_3 enters at $t = 3$ and starts at $t = 7$
Waiting time for $P_4 = (10 - 4) = 6$ ms as P_4 enters at $t = 4$ and starts at $t = 10$

Average waiting time $= (0 + 11 + 4 + 6)/4 = 5.25$ ms

Turnaround time for $P_1 = (7 - 0) = 7$ ms as P_1 enters at $t = 0$ and exits at $t = 7$
Turnaround time for $P_2 = (16 - 1) = 15$ ms as P_2 enters at $t = 1$ and exits at $t = 16$
Turnaround time for $P_3 = (10 - 3) = 7$ ms as P_3 enters at $t = 3$ and exits at $t = 10$
Turnaround time for $P_4 = (12 - 4) = 8$ ms as P_4 enters at $t = 4$ and exits at $t = 12$

Average turnaround time $= (7 + 15 + 7 + 8)/4 = 9.25$ ms

According to preemptive priority scheduling algorithm, the processes will be scheduled as depicted in the following Gantt chart.

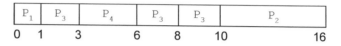

Waiting time for $P_1 = (10 - 1) = 9$ ms as P_1 enters at $t = 0$, executes for 1 ms, preempts at $t = 1$ and then resumes at $t = 11$
Waiting time for $P_2 = (8 - 2 - 1) = 5$ ms as P_2 enters at $t = 1$, executes for 2 ms, preempts at $t = 3$ and then resumes at $t = 8$
Waiting time for $P_3 = 0$ ms as P_3 enters at $t = 3$, starts immediately and executes completely
Waiting time for $P_4 = (6 - 4) = 2$ ms as P_4 enters at $t = 4$, starts at $t = 6$ and executes completely

Average waiting time $= (9 + 5 + 0 + 2)/4 = 4$ ms

Turnaround time for $P_1 = (16 - 0) = 16$ ms as P_1 enters at $t = 0$ and exits at $t = 16$
Turnaround time for $P_2 = (10 - 1) = 9$ ms as P_2 enters at $t = 1$ and exits at $t = 10$
Turnaround time for $P_3 = (6 - 3) = 3$ ms as P_3 enters at $t = 3$ and exits at $t = 6$
Turnaround time for $P_4 = (8 - 4) = 4$ ms as P_4 enters at $t = 4$ and exits at $t = 8$

Average turnaround time $= (16 + 9 + 3 + 4)/4 = 8$ ms

Highest Response Ratio Next (HRN) Scheduling

The highest response ratio next scheduling is a non-preemptive scheduling algorithm that schedules the processes according to their response ratio. Whenever CPU becomes available, the process having the highest value of response ratio among all the ready processes is scheduled next. The response ratio of a process in the queue is computed by using the following equation.

$$\text{Response ratio} = \frac{(\text{Time since arrival} + \text{CPU burst})}{\text{CPU burst}}$$

Initially, when a process enters, its response ratio is 1. It goes on increasing at the rate of (1/CPU burst) as the process's waiting time increases.

To understand HRN scheduling, consider four processes P_1, P_2, P_3 and P_4 with their arrival times and required CPU burst (in milliseconds) as shown in the following table.

Process	P_1	P_2	P_3	P_4
Arrival time	0	2	3	4
CPU burst (ms)	3	4	5	2

According to HRN scheduling algorithm, the processes will be scheduled as depicted in the following Gantt chart.

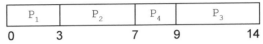

Waiting time for P_1 = 0 ms as P_1 starts immediately
Waiting time for P_2 = (3 − 2) = 1 ms as P_2 enters at t = 2 and starts at t = 3
Waiting time for P_3 = (9 − 3) = 6 ms as P_2 enters at t = 3 and starts at t = 9
Waiting time for P_4 = (7 − 4) = 3 ms as P_4 enters at t = 4 and starts at t = 7

Average waiting time = (0 + 1 + 6 + 3)/4 = 2.5 ms

Turnaround time for P_1 = (3 − 0) = 3 ms as P_1 enters at t = 0 and exits at t = 3
Turnaround time for P_2 = (7 − 2) = 5 ms as P_2 enters at t = 2 and exits at t = 7
Turnaround time for P_3 = (14 − 3) = 11 ms as P_3 enters at t = 3 and exits at t = 14
Turnaround time for P_4 = (9 − 4) = 5 ms as P_4 enters at t = 4 and exits at t = 9

Average turnaround time = (3 + 5 + 11 + 5)/4 = 6 ms

Round Robin (RR) Scheduling

The round robin scheduling is one of the most widely used pre-emptive scheduling algorithms which considers all the processes as equally important and treats them in a favourable manner. Each process in the ready queue gets a fixed amount of CPU time (generally from 10 to 100 milliseconds) known as time slice or time quantum for its execution. If the process does not execute completely till the end of time slice, it is pre-empted and the CPU is allocated to the next process in the ready queue. However, if the process blocks or terminates before the time slice expires, the CPU is switched to the next process in the ready queue at that moment only.

To implement the round robin scheduling algorithm, the ready queue is treated as a circular queue. All the processes arriving in the ready queue are put at the end of queue. The CPU is allocated to the first process in the queue and the process executes until its time slice expires. If the CPU burst of the process being executed is less than one time quantum, the process itself releases the CPU and is deleted from the queue. The CPU is then allocated to the next process in the queue. However, if the process does not execute completely within the time slice, an interrupt occurs when the time slice expires. The currently running process is pre-empted, put back at the end of the queue and the CPU is allocated to the next process in the queue. The pre-empted process again gets the CPU after all the processes before it in the queue have been allocated their CPU time slice. The whole process continues until all the processes in queue have been executed.

To understand RR scheduling algorithm, consider four processes P_1, P_2, P_3 and P_4 with their arrival times and required CPU burst (in milliseconds) as shown in the following table.

Process	P_1	P_2	P_3	P_4
Arrival time	0	1	3	4
CPU burst (ms)	10	5	2	3

Assuming that the time slice is 3 ms, according to RR scheduling algorithm, the processes will be scheduled as depicted in the following Gantt chart.

P_1	P_2	P_3	P_1	P_4	P_2	P_1	P_1

0   3   6   8   11   14   16   19 20

Waiting time for P_1 = (5 + 5) = 10 ms as P_1 enters at t = 0, starts immediately, waits for t = 3 to t = 8 and then again waits for t = 11 to t = 16
Waiting time for P_2 = (3 − 1 + 8) = 10 ms as P_2 enters at t = 1, starts at t = 3, waits for t = 6 to t = 14 and then resumes at t = 14
Waiting time for P_3 = (6 − 3) = 3 ms as P_3 enters at t = 3, starts at t = 6 and executes completely
Waiting time for P_4= (11 − 4) = 7 ms as P_4 enters at t = 4, starts at t = 11 and executes completely

Average waiting time = (10 + 10 + 3 + 7)/4 = 7.5 ms

Turnaround time for P_1 = (20 − 0) = 20 ms as P_1 enters at t = 0 and exits at t = 20
Turnaround time for P_2 = (16 − 1) = 15 ms as P_2 enters at t = 1 and exits at t = 16
Turnaround time for P_3 = (8 − 3) = 5 ms as P_3 enters at t = 3 and exits at t = 8
Turnaround time for P_4 = (14 − 4) = 10 ms as P_4 enters at t = 4 and exits at t = 14

Average turnaround time = (20 + 15 + 5 + 10)/4 = 12.5 ms

The performance of round robin scheduling is greatly affected by the size of the time quantum. If the time quantum is too small, a number of context switches occur which in turn increase the system overhead. The more time will be spent in performing context switching rather than executing the processes. On the other hand, if the time quantum is too large, the performance of round robin simply degrades to FCFS.

Q.13. (a) Discuss how deadlocks can be avoided and detected. (16)

Ans: **Deadlock Avoidance**

Deadlock can be avoided by never allowing allocation of a resource to a process if it leads to a deadlock. This can be achieved when some additional information is available about how the processes are going to request for resources in future. Information can be in the form of how many resources of each type will be requested by a process and in which order. On the basis of amount of information available, different algorithms can be used for deadlock avoidance.

The deadlock avoidance algorithm continuously examines the state of resource allocation ensuring that circular wait condition never exists in a system. The state of resource allocation can be either safe or unsafe. A state is said to be safe if allocation of resources to processes does not lead to the deadlock. More precisely, a system is in safe state only if there is a safe sequence. A safe sequence is a sequence of process execution such that each and every process executes till its completion. If no safe sequence of process execution exists then the state of the system is said to be unsafe. Note that a safe state is a deadlock-free state, whereas, all unsafe states may or may not result in a deadlock. That is, an unsafe state may lead to a deadlock but not always.

Two algorithms used for deadlock avoidance include resource allocation graph algorithm and banker's algorithm. The former is used in case of having single instance of each resource type while the latter is used in case of having multiple instances of each resource type.

Resource Allocation Graph Algorithm

The traditional resource allocation graph consists of two types of edges: request edge and assignment edge. In addition to these edges, another edge known as claim edge can also be introduced in this graph, which helps in avoiding the deadlock. A claim edge from a process to the resource indicates that the process will request for that resource in near future. This edge is represented same as that of request edge but with dotted line. Whenever the process actually requests for that resource, the claim edge is converted to the request edge. Also, whenever a resource is released by any process, corresponding assignment edge is converted back to the claim edge. The prerequisite of this representation is that all the claim edges related to a process must be depicted in the graph before the process starts executing. However, a claim edge can be added at the later stage only if all the edges related to that process are claim edges.

Whenever the process requests for a resource, the claim edge is converted to request edge only if converting the corresponding request edge to assignment edge does not lead to the formation of a cycle in a graph, as cycle in a graph indicates the deadlock. For example, consider the resource allocation graph shown in the following figure, the claim edge from process P_1 to the resource R_1 cannot be converted to the request edge as it will lead to the formation of cycle in the graph.

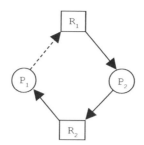

Resource Allocation Graph with Claim Edges

Banker's Algorithm

Refer **Q.13(b)(i)** BE/BTech Degree Examination May/June 2009.

Deadlock Detection

There is a possibility of deadlock if neither the deadlock prevention nor deadlock avoidance method is applied in a system. In such a situation, an algorithm must be provided for detecting the occurrence of deadlock in a system. Once the deadlock is detected, a methodology must be provided for the recovery of the system from the deadlock. Following are the ways by which deadlock can be detected in case of single instance of each resource type and multiple instances of each resource type.

Single Instance of Each Resource Type

When only single resource of each type is available, the deadlock can be detected by using variation of resource allocation graph. In this variation, the nodes representing resources and corresponding edges are removed. This new variation of resource allocation graph is known as wait-for graph, which shows the dependency of a process on another process for the resource allocation. For example, an edge from the process P_i to P_j indicates that the process P_i is waiting for the process P_j to release the resources required by it. If there exists two edges $P_n -> R_i$ and $R_i -> P_m$ in resource allocation graph, then the corresponding edge in the wait-for graph will be $P_n -> P_m$ indicating that the process P_n is waiting for the process P_m for the release of the resources. A resource allocation graph involving 6 processes and 6 resources and its corresponding wait-for graph is shown in the following figure.

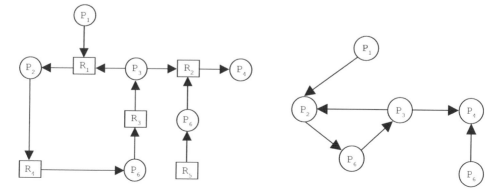

Converting Resource Allocation Graph to Wait-for Graph

If there exists a cycle in wait-for graph, there is a deadlock in the system and the processes forming the part of cycle are blocked in the deadlock. In wait-for graph (see figure on the previous page), the processes P_2, P_3 and P_6 form the cycle and hence are blocked in the deadlock. To take appropriate action to recover from this situation, an algorithm needs to be called periodically to detect existence of cycle in wait-for graph.

Multiple Instances of a Resource Type

When multiple instances of a resource type exist, the wait-for graph becomes inefficient to detect the deadlock in the system. For such system, another algorithm which uses certain data structures similar to the ones used in banker's algorithm is applied. The data structures used are as follows:

1. **Available resources, A:** A vector of size q stores information about the number of available resources of each type.
2. **Current allocation, C:** A matrix of order pxq stores information about the number of resources of each type allocated to each process. That is, C[i][j] indicates the number of resources of type j currently held by the process i.
3. **Request, Req:** A matrix of order pxq stores information about the number of resources of each type currently requested by each process. That is, R[i][j], indicates the number of resources of type j currently requested by the process i.

To understand the working of deadlock detection algorithm, consider a vector Complete of size p. Following are the steps to detect the deadlock.

1. Initialize Complete[i] = False for all i = 1, 2, 3, ..., p. Complete[i] = False indicates that the ith process is still not completed.
2. Search for an i, such that Complete[i] = False and (Req<=A), that is, resources currently requested by this process is less than the available resources. If no such process exists, then go to step 4.
3. Allocate the requested resources and let the process finish its execution. Set A=A+C and Complete[i]=True for that process. Go to step 2.
4. If Complete[i]=False for some i, then the system is in the state of deadlock and the ith process is deadlocked.

Or

Q.13. (b) Describe segmentation. (16)

Ans: Segmentation is a memory management scheme that implements the user view of a program. A user views a program as a collection of segments, such as main program, routines, variables, etc. All of these segments are variable in size and their size may also vary during execution. Each segment is identified by a name (or segment number) and the elements within a segment are identified by their offset from the starting of the segment. The following figure shows the user view of a program.

In segmentation scheme, the entire logical address space is considered as a collection of segments with each segment having a number and a length. The length of a segment may range from 0 to some maximum value as specified by the hardware and may also change during the execution. The user specifies each logical address consisting of a segment number (s) and an offset (d). This differentiates segmentation from paging in which the division of logical address into page number and page offset is performed by the hardware.

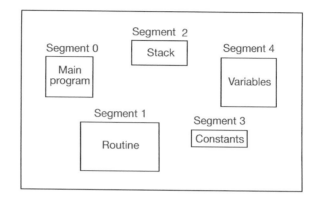

User View of a Program

To keep track of each segment, a segment table is maintained by the operating system. Each entry in the segment table consists of two fields: segment base and segment limit. The segment base specifies the starting address of the segment in physical memory and the segment limit specifies the length of the segment. The segment number is used as an index to the segment table.

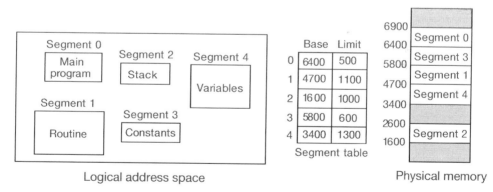

A Segment Table

When CPU generates a logical address, that address is sent to MMU. The MMU uses the segment number of logical address as an index to the segment table. The offset is compared with the segment limit and if it is greater, invalid-address error is generated. Otherwise, the offset is added to the segment base to form the physical address that is sent to the memory. The following figure shows the hardware to translate logical address into physical address in segmentation.

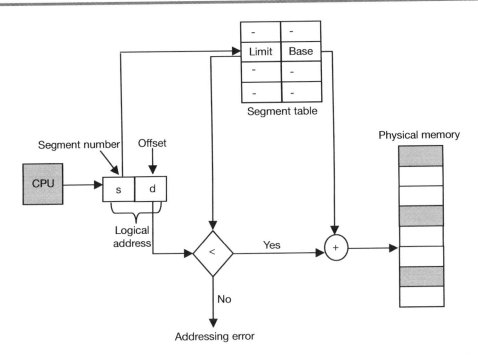

Segmentation Hardware

Example

Consider the following segment table.

	Base	Limit
0	5432	350
1	115	100
2	2200	780
3	4235	1100
4	1650	400

Segment Table

Now suppose we have to compute the physical address for segment 2 and offset 247.

It is clear from the segment table that limit of segment 2 = 780 and segment base = 2200. Since, the offset is less than the segment limit, physical address is computed as:

Physical address = offset + segment base

$$= 247 + 2200 = 2447$$

Following are some advantages of segmentation scheme.

- Since a segment contains one type of object, each segment can have different type of protection. For example, a procedure can be specified as execute only, whereas, a `char` type array can be specified as read only.
- It allows sharing of data or code between several processes. For example, a common function or shared library can be shared between various processes. Instead of having them in address space of every process, they can be put in a segment and that segment can be shared.

Q.14. (a) Explain the various page replacement algorithms with example.   (16)

Ans: When page fault occurs, page fault routine locates for a free page frame in memory and allocates it to the process. However, there is a possibility that the memory is full, that is, no free frame is available for allocation. In that case, the operating system has to evict a page from the memory to make space for the desired page to be swapped in. This is known as page replacement. There are various page replacement algorithms to select a page to be evicted, some of which are discussed below.

FIFO Page Replacement

The First-In First-Out (FIFO) is the simplest page replacement algorithm. As the name suggests, the first page loaded into the memory is the first page is to be replaced. That is, the page is replaced in the order in which it is loaded into the memory. To illustrate the FIFO replacement algorithm, consider the following reference string.

| 5 | 0 | 5 | 3 | 5 | 2 | 5 | 0 | 1 | 0 | 7 | 3 | Reference string

Assuming that initially, all the three frames are empty, the first two references made to page 5 and 0, and cause page faults. As a result, they are swapped in memory. The third reference made to page 5 does not cause page fault as it is already in memory. The next reference made to page 3 causes a page fault and that page is brought in memory. The reference to page 2 causes a page fault which results in the replacement of page 5 as it is the oldest page. Now, the oldest page is 0, so reference made to page 5 will replace page 0. This process continues until all the pages of reference string are accessed. It is clear from the following figure that there are nine page faults.

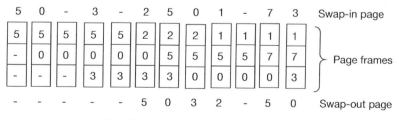

The FIFO Replacement Algorithm

Optimal Page Replacement

The Optimal Page Replacement (OPT) algorithm is the best possible page replacement algorithm. The basic idea behind this algorithm is that whenever a page fault occurs, some pages are in memory; out of these pages, one will be referenced at the next instruction while other pages may not be referenced until the execution of certain number of instructions. In case of page replacement, the page that is referenced at last will be replaced. That is, the page to be referenced in the most distant future is replaced. For this, each page can be labelled in the memory with the number of instructions to be executed before that page is referenced for the first time. The page with the highest label is replaced from the memory.

To illustrate this algorithm, consider the same reference string as used in previous algorithm. Like FIFO, the first two references made to page 5 and 0 cause page faults. As a result, they are swapped into the memory. The third reference made to page 5 does not cause page fault as it is already in memory. The reference made to page 3 causes a page fault and thus is swapped into memory. However, the reference made to page 2 replaces page 3 because page 3 is required at the last instruction, whereas, pages 5 and 0 are required at next instructions. The page faults and the pages swapped-in and swapped-out for all the page references are shown in the following figure. This algorithm causes seven page faults.

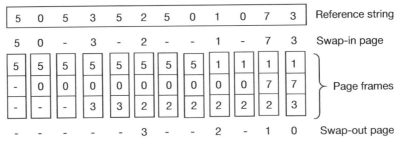

The Optimal Page Replacement Algorithm

The advantage of this algorithm is that it causes the lowest number of page faults as compared to other algorithms. The disadvantage of this algorithm is that its implementation requires prior knowledge of which page will be referenced next. Though this algorithm is not used in systems practically, it is used as the basis for comparing performance of other algorithms.

LRU Page Replacement

The Least Recently Used (LRU) algorithm is an approximation to the optimal algorithm. Unlike optimal algorithm, it uses the recent past behaviour of the program to predict the near future. It is based on the assumption that the page that has been used in the last few instructions will probably be referenced in the next few instructions. Thus, it replaces the page that has not been referenced for the longest time.

Consider the same reference string as used in previous algorithm. As a result of LRU page replacement algorithm, the page faults and the pages swapped-in and swapped-out for all the page references are shown in the following figure. Up to five references, page faults are same as that of optimal algorithm. When a reference is made to page 2, page 0 is replaced as it was least recently used. However, after page 5, it is being used again leading to a page fault. Regardless of this, the number of page faults is eight which is less than in case of FIFO.

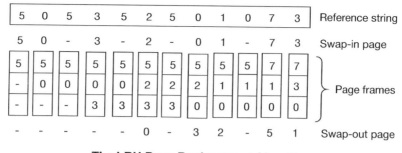

The LRU Page Replacement Algorithm

The Second Chance Page Replacement

The second chance page replacement algorithm (sometimes also referred to as clock algorithm) is a refinement over FIFO algorithm. It replaces the page that is both the oldest as well as unused instead of the oldest page that may be heavily used. To keep track of the usage of the page, it uses the reference bit (R) which is associated with each page. This bit indicates whether the reference has been made to the page while it is in memory. It is set whenever a page is accessed for either reading or writing. If this bit is clear for a page that means this page is not being used.

Whenever, a page is to be replaced, this algorithm uses the FIFO algorithm to find the oldest page and inspects its reference bit. If this bit is clear, the page is both the oldest and unused and thus, replaced. Otherwise, the second chance is given to this page and the reference bit of this page is cleared and its load time is set to the current time. Then the algorithm moves to the next oldest page using FIFO algorithm. This process continues until a page is found whose reference bit is clear. If the reference bit of all the pages is set (that is, all the pages are referenced), then this algorithm will proceed as pure FIFO.

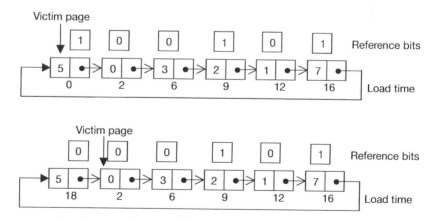

The Second Chance (Clock) Page Replacement Algorithm

To illustrate this algorithm, consider the same reference string as used in previous algorithm with reference bits as shown in the following figure. The algorithm starts with the page 5, say at time $t = 18$. Since, the reference bit of this page is set, its reference bit is cleared and time is reset to the current system time as though it has just arrived in the memory. The pointer is advanced to the next page that is page 0. The reference bit of this page is clear, so it is replaced by the new page. The pointer is advanced to the page 3 which will be the starting point for next invocation of this algorithm.

Counting-based Page Replacement Algorithm

Other than the page replacement algorithms discussed earlier, there are several other algorithms. Some of them keep record of how often each page has been referenced by associating a counter with each page. Initially, the value of this counter is 0, which is incremented every time when a reference to that page is made. That is, the counter counts the number of references that have been made to each page. A page with the highest value of the counter is heavily used while for a page with the lowest value of counter, there are following interpretations.

- That page is least frequently used.
- That page has just brought in and has yet to be used.

The algorithm based on the first interpretation is known as Least Frequently Used (LFU) page replacement algorithm. In this algorithm, when a page is to be replaced, the page with lowest value of counter is chosen for replacement. Clearly, the page that is heavily used is not replaced. The problem with this algorithm arises when there is a page that was used heavily initially, but afterwards never used again. For example, in a multipass compiler, some pages are used heavily during pass 1; after that pass, they may not be required. Still, these pages will not be replaced as they have high value of counter. Thus, this algorithm may replace useful pages instead of pages that are not in use. The algorithm that is based on the second interpretation is called the Most Frequently Used (MFU) page replacement algorithm.

Both these algorithms are not commonly used, as their implementation is expensive. Moreover, they do not approximate the OPT page replacement algorithm.

Or

Q.14. (b) Why is file protection necessary? Explain the techniques used for file protection.

(16)

Ans: The information stored in a system requires to be protected from the physical damage and unauthorized access. A file system can be damaged due to various reasons, such as a system breakdown, theft, fire, lightning or any other extreme condition that is unavoidable and uncertain. It is very difficult to restore the data back in such conditions. In some cases, when the physical damage is irreversible, the data can be lost permanently. Though, physical damage to a system is unavoidable, measures can be taken to safeguard and protect the data.

In a single-user system, protection can be provided by storing a copy of information on the disk to the disk itself or to some other removable storage media, such as magnetic tapes and compact disc. If the original data on the disk is accidentally erased or overwritten, or becomes inaccessible because of its malfunctioning, the backup copy can be used to restore the lost or damaged data. Apart, from protecting the files from physical damage, the files in a system also needs a protection mechanism to control improper access.

There are many protection mechanisms, each having some advantages and disadvantages. However, the kind of protection mechanism used depends on the need and size of the organization. A smaller organization needs a different protection mechanism while a larger organization with large number of people accessing the files needs a different protection mechanism.

Techniques for file protection

To protect the files from improper accesses, the access control mechanism can follow either of the two approaches.

- **Password:** A password can be assigned to each file and only a user knowing the password can access the file. This scheme protects the file from unauthorized access. The main drawback of this approach is the large number of passwords which are practically very difficult to remember (for each files separately). However, if only one password is used for accessing all the files, then if once the password is known, all the files become accessible. To balance the number of passwords in a system, some systems follow a scheme, where a user can associate a password with a subdirectory. This scheme allows a user to access all the files under a subdirectory with a single password. This scheme is also not very much safe. To overcome the drawbacks of these schemes, the protection must be provided at a more detailed level by using multiple passwords.
- **Access control list:** In this approach, access to a file is provided on the basis of identity of the user. An Access Control List (ACL) is associated with each file and directory, it stores user names and the type of access allowed to each user. When a user tries to access a file, the ACL is searched for that particular file. If that user is listed for the requested access, the access is allowed. Otherwise, the user is denied access to the file. This system of access control is effective but, in case if all users want to read a file, the ACL for this file should list all users with read permission. The main drawback of this system is that, making such a list would be a tedious job when number of users is not known. Moreover, the list need to be dynamic in nature as the number of users will keep on changing, thus resulting in complicated space management.

To resolve the problems associated with ACL, a restricted version of the access list can be used in which the length of the access list is shortened by classifying the users of the system into the following three categories.

- **Owner:** The user who created the file.
- **Group:** A set of users who need similar access permission for sharing the file is a group or work group.
- **Universe:** All the other users in the system form the universe.

Based on the category of a user, access permissions are assigned. The owner of the file has full access to a file and can perform all file operations (read, write and execute) whereas, a group user can read and write a file but cannot execute or delete a file. However, the member of the universe group can only read a file and are not allowed to perform any other operations on a file.

The above method of classifying users in groups will not work, when one user wants to access file of other user (for performing a specific file operation). For example, say, a user `comp` wants to access the file `abc` of other user `comp1`, for reading its content. To provide file specific permissions to a user, in addition to the user groups, an access control list is attached to a file. This list stores the user names and permissions in a specific format.

The UNIX operating system uses this method of access control, where the users are divided into three groups and access permissions for each file is set with the help of three fields. Each field is a collection of bits where, three bits are used for setting protection information and an additional bit is kept for a file owner, for the file's group and for all other users. The bits are set as $-$rwx where r controls read access, w controls write access and x controls execution. When all three bits are set to $-$rwx, it means a user has full permission on a file, whereas, if only $-$r$--$ field is set, it means a user can only read from a file and when $-$rw$-$ bits are set, it means user can read and write but cannot execute a file. The scheme requires total nine bits, to store the protection information. The permissions for a file can be set either by an administrator or a file owner.

Q.15. (a) Discuss the file system in Linux. (16)

Ans: The earliest file system used in Linux was the Minix file system. It was restricted by short filenames up to 14 characters and maximum file size of 64 MB. Therefore, after five years, a new improved file system, known as extended file system (extfs), was developed. This file system supported larger filenames and greater file size but it was slower than the Minix file system. So, the ext file system was redesigned to add the missing features and improve the performance of the file system and it gave rise to the ext2 file system also called second extended file system. The ext2fs has now become the standard file system of Linux. Apart from ext2fs, Linux offers a variety of other file systems also.

Linux also supports multiple disk partitions with each partition having the same or different file system on it. In order to facilitate the processes and applications to interact with different file systems at the same time, Linux offers a Virtual File System (VFS)—a layer of software between the process and file system—that hides the differences among the various file systems from the processes and applications. Thus, a user can use a file system of his/her choice irrespective of the file system implementation.

The Virtual File System

The virtual file system is an abstraction that supports a generic file model. It defines four types of objects, including `i-node`, `file`, `superblock` and `dentry`, and each object type is associated with a set of operations. The description of VFS object types is as follows:

- **i-node:** An i-node (a shortened form of index node) object describes a specific file. VFS defines an i-node object corresponding to each file in the file system. Since devices and directories in Linux are also treated as files, they have corresponding i-nodes also. An i-node is maintained on the physical disk as a data structure that contains pointers to the disk blocks storing the actual file contents.

- **File:** The file object describes an open file associated with a process. Before accessing the contents of an inode object, a process needs to obtain the file object which points to the inode. The file object also keeps track of the current position in file where the read/write operation is being performed. Note that there can be multiple file objects corresponding a single inode object with each file object belonging to a single process.

- **Superblock:** The superblock object describes a set of linked files that constitute an independent file system. The main task of superblock object is to provide access to the i-nodes. Each i-node is identified in VFS by a unique pair of file system and i-node number. Whenever an i-node is to be accessed, the VFS passes the request to the superblock object which then returns the i-node with that number.

- **Dentry:** The dentry object describes a directory entry which may comprise the actual file name or the name of the directory in path name of the file. For example, for a file with the pathname /bin/include/conio.h, there will be four dentry objects corresponding to four directory entries /, bin, include and conio.h.

The Linux ext2 File System

The Linux ext2fs is the most popular on-disk file system in use. It uses the same mechanism for storing the pointers to data blocks and finding the data blocks corresponding to a file as used in UNIX BSD Fast File System (FFS). In this file system, the i-nodes have a fixed size and can accommodate only a fixed number of pointer entries. An i-node holds only thirteen pointers out of which, first ten pointers are 'direct' pointers and remaining three pointers are 'indirect' pointers. Direct pointers point directly to the data blocks, whereas, indirect pointers point to index blocks which further point to data blocks.

Though in Linux the directory files are treated as normal files, they are interpreted in a different manner. Each data block of a directory file contains a linked list. Each entry of linked list stores the file name, i-node number of the i-node associated with that file, length of entry and the information about the group of blocks allocated to the file. The major thing that distinguishes ext2fs and FFS is the disk allocation policies. The ext2fs performs allocations in small units; block sizes of 1 KB, 2 KB or 4 KB, in contrast to FFS file system, where allocation is performed in large blocks of 8 KB each.

The Linux ext3 File System

The Linux ext2 file system improved the performance of the file system by allocating blocks of small size, but in case of sudden system failures and breakdowns, its performance was not satisfactory. The inefficiencies in the Linux ext2 file system gave rise to ext3 file system which uses the concept of journaling. The journaling refers to the process of maintaining a log (journal) in which the changes made to the file system are recorded in a sequential order. The changes written sequentially help in reducing the overheads due to disk head movements at the time of random disk accesses as already explained in log-structured file systems.

The Linux proc File System

The Linux proc (process) file system does not store files persistently; instead the files are read and used when required by the user. The basic idea is that for each individual process in system, a directory is created in the /proc file system. The name of this directory is the decimal number corresponding to process's PID such as `/proc/345`. Inside this directory are the virtual files (not actually stored on the disk) that seem to store process related information, such as its signal masks, command line, etc. When a user needs to read these virtual files, the system retrieves the desired information from the actual process at that time and returns it.

Or

Q.15. (b) Discuss in detail the disk management techniques followed in OS. (16)

Ans: An important function of the file system is to manage the space on the secondary storage, such as disk. It includes keeping track of the disk blocks allocated to files as well as the free blocks available for allocation.

Allocation of Disk Space

The two main issues related to disk space allocation are:

- Optimum utilization of the available disk space
- Fast accessing of files

For Disk space allocation techniques, Refer Q15(b) of BE/BTech Degree Examination May/June 2009.

Free Space Management

Whenever a new file is created, it is allocated some space from the available free space on the disk. The free space can be either the space on the disk that is never used for allocation or the space left by the deleted files. The file system maintains a free space **list** that indicates the free blocks on the disk. To create a file, the free space list is searched for the required amount of space and the space is then allocated to the new file. The newly allocated space is removed from the free space list. Similarly, when a file is deleted, its space is added to the free space list. Various methods used to implement free space list are bit vector, linked list, grouping and counting.

Bit Vector

Bit vector also known as bitmap is widely used to keep track of the free blocks on a disk. To track all the free and used blocks on a disk with total n blocks, a bitmap having n bits is required. Each bit in a bitmap represents a disk block where, a 0 in a bit represents an allocated block and a 1 in a bit represent a free block. The following figure shows bitmap representation of a disk.

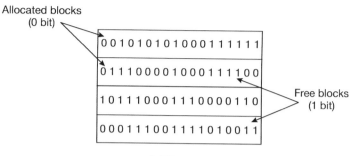

A Bitmap

The bitmap method for free space list implementation is simple. For instance, if a file requires four free blocks using contiguous allocation method, free blocks 12, 13, 14 and 15 (the first four free blocks on the disk that are adjacent to each other) may be allocated. However, for the same file using linked or indexed allocation, the file system may use free blocks 2, 4, 6 and 8 for allocation to the file.

Linked List

The linked list method for free space management creates a linked list of all the free blocks on the disk. A pointer to the first free block is kept in a special location on the disk and is cached in the memory. This first block contains a pointer to next free block, which contains a pointer to next free block and so on. The following figure shows the linked list implementation of free blocks, where block 2 is the first free block on the disk, which points to block 4, which points to block 5, which points to block 8, which points to block 9 and so on.

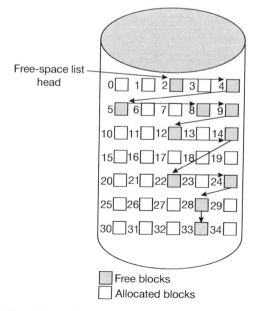

Free Space Management through Linked List

Linked list implementation for managing free-space list requires additional space. This is because a single entry in linked list requires more disk space to store a pointer as compared to 1 bit in bit map method. In addition, traversing the free-list requires substantial I/O operations as we have to read each and every block, which takes a lot of time.

Grouping

Grouping is a modification to the free list approach in the sense that instead of having a pointer in each free block to the next free block, we have pointers for first n free blocks in the first free block. The first $n-1$ blocks are then actually free. The nth block contains the address of next n free blocks and so on. A major advantage of this approach is that the addresses of many free disk blocks can be found with only one disk access.

Counting

When contiguous approach is used, creation or deletion of a file allocates or deallocates multiple contiguous blocks. Therefore, instead of having addresses of all the free blocks, as in grouping, we can have a pointer to the first free block and a count of contiguous free blocks that follow the first free block. With this approach, the size of each entry in the free space list increases because an entry now consists of a disk address and a count, rather than just a disk address. However, the overall list will be shorter, as count is usually greater than 1.

Anna University, Tiruchirappalli

B E/B Tech DEGREE EXAMINATION, APRIL/MAY 2010
FOURTH SEMESTER
COMPUTER SCIENCE AND ENGINEERING
CS1253 OPERATING SYSTEMS
Answer ALL Questions

◆◆◆

PART A — (10 × 2 = 20 marks)

Q.1. What is microkernel? Which operating system follows microkernel architecture?

Ans: Microkernel is an approach to structure the operating system that emphasizes on modularizing the kernel. The idea is to remove the less essential components from the kernel and keeping only a subset of mechanisms typically included in a kernel, thereby, reducing its size as well as number of system calls. Mach system and OS X are the examples of operating systems designed with microkernel approach.

Q.2. Which resources are used when a thread is created?

Ans: Whenever a thread (user-level or kernel-level) is created, the operating system allocates to it a data structure that holds a set of registers, stack and priority of the thread.

Q.3. What is busy-waiting? Is it preferable over blocking-wait? Give reason.

Ans: When a process is waiting for a condition to be satisfied in a tight loop without releasing the CPU, the process is said be busy-waiting. Busy-waiting results in wastage of CPU cycles. An alternative to busy-waiting is blocking-wait in which the process releases the CPU, blocks on the condition to be satisfied and waits to be awakened at some appropriate time in the future. Though blocking-wait does not result in wastage of CPU cycles, but incurs the overhead associated with putting a process to sleep and having to wake it up when the appropriate program state is reached. Thus, busy-waiting is preferable over blocking-wait.

Q.4. How to ensure that the circular wait condition never holds to prevent the deadlock?

Ans: The circular wait condition can be eliminated by assigning a priority number to each available resource and a process can request resources only in increasing order of priority. Whenever a process requests for a resource, the priority number of the required resource is compared with the priority numbers of the resources already held by it. If the priority number of a requested resource is greater than that of all the currently held resources, the request is granted. Otherwise, all the resources with greater priority number must be released first, before acquiring the new resource.

Q.5. Why is paging used?

Ans: Paging is a memory management scheme for multiprogramming systems. It allows the parts of a single process to occupy non-contiguous locations in the physical memory. It also avoids external fragmentation.

Q.6. Mention the importance of TLB.

Ans: TLB (Translation Look-aside Buffer) is a small high-speed associative memory. It is inside MMU and provides efficient memory access. In paging systems, TLB holds some page table entries—page number and the corresponding frame number. Whenever CPU generates a logical address and sends it to MMU, first the page number is searched in TLB. If it is found, its corresponding frame number is immediately available and is used to access the memory. Thus, the search is fast.

Q.7. List out the attributes associated with a file.

Ans: Each file is associated with certain attributes. Some of the common file attributes are as follows:

- **Name:** Helps to identify and locate a file in a system.
- **Size:** Stores information about the current size of the file (in bytes, words or blocks).
- **Type:** Helps the operating system to recognize and use the recommended program to open a particular file type. For instance, to open an `mpeg` (multimedia) file, operating system uses a media player.
- **Identifier:** A unique tag, usually a number that helps the file system to recognize the file within the file system.
- **Location:** A pointer that stores location information of the device and location of the file on that device.
- **Date and Time:** Stores information related to a file, such as creation, last modification and last use. Such information may be useful in case of protection, security and monitoring, etc.
- **Protection:** Stores information about the access permissions (read, write, execute) of different users. For example, it may specify who can access the file and which operations can be performed on a file by a user.

Q.8. What is Ext2fs?

Ans: Ext2fs (stands for extended 2 file system) is the most popularly used on-disk file system in Linux. In this file system, the i-nodes have a fixed size and can accommodate only a fixed number of pointer entries. An i-node holds only thirteen pointers out of which, first ten pointers are 'direct' pointers and remaining three pointers are 'indirect' pointers. Direct pointers point directly to the data blocks, whereas, indirect pointers point to index blocks which further point to data blocks.

Q.9. What are the functions of I/O subsystem?

Ans: The I/O subsystem of kernel is responsible for providing various I/O related services, which include:

- I/O scheduling
- Buffering
- Caching
- Spooling
- Device reservation
- Error handling

Q.10. What is the use of RAID?

Ans: RAID stands for Redundant Arrays of Independent Disks. The basic idea behind RAID is to have a large array of small independent disks. Presence of multiple disks in the system improves the overall transfer rates, if the disks are operated in parallel. Parallelizing the operation of multiple disks allows multiple I/Os to be serviced in parallel. This setup also offers opportunities for improving the reliability of data storage, because data can be stored redundantly on multiple disks. Thus, failure of one disk does not lead to loss of data. In other words, this large array of independent disks acts as a single logical disk with improved performance and reliability.

PART B – (5 × 16 = 80 marks)

Q.11. **(a)** Discuss the services provided by the operating system.   (8)

Ans: An operating system provides a variety of services. One set of operating system services provides functions to help the user. These services include the following:

- **User interface:** Providing a User Interface (UI) to interact with users is essential for an operating system. This interface can be in one of the several forms. One is command line interface, in which users interact with the operating system by typing commands. Another is batch interface, in which several commands and directives, to control those commands, are collected into files which are then executed. Another is Graphical User Interface (GUI), in which users interact with the system with a pointing device, such as a mouse.
- **Program execution:** The system must allocate memory to the user programs and then load these programs into memory so that they can be executed. The programs must be able to terminate either normally or abnormally.
- **I/O operations:** Almost all the programs require I/O involving a file or an I/O device. For efficiency and protection, the operating system must provide a means to perform I/O instead of leaving it for users to handle I/O devices directly.
- **File system manipulation:** Often, programs need to manipulate files and directories, such as creating a new file, writing contents to a file, deleting or searching a file by providing its name, etc. Some programs may also need to manage permissions for files or directories to allow or deny other programs requests to access these files or directories.

- **Communication:** A process executing in one computer may need to exchange information with the processes executing on the same computer or on a different computer connected via a computer network. The information is moved between processes by the operating system.
- **Error detection:** There is always a possibility of occurrence of error in the computer system. Error may occur in the CPU, memory, I/O devices or in user program. Examples of errors include an attempt to access an illegal memory location, power failure, link failure on a network, too long use of CPU by a user program, etc. The operating system must be constantly aware of possible errors and should take appropriate action in the event of occurrence of error to ensure correct and consistent computing.

In addition, the operating system provides another set of services that helps to ensure the efficient and secure execution of programs. These services include the following:

- **Resource allocation:** In case of multiprogramming, many programs execute concurrently, each of which require many different types of resources, such as CPU cycles, memory, I/O devices, etc. Therefore, in such an environment, operating system must allocate resources to programs in a manner such that resources are utilized efficiently and no program should wait forever for other programs to complete their execution.
- **Protection and security:** Protection involves ensuring controlled access to the system resources. In a multiuser or a networked computer system, the owner of information may want to protect information. When several processes execute concurrently, a process should not be allowed to interfere with other processes or with the operating system itself. Security involves protecting the system from unauthorized users. To provide security, each user should authenticate himself or herself to the system before accessing system resources. A common means of authenticating users is username/password mechanism.
- **Accounting:** We may want to keep track of usage of system resources by each individual user. This information may be used for accounting so that users can be billed or for accumulating usage statistics, which is valuable for researchers.

Q.11. (b) What is system call and explain its types? (8)

Ans: An operating system provides a wide variety of services and user programs interface to these services through system calls. A system call is similar to a procedure call except that it switches the mode of execution from user mode to kernel mode and invokes the operating system. The operating system then determines what the user program actually asks or wants, performs the system call and returns the control back to the instruction following the system call. The user program now again proceeds in the user mode.

In general, the services offered by these calls include creation and termination (or deletion) of processes, creation, deletion, reading, writing, opening and closing files, management of directories and carrying out input and output. In fact, the set of services that are offered through system calls determines a significant part of the operating system's responsibilities. All the system calls provided by an operating system can be roughly grouped into following five major categories.

- **Process management:** The system calls under this category includes the calls to create a new process, terminate a process, setting and retrieving process attributes (such as process priority, its maximum allowable execution time, etc), forcing a process to wait for some time or some event to occur, etc.
- **File management:** The system calls under this category includes the calls to create, delete, open, close, read and write a file.
- **Device management:** The system calls under this category includes the calls to request for device, releasing it and performing some operations (such as read or write) with the device.
- **Information maintenance:** The system calls under this category includes the calls to return information about the system, such as system's current data and time, number of current users, version of operating system, amount of free memory, etc.
- **Communications:** The system calls under this category includes the calls to open and close communication connection, reading and writing messages, etc.

Or

Q.12. (a) Explain about multithreading models. (8)

Ans: Refer **Q12(b)(i)** of BE/BTech Examination May/June 2009.

Q.12. (b) What is Process Control Block (PCB)? Describe the contents of PCB in detail. (8)

Ans: To keep track of all the processes in the system, the operating system maintains a structurally organized table called process table that includes an entry for each process. This entry is called Process Control Block (PCB)—a data structure created by the operating system for representing a process. A process control block stores descriptive information pertaining to a process, such as its state, program counter, memory management information, information about its scheduling, allocated resources, accounting information, etc., that is required to control and manage a particular process. The basic purpose of PCB is to indicate the so far progress of a process. Some of the important fields stored in a PCB are as follows:

- **Process ID:** Each process is assigned a unique identification number called Process Identifier (PID) by the operating system at the time of its creation. PID is used to refer the process in the operating system.
- **Process state:** It stores the current state of a process that can be new, ready, running, waiting or terminated.
- **Parent process ID:** It stores the PID of the parent, if the process has been created by some other process.
- **Child process IDs:** It stores the PIDs of all the child processes of a parent process.

- **Program counter:** It contains the address of the instruction that is to be executed next in the process. Whenever CPU switches from one process to another, the program counter of the old process is saved so that the operating system could resume with the same instruction whenever the old process is restarted.

- **Event information:** If the process is in waiting state then this field contains the information about the event for which the process is waiting to happen. For example, if the process is waiting for an I/O device, then this field stores the `ID` of that device.

- **Memory management information:** It includes information related to the memory configuration for a process, such as the value of base and limit registers, the page tables (if paging memory management technique has been used) or the segment tables (if segmentation memory management technique has been used).

- **CPU registers:** It stores the contents of index registers, general purpose registers, condition code information, etc., at the time when the CPU was last freed by the process or pre-empted from the process.

- **CPU scheduling information:** It includes information used by the scheduling algorithms, such as the process priority number (in case the priority scheduling is to be used for the process), the pointers to appropriate scheduling queues depending upon the current state of the process, the time when CPU was last allocated to the process, etc.

- **I/O status:** It includes information, such as I/O devices allocated to a process, pointers to the files opened by the process for I/O, the current position in the files, etc.

Q.13. Discuss the performance evaluation of scheduling algorithms.   (16)

Ans: To select a scheduling algorithm for a particular system, we need to evaluate the performance of different scheduling algorithms under given system workload and find out the most suitable one for the system. Some commonly used methods to evaluate scheduling algorithms include deterministic modelling, queuing models and simulation.

Deterministic Modelling

This is the simplest and direct method used to compare the performance of different scheduling algorithms on the basis of some specific criteria. It takes into account the prespecified system workload and measures the performance of each scheduling algorithm for that workload. For example, consider a system with workload as shown below. We have to select an algorithm out of FCFS, SJF and RR (with time slice 8 ms), which results in minimum average waiting time.

Process	P_1	P_2	P_3	P_4
Arrival time	0	1	3	4
CPU burst (ms)	7	15	2	5

According to FCFS, SJF and RR scheduling algorithms, the processes will be scheduled as depicted in the following Gantt charts.

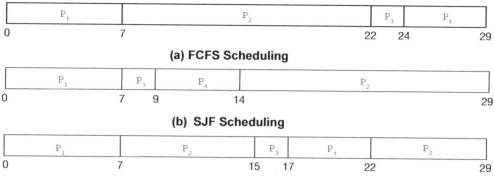

(a) FCFS Scheduling

(b) SJF Scheduling

(c) RR Scheduling

According to FCFS, the average waiting time = (0 + 6 + 19 + 20)/4 = 11.25 ms

According to SJF, the average waiting time = (0 + 13 + 4 + 5)/4 = 5.5 ms

According to RR, the average waiting time = (0 + 13 + 12 + 13)/4 = 9.5 ms

From the above calculation, we can study the comparative performance of scheduling algorithms. SJF scheduling algorithm results in average waiting time less than half of that in FCFS while the RR scheduling results in an intermediate value. Thus, for the given system workload, SJF scheduling will work best.

Though the deterministic modelling returns exact measures to compare the performance of scheduling algorithms, it requires the exact processing requirements of processes to be provided as input. Thus, deterministic modelling is suitable for systems in which same programs may run again and again, thereby, providing exact measures of CPU bursts and I/O bursts of processes.

Queuing Models

Generally, there is no fixed set of processes that run on systems, thus, it is not possible to measure the exact processing requirements of processes. However, we can measure the distributions of CPU bursts and I/O bursts during the lifetime of processes and derive a mathematical formula that identifies the probability of a specific CPU burst. Similarly, the arrival rate of processes in the system can also be approximated. The use of mathematical models for evaluating performance of various systems led to the development of queuing theory, a branch of mathematics. The fundamental model of queuing theory is identical to the computer system model. Each computer system is represented as a set of servers (such as CPU, I/O devices, etc.) with each server having its own queue. For example, CPU has a ready queue and an I/O device has a device queue associated with itself. By having knowledge of arrival rates of processes in each queue and service rates of processes, we can find out the average length of queue, average waiting time of processes in the queue, etc. For example, consider L denotes the average queue length, W denotes the average waiting time of a process in the queue and α denotes the average arrival rate of processes in the queue. The relationship between L, W and α can be expressed by the Little's formula, as given below:

$$L = \alpha \times W$$

Little's formula is based on the following facts:

- During the time a process waits in the queue ($\overline{W}$), (α x w) new processes enter into the queue.
- The system is in steady state, that is, the number of processes exiting from the queue is equal to the number of processes entering into the queue.

In spite of the fact that queuing analysis provides a mathematical formula to evaluate the performance of scheduling algorithms, it suffers from few limitations. We can use queuing analysis for only limited classes of scheduling algorithms, not for all. Moreover, it is based on approximations, therefore, the accuracy of calculated results depends on how closely the approximations match with the real system.

Simulations

This is the more accurate method of evaluating algorithms that mimic the dynamic behaviour of a real computer system over time. The computer system model is programmed and all the major components of system are represented by the data structures. The simulator employs a variable representing a clock. As the clock is incremented, the current system state is changed to reflect the changed actions of processes, scheduler, I/O devices, etc. While the simulation executes, the system parameters that affect the performance of scheduling algorithms, such as CPU burst, I/O burst and so on are gathered and recorded. The data to drive the simulation can be generated using the trace tapes, which are created by monitoring the system under study and recording the events taking place. The sequence of recorded events is then used to drive the simulation. Although trace tapes is the easier method to compare the performance of two different scheduling algorithms for the same set of real inputs, they need a vast amount of storage space. Moreover, simulation requires a lot of computer time; this makes it an expensive method.

Q.14. Consider the following snapshot of the system: (16)

Process	Allocation	Max. Demand	Available
P0	0 0 1 2	0 0 1 2	2 1 0 0
P1	2 0 0 0	2 7 5 0	
P2	0 0 3 4	6 6 5 6	
P3	2 3 5 4	4 3 5 6	
P4	0 3 3 2	0 6 5 2	

Write the Banker's algorithm and find out the following with the help of Banker's algorithm.

(a) How many resources the system still needs?

(b) Is the system currently safe? If it is safe state write the safe sequence.

(c) If a request from process P2 arrives for (0 1 0 0), can it be granted immediately?

Ans: Refer **Q13(b)(i)** of BE/BTech Examination May/June 2009.

(a) The resources the system still needs are:

Process	Required resources
P0	0 0 0 0
P1	0 7 5 0
P2	6 6 2 2
P3	2 0 0 2
P4	0 3 2 0

(b) Yes, the system is in safe state and the safe sequence is (P0, P3, P4, P1, P2).

(c) If the request from the process P2 for (0 1 0 0) resources is granted, the resulting system state will be:

Process	Allocation	Max. Demand	Available
P0	0 0 1 2	0 0 1 2	2 1 0 0
P1	2 0 0 0	2 7 5 0	
P2	0 0 3 4	6 6 5 6	
P3	2 3 5 4	4 3 5 6	
P4	0 3 3 2	0 6 5 2	

As the resulting system state is unsafe, the request from process P2 cannot be granted immediately.

Q.15. Discuss the hardware support for segmentation, paging and explain how logical address is mapped into physical address. (16)

Ans: **Hardware Support and Address Translation in Segmentation**

To keep track of each segment, a segment table is maintained by the operating system. Each entry in the segment table consists of two fields: segment base and segment limit. The segment base specifies the starting address of the segment in physical memory and the segment limit specifies the length of the segment. The segment number is used as an index to the segment table.

When CPU generates a logical address, that address is sent to MMU. The MMU uses the segment number of logical address as an index to the segment table. The offset is compared with the segment limit and if it is greater, invalid-address error is generated. Otherwise, the offset is added to the segment base to form the physical address that is sent to the memory.

Address Translation in Paging

In paging, address translation is performed using a mapping table, called **page table**. The operating system maintains a page table for each process to keep track of which page frame is allocated to which page. It stores the frame number allocated to each page and the page number is used as index to the page table.

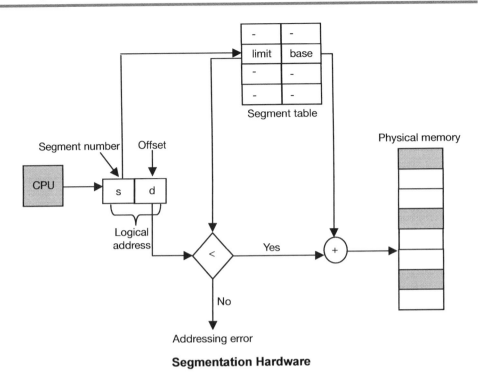

Segmentation Hardware

When CPU generates a logical address, that address is sent to MMU. The MMU uses the page number to find the corresponding page frame number in the page table. That page frame number is attached to the high-order end of the page offset to form the physical address that is sent to the memory.

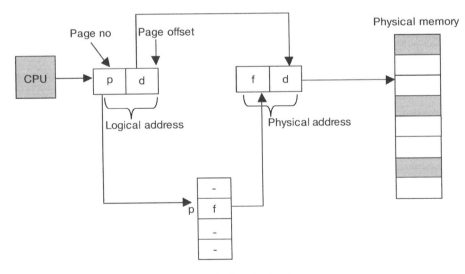

Address Translation in Paging

Hardware Support for Paging

Each operating system has its own way of storing page tables. The simplest way is to use registers to store the page table entries indexed by page number. Though this method is faster and does not require any memory reference, its disadvantage is that it is not feasible in case of large page table as registers are expensive. Moreover, at every context switch, the page table needs to be changed which in turn requires all the registers to be reloaded. This degrades the performance.

Another way is to keep the entire page table in main memory and the pointer to page table stored in a register called Page-Table Base Register (PTBR). Using this method, page table can be changed by reloading only one register, thus reduces context switch time to a great extent. The disadvantage of this scheme is that it requires two memory references to access a memory location; first to access page table using PTBR to find the page frame number and second to access the desired memory location. Thus, memory accessing is slowed down by a factor of two.

To overcome this problem, the system can be equipped with a special hardware device known as Translation Look-aside Buffer (TLB) (or associative memory). The TLB is inside MMU and contains a limited number of page table entries. When CPU generates a logical address and presents it to the MMU, it is compared with the page numbers present in the TLB. If a match is found in TLB (called TLB hit), the corresponding page frame number is used to access the physical memory. In case a match is not found in TLB (called TLB miss), memory is referenced for the page table. Further, this page number and the corresponding frame number are

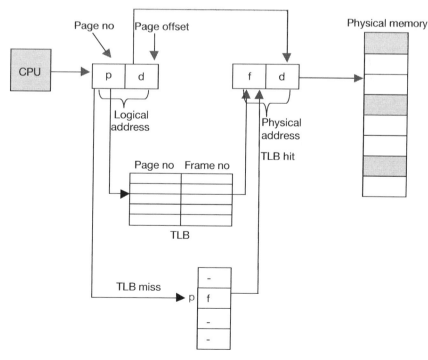

Paging with TLB

added to the TLB so that next time if this page is required, it can be referenced quickly. Since the size of TLB is limited so when it is full, one entry must be replaced.

TLB can contain entries for more than one process at the same time, so there is a possibility that two processes map the same page number to different frames. To resolve this ambiguity, a process identifier (PID) can be added with each entry of TLB. For each memory access, the PID present in the TLB is matched with the value in a special register that holds the PID of the currently executing process. If it matches, the page number is searched to find the page frame number, otherwise it is treated as a TLB miss.

Or

Q.16. Discuss the hardware support for demand paging and explain how logical address is translated into physical address. (16)

Ans: In demand paging, a page is loaded into the memory only when it is needed during program execution. Pages that are never accessed are never loaded into the memory.

A demand paging system combines the features of paging with swapping. To facilitate swapping, the entire virtual address space of a process is stored contiguously on a secondary storage device (usually, a disk). Whenever a process is to be executed, an area on secondary storage device is allocated to it on which its pages are copied. The area is known as swap space of the process. During the execution of a process, whenever a page is required, it is loaded into the main memory from the swap space. Similarly, when a process is to be removed from main memory, it is written back into the swap space if it has been modified.

Other than swap space, some form of hardware support is also needed to differentiate the pages that are in memory from that are on disk. For this, only an additional bit valid is maintained in each page table entry to indicate whether the page is in memory. If a page is valid (that is, it exists in the virtual address space of the process) and in memory, the associated valid bit is set to 1, otherwise it is set to 0. The following figure shows the page table in demand paging system.

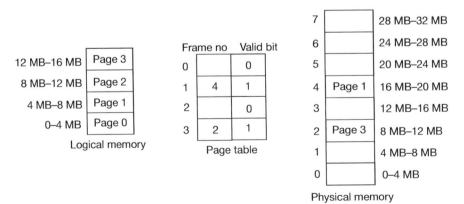

Page Table in Demand-paging System

Whenever a process requests for a page, the virtual address is sent to MMU. The MMU checks the `valid` bit in the page table entry of that page. If the `valid` bit is 1 (that is, the requested page is in memory), the corresponding frame number is extracted from the page table. That page frame number is attached to the high-order end of the page offset to form the physical address that is sent to the memory. Otherwise, the MMU raises an interrupt called page fault or a missing page interrupt and the control is passed to the page fault routine in the operating system.

To handle the page fault, the page fault routine first of all checks whether the virtual address for the desired page is valid from its PCB stored in the process table. If it is invalid, it terminates the process giving error. Otherwise, it takes the following steps.

1. Locates for a free page frame in memory and allocates it to the process.
2. Swaps the desired page into this allocated page frame.
3. Updates the process table and page table to indicate that the page is in memory.

After performing these steps, the CPU restarts from the instruction that it left off due to the page fault.

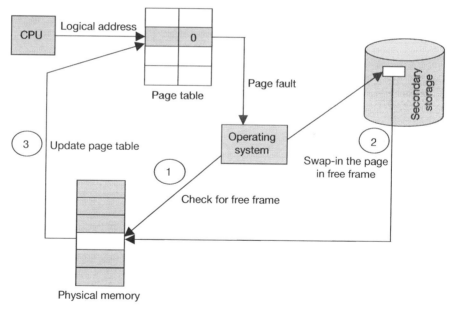

Handling a Page Fault

Q.17. Explain the file allocation methods on secondary storage device. (16)

Refer to Q15 (b) of BE/BTech Degree Examination May/June 2009.

Q.18. Explain the file system in Windows XP. (16)

Ans: On a system running Windows XP, one of three file systems, namely, FAT16, FAT32 and NTFS (New Technology File System) can be used. However, NTFS supersedes the FAT file systems and has become the standard file system of Windows XP because of several improvements. Some of the major improvements in NTFS over FAT file systems are as follows:

- It includes features, such as data recovery, file compression, large files and file systems, encryption, etc.
- It provides greater control over security and access of data within the file system.
- It supports large drives or partitions.
- It provides improved performance, reliability and efficient storage using advanced data structure.

NTFS Physical Structure

The basic entity of NTFS is volume. An NTFS volume can be a logical partition of the disk or the entire disk. It is organized as a sequence of clusters where a cluster is a collection of contiguous disk sectors, the number of disk sectors in a cluster is a power of 2. It is the smallest unit of disk space that can be allocated to a file. The size of a cluster for a volume varies from 512 bytes to 64 KB, depending on the size of volume. For example, the default cluster size for a 2 GB volume is 2 KB. Each cluster starting from the beginning of the disk to the end is assigned a number known as Logical Cluster Number (LCN). NTFS uses these logical cluster numbers instead of actual disk addresses while allocating space to files.

In NTFS, a file is considered to be a structured object consisting of a set of attributes which are nothing but independent byte streams. Some standard attributes, such as name, timestamp and the date of creation, are defined for all the files. Note that user data is also considered as an attribute and is stored in data attributes.

In order to keep track of information regarding each file on volume, NTFS maintains a Master File Table (MFT). It is created in addition to the boot sector and some system files when a volume is formatted using NTFS. The MFT is itself a file that contains at least one record for each file. Each MFT record consists of a sequence of (attribute header, value) pairs. The attribute header identifies the attribute and indicates the length of the value. If the value of attribute is short enough to fit in the MFT record, it is stored in the MFT record and is called resident attribute. On the other hand, if the value of attribute is too long, it is placed on one or more contiguous extents on the volume and a pointer to each extent is stored in the MFT record. Such attribute is known as non-resident attribute. Note that there may be a case when a file is extremely large or it has many attributes. In such case, two or more MFT records are required; the first one is known as base record that points to the other MFT records. Some of the attributes along with their description are listed in the following table.

Some Attributes in MFT Records

Attribute	Description
Standard information	Contains information, such as flag bits, timestamp.
Filename	Contains the filename in Unicode.
Attribute list	Lists the location of additional MFT records.
Object ID	Represents the file identifier unique to the volume.
Volume name	Contains the name of the volume, used in $Volume metadata file
Volume information	Contains the version of the volume, used in $Volume metadata file
Index root	Used to implement directories
Index allocation	Used to implement very large directories
Data	Contains stream data

NTFS associates each file with a unique ID known as file reference. It is of 64 bits where first 48 bit and last 16 bits represent the file number and the sequence number, respectively. The file number represents the record number in the MFT containing that file's entry and the sequence number shows the number of times that MFT entry has been used.

Metadata Files

In NTFS, the internal information about the data for a volume is stored in special system files known as metadata files. The MFT is also one of the metadata files, it not only stores information about itself but also about other metadata files. The first 16 MFT records are reserved for metadata files, the first one being the record for MFT itself. The second record is mirror copy of MFT that contains first 16 entries of original MFT file. It is used for recovery in case the original MFT file gets corrupted.

Metadata files are represented in the MFT using a dollar sign ($) at the beginning of the filename. Some of the metadata files other than MFT along with their file names and description are listed in the following table.

Some Metadata Files in MFT

System File	File Name	Description
Log file	$LogFile	Contains metadata updates to restore the data during recovery after a system failure
Volume	$Volume	Contains information about the volume, such as the volume label and the volume version
Attribute definitions	$AttrDef	Lists attribute names used in the volume and the operations that can be performed on them

Boot sector	$Boot	Contains the BIOS parameter that stores the information about the volume, such as name, size, etc., and boot code to load the operating system if the volume is bootable
Cluster bitmap	$Bitmap	Indicates the free clusters on the volume
Root file name index	.	The root folder
Security file	$Secure	Contains unique security descriptors for all files within a volume
Bad cluster file	$BadClus	Indicates the bad clusters on a volume

Directory Implementation

Like in MS-DOS and UNIX, the file system is organized as a hierarchy of directories, a directory can contain other directories. NTFS implements each directory using a data structure called B^+ tree; an index of the file names of that directory is stored in B^+ tree. B^+ tree not only makes insertion of new names in the directory at appropriate place easier but also facilitates efficient search of a file in a directory. This is because, in B^+ tree, the length of each path from the root of the tree to a leaf is same.

Q.19. Consider the following I/O request   (16)
98, 183, 37, 122, 14, 124, 65, 67.
The current head position is at 53. What is the total head movement to service the request for the following disk scheduling algorithm?

(a) SSTF
(b) SCAN
(c) C-SCAN
(d) LOOK
(e) C-LOOK

Ans:

(a) SSTF disk scheduling algorithm

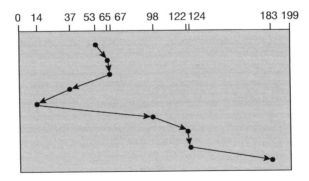

Total number of head movements = 12 + 2 + 30 + 23 + 84 + 24 + 2 + 59
= 236 cylinders.

(b) SCAN disk scheduling algorithm

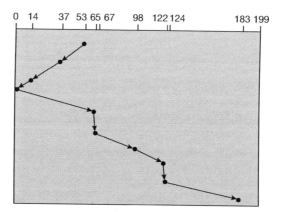

Suppose that the head is moving towards 0.
Total number of head movements $= 16 + 23 + 14 + 65 + 2 + 31 + 24 + 2 + 59 = 236$ cylinders

(c) C-SCAN disk scheduling algorithm

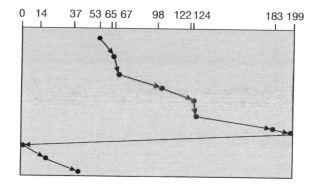

Total number of head
movements $= 12 + 2 + 31 + 24 + 2 + 59 + 16 + 199 + 14 + 23 = 382$ cylinders

(d) LOOK disk scheduling algorithm

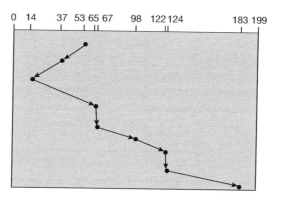

Suppose that the head is moving towards 0.

Total number of head movements $= 16 + 23 + 51 + 2 + 31 + 24 + 2 + 59 = 208$ cylinders

(e) C-LOOK disk scheduling algorithm

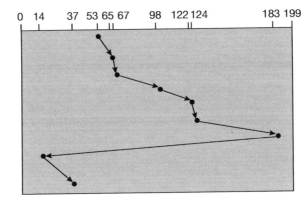

Total number of head movements $= 12 + 2 + 31 + 24 + 2 + 59 + 69 + 23$
$= 222$ cylinders

Or

Q.20. With the help of flowchart explain the lifecycle of I/O operation.   (16)

Ans: To understand the lifecycle of an I/O request, consider a process wishes to read data from a file. The following sequence of steps describes the typical lifecycle of a read (blocking) request.

1. The process invokes a blocking `read()` system call.
2. The kernel code determines whether the parameters passed are correct. After verification, the desired file blocks are checked in buffer and if available, are returned to the process. This completes the I/O request.
3. Otherwise, the desired data is to read from physical disk. The execution of the invoking process is suspended; the process is removed from the run queue and brought into the wait queue of appropriate device where it waits till it is scheduled. Finally, the kernel I/O subsystem passes the request to the appropriate device driver.
4. The device driver allocates buffer space in the kernel for receiving data and schedules the I/O request. Finally, it sends commands to the device controller.
5. The device controller functions the device hardware to transfer the data.
6. The driver may continuously monitor the device for its status and data (in case of programmed I/O) or may establish a DMA transfer in the kernel memory. In case of DMA, an interrupt is generated by the DMA controller after the transfer is complete.
7. The control is passed to the appropriate interrupt handler, which finds the interrupt, stores data (if required), sends signals to the device driver and then returns.
8. Upon receiving signals from the interrupt handler, the device driver identifies the I/O request that has accomplished, status of the request and informs the kernel I/O subsystem about I/O completion by sending signals to it.

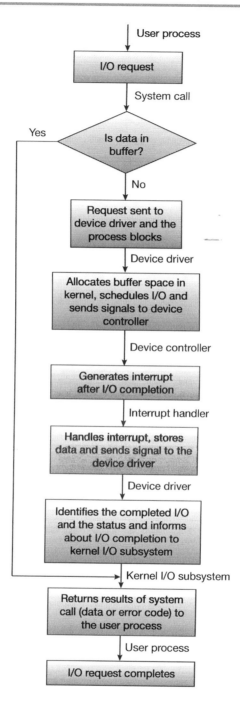

9. The kernel returns the results of system call (either data or the error code) to the invoking process. The process is unblocked by bringing it back into the run queue from the wait queue.

10. The I/O request is completed and the process continues its execution. The above figure depicts the lifecycle of a typical I/O request.

19632418R00184

Made in the USA
Lexington, KY
30 December 2012